T0375235

Beyond Technical Analysis

WILEY TRADING

Beyond Technical Analysis

How To Develop and Implement a Winning Trading System

SECOND EDITION

Tushar S. Chande, PhD

John Wiley & Sons, Inc.

New York • Chichester • Weinheim • Brisbane • Singapore • Toronto

Published by John Wiley & Sons, Inc.
Published simultaneously in Canada.

Data Scrambling is a trademark of Tushar S. Chande.
TradeStation, System Writer Plus, and Power Editor are trademarks of
Omega Research, Inc.
Excel is a registered trademark of Microsoft Corporation.
Continuous Contractor is a trademark of TechTools, Inc.
Portfolio Analyzer is a trademark of Tom Berry.

Library of Congress Cataloging-in-Publicaton Data:

Chande, Tushar S., 1958–
   Beyond technical analysis : how to develop and implement a winning
trading system / Tushar S. Chande.—2nd ed.
    p. cm.
   Includes bibliographical references and index.
   ISBN 0-471-41567-7 (cloth : alk. paper)
   1. Investment analysis. I. Title.

HG4529 .C448 2001
823'.914—dc21   00-065925

To my awesome co-inventors
Vidya, Ravi, and Aroon

Contents

viii   Contents

Preface

The new edition reflects my intense experiences as a Commodity Trading Advisor (CTA), developing systems, trading over 60 futures markets around the world and marketing services to clients. The additions to the second edition spring from my research to find effective answers to clients' questions about trading systems, risk control procedures, and expectations of future performance. For example, try giving a simple answer to the question, "What's a 'good' benchmark for performance comparisons of CTAs, hedge funds, and stocks?" I developed tools for comparing managers, analyzing equity curves, quantifying risk-adjusted performance, estimating drawdown risk, and projecting expected returns. These tools have been tested and accepted by many large allocators in the managed futures business and can be applied to stock indexes and mutual funds. Hence, they should be useful to many investors and allocators.

As part of the 24/7/365 experiences of a CTA, I faced my share of difficult markets and learned unforgettable lessons about the applications of sports psychology to the trading environment. Research by psychologists into the state of "flow" is also useful to build a framework for analyzing trader's reactions to the stresses of trading. This additional material in the second edition summarizes insights gained the expensive way. You can use it to cope with the inevitable stresses of trading.

In presentations to clients, there is rarely enough time to explain the nuances of design tradeoffs. Hence, marketing necessities led to the development of simplified schemes for classifying entry and exit strategies and system designs to explain the strengths of trading strategies. These classification schemes may be useful to you in your own iterations.

The new edition allowed me to give a true out-of-sample performance update for systems discussed in the first edition, and to show how to trade futures as well as stocks with the same system. This edition also includes an illustration of how CTAs derive their returns, and how to develop stabilized money-manager rankings. A review section of the basics of technical analysis is included at the request of many readers.

Since the publication of the first edition, I have had the good fortune to meet some of the most successful traders in the futures business, with individual net worths of $50 million to $100 million, and even beyond. They had reached the top of the mountain, and I tried to understand what got them there. I have summarized these impressions graphically in the form of the trader's mountain in the first section of the new edition. I am happy to report that the top traders agreed with the ideas in the first edition, and used many of them in one form or another. The discussions with top traders and the experiences of trading millions of dollars have convinced me that this book is useful in the "real world." I hope most readers will agree that the expanded scope of the new edition fulfills the original purpose of providing practical guidance for developing and implementing winning trading systems.

Chapter

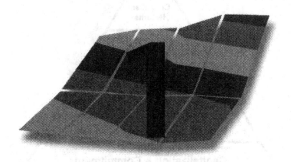

Developing and Implementing Trading Systems

Nothing is easier than developing a trading system by the usual process of trial and terror.

Introduction

Trading has been called the hardest way to make an easy dollar. To be consistently profitable, we must all climb the trader's mountain (see Figure 1.1). Top traders are internal attributors who take personal responsibility for their trading success. The foundation of their success is adequate capitalization coupled with an unwavering commitment to excel at trading. Successful traders have sufficient trading capital to withstand losing periods, as well as to trade many markets with multiple contracts. These traders simply love what they do, are constantly searching for better trading concepts, and devote the time and energy necessary to achieve their trading goals.

Capital conservation is just as important to top traders as capital appreciation. They know better than anyone the importance of having trading capital when the markets finally move in their favor. Top traders use sound money-management principles and rigid risk control to preserve capital during difficult market conditions.

Figure 1.1 The mountain a trader must climb for trading success.

All successful traders have developed specific trading competencies that match their style and objectives. They understand their trading preferences, and have developed the analytical tools and execution capabilities that allow their trading process to be implemented smoothly and, it seems, effortlessly. They have the patience and persistence to stick with a trading strategy and to review it periodically for upgrades and improvements. In essence, they test what they trade and trade what they test.

Winning traders are supremely confident about their abilities to be profitable over the long run. They are not surprised by losing periods, and they retain an optimistic and positive attitude under the most trying conditions. Their capitalization, money management, risk-control procedures, and competencies further help them keep the faith. Their confidence makes them disciplined and systematic in everything they do. This book will help you to develop the competencies needed for consistent performance, teach you the latest ideas on controlling risk, and give you the confidence to systematically trade what you test. Trading is analysis in action, and this book will empower you to go beyond technical analysis.

What's New in This Edition

This book can be divided into parts. The first part of the book, comprising the first five chapters, shows you how to build robust trading systems consistent with your beliefs. The second part, comprising the remaining chapters, discusses money management, risk control, and the implementation of trading systems. This second edition preserves the structure of the first edition and strengthens it by adding new material, derived primarily from personal research, that emphasizes capital preservation, robust system testing, and trading psychology. In response to reader comments, Chapters 1 and 3 contain new review material to help you to survey the basic principles of technical analysis, avoid common pitfalls in system testing, and assess the strategic design trade-offs in selecting entries and exits. Chapter 4 of this edition updates the performance of the key systems discussed in the first edition by testing these systems on a global portfolio with multiple contracts, to see how they would have fared in a true "out-of-sample" test on a million-dollar account. Next, we demonstrate that all the ideas in this book can be applied to stock trading by testing a new system on stocks and futures.

The bulk of the new material is concentrated in Chapters 6 and 7. Chapter 6, Equity Curve Analysis, now explains how to account for commodity trading advisor (CTA) performance by modeling CTA returns. It then discusses how to develop stabilized money manager rankings, so you can develop portfolios that are more efficient. A detailed discussion of risk-adjusted performance measures and an actual comparison of different measures allow you to choose the one you like best. Chapter 6 ends by developing a control chart of future performance so you can monitor CTA performance more effectively.

Chapter 7 features new material on estimating the three key unknowns of future performance: depth of drawdowns, duration of drawdowns, and expected returns. It builds quantitative models to estimate these key measures for a diversified portfolio of futures, hedge funds, or stocks. The application of these ideas is shown via the Chande Comfort Zone, an essential tool for systematic trading. This chapter shows how you can use these models to deal with drawdowns, and answers the crucial question: has the system stopped working? Additional models for scaling volatility, scaling leverage, and establishing benchmarks for calibrating risk-adjusted returns are included. Chapter 7 discusses empty diversification and shows an example comparing CTAs. The chapter ends by applying these ideas to the trading of stocks and mutual funds. The ideas in this book advance the state-of-the art in risk control and money management by providing portfolio-level solutions.

Chapter 9 shows how you can build an automated diary using a spreadsheet. The last of the new material in Chapter 9 applies sports psychology in trading. Trading exerts enormous pressures on traders, as does the field of sports on its professionals. Hence, it is natural to ask how the techniques of dealing with the mental demands of sports can be applied to trading. Chapter 9 shows how the basic ideas taken from sports can be adapted to the trading environment, to help traders deal with the stresses of trading. As with other issues in psychology, this is but one interpretation, and you may wish to apply these ideas differently. However, the ideas may provide a useful starting point for your own research into this important aspect of trading.

The Usual Disclaimer

Throughout the book, a number of trading systems are explored as examples of the art of designing and testing trading systems. This is not a recommendation that you trade these systems. I do not claim that these systems will be profitable in the future, nor that profits or losses will be similar to those shown in the calculations. In fact, there is no guarantee that these calculations are defect free. I urge you to review the section in Chapter 3 called a reality check. That section points out the inherent limitations of developing systems with the benefit of hindsight. You should use the examples in this book as an inspiration to develop your own trading systems. Do not forget that there is risk of loss in futures trading.

What Is a Trading System?

A trading system is a set of rules that defines conditions required to initiate and exit a trade. Usually, most trading systems have many parts, such as entry, exit, risk control, and money management rules.

The rules of a trading system can be implicit or explicit, simple or complex. A system can be as simple as "buy sweaters in summer," or "buy when she sells." By definition, the system must be feasible. Ideally, the system accounts for "all" trading issues, from signal generation, to order placement, to risk control. A good way to visualize effective system design is to stipulate that someone who is not a trader must be able to implement the system.

In practice, every trader uses a system. For most traders, a system could really be many systems. It could be discretionary, partly discretionary, or fully mechanical. The systems could use different types of data, such as 5-minute bars or weekly data. The systems may be neither consistent nor easy to test; the rules could have many exceptions. A system could have many variables and parameters. You can trade different combinations of parameters on the same market. You can trade different parameter sets on different markets. You can even trade the same parameter set on all markets.

What Is a Trading Program?

Clearly, no universal trading program exists, although the components of a successful trading program for stocks or futures can be easily identified (Table 1.1). The process of signal generation requires the trader to analyze data sources, determine the portfolio of markets or stocks to be traded, and feed that information continuously into the signal generator. The generated signals must then be correctly sized for the account equity, and the trade sizing algorithm must also

Table 1.1   Components of a successful trading program.

Signal Generation	Trading	Checks and Balances
Data sources	Entry/exit orders	Trading errors
Portfolio selection	Checking broker statements	Risk control
Entry package/exit package	Holidays/vacations	Trader psychology
Trade sizing/money management	Backup/redundant systems	Research into new ideas

include money management considerations. The output of this effort is a valid buy or sell order. The trader can then send the orders to a broker for execution. The trader must carefully monitor execution, check for fills and errors on the desks, and follow up by checks on the daily and monthly statements. Successful traders prepare for market holidays and their own vacations. They also have backup and redundant systems to allow for interruptions of data feeds, electrical power, and communication links. The last set of challenges, checks and balances, requires the trader to develop procedures for handling trading errors and overall risk controls. The trader must also monitor his or her own psychological condition and maintain a vigorous research program.

Every trader adapts a "system" to his or her style of trading. It would be helpful to classify trading systems into different types of return generation processes (RGPs) for ease of analysis and comparison. You will also find it easier to visualize your own trading style by understanding the classification scheme for RGPs proposed in the next section.

Classification of Return Generation Processes

A return generation process is simply a trading system or portfolio of systems. A simple and consistent system classification by style would facilitate a comparison of different RGPs. Such a method of classification should be useful for investors and allocators alike in their search for superior performers.

The RGP is the trading "system" by which equity is risked in order to seek profits. The variable that differentiates RGPs is the time frame over which prices are expected to move in favor of a given position. The time frame is quantified as the length of the average winning trade in trading, not calendar, days. On average, the longer the trade duration, the larger the amplitude of the expected move, and the larger the average profit per trade. A "slow" trading system tends to have trades of longer duration. Hence, the average duration of winning trades is a valid parameter for classifying RGPs.

We begin by separating the RGP into entry and exit strategies. Each RGP needs at least one of each, but may have one or more of both. We then·classify the "speed" of trading into two levels, fast and slow. The speed labels describe

Duration of Average Winning Trade (in trading days)			
		Exit Strategies	
		Fast	Slow
Entry	Fast	< 5	30~50
Strategies	Slow	5~30	>50

Figure 1.2　A classification of return generation processes by duration of winning trades.

the relative sensitivity of the entry and exit signals to price action. Faster entries and exits tend to be more sensitive to price movements. Because there are two levels each for the entry and exit, there are a total of four style combinations (Figure 1.2). The values of average trade duration assigned to the four style categories shown in Figure 1.2 are based on personal experience.

We can now convert the average trade duration into distinct RGP styles (Figure 1.3). Brute-force trend-following is an RGP that generally uses slow entry and exit strategies. Average trade lengths are typically greater than 50 days, and such RGPs are robust and have stood the test of time. These RGPs come in a variety of flavors, take moderate risks for large profits, and work best with large accounts using a diversified portfolio. They are susceptible to drawdowns when a large portion of open trade equity is lost due to slow exit strategies.

The diagonal opposite of brute-force trend-following is "hot-button" trading, which lasts less than 5 days. These high-speed RGPs use fast entries and fast exits, trade a relatively small number of markets, must control slippage and execution costs, and work best when there are "burst" moves lasting three or more days. They are susceptible to choppy price action, often take large risks for small profits, and are vulnerable to correlation shifts and pattern failures. Hot-button RGPs tend to have a low correlation to other RGPs, and are usually traded with small accounts or vast leverage.

An RGP that gets into an emerging trend early and stays until the trend is exhausted can be called an "early-bird special." This works best when markets

Description of Return Generation Process (RGP)			
		Exit Strategies	
		Fast	Slow
Entry	Fast	Hot-button trading	Early-bird special
Strategies	Slow	Selective trend-following	Brute-force trend-following

Figure 1.3　Descriptive classification of RGPs.

trend smoothly in a given direction (like migrating birds), but is susceptible to false breakouts or early trend reversals. Hence, this strategy can also be viewed as optimistic trend-following. Such RGPs are also robust, but tend to give up some equity before closing successful trades. An antitrend strategy may be visualized as belonging to this category.

The last remaining RGP style can be called selective trend-following because it seeks well-established trends. Because such RGPs are slow to enter and quick to exit, they are less vulnerable to early reversals or late setbacks during trends. However, the price of such RGPs is lost market opportunities when trends are smooth and orderly, even though they have excellent risk adjusted performance.

Figures 1.2 and 1.3 can help you to classify your own style or that of a trading advisor. If the advisor uses a blend of strategies, then a weighted average trade duration can be used to classify that manager. The investor or allocator can now create portfolios with a blend of these RGPs, or a preponderance of these RGPs, in order to meet their investment goals. For example, a portfolio may include a brute-force trend-follower and a selective trend-follower to add extra returns when trends are strong while reducing down-side volatility when trends are particularly scarce.

The strengths and weaknesses of each style are summarized in Table 1.2. An investor or allocator can use this generalized classification scheme to understand or test the strengths and weaknesses of any particular RGP. It is easier to sort through conflicting claims by identifying the style of a manager because performance should be generally similar within a style classification. You can also use your own data to have three speed categories, fast, medium, and slow. In conclusion, you can use this approach to construct effective portfolios. Yet another approach to classifying RGPs is discretionary versus fully systematic, as discussed in the next section.

Table 1.2 Comparison of RGP strengths and weaknesses.

Strategy	Pros	Cons
Hot-button trading	Low correlation to other RGPs, does not require sustained trends	Execution costs, diversification, vulnerable to random noise
Early-bird special	Gets in early into emerging trends	Vulnerable to early reversals, and late collapses
Selective trend-following	Good compromise between being too quick to enter and too slow to exit	Not immune to rapid reversals at the start or end of the trend
Brute-force trend-following	Robust, has stood the test of time	Requires sustained trends, gives up equity at the end of the trend

Comparison: Discretionary versus Mechanical System Trader

Table 1.3 compares two extremes in trading: a discretionary trader and a 100 percent mechanical system trader. Discretionary traders use all inputs that seem relevant to the trade: fundamental data, technical analysis, news, trade press, phases of the moon—their imagination is the limit. System traders, on the other hand, slavishly follow a mechanical system without any deviations. Their entire focus is on implementing the system "as is," with no variations, exceptions, modifications, or adaptations of any kind.

Exceptional traders are discretionary traders, and they can probably outperform all mechanical system traders. Their biggest advantage is that they can change the key variable driving each trade, and therefore vary bet size more intelligently than in a mechanical system. Discretionary traders can change the relative importance of their trading variables so they can easily switch between trend-following and anti-trend modes. They can instantly switch between time frames of analysis, going from 5-minute bars to weekly bars as their assessment of the trading opportunity changes.

Discretionary traders can make better use of market information other than price. For example, they can react to news or fundamental information to change bet size. Discretionary traders can adjust their perceived risk constantly, so they can increase or decrease positions more intelligently than mechanical traders. These infrequent "home runs" often make all the difference between good and great trading performance. However, for the average trader, being a mechanical system trader probably maximizes the chances of success.

The goals of a mechanical system trader are to pick a time frame (for example, hourly, daily, weekly), identify the trend status, and anticipate the direction of the future trend. The system trader must then trade the anticipated trend, control losses, and take profits. The rules must be specific, and cover every aspect of trading. For example, the rules must specify how to calculate the

Table 1.3   Comparison of the information-based style of a discretionary trader to the data-driven style of the fully systematic trader.

Discretionary Trader	100% Mechanical System Trader
Trades "information" flow	Trades "data" flow
Anticipatory traders	Participatory traders
Subjective	Objective
Many rules	Few rules
Emotional	Unemotional
Varies "key" indicator from trade to trade	"Key" indicators are always the same
Few markets	Many markets

number of contracts to trade and what type of entry order to use. The rules must indicate where to place the initial money management stop. The trader must execute the system "automatically," without any ambiguity about the implementation.

Mechanical system traders are objective, use relatively few rules, and must remain unemotional as they take their losses or profits. The most prominent feature of a mechanical system is that its rules are constant. The system always calculates its key variables in the same way regardless of market action. Even though some indicators vary their effective length based on volatility, all the rules of the system are fixed, and known a priori. Thus, mechanical system traders have no opportunity to vary the rules based on background events, nor to adjust position size to match the markets more effectively. This is at once a strength and a weakness. A major benefit for system traders is that they can trade many more markets than can discretionary traders, and achieve a level of diversification that may not otherwise be possible.

You can create different flavors of trading systems that use a small or limited amount of discretion. You could, for example, have specific criteria to increase position size. This could include fundamental and technical information. You can be consistent only if you are specific. This discussion really begs the question of why to use trading systems, answered in the next section.

Why Should You Use a Trading System?

The most important reason to use a trading system is to gain a "statistical edge." This often-used term simply means that you have tested the system, and the profit of the average trade—including all losing and winning trades—is a positive number. This average trade profit is large enough to make this system worth trading—it covers trading costs, slippage, and is, on average, likely to perform better than competing systems. Later in the book, I discuss all of these criteria in greater detail.

The statistical edge is relevant to another statistical quantity called the probability of ruin. The smaller this number, the more likely you are, on paper, to survive and prosper. For example, if you have a probability of ruin less than, say, 1 percent, your risk control measures and other measures of system performance are typically sufficient to prevent instant destruction of your account equity.

My biggest source of concern about these statistical numbers is they assume you will trade the system exactly as you have tested it, with not one deviation. This is difficult to achieve in practice. Thus, your risk of ruin—and it is only a risk until it becomes a fact—could be higher than your calculations. Despite this concern, you should develop systems that meet sound statistical criteria, for that greatly enhances your odds of success. As usual, there are no guarantees, but at least the odds, if not the gods, will be on your side.

Another reason to use a trading system is to gain objectivity. If you are steadfastly objective, you can resist the siren call of news events, hot tips, gossip, or boredom. Suppose you are a chart trader and you enjoy some flexibility in interpreting a given chart formation. It is very easy to identify a pattern after the fact, but it is rather difficult to do so as the pattern evolves in real time. Hence, analysis can paralyze you, and you may never make an executable trading decision. Being objective frees you to follow the dictates of your analysis.

Consistency is another vital reason to use a trading system. Since the few rules in a trading system are applied in precisely the same way each time, you are assured of a rare consistency in your trading. In many ways, objectivity and consistency go together. Although consistency is known as the hobgoblin of little minds, it is certainly a useful trait when you are not quite a champion trader.

A trading system gives another crucial advantage: diversification, particularly across trading models, markets, and time frames. No one can be certain when the markets will have their big move, and diversification is another way to increase your odds of being in the right place at the right time.

In summary, you can use a trading system to gain a statistical edge, objectivity, consistency, and diversification across models and markets. A key assumption underlying this section is that the system you are using is well designed and robust. The next section discusses examples of a robust trading system.

Robust Trading Systems: TOPS COLA

A robust trading system is one that can withstand a variety of market conditions across many markets and time frames. A robust system is not overly sensitive to the actual values of the parameters it uses. It is not likely to be the worst or best performer, when traded over a "long" time (perhaps 2 years or more). Such a system is usually a trend-following system, which cuts losses immediately and lets profits run. This philosophy, called TOPS COLA, merely says "take our profits slowly" and "cut off losses at once."

Two examples of robust systems are a moving-average cross-over system and a price-range breakout system. Both systems are well known, and are widely traded in some form or another. The trades from these systems typically last more than 20 days. Hence I classify them as intermediate-term systems. They are trend-following in nature, in that they make money in trending markets and lose money in nontrending markets. The typical system has a winning record of 35 to 45 percent, with an average trade of more than $200. I will discuss these systems in detail later.

The key feature to note is that, when systematically implemented over a "long" time and over many markets, robust systems tend to be, on the whole, profitable. If executed correctly, they guarantee entry in the direction of the intermediate trend, cut off losses quickly, and let profits run. Countless variations of these systems exist, and trend-following systems seem to account for a large percentage of professionally managed accounts.

Robust systems do not make many assumptions about market behavior, have relatively few variables or parameters, and do not change their parameters in response to market action. There is no sharp drop in performance due to small changes in the values of system variables. Such systems are worthy of consideration in most portfolios, and are reasonably reliable. In addition, they are easy to implement.

What Is a "Good" Trading Program?

You can use the tools in this book to develop "good" mechanical systems; that is, systems you can trade systematically, without any deviations, and without worrying about each position every day. Systems must be combined with risk control guidelines and money-management algorithms to construct trading programs. But how do you know you have a good program? Table 1.4 presents a simple checklist that you can use as a guide or benchmark. Remember, there are no guarantees; however, the following suggestions should put you on the right track and are typical of the long-term performance of professional money managers. You can expect to see considerable variation, depending on the time period used for the comparison. For example, the return efficiency can range from 0.1 to 0.5, with mutual funds in the 0.35 to 0.40 area, given the recent strong market performance. The expected drawdown is about four to five times

Table 1.4   A proposed benchmark for a "good" mechanical trading program consistent with your trading beliefs.

Description		Units
Total Entry Conditions/Parameters	≤ 10	#
Total Exit Conditions/Parameters	≤ 10	#
Number of markets traded	≥ 10	#
Test period/data	≥ 24	Months
Equity risked per trade	≤ 2	%
Proportion of profitable trades	≤ 50	%
Average monthly return (μ)	1	%
Standard deviation of monthly returns (σ)	5	%
Return Efficiency (μ/σ)	≥ 0.2	#
Expected depth of drawdown	20	%
Expected duration of drawdown	≤ 9	Months
Proportion of profitable months	≤ 65	%
Expected Return	> 13	%

the standard deviation of monthly returns; hence, it makes little sense to trade a program with monthly standard deviations greater than 15 percent. These guidelines assume that you are trading daily data, selecting systems using risk-adjusted performance (via return efficiency) and willing to tolerate drawdowns equal to four times the standard deviation of monthly returns. The goal of any parameter choices is to maximize the number of trades over the test period with an eye toward robustness.

These guidelines are probably a good indicator of when you can stop your "search for the Holy Grail" and start trading the program. With sufficient work and originality, you can probably develop a program that can beat these guidelines. However, it is not enough to design a good program—you must also be able to implement it seamlessly.

How Do You Implement a Trading System?

Begin with a trading system you trust. After sufficient testing, you can determine the risk control strategy necessary for that system. The risk control strategy specifies the number of contracts per signal and the initial dollar amount of the risk per contract. The risk control strategy may also specify how the initial stop changes after prices move favorably for many days.

The system must clarify portfolio issues such as the number and type of markets suitable for this account. The trading system must also specify when and how to put on initial positions in markets in which it has signaled a trade before commencement of trading for a particular account.

A trade plan is at the heart of system implementation. The trade plan specifies entry, exit, and risk control rules along with the statistical edge. You should record a diary of your feelings and the quality of your implementation, plus any deviations from the plan and the reasons for those deviations. You should monitor position risk and the status of all exit rules.

Last, take the long view: Imagine you are going to implement 100 trades with this plan, not just one. Thus, you can ignore the performance of any one trade, whether profitable or not, and focus on executing the trade plan. These and other implementation issues are discussed in detail in Chapter 9.

Is Systematic Trading Easy?

Systematic trading is not easy because it is against human nature. Trading is an emotional endeavor, and systematic trading requires the trader to execute a set strategy for a "long" time without deviations (i.e., without emotions). This makes trading a boring activity, and thus counter to human nature. It takes a lot of patience and discipline to stick with your plan when the markets are going

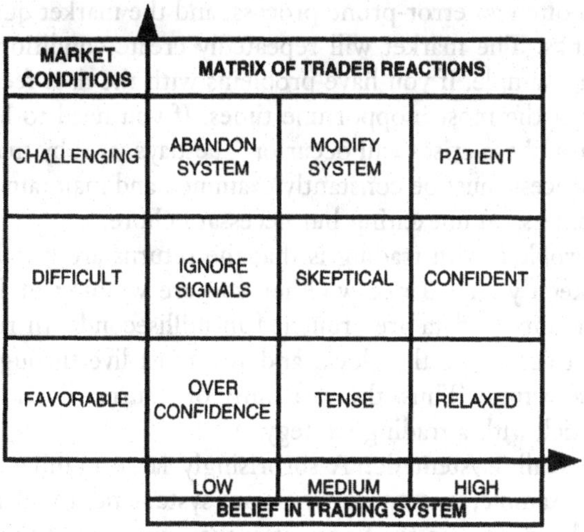

MARKET CONDITIONS	MATRIX OF TRADER REACTIONS		
CHALLENGING	ABANDON SYSTEM	MODIFY SYSTEM	PATIENT
DIFFICULT	IGNORE SIGNALS	SKEPTICAL	CONFIDENT
FAVORABLE	OVER CONFIDENCE	TENSE	RELAXED
	LOW	MEDIUM	HIGH
	BELIEF IN TRADING SYSTEM		

Figure 1.4   Typical reactions of traders to the stresses of trading.

against your strategy. The markets are constantly presenting traders with information to challenge their trading beliefs, encouraging deviations from the predefined plan. For example, if you are an antitrend trader, the market will present you with a series of trends that go through your risk control stops instead of reversing as expected. Or, if you are a breakout-style trader, the market will confront you with a sequence of false breakouts that tempt you into an antitrend strategy.

You need very strong beliefs in your trading process to stay with it without constantly tampering with the parameters (Figure 1.4). For example, the trader who truly believes in the system is prepared for drawdowns when they arrive, and can patiently grind out the worst periods, perhaps deleveraging the system if necessary. A trader with only moderate confidence goes from a state of tensely monitoring performance to increasing skepticism, and then a strong desire to modify or optimize the system. The trader with weak beliefs often starts out with excessive confidence in the system, which evaporates rapidly, so that he or she begins to ignore trading signals; this trader is late to get in and quick to get out. This trader abandons all hope as well as the system itself, and begins the destructive cycle anew with another system he or she barely believes in.

How, then, can you build confidence in a system? It begins with a knowledge of your trading beliefs, a topic covered in detail in Chapter 2. Then, you must have confidence in your testing. All the material in this book is designed to give you that confidence. Next, you must have realistic expectations. Guidelines for a "good" program as well as a discussion of return-efficiency benchmarks appear in Chapter 7. Last, you must trade what you test; Chapter 8 and the discussion on sports psychology in Chapter 9 will help.

Trading is often an error-prone process, and the market quickly discovers your weakest links. The market will repeatedly create conditions to test your weaknesses. For example, if you have problems with the data feed, those problems will occur at the most inopportune times. If you need to leave the office early on Tuesdays, these crises will occur on Tuesdays, as if by magic. Thus, the entire trading process must be constantly examined and maintained at the highest state of readiness, an unexciting but necessary chore.

Another problem with trading is that the returns are variable, and it can be difficult to keep your balance whether you are winning or losing. During testing, vast amounts of data are crunched in milliseconds. In real time, however, you cannot accelerate the clock, and you must live through every drawdown one day at a time. Thus, the variability of returns can also work against your desire to stick with a trading strategy.

Is anyone really systematic? A surprisingly large number of the professionals are. For example, money managers are systematic. Index fund managers are systematic. Even casinos are systematic; they understand they have a small edge, and the more bets people place, the more likely it is that the "house" will be profitable. Insurance companies understand that the more people they insure, the less the risk to the entire portfolio. Thus, systematic trading can be profitable over the long run, if you understand that you have to live through the difficult times to be around when the market conditions favor your strategy. Systematic trading is difficult to execute over a long time, but if you master the psychological challenges, you will clearly have an edge. If you do not wish to be systematic, then find out who wins and who loses in the next section of this chapter.

Who Wins? Who Loses?

Tewles, Harlow, and Stone (1974) report a study by Blair Stewart of the complete trading accounts of 8,922 customers in the 1930s. That may seem like a long time ago, but the human psychology of fear, hope, and greed has changed little in the last 70 or so years. The results of the study are worth considering seriously.

Stewart reported three mistakes made by these customers: (1) Speculators showed a clear tendency to cut profits short, while letting their losses run; (2) Speculators were more likely to be long than short, even though prices generally declined during the nine years of the study; and (3) Longs bought on weakness and shorts sold on strength, indicating they were price-level rather than price-movement traders.

I should contrast this experience with the TOPS COLA philosophy discussed earlier. By taking profits slowly and cutting off losers at once, you will avoid the first mistake reported by Stewart. Second, by being a trend follower, you will avoid the next two mistakes. If you follow trends, you will be long or short per the intermediate trend, and avoid any tendency to be generally long. Third, if you follow trends, you will follow price movement, rather than being a price-level trader.

You will win in the trading business if you have a specific trade plan that contains all the necessary details. You should focus much of your effort and energy on implementing the trade plan as accurately and consistently as possible. Thus, you must go beyond technical analysis, deep into trade management and organized trading, to win.

Appendix to Chapter 1: A Brief Technical Analysis Primer

Introduction

This primer is intended for anyone unfamiliar with the fundamental ideas of technical analysis. If you are familiar with the basic ideas of technical analysis and can use commercial technical analysis software programs, then you can skip this appendix entirely. However, it does include the code for adaptive oscillators and adaptive moving averages that some of you advanced readers might find useful.

There are two types of market data: external and internal. External data are generated by economic activity, regulators, or governments—factors influencing supply and demand, production, and consumption. External data are called fundamental data. Internal market data are generated by the process of trading an instrument such as stocks, futures, or options, and are collected and disseminated by the trading exchanges. Trading data are called technical data. Hence, technical analysis is the analysis of internally generated market data. There are different kinds of internal data, depending on how and where an instrument is traded.

Trading a stock or futures contract generates such information as the price at which the instrument was traded, the number of contracts or units traded, and whether a new position was opened or an existing position was closed. When all the trades in a day are collected and summarized, the exchanges report the daily trading range (high and low), the opening price, the closing price, the trading volume, and the open interest. If you do not understand what each of these terms means, you can visit the Web sites of any futures or stock exchange.

Technical market data are analyzed by plotting them on a graph or chart, in which the horizontal axis is time and the vertical axis describes the units of technical data. The horizontal (time) axis of the graph may depict yearly, monthly, weekly, daily, or intraday periods. The vertical axis shows the price activity: the opening, high, low, and closing prices in local currency. For stocks in particular, the volume of activity during the period is plotted immediately beneath the price bar. Because the price range looks like a bar, this is usually called a bar chart.

Over time, creative traders have observed, invented, tested, and cataloged hundreds of ideas about analyzing bar charts. The advent of computers has simplified this analysis, while permitting other more computationally intensive analytical approaches. It is impossible to describe the myriad ideas in a few short paragraphs, but some important elements that are relevant to understanding the material presented in this book are summarized here.

Assumptions of Technical Analysis

Perhaps the most important assumption of technical analysis is that history repeats itself, and past price action has important implications for future price action. The second major assumption is that a trend in force continues in that direction until replaced, and the trend in a longer time frame (say monthly) is more important than a trend in a shorter time span (say daily). The third assumption is that all currently available information in the public domain about the instrument being traded is fully reflected in the market. This implies that no trader has an information edge, which is not necessarily true. You can debate the validity of these assumptions, and a number of academic studies are available that raise questions about them, insider trading and the random walk theory being two obvious examples. However, for all practical purposes, we will take these assumptions to be generally correct.

Technical analysis relies on detecting patterns in the past that can be traded with confidence in the future. The identification and quantification of patterns can be subjective or objective. Subjective patterns include various types of price formations on a chart, such as channels or triangles. Objective measures of prices are algorithmic formulations, such as moving averages and oscillators. Here we focus on the quantitative elements of technical analysis and refer you to other books on technical analysis for a discussion of chart patterns.

Typical Price Patterns and Chart Formations

Some common price patterns and chart formations using data from the futures markets are shown in Figures 1.5 through 1.13. The same terms are used with stock charts.

A *trending market* shows prices that move steadily in one direction, either up or down (Figure 1.5). These trends can be traded by taking a position in the direction of the trend. Trends occur in response to fundamental developments that attract buyers willing to pay ever-higher prices or draw out sellers willing to sell at ever-lower prices. In the language of economics, the equilibrium price is far away from the current price, and prices move toward the perceived future

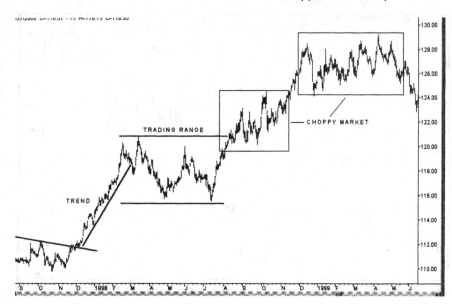

Figure 1.5   A continuous contract of the Eurex Swiss Federal Bond illustrating basic chart patterns.

equilibrium price. Trends can cover a very wide range in prices, with stocks covering a much larger range in prices than futures.

A *trading range* usually occurs at the end of trends, when the prices are close to the perceived equilibrium price and "move sideways" or are contained within some range of values (see Figure 1.5). The usual interpretation here is that the market finds supply at the high end of the trading range (more aggressive sellers) and support at the lower end of the range (more aggressive buyers). One cannot say that there are more buyers than sellers because each trade must match buyers and sellers. Note that there can be an increase in the open interest or in the short interest for stocks if there is a preponderance of sellers or buyers. Such markets are best traded with an antitrend approach that buys lows and sells highs. A trend-following approach using moving averages will be unprofitable because prices move back and forth, producing a succession of losing signals in both directions.

A *choppy market* lacks conviction about price direction, with drifts in one direction and rapid moves in the other direction (see Figure 1.5). A choppy market may be viewed as a market trading within an expanded trading range. A choppy region could occur within a broad uptrend or downtrend, and could last from 1 to 5 months. Trend-following strategies using moving averages and breakout-style strategies are prone to losses within choppy markets. The markets

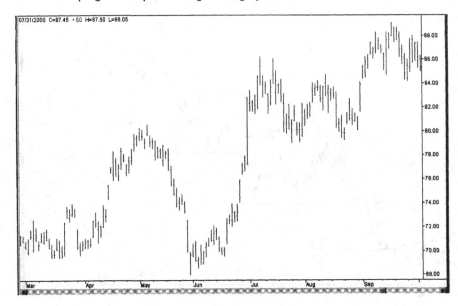

Figure 1.6   A continuous contract of the New York High Grade Copper showing swing moves in 1999.

generally break out of such ranges, but it is difficult to single out false breakouts with accuracy.

A market is making *swing moves* (see Figure 1.6) when it moves smoothly from one price level to another within a very wide trading range over a 7 to 20 day interval. Trend-following strategies using moving averages will be more profitable than breakout-style strategies, and antitrend strategies will be unprofitable in such a market. Periods of swing moves may be viewed as extended consolidations and are usually followed by a trading range or choppy trading. Although such regions can be easily detected (after the fact) by the human eye, they are difficult to detect in real time using quantitative measures.

Cyclic markets make swing moves lasting 3 to 7 days covering a narrow trading range (Figure 1.7). They can be detected using computer-intensive methods and traded by anticipating turning points. Such conditions occur somewhat less frequently than is popularly believed.

Price channels form when swing moves or cyclic markets are superimposed on strong trends. When detected, they are easy to trade using simple trend-following tools. The London International Petroleum Exchange (IPE) Brent Crude futures contract showed a particularly neat channel during its uptrend in 1999–2000 (Figure 1.8). The initial rise in early 1999 was sufficient to define the channel that carried well into 2000. Discretionary traders would have enjoyed low-risk buying opportunities near the bottom of the channel with little follow through below the channel. The same discretionary traders were offered

08/03/2000 C=12590.0 -450.0 H=12910.0 L=12450.0

CYCLIC PRICE PATTERN

Figure 1.7   A continuous contract of the Stockholm Options Market OMX Index showing strong cyclic pattern in 2000.

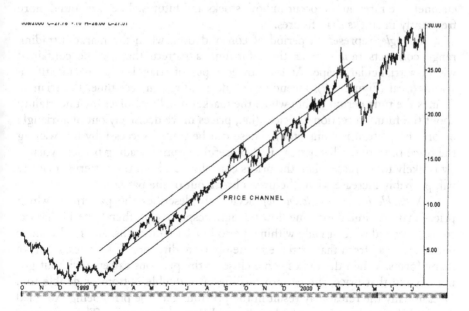

PRICE CHANNEL

Figure 1.8   The London IPE Brent Crude futures continuous contract showing a well-defined price channel in the 1999–2000 period.

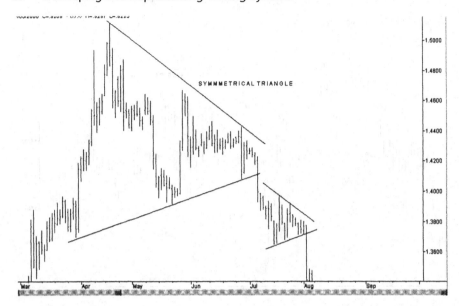

Figure 1.9 A continuous chart of the Chicago IMM Japanese Yen futures contract showing massive triangular consolidation in 1995.

low-risk shorting opportunities near the top of the channel. Such powerful channels are rare, but do occur in both stocks and futures. They are found more frequently in stocks than futures.

Triangles represent a period of consolidation, when the market's trading range contracts rapidly over time, forming a pattern that can be contained within a triangular shape. At least three types of triangles can be identified: symmetrical (Figure 1.9), ascending, or descending. In real time, the triangle defines the time period within which the market usually resolves the uncertainty about the future direction of prices (i.e., prices move decisively out of a triangle before the pattern is completed). These can be traded successfully by awaiting the price breakout. This pattern is also useful in option trading because volatility is likely to decrease when the prices consolidate within the pattern; volatility will probably increase when the prices break out of the pattern.

A *double bottom* or *double top* accurately describes the pattern in which prices make an initial extreme (low or high, respectively), then "retest" that extreme a second time, usually within a period of 1 to 4 months, and finally move decisively away from that extreme in the opposite direction. The retest can take many forms. When the prices come close to the previous extreme without going beyond that price, the pattern qualifies as a double bottom or double top. Occasionally the retest may result in the previous extreme price being exceeded by a small amount, without a close beyond the prior extreme. These patterns represent a loss of momentum, and are easy to detect by eye, but somewhat

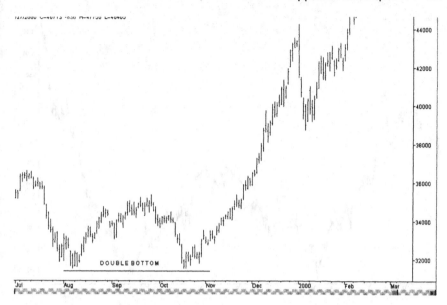

Figure 1.10   A double bottom in a continuous contract of Italy's Milan 30-Stock Index Futures (MIF) in late 1999.

more difficult to define programmatically because the time between retests can vary widely.

Compare, for example, the double bottom formed over a typical period of 1 to 4 months in the Milan 30-Stock Index Futures (MIF) (Figure 1.10) to the massive double bottom that took about 10 months to form in the New York CSCE Sugar #11 futures contract (Figure 1.11). The definition of a double bottom embodies considerable subjectivity. However, as both charts indicate, it can be traded successfully. The aggressive trader may try to enter as close to the double bottom as possible in anticipation of the pattern. A more conservative approach is to buy above the high formed between the test of the low prices on either side of the double bottom. In the conservative approach, the early entrants are typically selling out to the late buyers, and a retest of the double bottom or a minor consolidation can occur here. A close above the high between the double bottoms is said to confirm the double bottom.

Measured Objectives from Chart Formations

Empirical observations have resulted in a consensus about the amplitude of future moves when prices show certain definable chart formations. Such amplitude projections are called *measured objectives*. In any given occurrence, the market may or may not achieve the expected amplitude, or may easily go on to significantly exceed the projected amplitude. However, the ability to recognize

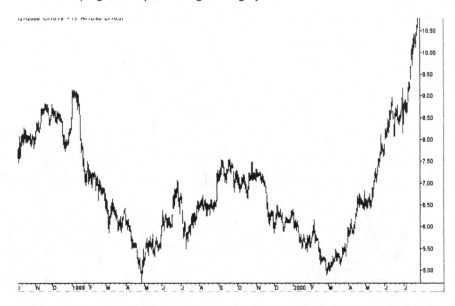

Figure 1.11   A massive double bottom in a continuous contract of the New York CSCE Sugar #11 futures that led to a powerful rally in 2000.

and categorize the pattern and make a projection about future price objectives permits the creation of a trading strategy around such patterns. The two examples shown here illustrate this idea, but are by no means a complete or exhaustive catalog of such patterns.

One often finds a *rectangular price pattern* on price charts, in which the prices have been trading in a "rectangle" for 4 to 6 months. The height of the rectangle can be used to derive a target for prices when they break outside the rectangle. Figure 1.12 shows a continuous chart for New York Cotton futures, with a rectangular price consolidation that occurred in the first half of 1999. The height of the rectangle was $7.25, and the projected downside target was 61.11. Once prices broke out of the consolidation, they reached the price target in less than a month.

Another well-known consolidation price pattern is the *head-and-shoulder pattern*, in which prices form an initial high, then the actual high, followed by a weak retest of that high. The retest fails at a lower level than the high for the move, forming the right shoulder. A trend line can be drawn under the lows of the pattern to form the "neck line." Ideally, the neck line should be horizontal on the chart, but inclined neck lines are not unusual. This pattern can also be occasionally seen at market bottoms. The expected outcome after the formation of the pattern is a powerful move below the neck line for tops and above the neck line for bottoms. The head-and-shoulders pattern should be traded with caution because it has a relatively high failure rate. However, it does provide a

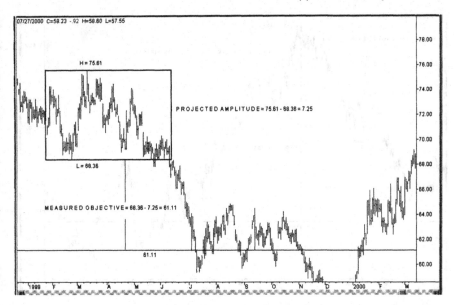

07/27/2000 C=58.23 -.92 H=58.60 L=57.55

H = 75.61

PROJECTED AMPLITUDE= 75.61 - 68.36 = 7.25

L = 68.36

MEASURED OBJECTIVE= 68.36 - 7.25 = 61.11

61.11

Figure 1.12 The measured objective is derived from a price rectangle as the height of the rectangle in this price chart of New York Cotton futures market.

means to derive a price target, measured from the highest high (or lowest low) to the neck line.

Figure 1.13 shows a head-and-shoulders pattern in the London LIFFE Long Gilt futures continuous contract. The highest high on the continuous chart was 125.15, and the neckline intersects a vertical line from the highest high bar at 118.15, indicating a projected price target a full 7 points below the intersection price at 111.15. The Long Gilt broke below the neckline in May 1999, followed by a retest of the neck line seven days later. Once the retest failed, the Long Gilt traded lower in a choppy downtrend and reached the downside target 4 months later. Observe that the price target can be easily exceeded, as was the case with the Long Gilt in Figure 1.13.

Many classical books on technical analysis of stocks that describe measured objectives for patterns such as triangles, pennants, waves, and so on are available for further research in this area. You can probably derive many measurements on your own. You can use these targets as potential entry points or exit points in your systems, as long as you remember that the market will do what it wants.

Statistical Review

The arithmetic average, or mean, of a set of numbers is a summary statistic that summarizes some chosen property of the sample. The arithmetic average sums

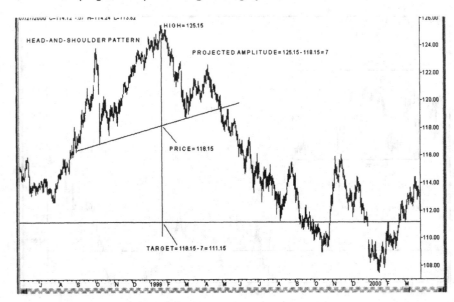

Figure 1.13   A downside target derived for the London LIFFE Long Gilt futures contract using a head-and-shoulder pattern for measurement.

the chosen parameter over every item in the sample, and then divides that total by the number of items in the sample. For example, to find the average weekly closing price, add the daily closing prices from Monday through Friday, and then divide that sum by 5 to get the average weekly closing price. The average may be viewed as a weighted sum over all data points:

$$\text{Average} = \mu = \text{sum}(w_i{}^* V_i)$$

where the weight $w_i = (1/n)$, n = total number of data points, and V_i is the value of each data point. Hence, the average is an equally weighted sum of all the values in the sample, where the weight for each data point is simply the inverse of the total number of data points.

The *average*, or *mean*, of a sample does not give us any idea of how the data are scattered (or dispersed) about the mean; that is, we do not know how close to or how far away from the mean we will find data points. For example, calculating the average height of all the children in a class does not tell us either the range (the tallest minus the shortest) or the frequency of occurrence of different heights. We quantify the spread or dispersion in the data by the *standard deviation*.

To calculate the standard deviation, we first calculate the deviation of each data point from the mean $(V_i - \mu)$. The deviations are squared (to eliminate negative values) and averaged (as above) by summing the squared deviations and

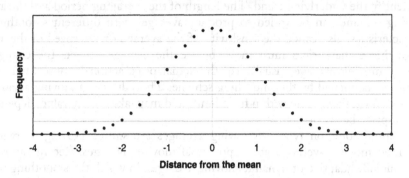

Figure 1.14   Frequency distribution of a normal distribution with mean = 0 and standard deviation of 1 unit. Notice that most of the data are located in a region close to the mean, and there are relatively few data points "far" from the mean. The standard deviation is the yardstick used to quantify the distance of a data point from the mean.

dividing by the number of data points. This is called the *sample variance*. Last, we reverse the effect of squaring the deviations to compute the sample standard deviation as the square root of the variance, obtaining a measure of the dispersion of the data. The standard deviation may be viewed as the square root of the equally weighted average of the squared deviations. The actual formula is:

$$\text{Sample standard deviation} = \sigma = \sqrt{\text{sum}(w_i(V_i - \mu)^2)}$$

In a *normal distribution* (Figure 1.14), the frequency of occurrence of the data in the sample is distributed like a bell curve around the mean. This means that the density of the data is highest near the center of the range of values. We expect to find more data points closer to the mean and relatively fewer points as we move away from the mean. If the data are normally distributed, then we expect about 67 percent of the data to occur inside a region one standard deviation on either side of the mean. In a normal distribution, approximately 99 percent of the data will lie in a region within three standard deviations on either side of the mean. This clarifies the description of the standard deviation as a measure of dispersion.

Moving Averages

Moving averages are simply average values of some variable, such as the close, calculated over a certain time interval, say nine periods. Moving averages are frequently calculated using the closing prices on a bar chart, but you could use anything else you wish. Moving averages are used to smooth prices and are used to identify the underlying trend. The length of the averaging period and the averaging scheme can be varied to produce averages with different smoothing characteristics, also called the sensitivity of the average or the speed of the average. Note that prices must move before the average reflects the change. Hence, moving averages usually lag the actual price action because their response is dampened by the smoothing scheme. The values of a moving average are not constrained to lie within fixed limits and may take on any value, depending on price behavior.

Some common types of moving averages are simple moving averages, weighted moving averages, and exponential moving averages. Recent innovations include adaptive or dynamic moving averages, in which the smoothing period is not fixed but can be varied with market volatility.

The weighting scheme in a simple moving average (SMA) is such that it gives equal weight to all data points. The weight is (1/n), where n is the number of time periods in the calculation. Because the length of the calculation period is fixed, at the end of each time period, a new data point is added and the oldest data point is discarded. In a weighted moving average (WMA), the weights are adjusted so that the sum of all the weights is one, but recent data are given more weight than data toward the end of the sampling period. A weighted average also drops the oldest data point when a new data point arrives. Some traders feel that the oldest data should also be included in the smoothing scheme. This led to the acceptance of exponential moving averages (EMA), which never actually drop the oldest data when new data arrive, but continuously reduce their weight in the calculation.

Which moving average is used is largely a matter of personal preference. Figure 1.15 shows the Tokyo Palladium contract as it experienced a vigorous rally in January and February 2000. The figure also shows three different 20-period moving averages of the close. Notice how the EMA responds more quickly than the WMA, which is more sensitive than the SMA. The EMA and the WMA give greater weight to recent data, and hence proved to be more sensitive to the rapid price move in that market.

Moving averages form the bases of trend-following trading systems, when two or more averages are used to identify changes in trend, and positions are established in the direction of the new trend. The simplest of these strategies uses two simple moving averages of different length, one shorter than the other. The shorter the length of a moving average, the fewer the time periods used in its calculation. Thus, the longer average is the "old" trend and the shorter average is the "new" trend. If the shorter moving average crosses over the longer moving average, then a new uptrend is about to occur, and long positions are established. Likewise, the shorter average crossing under the longer average indicates a downtrend and short positions. Many variations of this strategy can be developed.

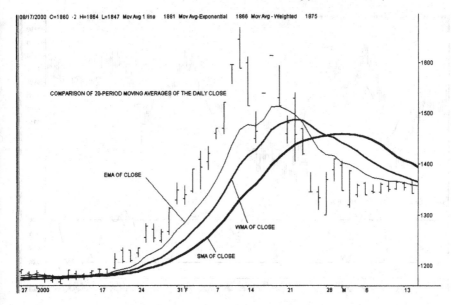

Figure 1.15   The 20-period simple (SMA), weighted (WMA), and exponential (EMA) moving averages of the daily closing price during a sharp rally in the Tokyo Palladium market in the first two months of 2000.

Oscillators

Oscillators are derived from market prices but "normalized" so they fluctuate about some fixed value, such as zero, between fixed upper and lower bounds. Oscillators are just another measure of market momentum. Various smoothing schemes are used to create oscillators that move about smoothly. The time period over which the values are calculated is usually fixed, and the oscillators are used to indicate when prices are "overbought" or "oversold" (i.e., have been pushed too far in one direction). The trading thesis is that such extremes in prices cannot be sustained, and prices are expected to go sideways or even reverse direction for brief periods.

A class of "range location oscillators" identifies the location of current prices within the range of prices over a fixed time period. The so-called stochastic oscillator is an example of a range location oscillator. Figure 1.16 shows the Eurex EuroBund contract with a stochastic oscillator plotted below prices. Note how the oscillator shows the location of the close within the range of recent prices. The oscillator heads higher when prices rise and falls when prices decline. Because the time period for calculating the price range is fixed, the price range used to compute the relative location of the close changes continuously. For example, the oscillator shows that prices were near the bottom of

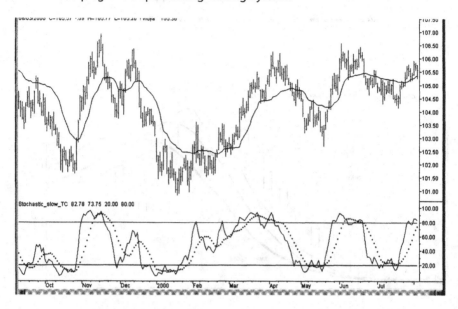

Figure 1.16   Eurex EuroBund contract with a slow stochastic oscillator showing market momentum.

their recent trading range in January 2000 and May 2000, even though the price range leading into those bottoms was larger in January. Oscillators are useful in identifying turning points in markets locked in a trading range.

During trends, a second application of oscillators is to detect divergences between market momentum and price action. The so-called momentum divergences are a direct result of calculating the oscillator using a fixed time period. For example, a divergence occurs when prices make a new low but the oscillator does not. This occurs when the initial low is accompanied by an expansion in the price range traversed over the calculation period. If the subsequent low occurs with a smaller price range over the calculation period, the value of the oscillator is higher than the oscillator value at the previous price extreme, thereby producing a divergence. The reverse of this situation (i.e., prices make a new high, but the oscillator does not) also is a divergence. Divergences are usually observed at key turning points, but not every divergence leads to a key turning point. Figure 1.17 shows the Eurex EuroBund contract with divergences between prices and the momentum oscillator highlighted for quick visual reference.

Price Channels and Bands

Price channels are used to plot the highest high and lowest low prices over a fixed calculation period. This is a different graphical device than the channel chart formation discussed earlier. Price channels as used here define the range of

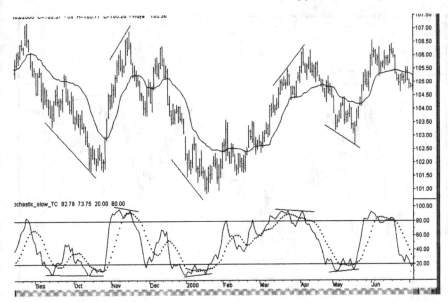

Figure 1.17   Divergences between prices and the momentum of prices are isolated using the stochastic oscillator for the Eurex EuroBund futures continuous contract. The divergences here occur when prices make a new extreme but the momentum oscillator does not.

price action over the given time period (Figure 1.18). They are used to make trading decisions when prices make new highs or lows. New highs or lows can be interpreted to signal the start of new trends, and positions can be established in the direction of the trend or liquidated against the direction of the previous trend.

Price bands are usually plotted around moving averages and are used to measure the range of price action on either side of the average. The bands can be created by plotting them a fixed percentage on either side of the moving average or by adding some measure of volatility, such as the standard deviation of prices over the length of the moving average. The bands can be used to measure price extremes or strong trends. Figure 1.19 shows the Eurex EuroBund contract with a 50-day simple moving average surrounded by 2 percent bands. Consolidations tend to occur within the bands, and trends tend to occur outside the bands. The bands around a moving average can be defined in a variety of ways, including those based on volatility.

It is possible to develop trend-following or antitrend trading systems using price channels or price bands or both. However, even though every major trend starts with the penetration of channels or bands, not every penetration of the bands or channels leads to a major trend.

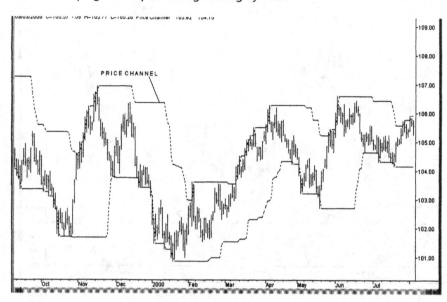

Figure 1.18   A 20-bar price channel overlaid in a continuous contract of the Eurex EuroBund futures contract. A penetration of the upper channel indicates an uptrend, a penetration of the lower channel indicates a downtrend. Note that the amplitude and duration of market movement after the initial penetration is unpredictable.

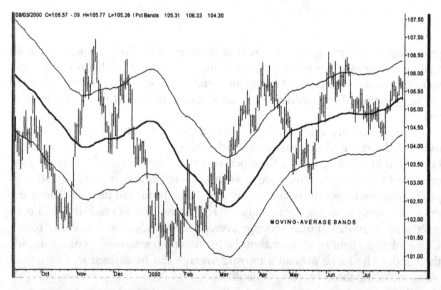

Figure 1.19   A continuous contract of the Eurex EuroBund contract overlaid with a 50-day simple moving average surrounded by 2 percent bands. The upper band is 2 percent above, and the lower band is 2 percent below, the value of that day's 50-day moving average.

Trendiness Indicators

The timely detection of trends can be potentially profitable; therefore, a number of price-based indicators have been created to measure "trendiness" in the markets. A high value on such measures would indicate the presence of a trend, and hence trend-based trading strategies could be used. These indicators can be approximated by twice-smooth momentum measures such as moving averages.

The *average directional index* (ADX) is one indicator of trendiness with a rather complex calculation after the user specifies the length of the look-back period. An ADX value greater than 20 or a rising trend in the ADX is presumed to indicate a trend. In every major trend, the 14-period ADX will usually exceed 20, but not every occurrence of ADX greater then 20 leads to a major trend.

The recently proposed Chande Trend Index is based on option pricing theory. If L is the length of the look-back period, then the formula may be written as:

$$\text{Chande Trend Index (CTI)} = \tau = \ln(c/c[L])/(\text{stdev}(\ln(c/c[1]),L) * \text{sqrt}(L))$$

where τ is the trend index, ln is the natural logarithm, stdev is the standard deviation, c[1] is yesterday's close, c[L] is the close L days ago, and sqrt is the square root function. A value greater than 1 indicates the presence of a trend. The reasoning behind this measure of trendiness is as follows. The theory of Brownian motion suggests that prices move as the standard deviation of daily logarithmic changes multiplied by the square-root of the length of the time interval over which the price change is measured. This is the quantity in the denominator. The numerator is the logarithm of the ending and starting prices over the same interval. If prices are moving randomly, then the Chande Trend Index should be less than or equal to 1. Conversely, if prices are trending strongly, then the CTI should be greater than 1. Figure 1.20 shows a 50-day moving average with 2 percent bands along with the Chande Trend Index on a continuous contract of the Eurex Bund contract. Notice how trends generally occur outside the band, and are confirmed with values of CTI greater than 1. When the market began to lose momentum, near the right edge of the chart, the CTI values trended lower and were generally below 1.

The CTI can be applied to stocks with equal ease. For example, Ariba, Inc. stock, shown in Figure 1.21, shows how strong trends raise the CTI to values well above 1. In that case, the CTI can be used as an overbought indicator.

Dynamic Indicators

The indicators discussed thus far require the user to select the time period over which the indicator is computed. In many instances, it would nice to create indicators that adjust their calculation period automatically based on underlying

Figure 1.20   The Chande Trend Index plotted below a continuous chart of the Eurex EuroBund futures and 2 percent bands around a 50-day simple moving average. A value of the CTI greater than 1 indicates the presence of a trend over the time period of the calculation.

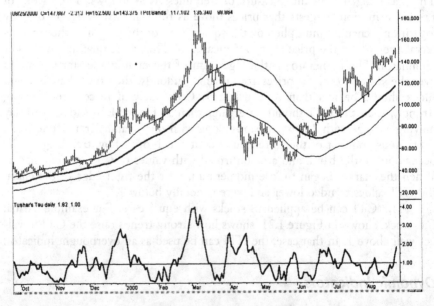

Figure 1.21   Ariba, Inc. (ARBA) stock showing the Chande Trend Index and a 50-day moving average with 2 percent bands. Values of CTI greater than 1 indicate the presence of trends, confirmed by prices rising above or falling below the price bands.

price action. These ideas are detailed in Chande and Kroll's *The New Technical Trader* (John Wiley & Sons, 1994). In particular, Chande and Kroll's "Stochastic RSI and Dynamic Momentum Index" (see bibliography for reference) explains how to use adaptive indicators.

The strategy behind dynamic indicators is to change the look-back length of the indicator by connecting it to market volatility. We would like the indicator to have a "long" look-back period when prices are in a trading range (volatility is low). Conversely, we want a "short" look-back length when prices are moving rapidly. Changing the look-back length for calculating indicators is more responsive than smoothing them with adaptive moving averages. The actual definition of "long" and "short" look-back length depends on your trading horizon.

Figure 1.22 presents a sample Omega Research TradeStation code to create an adaptive stochastic oscillator that uses the 20-day standard deviation of closing prices to vary the length between 7 and 28 days. First, determine if the 20-day standard deviation is at its highest level. To do so, compute a stochastic oscillator using the 20-day standard deviation (variables v1 through v4). If the 20-day standard deviation is at its highest level (v1 = v2), then v4 = 1, and the oscillator length is set at its shortest value, variable lenmin (= 7 days). If the 20-day standard deviation is at its lowest value (v1 = v3), hence v4 = 0, and the current length is set to the maximum length, variable lenmax (= 28 days). All that remains is to calculate the stochastic oscillator, stoch, for the close and smooth it using a 3-day exponential moving average. The same approach can be used to develop other adaptive indicators or averages.

Figure 1.23 shows the Eurex EuroBund contract with the adaptive stochastic oscillator (thin line) superimposed on an 18-day stochastic oscillator. The adaptive oscillator clearly adapts to price action, reaching extreme levels more quickly than the fixed-length equivalent oscillator.

The variable-index dynamic moving average (VIDYA) essentially modifies the equation of an exponential average by varying the index of the exponential average using market volatility. Such averages adjust their length automatically and are more responsive to price action. The effective length of the average shortens when market volatility increases. Conversely, the effective length of the average lengthens when market volatility decreases. Figure 1.24 examines the Milan Index Futures (MIF) by plotting the 9-day exponential moving average and the variable-index dynamic moving average. When the market is moving rapidly, the VIDYA converges to a 9-day exponential moving average. When volatility is at its lowest levels, VIDYA flattens out and its effective length becomes "infinite," proving that it has a large dynamic range of effective lengths. In Figure 1.24, as the Milan stock futures accelerated out of a consolidation in June 1997, the VIDYA was effectively the same length as a 9-day exponential moving average. As the MIF consolidated in June through September, VIDYA flattened out. This flattening of the VIDYA is an effective tool for identifying consolidations.

```
{--- © 2K Tushar Chande; Adaptive Stochastic Oscillator ---}

    vars: v1(0), v2(0), v3(0), v4(0) ;
    vars: lenmax(28), lenmin(7), currlen(0) ;
    vars: hh(0), ll(0), stoch(0), stochma(0) ;

{--- Calculate 20-day std. Dev. And its 20-day range  ---}

    v1 - stddev(c,20) ;
    v2 - highest(v1, 20) ;
    v3 - lowest(v1, 20) ;

{--- Create v4: stochastic oscillator for 20-day std. dev. ---}
{--- if v1-v2 (highest level) -> v4 - 1; if v1-v3 (lowest level) ->
     v4-0 ---}

    if (v2-v3) > 0 then v4 - ((v1 - v3)/(v2-v3)) Else v4 - 0 ;

{--- Calculate current effective length; if v4 - 1, then length -
     mininum ---}

    currlen - IntPortion(lenmin + (lenmax-lenmin)*(1-v4)) ;

{--- Calculate stochastic oscillator and its 3-day exponential
     average ---}

    hh - highest(h, currlen) ;
    ll - lowest(l, currlen) ;
    if (hh-ll) > 0 then stoch - ((close - ll)/(hh - ll)) * 100 ;
    if currentbar - 1 then stochma - 0 else
    stochma - 0.5*stoch + 0.5*stochma[1] ;

{--- Plot data ---}

    plot1(stoch, "adapt_stoch") ;
    plot2(slowk(18), "stochma") ;
    plot3(80, "hi_ref") ;
    plot4(20, "lo_ref") ;

{--- End of code ---}
```

Figure 1.22 Sample code for Omega Research TradeStation program.

The TradeStation code for VIDYA is provided in Figure 1.25. It modifies the code for the adaptive stochastic oscillator discussed previously (Figure 1.22). The sensitivity of the average can be increased by increasing the scale factor (sfac) variable in the code in Figure 1.25. Other ways to calculate VIDYA are discussed in *The New Technical Trader.*

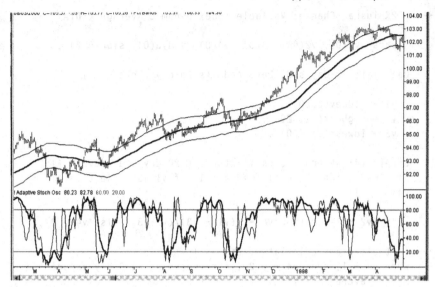

Figure 1.23   A continuous contract for the Eurex EuroBund futures shown with the adaptive stochastic oscillator, in which the time period of the calculation is adjusted from 7 to 28 days based on the 20-day standard deviation of daily closing prices. The thin line is the adaptive stochastic oscillator, and the thick line is a 18-day stochastic oscillator. The adaptive stochastic oscillator is more sensitive to price changes. A 50-day simple moving average is used to plot 2 percent bands for visual reference.

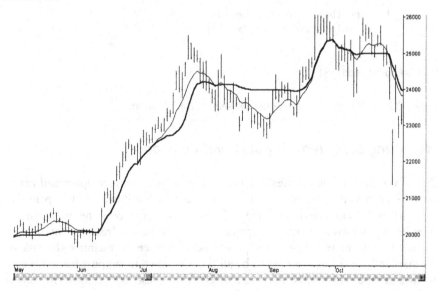

Figure 1.24   A continuous contract for the Milan Index Futures in Italy plotted with the 9-day EMA (thin line) and a 9-day VIDYA (thick line). The dynamic average changes its effective length based on the 20-day standard deviation of closing prices. Notice how VIDYA flattens out during price consolidation.

```
{--- © 2K Tushar Chande; Variable Index Dynamic Average VIDYA ---}

    vars: v1(0), v2(0), v3(0), v4(0), vidya(0), sfac(0.2) ;

{--- Calculate 20-day std. Dev. And its 20-day range  ---}

    v1 = stddev(c,20) ;
    v2 = highest(v1, 20) ;
    v3 = lowest(v1, 20) ;

{--- Create v4: stochastic oscillator for 20-day std. dev. ---}
{--- if v1=v2 (highest level) => v4 = 1; if v1=v3 (lowest level) =>
    v4=0 ---}

    if (v2-v3) > 0 then v4 = ((v1 - v3)/(v2-v3)) Else v4 = 0 ;

{--- Initialize and calculate VIDYA ---}
{--- When v4 = 1, sfac*v4 = 0.20, corresponding to 9-day exponential
    moving average ---}

    if currentbar <=50 then vidya = c ;
    if currentbar > 50 then vidya = sfac*v4*close +
       (1-sfac*v4)*Vidya[1] ;

{--- Plot data ---}

    if currentbar > 50 then begin
         plot1(vidya, "vidya") ;
    end ;

{ --- End of code -}
```

Figure 1.25   VIDYA code for OmegaResearch TradeStation.

Estimating Long-Term Support and Resistance

One of the most common uses of a price chart is to estimate support and resistance. *Support* is the approximate price level at which a downtrend in prices is likely to stop, "supported" by buyers. Conversely, *resistance* is the approximate price level at which an uptrend in prices is likely to pause, "resisted" by sellers. We want to estimate long-term support and resistance, to quantify the risk in the market. The risk is assumed to be all the way down to support for longs and up to resistance for shorts. A review of charts suggests that long-term moves in the futures markets seem to last about 18 to 20 months, or about 400 days, assuming 20 trading days in a month. Hence, here we define long-term support and resistance at the 400-day simple moving average. Because the markets

Figure 1.26   A continuous chart of the S&P-500 daily futures with 400-day simple moving average and bands set at one-half of the 400-day standard deviation of closing prices. The long-term support and resistance seem to lie near the bands.

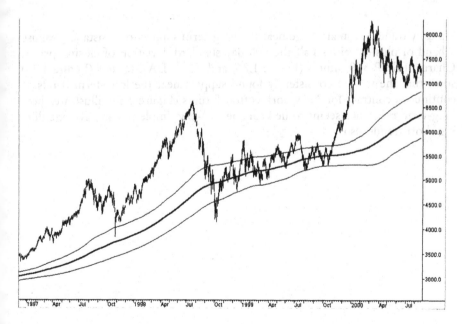

Figure 1.27   The Eurex DAX futures contract found support at the 400-day moving average and the bands set at one-half the 400-day standard deviation of closing prices.

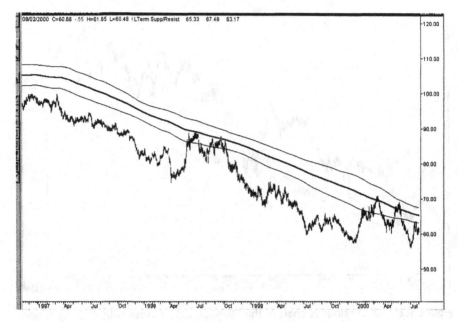

08/02/2000 C=60.86 -.55 H=61.65 L=60.48 ! LTerm Supp/Resist 65.33   67.48   63.17

Figure 1.28   A continuous contract for New York Cotton showing resistance at the 400-day simple moving average during a multiyear downtrend.

typically trade in a small range near the long-term support or resistance, we use a band of plus or minus half the 400-day standard deviation of closing prices. Charts of S&P-500 futures (Figure 1.26) and Eurex DAX futures (Figure 1.27) show that the market consistently found support near the long-term bands. A continuous contract for New York cotton futures (Figure 1.28) illustrates how long-term resistance seems to lie near the 400-day simple moving average during short trends also.

Chapter

Principles of Trading System Design

If not the gods, put the odds on your side.

Introduction

This chapter presents some basic principles of system design. You should try to understand these issues and adapt them to your preferences.

First, assess your trading beliefs—these beliefs are fundamental to your success and should be at the core of your trading system. You may have several strong beliefs, and they can all be used to formulate one or more trading systems. After you have a list of your core beliefs, you can build a trading system around them. Remember, it will not be easy to stick with a system that does not reflect your beliefs.

The six major rules of system design are covered in this chapter in considerable detail. The specific issues to be examined are why your system should have a positive expectation and why you should have a small number of robust rules. The focus in the later sections of this chapter is on money-management aspects such as trading multiple contracts, using risk control, and trading a portfolio of markets. The real difficulties lie in implementing a system, and hence, the chapter ends by explaining why a system should be mechanical.

By the end of this chapter, you should be able to write down your trading beliefs, as well as explain and apply the six basic principles of system design.

What Are Your Trading Beliefs?

You can trade only what you believe; therefore, your beliefs about price action must be at the core of your trading system. This will allow the trading system to reflect your personality, and you are more likely to succeed with such a system over the long run. If you hold many beliefs about price action, you can develop many systems, each reflecting one particular belief. As we will see later, trading multiple systems is one form of diversification that can reduce fluctuations in account equity.

The simplest way to understand your trading beliefs is to list them. Table 2.1 presents a brief checklist to help you get started.

You can expand the items in Table 2.1 to include many other items. For example, you can include beliefs about breakout systems, moving-average methods, or volatility systems. Your trading beliefs are also influenced by what you do. For example, you may be a market marker, with a very short term trading horizon. Or, you may be a proprietary trader for a big bank, trading currencies. You may wish to keep an eye on economic data as one ingredient in your decision process. As a former floor trader, you may like to read the commitment of traders report. Perhaps you were once a buyer of coffee beans for a major manufacturer, and you like to look at crop yield data as you trade coffee. The range of possible beliefs is as varied as individual traders.

You must ensure that your beliefs are consistent. For example, if you like fast action, you probably will not use weekly data, nor hold positions as long as necessary. Nor are you likely to use fundamental data in your analysis. Hence, a need for fast action is more consistent with day trading, and using cycles, patterns, and oscillators with intraday data. Similarly, if you like a trend-following approach, you are more likely to use daily and weekly data, hold positions for more than five days, trade a variable number of contracts, and trade a diversified portfolio. If you hold multiple beliefs, ensure that they are a consistent set and develop models that fit those beliefs. A set of consistent beliefs that can be used to build trading systems is listed below as an example.

1. I like to trade with the trend (5 to 50 days).

2. I like to trade with a system.

3. I like to hold positions as long as necessary (1 to 100 days).

4. I like to trade a variable number of shares or contracts.

5. I like to use stop orders to control my risk.

Pare down your list to just your top five beliefs. You can review and update this list periodically. When you design trading systems, check that they reflect your five most strongly held beliefs. The next section presents other rules your system must also follow.

Table 2.1   A checklist of your trading beliefs.

Beliefs That Can Influence Your Trading Decisions	Yes, I Agree	No, I Disagree
I like to trade using fundamentals only.	☐	☐
I like to trade with technical analysis only.	☐	☐
I like to trade with the trend (you define time frame).	☐	☐
I like to trade against the trend (you define time frame).	☐	☐
I like to buy dips (you define time frame).	☐	☐
I like to sell rallies (you define time frame).	☐	☐
I like to hold positions as long as necessary (1 to 100 days).	☐	☐
I like to hold positions for a short time (1 to 5 days).	☐	☐
I like to trade intraday only, closing out all positions.	☐	☐
I like to trade a fixed number of shares or contracts.	☐	☐
I like to trade a variable number of shares or contracts.	☐	☐
I like to trade a small number of markets or stocks (1 to 5).	☐	☐
I like to trade a diversified portfolio (more than10 stocks or markets).	☐	☐
I like to trade using cycles because I can anticipate changes.	☐	☐
I like to trade price patterns because I can react immediately.	☐	☐
I like to trade with price oscillators.	☐	☐
I like to read the opinions of others on the markets I trade.	☐	☐
I like to use only my own analysis of price action.	☐	☐
I like to use daily data in my analysis.	☐	☐
I like to use intraday data in my analysis.	☐	☐
I like to use weekly data in my analysis.	☐	☐
I like to trade with a system.	☐	☐
I like to use discretion, matching wits with the market.	☐	☐
I like lots of fast action in my trading.	☐	☐
I like to use stop orders to control my risk.	☐	☐
I like to trade with variable-length moving-average systems.	☐	☐

Six Cardinal Rules

Once you identify your strongly held trading beliefs, you can switch to the task of building a trading system around those beliefs. The six rules listed below are important considerations in trading system design. You should consider this list a starting point for your own trading system design. You may add other rules based on your experiences and preferences.

1. The trading system must have a positive expectation, so that it is "likely to be profitable."

2. The trading system must use a small number of rules, perhaps ten rules or less.

3. The trading system must have robust parameter values, usable over many different time periods and markets.

4. The trading system must permit trading multiple contracts, if possible.

5. The trading system must use risk control, money management, and portfolio design.

6. The trading system must be fully mechanical.

There is a seventh, unwritten rule: you must believe in the trading principles governing the trading system. Even as the system reflects your trading beliefs, it must satisfy other rules to be workable. For example, if you want to day-trade, then your short-term, day-trading system must also follow the six rules.

You can easily modify this list. For example, rule 3 suggests that the system must be valid on many markets. You may modify this rule to say the system must work on related markets. For example, you may have a system that trades the currency markets. This system should "work" on all currency markets, such as the Japanese yen, deutsche mark, British pound, and Swiss franc. However, you will not mandate that the system must also work on the grain markets, such as wheat and soybeans. In general, such market-specific systems are more vulnerable to design failures. Hence, you should be careful when you relax the scope of any of the six cardinal rules.

Another way to modify the rules is to look at rule 6, which says that the system must be fully mechanical. For example, you may wish to put in a volatility-based rule that allows you to override the signals. Be as specific as possible in defining the conditions that will permit you to deviate from the system. You can likely test these exceptional situations on past market data, and then directly include the exception rules in your mechanical system design.

In summary, these rules should help you develop sound trading systems. You can add more rules, or modify the existing ones, to build a consistent framework for system design. The following sections discuss these rules in greater detail.

Rule 1: Positive Expectation

A trading system that has a positive expectation is likely to be profitable in the future. The expectation here refers to the dollar profit of the average trade, including all available winning and losing trades. The data may be derived from actual trading or system testing. Some analysts call this your mathematical edge, or simply your "edge" in the markets.

The terms "average trade" and "expectation" represent the same object, so they are freely interchanged in the following discussion. Expectation can be written in many different ways. The following formulations are identical:

Expectation($) = Average Trade($),

Expectation($) = Net profit($)/(Total number of trades),

Expectation($) = [(Pwin) × (Average win($))] − (1 − Pwin)
× (Average loss($))].

The expectation, measured in dollars, is the profit of the average trade. The net profit, measured in dollars, is the gross profit minus the gross loss over the entire test period. Pwin is the fraction of winning trades, or the probability of winning. The probability of losing trades is given by (1−Pwin). The average win is the average dollar profit of all winning trades. Similarly, the average loss is the average dollar loss of all losing trades.

The expectation must be positive because, on balance, we want the trading system to be profitable. If the expectation is negative, this is a losing system, and money management or risk control cannot overcome its inherent limitations.

Assume that you are using system test results to estimate your average trade. Note that your estimate of the expectation is limited by the available data. If you test your system on another data set, you will get a different estimate of the average trade. If you test your system on different subsets of the same data set, you will find that each subset gives a different result for the average trade. Thus, the expectation of a trading system is not a "hard and fixed" constant. Rather, the expectation changes over time, markets, and data sets. Hence, you should use as long a time period as possible to calculate your expectation.

Since the expectation is not constant, you should stipulate a minimum acceptable value for the average trade. For example, the minimum value should cover your trading costs and provide a "risk premium" to make it attractive. Hence, a value such as $250 for the expectation could be used as a threshold for accepting a system. In general, the larger the value of the average trade, the easier it is to tolerate its fluctuations.

Note that the expectation does not provide any measure of the variability of returns. The standard deviation of the profits of all trades is a good measure of system variability, system volatility, or system risk. Thus, the expectation does not fully quantify the amount of risk (read volatility) that must be absorbed to benefit from its profitability.

The expectation is also related to your risk of ruin. You can use statistical theory to calculate the probability that your starting capital will diminish to some small value. These calculations require assumptions about the probability of winning, the payoff ratio, and the bet size. The payoff ratio can be defined as the ratio of the average winning trades to the average losing trades. As your payoff ratio increases, and your Pwin increases, your risk of ruin decreases. The risk of ruin is also governed by bet size, that is, percentage of capital risked on every trade. The smaller your bet size, the lower the risk of ruin. Detailed calculations of risk of ruin are presented in Chapter 7.

In summary, it is essential that your system have a positive expectation, that is, a profitable average trade. The value of the average trade is not fixed, but changes over time. Hence, you can specify a threshold value, such as $250, before you will accept a trading system. The expectation is also important because it affects your risk of ruin. Avoid trading systems that have a negative expectation when tested over a long time.

The expectation of your system is determined by its trading rules. The next section examines how the number of trading rules affects your system design.

Rule 2: A Small Number of Rules

This book deals with deterministic trading systems using a small number of rules or variables. These trading systems are similar to systems people have developed for tasks such as controlling a chemical process. Their experience suggests that robust, reliable control systems have as few variables as possible.

Consider two well-known trend-following systems. The common dual moving-average system has just two rules. One says to buy the upside crossover, and the other says to sell the downside crossover. Similarly, the popular 20-bar breakout system has at least four rules, two each for entries and exits. You can show with testing software that these systems are profitable over many markets across multiyear time frames.

You can contrast this approach with an expert system-based trading system that may have hundreds of rules. For example, one commercially available system apparently has more than 400 rules. However, it turns out that only one rule is the actual trigger for the trades. The deterministic systems differ from neural-net–based systems that may have an unknown number of rules.

The statistical theory of design of experiments says that even complex processes are controllable using five to seven "main" variables. It is rare for a process to depend on more than ten main variables, and it is quite difficult to reliably control a process that depends on 20 or more variables. It is also rare to find processes that depend on the interactions of four or more variables. Thus, the effect of higher-order interactions is usually insignificant. The goal is to keep the overall number of rules and variables as small as possible.

There are many hazards in designing trading systems with a large number of rules. First, the relative importance of rules decreases as the number of rules increases. Second, the degrees of freedom decrease as the number of rules or variables increases. This means larger amounts of test data are needed to get valid results as the number of rules or variables increases.

A third problem is the danger of curve-fitting the data in the test sample. For example, given a data set, a simple linear regression with just two variables may fit the data adequately. As the number of variables in the regression increases to, say, seven, the line fits the data more closely. Therefore, we can pick up nuances in the data when we curve-fit our trading system, only to pick up patterns that may never repeat in the future. The total degrees of freedom decrease by two for the simple linear regression, but will decrease by seven for the polynomial regression.

These ideas can be illustrated by using regression fits of daily closing data for the December 1995 Standard and Poors 500 (S&P-500) futures contract. The data set covers 95 days from August 1, 1995, through December 13, 1995. Two regression lines are fitted to the same data: Figure 2.1 presents a simple linear regression; Figure 2.2 fits higher-order polynomial terms, going out to the fifth power. As higher-order terms are added, the regression line becomes a curve, and we pick up more nuances in the data.

For simplicity, the daily closes are numbered 1 through 95 and denoted by D. All numbers represented by C (such as C_1) are constants. Est Close is the closing price estimated from the regression.

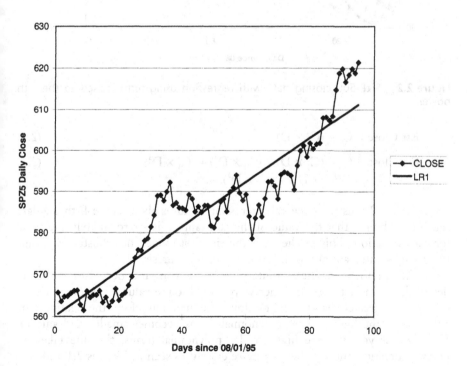

Figure 2.1   S&P-500 closing data with simple linear regression straight line.

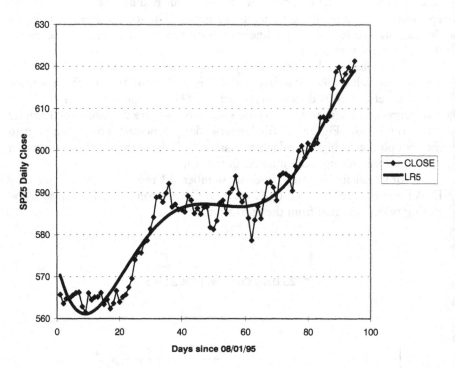

SPZ5 daily close with 5th order regression

Figure 2.2   S&P-500 closing data with regression using terms raised to the fifth power.

$$\text{Est Close} = C_0 + (C_1 \times D) \tag{2.1}$$

$$\text{Est Close} = C_0 + (C_1 \times D) + (C_2 \times D^2) + (C_3 \times D^3) \\ + (C_4 \times D^4) + (C_5 \times D^5) \tag{2.2}$$

Table 2.2 illustrates several interesting features about curve-fitting a data set. First, observe that the value of the constant C_0 is approximately the same for each equation. This implies that the simplest model, the constant C_0, captures a substantial amount of information in the data set.

Then, notice that the absolute value of the constants decreases as the order of the term increases. In other words, in absolute value, C_0 is greater than C_1, which is greater than C_2 and on down the line. Therefore, the relative contribution of the higher-order polynomial terms becomes smaller and smaller. However, as you add the higher-order polynomial terms, the line takes on greater curvature and fits the data more closely, as seen in Figures 2.1 and 2.2.

This exercise illustrates many important ideas. First, any model you build for the data should be as simple as possible. In this case, the simple linear

Table 2.2   Comparison of linear regression coefficients.

	C_0	C_1	C_2	C_3	C_4	C_5
Equation 2.1	560.0865	0.537870				
Equation 2.2	570.2379	−1.94509	0.131279	−0.00154	−0.00003	0.0000006

regression, with a slope and intercept, captured essentially all the information in the data. Second, adding complexity by adding higher-order terms (read rules) does improve the fit with the data. Thus, we pick up nuances in the data as we build more complex models. The probability that these nuances will repeat exactly is very small. Third, the purpose of our models is to describe how prices have changed over the test period. We used our data to directly calculate the linear regression coefficients. Thus, our model is hostage to the data set. There is no reason why these coefficients should accurately describe any future data. This means that over-fitted trading systems are unlikely to perform as well in the future.

Another example, a variant of the moving-average crossover system, illustrates why it makes sense to limit the number of rules. In the usual case, the dual moving average system has just two rules. For example, for the long entry the 3-day average should cross over the 65-day average and vice versa.

Now, consider a variant that uses more than two averages. For example, buy on the close if both the 3-day and the 4-day moving averages are above the 65-day average. Since there are two "short" averages, this gives us four rules, two each for long and short trades. Using more and more "short" averages rapidly increases the number of rules. For example, if the 3-, 4-, 5-, 6-, and 7-day moving averages should all be above the 65-day average for the long entry, ten rules would apply.

Consider 10 years of Swiss franc continuous contract data, from January 1, 1985, through December 31, 1994, without any initial stop, but allowing $100 for slippage and commissions. The number of rules is varied from 2 to 128 to explore the effects of increasing the number of rules. As the number of rules increases, the number of trades decreases, as shown in Figure 2.3. This illustrates the fact that as you increase the number of rules, you need more data to perform reliable tests.

Figure 2.4 shows that the profit initially increased as we added more rules. This means that the extra rules first act as filters and eliminate bad trades. As we add even more rules, however, they choke off profits and moreover increase equity curve roughness. Thus, you should be careful to not add dozens of rules.

As stated, this example did not include an initial stop. Hence, as we increase the number of rules, the maximum intraday drawdown should increase because both entries and exits are delayed. You can verify this by using Figure 2.5.

More rules need more data

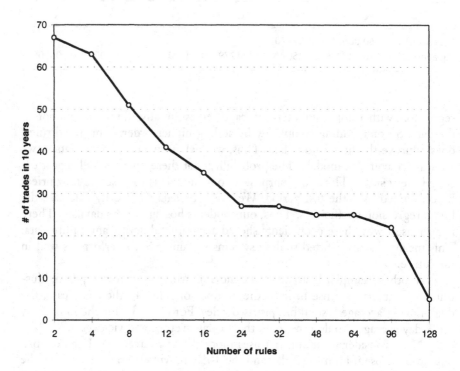

Figure 2.3   Adding rules reduced the number of trades generated over 10 years of Swiss franc data. Note that the horizontal scale is not linear.

Calculations for the U.S. bond market from January 1, 1975, through June 30, 1995, illustrate that the general pattern still holds. Figure 2.6 shows that as the number of rules increases, the profits decrease. The exact patterns will depend on the test data. Data from other markets confirm that increasing rules decreases profits.

Thus, adding rules does not produce endless benefits. Not only do you need more data, but the rising complexity may lead to worsening system performance. A complex system with many rules merely captures nuances within the test data, but these patterns may never repeat. Hence, relatively simple systems are likely to perform better in the future.

Rule 3: Robust Trading Rules

Robust trading rules can handle a variety of market conditions. The performance of such systems is not sensitive to small changes in parameter values.

Increasing rules first filter, then choke profits

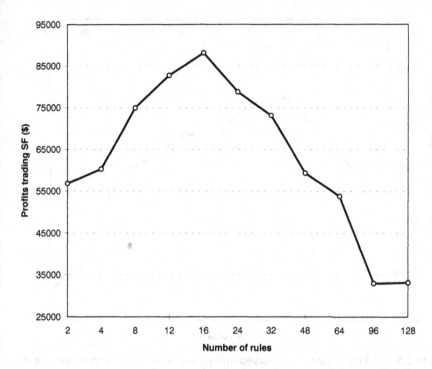

Figure 2.4   Adding rules increased profits moderately on 10-years of Swiss franc continuous contracts from January 1, 1985, through December 31, 1994. Note that the horizontal scale is not linear.

Usually, these rules are profitable over multiperiod testing, as well as over many different markets. Robust rules avoid curve-fitting, and are likely to work in the future.

An example of a system with delayed long entries illustrates the use of nonrobust parameters. The entry rule is as follows: if the crossover between 3- and 12-day simple moving averages (SMAs) occurred x days ago, and the low is greater than the parabolic, then buy tomorrow at the today's high + 1 point on a buy stop. A $1,500 initial stop was used and $100 was charged for slippage and commissions (Figure 2.7).

The results above are for an IMM (International Monetary Market) Japanese yen futures continuous contract, from August 2, 1976 through June 30, 1995. The dollar profits are sensitive to the number of days of delay, and can vary widely due to small changes in parameter values. It also does not seem reasonable to wait 12 days after a crossover for such short-term moving averages. Hence, the flattening out of the curve after a 9-day delay is of little practical

MIDD follows same pattern as profits

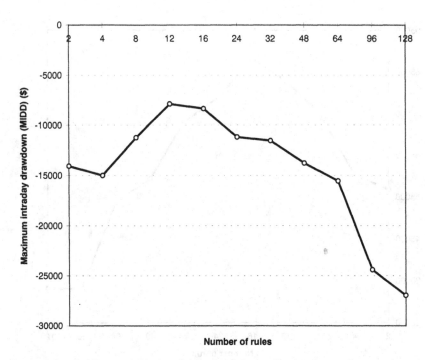

Number of rules

Figure 2.5   Adding more rules delayed entries and exits, increasing maximum intraday drawdown. Note that the horizontal scale is not linear.

relevance. The delay parameter is not robust because a small change in the value of this parameter can make system performance vary widely with markets and time frames.

Next consider the effect of nonrobust, curve-fitted rules, illustrated by the August 1995 N.Y. light crude oil futures contract (Figure 2.8). The market was in a narrow trading range during February and March, and then broke out above the $18.00 per barrel price level. The market moved up quickly, reaching the $20 level by May. A volatile consolidation period ensued through June, before prices broke down toward the $17 per barrel level by July.

The following trading rules were derived simply by visual inspection of the price chart in an attempt to develop a curve-fitted system that picked up specific patterns in this contract.

Rule 1: Buy tomorrow at highest 50-day high + 5 points on a buy stop (breakout rule).

Rule 2: Sell tomorrow at low –2 × (h–l) – 5 points on a sell stop (downside range-expansion rule).

More rules, less profit in US Bonds

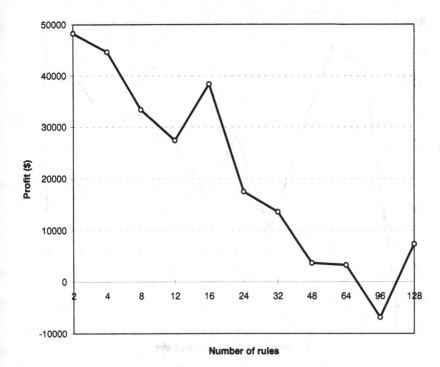

Figure 2.6   Increasing the number of rules decreased profits in the U.S. bond market from January 1, 1975 through June 30, 1995. Note that the horizontal scale is not linear.

Rule 3: If this is the twenty-first day in the trade, then exit short trades on the close (time-based exit rule).

Rule 4: If Rule 3 is triggered, then buy two contracts on the close (countertrend entry rule).

Rule 5: If short, then sell tomorrow at the highest high of last 3 days +1 point limit (sell rallies rule).

The first rule is a typical breakout system entry rule, albeit for a breakout over prior 50-bar trading range. The second rule is a volatility-inspired sell rule. The idea was to sell at a point five ticks below twice the previous day's trading range subtracted from the previous low. This will typically be triggered after a narrow-range day, if the daily range expands on the downside due to selling near an intermediate high. The third rule is a time-dependent exit rule, optimized by visual inspection over the August contract. The idea behind time-based exits is that one expects a reaction opposite the intermediate trend after x

Effect of delayed entry on profits: 3/12 SMAXO

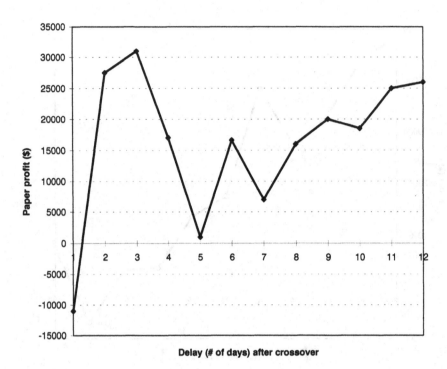

Figure 2.7   The effect on profits of changing the number of days of delay in accepting a crossover signal of a 3-day SMA by 12-day SMA system is highly dependent on the delay.

days of trending prices. Rule 4 merely reinforces rule 3 by not only exiting the short position but putting on a two-contract long position at the close. Rule 5 is a conscious attempt to sell rallies during downtrends. In this case, limit orders were used to sell, to avoid slippage. These rules assumed that as many as nine contracts could be traded at one time, using a $1,000 initial money-management stop.

The results of the testing are summarized in Table 2.3. The first clue that this may be a curve-fitted system is the number of profitable trades. As many as 87 percent of all trades (20 out of 23) were profitable. A second clue was in the 14 consecutive profitable trades. A third clue was in a suspiciously large profit factor (= gross profit/gross loss) of 13.49. These results are what you might see in curve-fitted systems tested over a relatively short time period. The computer-generated buy and sell signals are shown in Figure 2.8.

This curve-fitted system was tested by using a continuous contract of crude oil futures data from January 3, 1989, through June 30, 1995. Not surprisingly,

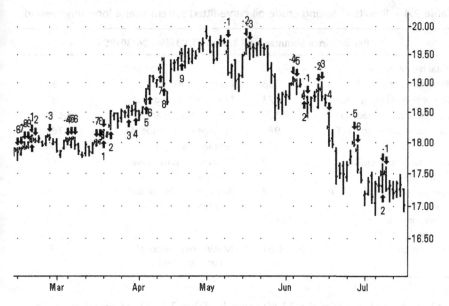

Figure 2.8   The August 1995 crude oil contract with curve-fitted system.

this system would have lost $107,870 on paper, as shown in Table 2.4. Note how only 32 percent of the trades would have been profitable. There would have been as many as 48 consecutive losing trades, requiring quite an act of faith to continue trading this system. Also, the profit factor was a less impressive

Table 2.3   Results of testing August 1995 crude oil curve-fitted system.

N.Y. Light Crude Oil 08/95-Daily 12/01/94 – 07/20/95			
Total net profit ($)	12,990.00	Open position profit/loss ($)	520.00
Gross profit ($)	14,030.00	Gross loss ($)	–1,040.00
Total number of trades	23	Percent profitable	87
Number of winning trades	20	Number of losing trades	3
Largest winning trade ($)	1,370.00	Largest losing trade ($)	–860.00
Average winning trade ($)	701.50	Average losing trade ($)	–346.67
		Average trade ($)	564.78
Maximum consecutive winners	14	Maximum consecutive losers	2
Average number of bars in winners	20	Average number of bars in losers	1
Maximum intraday drawdown ($)	–1,670.00		
Profit factor	13.49	Maximum number of contracts held	9

Table 2.4   Results of testing crude oil curve-fitted system over a long time period.

Performance Summary: All Trades 01/03/89 – 06/30/95			
Total net profit ($)	–107,870		
Total number of trades	538	Percent profitable	32
Number of winning trades	173	Number of losing trades	365
Largest winning trade ($)	7,160	Largest losing trade ($)	–3,670
Average winning trade ($)	983	Average losing trade ($)	–761
		Average trade ($)	–200
Maximum consecutive winners	9	Maximum consecutive losers	48
Average number of bars in winners	12	Average number of bars in losers	6
Maximum intraday drawdown ($)	–120,950		
Profit factor	0.61	Maximum number of contracts held	9

0.61, a sharp drop from the 13.49 value in Table 2.3. These calculations show that curve-fitted systems may not work over long periods of time.

Interestingly, this system has its merits. When tested over 12 other markets to check if these rules were robust enough to use across many markets (Table 2.5), the results were better than expected; on some markets the system tested very well. This result was surprising because (1) this particular combination of rules had never been tested on these markets and were derived by

Table 2.5   A check for robustness: crude oil curve-fitted system over 12 markets (test period: 1/3/89–6/30/95, using continuous contracts, $100 slippage, and commission charge).

Market	Paper Profit ($)	Average Trade ($)
Coffee	132,908	445
S&P-500	145,545	547
Cotton	84,925	284
U.S. bond	84,319	324
Japanese yen	67,975	176
Swiss franc	17,975	51
10-year T-note	13,538	48
Gold, Comex	–13,270	–33
Copper, high-grade	–22,167	–49
Soybeans	–41,656	–117
Heating oil	–45,868	–80
Sugar #11	–56,394	–136

inspection of just one chart; and (2) the long entries and short entries are asymmetric. A symmetrical trading system uses identical rules for entries and exits, except that the signs of the required changes are reversed. For example, a moving average system would require an upside crossover or a downside crossunder for signals.

A closer look at the rules shows that they do follow some sound principles. For example, during an uptrend, each successive 50-bar breakout adds a contract until nine contracts are acquired. Thus, market exposure is increased during strong uptrends. The sell rule tends to lock in profits close to intermediate highs. As we sell rallies in downtrends, we are increasing exposure in the direction of the intermediate term trend. Also, a relatively tight $1,000 initial money management stop was used. Thus, even though these rules were derived by inspection, they followed sound principles of following the trend, adding to with-the-trend positions, letting profits run, and cutting losses quickly.

In summary, it is easy to develop a curve-fitted system over a short test sample. If these rules are not robust, they will not be profitable over many different market conditions. Hence, they will not be profitable over long time periods and many markets. Such rules are unlikely to be consistently profitable in the future. Hence, you should try to develop robust trading systems.

Rule 4: Trading Multiple Contracts

Multiple contracts allow you to make larger profits when you are right. However, the drawdowns are larger if you are wrong. You are betting that with good risk control, the overall profits will be greater than the drawdowns. An essential requirement is that your account equity must be sufficiently large to permit trading multiple contracts. Your risk control guidelines must permit multiple contracts to benefit from this approach. If your account permits you to trade just one contract at a time, then this approach must be deferred until your equity has increased.

Multiple contracts also allow you to add a nonlinear element to your system design. This means the results of trading, say, five contracts using this nonlinear logic are better than trading five contracts using the usual linear logic. The linear logic trades one contract per signal. The nonlinear logic uses a price-based criterion such as volatility. The volatility rule buys more contracts when volatility is low. Markets often have low volatility after they have consolidated for many weeks. If a strong trend develops as the market emerges from the consolidation, then the nonlinear effect is to boost profits significantly.

A simple example illustrates these ideas. Assume that your account is so large that trading up to 15 contracts in the 10-year T-note market is well within your risk control guidelines. For example, with a 1 percent risk per position and a $1,000 initial money management stop, you would need $1,500,000 in equity to trade 15 T-note contracts. This assumes that the 15-lot margin is also within your money-management guidelines.

Consider a simple moving average crossover system using 5-day and 50-day simple moving averages. The trade day is one day after the crossover day. You will buy or sell on the next day's open if you get a 5/50 crossover tonight after the close. Use a $1,000 initial stop on each contract and allow $100 for slippage and commissions.

Let us compare system performance with one contract versus variable contracts, rising to a maximum of 15 contracts. The test period is from January 3, 1989, through June 30, 1995, using a continuous contract. Table 2.6 compares four variations of the 5/50 crossover system. The column labeled "fixed 1 contract" shows the results over the test period for always trading one contract per trade. The next column, "fixed 15 contracts" shows the calculated results for always trading 15 contracts per trade. The column, "variable #1" trades a maximum of 15 contracts with the contracts added at the open on successive days. The "variable #2" trades a maximum of 15 contracts with all the contracts bought on the same day. The volatility in dollars here is four times the average 20-day true range. The volatility divided into $15,000 gives the number of contracts. Thus, variable #2 uses a volatility-based criterion for calculating the number of contracts, always trading 15 or less.

Table 2.6   Performance comparison using variable number of contracts.

Item	Fixed 1 Contract	Fixed 15 Contracts	Variable #1 Maximum 15 Contracts	Variable #2 Maximum 15 Contracts
Net profit ($)	24,018.75	360,281	339,774	294,869
Maximum intra-day drawdown (MIDD) ($)	–6,918.75	–103,781	–66,650	–62,763
Net profit /MIDD	3.47	3.47	5.10	4.70
Largest losing trade ($)	–1,100	–16,500	–1,350	–13,200
Total number of trades	48	48	594	48
Number of winning trades	15	15	215	15
Average trade ($)	500.39	7,506	572	6,143
Standard deviation of trades ($)	2,448	36,721	5,836	25,506
Average trade/ standard deviation	0.09	0.20	0.10	0.24
Standard deviation: losing trades ($)	340	5,092	364	3,362

Let us compare the net profit produced by the four strategies. It should come as no surprise that the absolute amount of profit increases as we trade more contracts. However, as the next row of Table 2.6 shows, the maximum intraday drawdown also increases as we trade more contracts. The ratio of net profits to maximum intraday drawdown shows whether we gain anything by trading multiple contracts. This ratio is 3.47 for fixed contract trading strategy. The ratio increases to 4.7 or 5.1 for the variable contracts strategies. This is a 39 to 47 percent improvement, a strong reason to consider multiple contracts. Hence, profits can increase without proportionately increasing drawdowns.

Observe from Table 2.6 that the largest losing trade for variable #1 is considerably less than simply trading a fixed number of 15 contracts. Similarly, the largest losing trade in variable #2 is less than always trading 15 contracts. This too confirms the benefits of going to the multiple-contract strategy.

The total number of trades remains the same for the fixed-1, fixed-15 and variable #2 strategies, since all the contracts are bought on the same day. The number of trades increases for variable #1 since not all the contracts are bought on the same day.

The average trade for each strategy is relatively high, suggesting that this simple model seems to catch significant trends. The average trade is higher when all the contracts are bought at the same time. This is merely an artifact of system design. As pointed out before, the average trade does not provide a measure of variability in system results.

The standard deviation per trade is naturally smaller when we trade one contract at a time rather than all at once. The standard deviation in trade returns increases as the number of contracts increases. As Table 2.6 shows, there is a higher volatility in trade returns ($36,721) for fixed 15-contract trading than either of the variable contract strategies. This means volatility can be reduced by trading a variable number of multiple contracts, rather than a fixed number of multiple contracts. This is another desirable design goal.

Dividing the average trade profit by the standard deviation in trade profitability yields a composite picture of model performance. The higher this number, the more desirable the system. For the fixed 1-contract strategy, this reward to risk ratio is only 0.09, and it increases to 0.24 for the variable #2 strategy. Remember, however, that the volatility in trading profits increases significantly with multiple contracts.

The last line of Table 2.6, the downside volatility, explains that the increased volatility occurs due to rising profits of winning trades. Note that the fixed 15-contract downside volatility is the highest, followed by the variable #2 and variable #1 strategies. There is not a large difference in downside volatility between the fixed 1-contract strategy and variable #1 strategy, which buys one contract at a time but on multiple days. Note also that the standard deviation of all trades (including winning trades) is much greater than the downside volatility. Thus, rather than all volatility being undesirable, note that adding multiple contracts increases upside volatility more than downside volatility. Increasing upside volatility is easier to cope with than sharply rising downside volatility.

In summary, if your account equity and mental makeup permit, consider the benefits of a multiple contract strategy.

Rule 5: Risk Control, Money Management, and Portfolio Design

All traders have accounts of finite size as well as written or unwritten guidelines for expected performance over the immediate future. These performance guidelines have a great influence over the existence and longevity of an account. For example, consider a trading system that produces a 30 percent loss over five months. The same trading system then goes on to perform extremely well. One person may close the account after the 30 percent drawdown. Another may go on to reap excellent returns. Your money management rules could cause you to close out an account too soon, or keep it open too long. Thus, money management guidelines are crucial to trading success.

Given performance expectations and finite size of the trading account, it is essential to maintain good risk control, sensible money management, and good portfolio design. Risk control is the process of managing open trades with predefined exit orders. Money management rules determine how many contracts to trade in a given market and the amount of money to risk on particular positions. Portfolio-level issues must be considered to obtain a smoother equity curve.

Table 2.7 illustrates the effects of not using an initial money management stop versus adding an initial money management stop of $2,000. The trading system, a "canned" system using four consecutive up or down closes to initiate a trade, comes with the Omega Research's System Writer Plus™.

As expected, the largest losing trade can be horrifying, and most real-world accounts would probably close before swallowing such huge losses. Of course, recent headlines of billion-dollar plus losses in sophisticated trading firms illustrate that trading without adequate risk control is not uncommon.

Adding a money management stop constrains the worst initial loss to predictable levels. Even with slippage, the largest loss is usually lower than trading without any stop at all. Thus, your profitability is likely to improve with improved risk control. Observe that average net profits improved from a loss of –$5,085 with no stop to a loss of –$424 using risk control. The maximum drawdown also improved with the added risk control. The lesson from this comparison is clear. There is much to gain if you use proper risk control.

You can reduce swings in equity and improve account longevity if you combine risk control with sound money management ideas. Your money management guidelines will specify how much of your equity to risk on any trade.

Table 2.7   Effect of adding an initial money management stop, May 1989–June 1995 (dollars).

	No Stop			$2000 Stop		
Market	Net Profit	Largest Loss	Maximum Drawdown	Net Profit	Largest Loss	Maximum Drawdown
Coffee	–4,206	–50,868	–24,149	33,776	–2,594	–13,970
Copper	5,082	–3,542	–14,810	–5,455	–2,302	–20,430
Cotton	4,370	–4,620	–14,585	7,580	–3,025	–13,800
Crude oil	–14,350	–12,350	–20,760	–8,690	–2,870	–15,100
Gold, Comex	7,180	–2,250	–6,560	3,750	–2,340	–6,650
Heating oil	16,758	–4,174	–16,350	–378	–3,989	–16,334
Japanese yen	–36,800	–6,550	–65,673	–23,675	–3,388	–50,300
Sugar	–9,770	–3,594	–14,428	–7,799	–2,194	–12,456
Swiss franc	8,225	–7,613	–16,438	15,688	–2,663	–15,263
10-year T-note	–15,913	–4,413	–29,444	–8,788	–2,100	–21,881
U.S. bond	–16,506	–6,194	–28,969	–10,625	–2,100	–22,856
Worst	–36,800	–50,868	–65,673	–23,675	–3,989	–50,300
Best	16,758	–2,250	–6,560	33,776	–2,100	–6,650
Average	–5,085	–9,652	–22,924	–424	–2,688	–19,004

These guidelines convert the initial stop into a specific percentage of your equity. One common rule of thumb is to risk or "bet" just 2 percent of your account equity per trade.

The 2-percent rule converts into a $1,000 initial stop for a $50,000 account. This $1,000 initial stop is often called a "hard dollar stop," applied to the entire position. A position could have one or more contracts. Thus, if you had two contracts, you would protect the position with a stop loss order placed $500 away from the entry price. Chapter 7 discusses the bet size issue in detail.

Overtrading an account is a common problem cited by analysts for many account closures. For example, if you consistently bet more than 2 percent per trade, you are overtrading an account. If you do not use any initial money management stop, then the risk could be much greater than 2 percent of equity. In the worst case, you risk your entire account equity. Some extra risk, say up to 5 percent of equity, may be justified if the market presents an extraordinary market opportunity (see Chapter 4). However, consistently exceeding the 2 percent limit can cause large and unforeseen swings in account equity.

As another rule of thumb, you are overtrading an account if the monthly equity swings are often greater than 20 percent. Again, there may be an occasional exception due to extraordinary market conditions.

You must also consider the benefits and problems of diversification, that is, trading many different markets in a single account. The main advantage of trading many markets is that it increases the odds of participating in major moves. The main problem is that many of the markets respond to the same or similar fundamental forces, so their price moves are highly correlated in time. Therefore, trading many correlated markets is similar to trading multiple contracts in one market.

For example, the Swiss franc (SF) and deutsche mark (DM) often move together, and trading both these markets is equivalent to trading multiple contracts in either the franc or the mark. Let us look specifically at SF and DM continuous contracts from May 26, 1989, through June 30, 1995, with a dual moving average system using a $1,500 stop and $100 for slippage and commissions. The two moving averages were 7 and 65 days. As Figure 2.9 shows, the equity curves have a correlation of 83 percent. For example, you would have made $60,619 trading one contract each of SF and DM, but your profits would have been $63,850 trading two contracts of DM and $57,388 trading two contracts of SF.

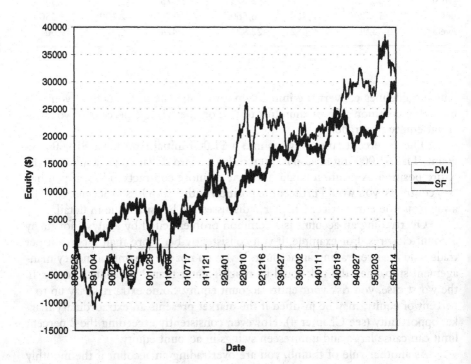

Comparison of equity curves: DM and SF

Figure 2.9 Swiss franc and deutsche mark equity curves are highly correlated at 83 percent.

Note one important difference between the two cases. Since the two markets may have negative correlation from time to time, the drawdown for both SF and DM together may be in between trading two contracts of just DM or SF. For example, the drawdown for SF and DM in this case was –$10,186 versus –$22,375 for two DM contracts and –$9,950 for two SF contracts. Hence, the benefits of trading correlated markets are relatively small. Thus, it may be better to trade uncorrelated or weakly correlated markets in the same portfolio.

The benefits of adding usually unrelated markets to a portfolio can be illustrated by an example of trading the Swiss franc (SF), cotton (CT) and 10-year Treasury note (TY) in a single account, using the same dual moving average system as above. The paper profits from trading three SF contracts add up to $86,801 versus $85,683 for SF plus TY and CT. The equity curve for the two combinations is shown in Figure 2.10. The smoothness of the two curves can be compared by using linear regression analysis to calculate the standard error (SE) of the daily equity curve. The SE for trading three SF contracts in $6238, and the SE for SF and TY plus CT is just $4,902, a reduction of 21 percent. Thus,

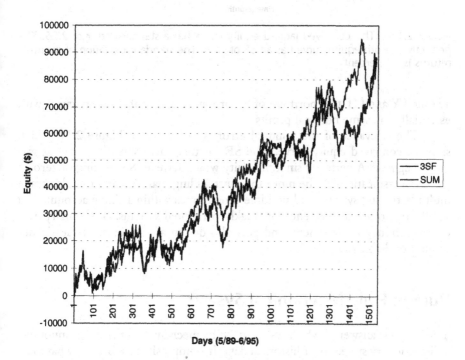

Figure 2.10 Adding 10-year T-note (TY) and cotton to the portfolio trading just Swiss francs provides a smoother equity curve versus trading three SF contracts.

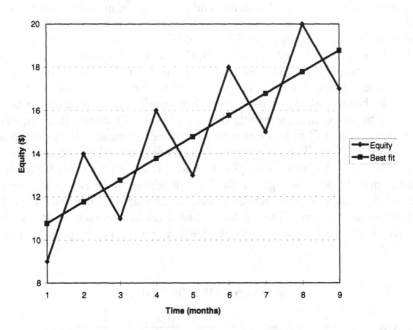

Figure 2.11   This contrived jagged equity curve has a standard error of 2.25. The perfectly smooth equity curve has an SE of zero. The standard deviation of monthly returns is 33 percent.

adding TY and CT to a portfolio of SF produced a smoother equity curve with essentially the same nominal profits.

The relevance of the standard error is illustrated in Figure 2.11, which shows a contrived equity curve. The SE for that curve was 2.25, since it was quite "jagged." A perfectly smooth equity would have an SE reading of zero.

Diversification can be more than just adding markets. You can also trade multiple trading systems and multiple time frames within a single account. You should try to use uncorrelated or weakly correlated systems. In summary, risk control, money management, and portfolio design are important issues in designing trading systems.

Rule 6: Fully Mechanical System

The simplest answer to why a system must be mechanical is that you cannot test a discretionary system over historical data. It is impossible to forecast what market conditions you will face in future and how you will react to those conditions. Therefore, in this book, we will restrict ourselves to fully mechanical systems.

If you can define how you make discretionary decisions, then these rules could be formalized and tested. The process of formalization could itself provide many interesting ideas for further testing. Hence you are encouraged to move toward mechanical systems.

You are more likely to make consistent trading decisions if you use mechanical systems. The manner in which a mechanical system will process price data is predictable, and hence assures that you will make consistent trading decisions. However, there is no assurance that these logically consistent decisions will also be consistently profitable. Nor is there any assurance that these trading decisions will be implemented without modification by the trader.

Summary

This chapter developed a checklist for narrowing your trading beliefs. You should narrow your beliefs down to five or less to build effective trading systems around them.

This chapter also reviewed six major rules of the system design. A trading system with a positive expectation is likely to be profitable in the future. The number of rules in a system should be limited because increasing complexity often hurts performance. Relatively simple systems are likely to fare better in the future. The rules should be robust, so they will be profitable over long periods and over many markets. You should trade multiple contracts if possible because they allow you to make more profits when you are right. Risk control, money management, and portfolio design give you a smoother equity curve and are the keys to profitability. Lastly, a system should be mechanical to provide consistent, objective decision making. You should follow the six major rules to build superior systems that are consistent with your trading beliefs.

Chapter

Foundations of System Design

The best system provides instant gratification and constant satisfaction.

Introduction

This chapter examines many key system design issues. Now that you understand some basic principles of system design, you can consider more complex issues. And as you understand these issues, you can design more powerful systems.

We will begin by asking the question: Do markets trend? The answer to the next big question, whether you should trade with the trend or against the trend, is that you should trade with the trend. This chapter presents some test results to support this answer. You can then ask whether you should or should not optimize your trading system. We explore here how well you can predict future performance based on optimization of historical data.

The chapter begins the discussion on risk control issues by addressing whether the initial stop is a problem or a solution and discussing the different types of risk you may face in your trading. You should consider these issues early in your design process. We then look at the different types of data you can use for your testing and what difference, if any, they make. Finally, the chapter explains what is found as well as what is lacking in the system performance summary.

At the end of this chapter, you will be able to:

1. Explain how you can diagnose trending markets.

2. Know whether to use a trend-following (TF) or countertrend strategy.

3. Explain the benefits and pitfalls of optimization.

4. Understand the type of risks you may encounter.

5. Know how to select data for tests.

6. Effectively use the performance summary of system testing results.

7. Understand and explore what is not covered in the performance summary.

8. Explain why system design has its limits.

Diagnosing Market Trends

You can design a profitable trading strategy if you can correctly and consistently diagnose whether a market is trending. In simple terms, the market exists in two states: trending and ranging. A market is trending if it moves steadily in one direction. If the market is going back and forth within a relatively narrow price range, then it is ranging.

Longer-term strategies are likely to succeed in trending markets, and shorter-term strategies in ranging markets. As always, the market may not make a crisp transition from trending to ranging and back again. Sometimes the market begins to range only to break out into a trend, or vice versa.

There are many different ways to determine if a market is trending. Clearly, you must make a number of trade-offs, and these trade-offs largely define your answer. For example, one well-known measure is the average directional index (ADX) developed by J. Welles Wilder Jr. (see bibliography for references). This is usually a built-in function in most technical analysis software programs. The ADX describes double-smoothed, absolute market momentum. A rising ADX line usually indicates trend. You have to choose the number of days to calculate the ADX; the sensitivity of the indicator decreases as the time increases. A value of 14 days is common, although 18 days works well. You must also define two reference levels to screen out false signals. An ADX value of 20 is useful as a reference level—that is to say a market is not trending unless the rising 18-day ADX is above 20. A second useful barrier level is 40, which says that when the ADX rises above 40 and then turns down, a consolidation is likely. You will find that in particularly strong trends, the "hook" from above 40 often signals just a brief consolidation phase. The trend then has a strong second "leg" toward higher highs or lower lows.

Sometimes you will find that the ADX will rise above 20 in markets that are in a broad trading range. Another quirk is that the ADX can head lower even though prices march steadily and smoothly in either direction. In short, this is not a perfect indicator. The main difficulty with the ADX is that it has two levels of smoothing, which produces disconcerting lags between price movement and indicator response. Chapter 5 shows that the absolute level of the ADX indicator is not as useful for system design as is its trend.

An indicator that is more directly based on market momentum, and that responds more predictably than the ADX, is the range action verification index (RAVI). This strategy, which focuses on identifying ranging markets, is different from the ADX, which looks at how much of today's price action is beyond yesterday's price bar.

To define RAVI, we begin by selecting the 13-week simple moving average, since it represents a quarter of a year. Because we want to use daily data, we convert the 13-week SMA into the equivalent 65-day SMA of the close. This is the long moving average. The short moving average is chosen as only 10 percent of the long moving average, which is 6.5 days, or, rounding up, 7 days. Thus, we use 7-day and 65-day simple moving averages. This choice of lengths is purely arbitrary. Next, the RAVI is defined as the absolute value of the percentage difference between the 7-day SMA (7-SMA) and the 65-day SMA (65-SMA):

RAVI = Absolute value (100 × (7-SMA–65-SMA)/65-SMA)

An arbitrary reference level of 3 percent means a market is ranging if the RAVI is less than 3 percent, and trending strongly if the RAVI is greater than 3 percent. In some markets, such as Eurodollars, this is too high a hurdle. Hence, you may want to experiment with a smaller level, such as 1 percent, or use a relative measure, such as a 65-day SMA of the RAVI. You can also require that the RAVI be above 3 percent and rising for there to be a strong trend.

Note the following design features of the RAVI: (1) There is only one level of smoothing. (2) The 7-day moving average is relatively sensitive, so that the lags between price action and indicator action should be small. (3) Markets can still move more quickly than the RAVI indicates. You can verify this by looking at the currency markets. (4) Markets in a slowly drifting, choppy trend will pin the RAVI below 3 percent, indicating ranging action.

Figure 3.1 compares the 18-day ADX (bottom graph) to the RAVI (middle graph) with a horizontal line at the 3 percent RAVI level. There is a general similarity between the two indicators, with the RAVI responding more quickly than the ADX because it has only one level of smoothing versus two levels for the ADX. A double-smoothed RAVI indicator created by smoothing the RAVI with a 14-day SMA is very similar to the 18-day ADX, as shown in Figure 3.2. Thus the ADX closely describes double-smoothed momentum and can lag price movements.

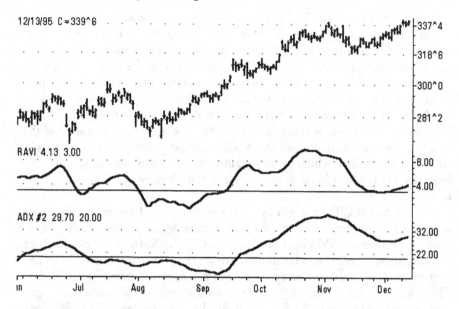

Figure 3.1   Comparison between the ADX (bottom) and RAVI (middle) to measure ranging behavior.

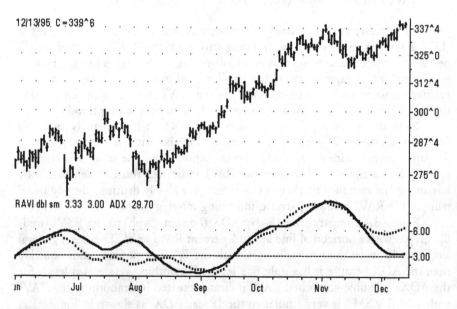

Figure 3.2   A double-smoothed RAVI (solid line) compared to the 18-day ADX (dotted line) shows that the two indicators are very similar.

Table 3.1   Proportion of market days showing definite trend, using ADX and RAVI.

Market (1/1/89–6/30/95)	Percentage of Days ADX Rising, ADX>20	Percentage of Days RAVI Rising, RAVI > 3
Coffee	30.2	43.3
Copper, high-grade	27.0	35.3
Cotton	29.2	39.4
Crude oil	30.2	39.9
Deutsche mark	32.6	25.7
Gold, Comex	25.0	15.8
Japanese yen	27.7	20.6
Soybeans	30.1	23.9
S&P-500	24.0	17.9
Sugar	31.3	41.7
Swiss franc	30.7	28.9
10-year T-note	32.8	6.0
U.S. bond	37.5	16.0

We now compare the ADX and RAVI and use them both to measure how often trends occur. In this example, we use continuous contracts from January 1, 1989, through June 30, 1995, a rising 18-day ADX above 20, and a rising RAVI greater than 3 percent. The ADX and RAVI are considered to be rising if today's value is greater than the value 10 days ago. These choices of length and reference levels are arbitrary.

The calculations shown in Table 3.1 suggest that markets seem to show some form of trendiness about 20 to 40 percent of the time. Some markets, such as the 10-year T-note, have not shown very strong trends as measured by the RAVI. However, this may just be due to using a 3 percent barrier with the RAVI to measure trend strength. The "soft" markets, such as coffee and sugar, show the highest tendency to trend. Other fundamentals-driven markets, such as cotton, copper, and crude oil, also show a tendency to have strong trends, with a RAVI rating above 35 percent. The more mature markets, such as S&P-500 and U.S. bond markets, show fewer strong trends than the softs. RAVI calculations correctly tagged the prolonged sideways ranging action in gold with a low rating of 15.8.

A separate calculation showed that the average length of these trending intervals was about 15 to 18 days in most markets, with values ranging from as low as 1 to more than 30. Thus, the trending phase of these markets was long enough to allow profitable trading. These calculations show that markets have provided sufficient opportunities for trend-following systems in the "trendless nineties."

In summary, you can use momentum-based indicators to measure ranging or trending action. The calculations show that markets have trends lasting 15 to 18 days on average. Hence, trend-following strategies are worth considering for system design. The next section examines whether you should use trend-following strategies over the long run.

To Follow the Trend or Not?

If you are not a large hedger or an institutional trader, you can follow either of two basic strategies when you design a trading system. You can be a trend follower, or you can take antitrend positions. If you are a trend follower, you will typically take intermediate-term positions. In contrast, with a countertrend strategy, you take shorter-term positions that anticipate trends. This section explores both strategies and shows that a trend-following approach is more likely to be profitable over the long run than an antitrend approach.

Table 3.2 shows test results for a stochastic-oscillator–based antitrend trading system provided with System Writer Plus™ software from Omega Research. The stochastic oscillator is a range-location oscillator that shows where today's close is within its trading range over the last x days. If the close is near the top of the range, then oscillator values are greater than 80. The next move in prices will probably be toward the lower end of the range. Similarly, if the close is near the lower end of the range, then oscillator values are below 20. We assume that the next move will take prices toward the top of the range. The "range" between the x-day high and low changes continuously. Hence, this oscillator cannot predict the amplitude of the next move.

Table 3.2   Stochastic-oscillator antitrend trading system results.

	Paper Profits ($)	Number of Trades	Percent-age of Winners	Largest Winner ($)	Biggest Loser ($)	Max-imum Consecu-tive Losers	Maximum Intraday Drawdown ($)
Coffee	1,837	276	32	27,065	–11,215	9	–44,931
Cotton	–98,725	296	24	4,955	–2,800	14	–102,205
Crude oil, light	–61,940	301	29	5,210	–7,850	17	–63,180
Gold, Comex	–29,830	256	29	2,630	–2,920	21	–31,150
Japanese yen	–47,713	309	32	8,633	–2,762	9	–60,813
Swiss franc	–55,350	285	32	9,175	–3,225	10	–63,513
U.S. Bond	–49,313	310	28	4,400	–1,694	13	–61,469

The system tested uses a 10-day period to calculate the so-called fast-K and fast-D moving averages. When the fast-K is above the fast-D line, the system buys on the open and vice versa. The System Writer Plus™ software guide gives the exact method for the calculations.

This example uses continuous contracts for seven unrelated markets, allows $100 for slippage and commissions, and uses a $1,500 initial money management stop. The test period was from May 26, 1989, through June 30, 1995. This simple system was a net loser over these markets. It also had substantial drawdowns, largely due to the many successive losing trades. Note the large number of trades and the relatively low proportion of winners.

The main implication of these calculations is that although markets may trend for short periods only, the profits during trending periods can far exceed the profits during trading ranges. The reason for this is that the amplitude of price moves during trends is many times the amplitude during trading ranges.

This example assumes that you pay the "discounted" trading commissions offered on the street. If your trading commissions are very low or negligible, then the antitrend strategy, with its high trading frequency, takes on a different dimension.

Table 3.3 compares paper profits with and without slippage and commissions (S&C). The difference in profitability is striking. The stochastic oscillator system performance improved significantly with low commissions. This result indicates that an antitrend strategy would not be attractive if you had to pay high commissions.

There are a number of "antitrend" strategies. Table 3.4 presents another set of calculations using a different trading strategy to illustrate this point. The moving average crossover (MAXO) system is the simplest trend-following strategy, but it can also be used as an antitrend strategy. For example, if the shorter moving average crosses over the longer moving average, you can go short in an antitrend strategy. Of course, this "upside" crossover would be a signal to buy long in a trend-following strategy.

Table 3.3   Impact of trading costs on profitability of antitrend trading strategies (dollars).

Market	Paper Profit $100 S&C	Paper Profit no S&C
Coffee	1,837	29,438
Cotton	−98,725	−69,125
Crude oil, light	−61,940	−31,840
Gold, Comex	−29,830	−4,230
Japanese yen	−47,713	−16,813
Swiss franc	−55,350	−26,850
U.S. bond	−49,313	−18,313

Table 3.4   Comparison of trading systems using 5-day and 20-day simple MAXO tests, 5/89–6/95 (dollars).

	Antitrend Trading MAXO		Trend-Following MAXO	
	Paper Profit, $100 S&C	Maximum Intraday Drawdown	Paper Profit, $100 S&C	Maximum Intraday Drawdown
Coffee	–42,719	–59,344	59,241	–17,216
Cotton	–14,670	–36,895	–6,845	–18,010
Crude oil, light	2,580	–21,500	–30,730	–35,460
Gold, Comex	–12,740	–21,780	–8,560	–12,950
Japanese yen	–34,650	–58,540	–9,025	–22,738
Swiss franc	–7,812	–45,688	–23,500	–40,175
U.S. bond	–28,119	–33,019	–9,643	–23,568
Average	–19,733	–39,538	–4,152	–24,302

Here we have arbitrarily picked 5-day and 20-day moving averages as examples of short- to intermediate-term averages. The test period was from May 26, 1989, through June 30, 1995, with $100 for slippage and commissions and a $1,500 initial stop. The antitrend strategy was a net loser on average, with significant potential for intraday drawdowns. The trend-following strategy cut the average loss by 79 percent and drawdown is lower by 39 percent—a better situation on both counts.

Table 3.5 presents another combination: the moving average antitrend and trend-following strategies with 7-day and 50-day simple moving averages. This combination is good for no-nonsense trend following. The assumptions are the same as before: $100 for slippage and commissions and a $1,500 initial stop with the calculations performed from May 26, 1989, through June 30, 1995.

Under antitrend trading, the 7/50-day SMA combination was also a net loser. On the other hand, it was a net winner with trend following, with profitability across all seven markets. The trend-following strategy had approximately one-fifth the drawdowns of the antitrend approach. Thus, the trend-following approach was the better choice on both counts.

These calculations show that a trend-following strategy is probably the better choice for the average position trader. However, the antitrend strategy may be attractive if you have low commission costs and little slippage.

The example tests in this chapter used arbitrary combinations of moving averages. However, you can test your system over historical data to find other combinations with better performance. Optimization is the process of finding the "best" performing variable set on historical data. The next section examines whether optimization is a good design strategy.

Table 3.5 Comparison of performance for 7-day and 50-day simple MAXO tests, 5/89–6/95 (dollars).

	Antitrend Trading MAXO		Trend-Following MAXO	
	Paper Profit $100 S&C	Maximum Intraday Drawdown	Paper Profit $100 S&C	Maximum Intraday Drawdown
Coffee	−22,716	−68,534	38,689	−27,615
Cotton	−44,375	−52,275	23,155	−9,795
Crude oil, light	−43,440	−47,570	20,430	−5,020
Gold, Comex	−14,540	−20,980	4,560	−5,730
Japanese yen	−39,663	−71,225	23,662	−23,075
Swiss franc	−49,325	−70,800	32,988	−13,163
U.S. bond	−34,606	−36,756	18,131	−14,619
Average	−37,658	−49,934	20,488	−11,900

To Optimize or Not To Optimize?

If you have a computer, you can easily set up a search to find the "optimum" values for a system over historical data. The results can be truly astonishing. Imagine your profits if you could only have known ahead of time what the most profitable parameter combination was going to be. Therein lies the rub. The unfortunate fact is that parameters that work best on past data rarely provide similar performance in the future.

The term "optimization" is used rather loosely here to include all the activities affecting selection of parameter values in a trading system. We have already seen the difficulties of curve-fitting a model. You can also consider lower levels of optimization, in which you test variables over a broad range of values and markets, and try to select the one you like "best." But the real issue is not whether a particular set is the best. It is whether you believe sufficiently in the system to trade it without deviations. The primary benefit of optimization may be that you improve your comfort level with a particular system.

The problem with system optimization is that past price patterns do not repeat exactly in the future. The same is true of intermarket relationships. Although broad relationships follow from historical data, there can be differences in the time-lags between events and the relative magnitudes of the effects.

You must also resolve other conflicts. For example, you must choose the period you will use to optimize your trading system values. As you will quickly discover, the values you choose depend on the length of the test period. You must also determine how often you will reoptimize your system in the future. You must then prescribe the time for which the optimized values are valid.

For example, you may decide to use 3 years of data to optimize the values and recalculate them after 3 months. Thus, one solution may be to reoptimize after 3 months on the latest 3 years of data available. This is equivalent to retraining your favorite neural net. If you do reoptimize, you must determine how to treat trades that may be open from the previous period or values of the trading system.

You must also decide if you want to use the same values of your system parameters on all markets. If not, you will have to optimize the system on each market separately. In that case, you must keep up a program of reoptimization and recalibration for each of your systems over every market that you trade. Is all this effort worth the trouble? The results of deterministic testing do not support any attempts at finding the "best" or optimized variables.

Consider the following test using actual deutsche mark futures contracts. The rollover dates are the twenty-first day of the month before expiration. For simplicity, we will trade just one contract, allowing $100 for slippage and commissions, with a $1,500 initial money management stop. We will use a variation of the moving average crossover system, trading not the crossover, but a 5-day breakout in prices after the crossover. Thus, if the shorter moving average was above the longer moving average, then a 5-day breakout above the highs would trigger a long entry. Also included is a simple exit condition, ending the trade on the close of the twentieth day in the trade. One attractive feature of this arbitrary system is that the lengths of the short and long moving average can be optimized.

The calculations are simplified by fixing the length of the short average to a 3-day simple moving average of the close. The length of the longer simple moving average varies from 20 to 50 days, with an increment of 5 days. The test period was from November 14, 1983, through November 21, 1989. The performance of the various models was observed 3, 6, 9, and 12 months into the future. As Tables 3.6 and 3.7 show, there is no predicting how the model will do over a future period. The relative rankings change from period to period without any pattern or consistency.

Table 3.6   Data showing that past performance does not predict future performance.

Length of SMA (Days)	Optimized Profit ($)	3 mo. 1990 Profit ($)	6 mo. 1990 Profit ($)	9 mo. 1990 Profit ($)	12 mo. 1990 Profit ($)
20	31,238	−2,200	−1,538	1,863	650
25	28,275	−2,475	−3,112	−488	−2,300
30	24,175	338	−300	2,325	2,113
35	18,088	338	63	2,175	1,963
40	15,475	338	−525	2,625	4,000
45	7,950	338	−4,363	2,038	3,600
50	7,013	338	−4,363	−1,800	−238

Table 3.7   Data showing that relative rankings from the past do not predict future relative ranks.

Length of SMA (days)	Optimized Relative Rank	3 mo. 1990 Relative Rank	6 mo. 1990 Relative Rank	9 mo. 1990 Relative Rank	12 mo. 1990 Relative Rank
20	1	6	4	5	5
25	2	7	6	6	7
30	3	1	2	2	3
35	4	1	1	3	4
40	5	1	3	1	1
45	6	1	6	4	2
50	7	1	6	7	6

We next test the hypothesis that if the optimization period were closer to the actual trading period, the predictions would be more reliable. However, as Tables 3.8 and 3.9 show, there is again no way to predict what the model will do in the succeeding periods. This should be expected because there is no cause-and-effect relationship between our optimized model and market forces. Since we are merely fitting a model to past data, we are not capturing all the fundamental and psychological forces driving the market. Our poor ability to predict the future based only on past price data is not surprising.

Let us carry our argument one step forward. Because we do not capture any cause-and-effect relationships, optimization on one market should have little or no benefit for trading other markets. Indeed, as Table 3.10 shows, optimizing a system on one market (here the deutsche mark) does little to improve performance in other markets.

Any optimization exercise has many potential benefits. The first benefit is recognition of the type of market conditions under which the trading system is

Table 3.8   Data showing that bringing the optimization period closer to the trading period (11/88–11/89) does not predict future performance.

Length of SMA (Days)	Optimized Profit ($)	3 mo. 1990 Profit ($)	6 mo. 1990 Profit ($)	9 mo. 1990 Profit ($)	12 mo. 1990 Profit ($)
20	3,525	−1,625	−1,000	2,650	2,438
25	5,225	−1,900	−2,575	400	−413
30	4,250	5,338	4,713	7,688	8,475
35	513	5,338	4,713	7,213	8,000
40	63	5,338	4,437	6,213	8,813
45	−2,800	5,338	3,138	4,913	7,638
50	−1,525	5,338	913	2,688	5,413

Table 3.9   Data showing that relative rankings over recent past (11/88–11/89) do not predict future relative ranks.

Length of SMA (Days)	Optimized Relative Rank	3 mo. 1990 Relative Rank	6 mo. 1990 Relative Rank	9 mo. 1990 Relative Rank	12 mo. 1990 Relative Rank
20	2	6	6	6	6
25	1	7	7	7	7
30	3	1	1	1	2
35	4	1	1	2	3
40	5	1	3	3	1
45	7	1	4	4	4
50	6	1	5	5	5

unprofitable. For any rules that you can construct, you can find market action that produces losses. This happens because the market triggers the signal, and then does just the opposite instead of following through.

The second benefit is verification of the general ideas underlying the model. For example, you can check to see if the model is profitable in trending markets or trendless markets. You have designed the rules to be profitable under certain market assumptions. The optimization exercise allows you to verify if your broad assumptions are correct.

A third benefit is understanding the effect of initial money management stops. You can quantify what level of initial stop allows you to capture the majority of potential profits. For example, if your stop is too wide, your losing trades will be relatively large. On the other hand, if your stop is too close to the starting position, you will be stopped out frequently. Your loss per trade will be

Table 3.10   Data showing that optimization over one market does not predict performance in other markets.

Length of SMA (Days)	Deutsche Mark 11/88–11/89 Profit ($)	Japanese Yen 11/90–7/95 Profit ($)	Gold 11/90–7/95 Profit ($)	Coffee 11/90–7/95 Profit ($)	Heating Oil 11/90–7/95 Profit ($)
20	3,525	8,188	−16,190	30,956	−26,771
25	5,225	7,838	−15,370	29,206	−21,938
30	4,250	8,938	−13,920	40,781	−21,230
35	513	7,013	−10,860	−5,013	−18,028
40	63	3,963	−11,400	−6,343	−14,316
45	−2,800	3,250	−7,940	6,188	−18,873
50	−1,525	11,245	−8,310	6,625	−13,773

small. However, the higher frequency of losing trades means your total drawdown could exceed a larger initial stop.

The biggest benefit of optimization is reinforcing your beliefs about a particular trading system. Ultimately, it is more important for you to implement the trading system exactly as planned. Hence, any testing you do that allows you to understand system performance and become more comfortable with its profit and loss characteristics will help you to execute it with greater confidence in actual trading.

The main point of this section is that you cannot assume your system is going to be as profitable in the future as it has been in the past. This raises the issue of how you control your risks to cope with uncertain future performance. The next section presents risk-control ideas.

Initial Stop: Solution or Problem?

Many traders have raised stop placement to an art form because it is not clear if the initial stop is a solution or a problem. The answer depends on your experiences. Often, the stop acts as a magnet for prices. It seems the market hits the stop, only to reverse and resume the previous trend. Thus, initial stops can easily test your patience. Even so, initial stops should be an essential part of managing trading risk. This section discusses some general issues related to selecting an initial stop. Detailed examples appear in the following chapters.

If you use an initial stop at all, use stops that follow money-management rules but are derived from system design and market volatility. A good idea is to use a 2 percent of equity initial stop, and then use maximum adverse excursion (MAE), a distribution of the worst loss in winning trades, to select the dollar value of the stop for a particular system. Relate the MAE to some measure of market volatility before calculating the number of contracts. Thus, the initial stop meets three criteria: money management, MAE, and volatility.

Another issue involves whether you should place your stop loss order with your broker. Many traders will have a well-defined exit price, but will not place an order in the market. They like to monitor the market in real time, and will place the exit order themselves if needed. This is termed the "discretionary initial stop." If you have good discipline and judgment, the discretionary initial stop could work well for you. However, if you cannot monitor the market continuously, it may be prudent to enter the exit order with your broker.

What values of the initial stop should you use during system testing? That depends on the type of data you have and the nature of the system design. The issue is whether to use a tight stop or a loose stop. A tight stop may have a dollar value less than $500 per contract. A loose stop could be as high as $5,000.

Let us assume you have only daily data. In this case, it is difficult to test a tight stop accurately because the exact track of prices during the day is unknown. Suppose you are trading the bond market, and the typical daily range is

$1,000. Now, say you want to test a $100 stop with daily data. Most system-testing software will stop you out on the day of entry because it does not know the exact track of prices. Of course, if you have intraday data, then you can more accurately test a $100 stop. Thus, if your stop is very tight, you need intraday data for accurate tests.

There are two broad types of systems, those that are self-correcting and those that are not self-correcting. Self-correcting systems have rules for long and short entries. Such systems will eventually generate a long signal for short trades and vice versa. Because these systems are self-correcting, the reverse signal will limit losses, even without an initial stop. Of course, the losses will depend on market volatility, and easily could be as large as –$10,000 per contract.

Systems that are not self-correcting include those that trade the long side or the short side only. Thus, you could get a false short signal and remain short through a long up trend. The losses in these systems can be unlimited, and hence must be protected by an initial stop. A one-sided system with an exit strategy can become self-correcting. The exit strategy will limit losses in a one-sided system by closing out the trade at some preselected point. For example, a self-correcting, longside-only system has an exit stop at the most recent 14-day low.

You can get a better feel for the efficiency of entry rules if you test a self-correcting system without initial stops. However, if the system is not self-correcting, then you must test it with an initial stop. There is still the issue of how wide the stop should be. Relatively wide stops, defined as three times the 10-day average of the daily range, are a good choice. In this way the stop has a smaller influence on results than do the entry rules. If you like tight stops, then use intraday data, or use an amount larger than the recent daily trading range.

Your data set will strongly influence the results of your initial stop selection. If your data set has many trading range markets, then a tight stop will produce whipsaw losses. Even though each loss may be small, the sum of a series of losses can be large. A loose stop will prevent whipsaw losses in a trading range. If the market is trending, then the value of the initial stop is not critical. Thus, a trending market will rescue a system with tight stops, and you can get some astonishing results.

Relatively loose stops, between $1,500 and $5,000, work well. If the stops are relatively "loose" then there is little difference between nearby values. Conversely, if the stop is "tight," then small changes in the stop can produce big swings in equity. Hence, the system tests in this book use daily data and stops ranging from $1,000 to $5,000.

Often, the point of discussion in this book does not depend on the amount of the stop. Sometimes the loose stop is a necessary design feature. In such cases the reason for choosing the wider stop is stated. Ultimately, if you do not like my stop, you can retest the system to suit your preferences.

Some actual calculations will clarify this discussion. Here we use the standard 20-day channel breakout on the close (CHBOC) trading system. This system buys on the close if today's close is higher than the highest high of the last 20 days. The short sale condition is symmetrical. The system sells short on the close if today's close is lower than the lowest low of the past 20 days. We will test this system on the coffee market, which has seen much volatility as well as strong trends. We will vary the initial stop from $0 to $8,000 in $500 increments and allow $100 for slippage and commissions.

Consider for a moment what the $0 initial stop means. The system goes long or short on the close. Thus, the trade will remain open only if prices continue to move strongly beyond today's close. This is the toughest stop you can impose because the only trades that survive are the ones that are profitable immediately.

Observe that profits increase steadily as we loosen the initial stop (see Figure 3.3). There was a surprising profit of $158,103 with a $0 initial stop on just 20 (of 434) trades. This confirms a common piece of market wisdom that the best trades are profitable immediately. It also confirms that only 5 percent or so of the trades are the "big ones." So you should work hard not to miss them.

Figure 3.4 shows that a tight stop can produce a drawdown greater than using no stop at all. More and more trades recover their losses and close at a

20-day CHBOC with varying initial stop

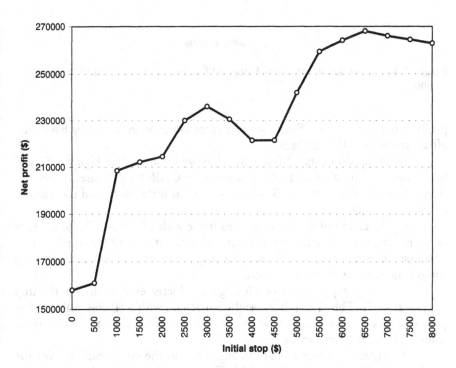

Figure 3.3 Profit increases steadily and then levels off as the initial stop increases.

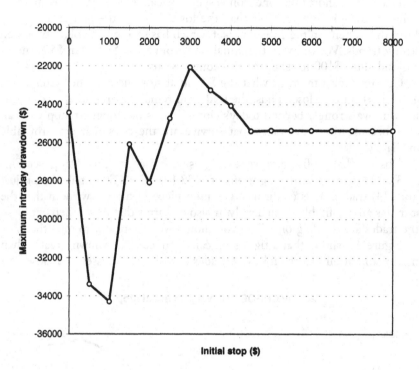

Figure 3.4 As we loosen the initial stop, MIDD first increases and then stops declining.

profit as the stop widens. Eventually the stops are so large that they have little effect, and so MIDD stabilizes.

The initial stop cuts off fewer trades as we loosen it (see Figure 3.5), and hence the total number of trades produced by CHBOC decreases. Once the stop is "too loose" (more than $3,000 or so), it has little effect, and the number of trades stops declining.

Only 5 percent of the trades are profitable with a $0 stop. The percentage of winners increases quickly as we loosen the initial stop until the stop has little effect (see Figure 3.6). As we loosen the stop, more of the winning trades can survive the vagaries of market action.

As you may expect, the worst losing trade increases as we loosen the stop (see Figure 3.7). This occurs because the worst case with a $0 stop reflects slippage due to a weak opening. However, as we loosen the stop, the losing trade from a false signal can survive longer.

The highest average 10-day trading range in the coffee market over the last 20 years was approximately $5,025. The average value was $1,015 and the

Number of trades for 20-day CHBOC on Coffee

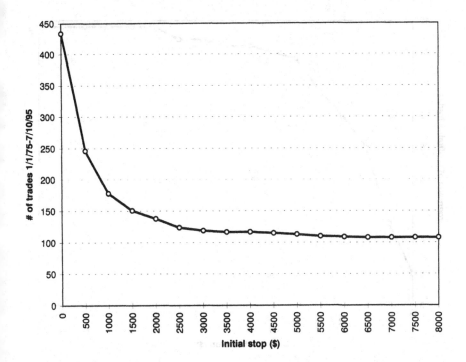

Figure 3.5   The number of trades drops and levels off as we loosen the initial stop.

standard deviation was $641. The cumulative distribution (Figure 3.8) shows that a stop of $3,000 exceeds 98.3 percent of all the 10-day average trading range values seen in coffee over the last 20 years. Hence, $3,000 should be a loose stop. Figures 3.3 through 3.7 show that the changes in performance begin to level off beyond $3,000. Thus, you can view stops greater than $3,000 as "very loose" stops. A $500 stop that covers less than 20 percent of all observed values of the 10-day average daily range qualifies as a "tight" stop.

You can now use the cumulative frequency distribution to select a stop based on market volatility. An arbitrary stop may be too tight or too loose. This analysis assumes that you use the same dollar stop on every trade. If you vary the initial stop on every trade then this analysis will be of little use to you. We already know that stops are hit more frequently during trading range markets. Hence, you could use some measure of trendiness to vary your initial stop.

Many traders feel an aversion to taking a big loss, even though they have no problem taking many small ones. The maximum drawdown usually decreases as the stop increases (see Figure 3.4). Thus, you should try to take the long-term view when you set your stops. If you use a constant stop based on

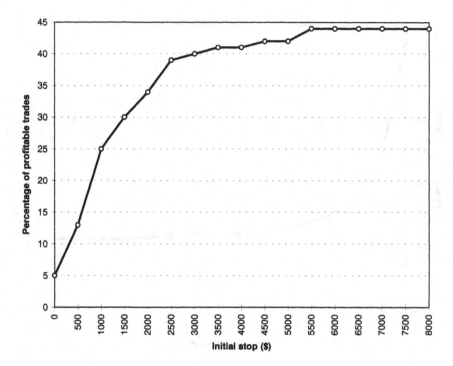

Changes in percent profitable trades, 20-day CHBOC on Coffee

Figure 3.6   The proportion of profitable trades increases and levels off as we loosen the initial stop.

system design, then use loose stops. If you set the stop differently for each trade, then you have probably mastered the fine art of placing stops.

The risk of being stopped out is highest near trade inception, as shown by the calculations in Table 3.11. This table shows the effect on the length of the average losing trade of using no stop, a $1,500 stop, and a variable stop. A simple 20-day CHBOC model, with no exits other than an initial money management stop, is used, allowing $100 for slippage and commissions. The tests were over a 6-year period commencing May 26, 1989, using continuous contracts.

The data in Table 3.11 show that inserting an initial money management stop of $1,500 reduced the length of the average losing trade by approximately 40 percent to 17 days from 28 days. These calculations confirm that the risk of being stopped out is highest near trade inception. The average winning trade was typically 2 to 3 times longer than the average losing trade.

If you look more closely at Table 3.11, you will see that for some markets, such as gold, sugar, and soybeans, the length of the average losing trade did not decrease much even after adding a stop. This means that the volatility in these

Variation in biggest losing trade: 20-day CHBOC on Coffee

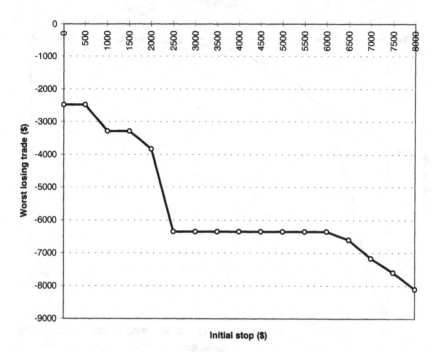

Figure 3.7　The worst losing trade increases as we loosen the stop.

markets is not as large as, say, the currency or bond market. An approximate initial stop that will produce an average losing trade length of 10 or 11 days is also shown in Table 3.11. The S&P-500 index futures contract and coffee were the two most volatile markets, followed by cotton, Swiss franc, and the U.S. bond markets. Conversely, gold, sugar, and crude oil were relatively less volatile. Hence, you may find it useful to consider overall market volatility when placing your initial stop.

In summary, you can get a better feel for system performance if you use loose stops with a self-correcting system. If a stop is "tight," then a small change in the stop can affect long-term performance. If a stop is "very loose," then changing the stop will have little effect. As you loosen your initial stop, the profits increase and then change more slowly. This means that once you pass some volatility threshold, increasing the initial stop adds little value.

Another reason to use loose stops is that you cannot properly test stops that are smaller than the daily price range. Ideally, you should base your initial stop on money management guidelines, the maximum adverse excursion of the system, and on market volatility. There are many ways to select an initial stop; once you pick a method, you should use it consistently.

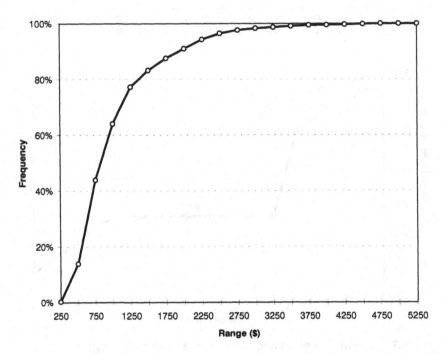

Cumulative frequency distribution average 10-day daily range in coffee

Figure 3.8   The cumulative frequency distribution of the 10-day average daily range shows that an initial stop of $3,000 or more covers 98.3 percent of all trading ranges.

Does Your Design Control Risks?

As you design your trading system, remind yourself that one of your key goals is to control the downside risk. You will quickly discover that risk is a many-splendored thing. This section briefly discusses some of the areas of risk you may wish to consider as you take a portfolio-level look at your trading system.

A trailing stop is a popular method to control portfolio volatility and protect profits. A trailing stop is simply a stop order that is placed some fixed distance away from the highest profit point in the trade. When the market reverses, or when market volatility increases, this stop will be touched off and will protect your profits. If you are using long-term systems that are slow to react to trend changes, then such a stop may smooth out your equity curve.

An important type of risk arises from correlation among markets. You know that correlated markets move roughly together. A good example is the currency markets such as the Swiss franc and deutsche mark (see Figure 2.10).

Table 3.11   Effect of initial money management stop on length of average losing trade.

Market	Average Days in Losing Trades (–1,500 stop)	Average Days in Losing Trade (no stop)	Initial Stop Required to Give 10–11 days in Average Losing Trades (variable stop) ($)
Coffee	92	6	1,600
Copper, high grade	21	28	500
Cotton	14	20	1,250
Crude oil	23	27	500
Deutsche mark	16	27	1,000
Gold, Comex	28	31	400
Heating oil	27	37	700
Japanese yen	13	26	1,000
Soybeans	24	27	500
S&P-500	7	26	2,000
Sugar	32	32	500
Swiss franc	13	27	1,250
10-year T-note	23	35	850
U.S. bond	12	27	1,250

These markets tend to experience broadly similar moves versus the U.S. dollar. As we saw in Chapter 2, trading correlated markets in the same portfolio is equivalent to trading multiple contracts in a single market. This may increase your risk to market events such as unexpected and unexplained news events.

There is an execution risk to your portfolio due to market liquidity or lack of it. For example, lightly traded markets can produce significant slippage. You experience slippage getting in and out, reducing profits, and increasing losses. In these markets your paper testing may not adequately account for slippage and commissions, thereby overestimating potential profitability.

Liquidity can be a particular problem near major holidays, such as Christmas and New Year's Day. During these thin market periods, it is common to see large one-day moves (see Figure 3.9) that can scramble the best-laid risk-control plans. These moves do not change the underlying trend, but can be difficult to model when you test your trading system.

Global trading produces a new set of risks to your portfolio. If news events occur when the U.S. markets are closed, then large price moves could occur in foreign markets. This is particularly true for currencies such as the Swiss franc, Japanese yen, or deutsche mark; energy markets such as crude oil; and metals markets such as gold and silver. Often, an emotional reaction in foreign markets will produce a large opening gap stopping you out at extraordinary

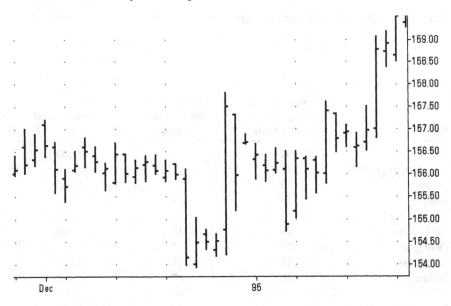

Figure 3.9   Increased volatility in the British pound market caused by thin markets at year end 1994 is clearly visible.

slippage. You may find that your profits are lower than anticipated due to these large opening gaps. Then to make matters worse, the markets may stage a recovery to close well inside your stop loss point. Thus, round-the-clock trading adds new risks to your portfolio.

The DM contract in 1995 showed some large gaps during a volatile period (see Figure 3.10). Large overnight moves in foreign currency markets produced these large gaps, which are difficult to simulate correctly in historical testing. The first encircled gap was for $2,112.50, a big move against you if you were short. The island reversal in the middle ellipse in late March 1995 also left huge gaps, about $1,300 per contract. The gap circled in May was about $1,500. Here, your signal a day off on either side would show significantly different results.

The large intraday ranges in this contract also increases the difficulty with entering a market on the close. For example, you may lose a big move if you had the right signal on the right day, but entered the market on the close rather than on a stop. Say you had a sell order at 71.80 stop close only. Your fill would have been after a slippage of $2,400, quite unacceptable to most traders (see Figure 3.11).

The type of data you use often poses hidden risk. Consider a situation in which you are using weekly data to develop your trading system. Let us suppose you generate a signal at the Friday close, and purchase with a delay on Tuesday open. Since daily opening gaps are missing from weekly data, you can easily

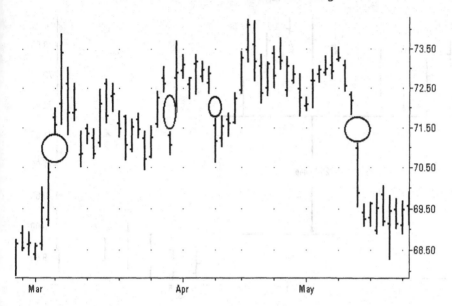

Figure 3.10   The large gaps are due to big moves overnight in overseas markets. Note the large close-to-open gaps in the bars highlighted by the ellipse in the middle of the chart.

underestimate the slippage from actual trading. Another potential problem area is using systems that generate signals this week and ask you to trade next week. You could have a large move this week, and have missed a big portion of the profits by the time you enter the trade next week.

Your system could also experience a time-based risk. For example, the best moves seem to occur when the market moves rapidly immediately after a signal. Suppose the market consolidates immediately after giving you a new breakout signal. The risk of being stopped out is significantly higher in a sideways trend. Hence, you may want a filter that will exit within 5 days of entry if the trade shows a loss.

Another quirky situation arises when you get a new signal very close to a rollover date. It is possible to generate an entry signal on the contract about to expire, but not on the next active futures contract. In this case you must decide whether to take the signal as is, and then rollover immediately or in a few days, or just to wait until the next active contract generates its signal.

In testing with continuous contracts, you could easily underestimate the effects of rollovers on trading costs and profitability. You must also resolve the issue of where to place your initial stop on the new rollover position. Your real position may hit the stop, while your continuous contract merrily rolls along with its position intact.

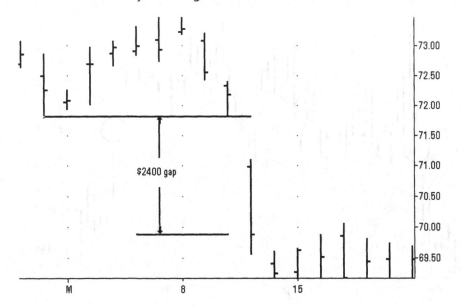

Figure 3.11 A stop close only sell order would have a $2,400 slippage due to market volatility.

This discussion does not include all types of risk, but highlights why you should consider risk control early in your trading system design process.

Data! Handle with Care!

You have many choices when you select data for your system testing. You should therefore exercise great care in choosing your test data because they have a big influence on test results.

Choose your data vendor with care, since data vendors differ in accuracy, depth of coverage, and reporting conventions. For example, there can be differences in the opening price of a contract between data vendors. Another policy difference is how errors are detected and corrected. You want a vendor with "clean" data all around.

If you are testing futures contracts, use a continuous contract or the actual contracts with rollovers. Unlike a cash market index, futures data are not continuous: contracts are dormant, become active, and expire. Hence, to produce a continuous, albeit "synthetic," data stream, different contracts must be combined in some consistent manner. You have two choices when you combine futures contracts. You can preserve the prices or price levels, at the cost of incorrectly preserving the amplitude of price movements, or, alternately, you can preserve the amplitude of price movements at the cost of adjusting prices.

Continuous contracts that preserve amplitudes are preferred for testing. Each type of continuous contract will give slightly different numerical results.

A good choice is using actual data with rollovers if the software allows it. Results from continuous contracts come closest to data with rollovers, but they tend to underestimate the number of trades and hence the losses due to slippage and commissions. They also underestimate the difficulty with placing stops on rollover trades. For example, after rollovers, you can get stopped out on a real trade, while the system trading the continuous contract continues to hold its position.

Other than type of data, you must also choose the amount of data. In general, the more data you can use, the better, because you can then test a model over a wide variety of market conditions. There is also a statistical requirement, to start using tests based on the normal distribution, usually quoted as sufficient data to produce 30 or more trades over the test period. The idea here is simply that the more trades you have in a given sample, the better your estimate of the average properties for the entire universe. Hence, you can use the average properties (such as average trade) to estimate how the system will do in the future.

Although 30 trades may not seem like a large number, you may have difficulty obtaining 30 trades with weekly data using certain trend-following models. Thirty trades is probably too small a number to fully eliminate any effects of the data used for the tests. Hence, more than 100 tests is preferable, if possible, and you can obtain sufficient numbers by combining tests over multiple markets and multiple time frames. Later in the book you will learn how to generate synthetic data to generate a large sample of trades.

The point of this discussion is that different input data will give you different results. Besides, you cannot be certain that your trading will ever achieve those results because you do not actually trade the synthetic data. We now look at the results of testing a dual-moving average crossover system using 5-day and 50-day simple moving averages, an initial money management stop of $1,500, and $100 for slippage and commissions.

Table 3.12 was created by Continuous Contractor™ software from Tech Tools, Inc. to show different types of continuous contracts for the Swiss franc. Over the same period, model performance was calculated using actual contracts with automatic rollover on the twenty-first day of the month prior to expiration. The cautionary tale here is that test results vary widely with the type of data used.

Focus on the number of trades for the same entry and exit rules. There are 111 trades with the actual data, almost 37 percent more than the average number of trades created using continuous contracts. The extra trades result primarily from rolling over existing positions into the next active contract.

Notice also that the ratio of average winning to losing trades is the smallest (1.80) with actual data. This occurs because rolling over positions decreases the amount of profit in winning trades. During a long trend the continuous

Table 3.12   Comparison of test results with different types of continuous contracts.

Data Type	Profit ($)	MIDD ($)	Number of Trades	Wins (%)	Win/Loss Ratio
Actual with rollovers	17,963	−21,663	111	40	1.80
Continuous type 38/13	18,450	−24,813	79	31	2.74
Continuous type 49/25	20,413	−22,137	77	31	2.89
Continuous type 55/25	20,350	−21,115	86	34	2.42
Continuous type 56/25	10,625	−27,800	91	31	2.43
Continuous type 60/25	39,862	−18,363	70	35	3.12

contract goes on without any rollovers. Hence, the duration of the trade is longer and therefore its profit figure is also greater with continuous contracts. Thus, continuous contracts may underestimate the number of trades and overestimate the win/loss ratio and the duration of trades.

Choosing Orders for Entries and Exits

You have three basic choices for orders that you use to initiate or exit your trades: market, stop, or limit orders. There are three philosophies at work here. One says to get your price, implying you should use limit orders or stop limit orders to get into the trade. Another philosophy says to guarantee entry into trade, implying you should use market orders or stop orders. The third philosophy insists that you should exit positions with market orders, but can enter on a stop or a limit.

Timed-market orders on the open or the close are a good way to both exit and enter positions. Many traders recommend entering on the open, and avoiding the rush of orders at the close. Using stop orders can cause you extra slippage if the market opens beyond the stop price.

Remember that there can be divergences between what the testing software assumes and what actually happens in practice. You may get a fill from the software, but not from the floor due to the peculiarities of the market. For example, the software testing daily data has no idea if there were fast market conditions on a particular day. Hence, you may or may not get a fill when the software says you did. It is important to understand how the software fills a particular order.

One other important feature is the difference between the signal day (or date) and execution day (or date). This means you can get your signal and open the trade the same day. For example, if you are trading a simple moving-average crossover system, you can calculate that a close beyond a particular point will give you a crossover today. Hence, your order may say buy (or sell) at x, stop close only. Alternatively, you can generate your signals after the close, and enter them the next day. The latter approach is preferable only because it is simpler, and when coupled with an order to enter on the open, it is a reliable way to measure system performance.

Entering tomorrow on a stop above the high or low of today is an effective filter when compared to buying tomorrow on the open. In effect, it filters out some whipsaw trades. Generating orders today and entering on the next day on a stop, on the open or on the close, is a consistent and realistic way to assess model performance.

Understanding Summary of Test Results

This discussion of the detailed summary of test results found in technical analysis programs uses in part the report from Omega Research's TradeStation™ software. The purpose of the summary is to show how a particular trading system would have done on historical data.

The summary shown in Table 3.13 is for the British pound continuous contract for the 65-day simple moving average, three consecutive closes (65sma-3cc) trend-following system. The 65sma-3cc trading system is discussed in detail in the next chapter. The summary here is for all trades, long and short. The software shows the same information for long trades only and for all short trades.

The summary is broken down into five blocks. The top-most block describes profitability. The second block gives physical trade count. The third block presents average trade data. The fourth block shows trade duration or length data. Finally, the fifth block gives important information on drawdowns, profit factor, and returns.

The total net profit is the difference between the gross profit and gross loss. The gross profit is the sum of the profits on all profitable trades. Similarly, the gross loss is the sum of losses on all losing trades. The open trade profit or loss is the value on a trade still open at the end of the test period. The net profit is an important figure that influences other calculations below. Note that the profit factor shown in block five is simply the absolute value of the ratio of gross profit divided by gross loss. In trading system design, a profit factor of more than 1 is highly desirable, since it says that gross profits exceeded gross losses over the test period.

The trade count block shows the total number of trades, and the breakdown into number of winning and losing trades. The percentage of winning trades is a function of both the trading system rules and the test data, and helps influence the risk of ruin. Naturally, the larger this number, the better. It is common to have trend-following systems report in with a winning percentage

Table 3.13   Typical performance summary for 65sma-3cc system.

British Pound 38/13-daily 02/13/75 – 7/10/95 Performance Summary: All Trades			
Total net profit ($)	155,675.00	Open trade profit or loss ($)	–1,212.50
Gross profit ($)	266,918.75	Gross loss ($)	–111,243.75
Total number of trades	71	Percentage profitable	45
Number of winning trades	32	Number of losing trades	39
Largest winning trade ($)	40,768.75	Largest losing trade ($)	–7,993.75
Average winning trade ($)	8,341.21	Average losing trade ($)	–2,852.40
Average win/average loss	2.92	Average trade (win and loss) ($)	2,192.61
Maximum consecutive winners	6	Maximum consecutive losers	7
Average number of bars in winners	123	Average number of bars in losers	29
Maximum intraday drawdown ($)	–27,881.25		
Profit factor	2.40	Maximum number of contracts held	1
Account size required ($)	30,881.25	Return on account (%)	504

of 30 to 50 percent. A number above 60 percent is difficult to find, and anything over 70 percent is remarkable.

The average trade performance block merely combines data from the two blocks above to report average numbers. The largest winning trade and largest losing trade are new numbers in this block. They are usually functions of the test data, trading system rules, and risk control specifications. If you do not use stops and the markets are volatile, there will be a large losing trade. Exceptional trends can give you a large winning trade. Beware if the largest winning trade is more than 50 percent of your net profits. It probably means you should deduct this amount from net profits to evaluate true system potential.

The average winning trade is simply the ratio of gross profit divided by number of winning trades. The ratio of the average winning to average losing trade is useful for calculating risk of ruin. This is called the payoff ratio, and is a function of the test data, trading system rules, and the length of trades. The typical trend-following systems will return values greater than 2.

The average trade reported in the third block is one of the most important numbers in the summary. It is simply the ratio of net profit divided by the total number of trades. This number depends on the test data and trading system rules. This number would ideally be as large as possible. If this number is negative or less than $200, avoid trading this system unless you test it on other markets and other time frames. This number is the statistical edge for this system.

The trade duration block gives the length of the average winning and losing trades (average number of bars in winners equals length of average winning trade). This ratio should be greater than 1, and it could be greater than 5 for trend-following systems. Ask yourself if you would be comfortable holding a trade for the number of days shown in the length of average winning trade. Do you have the discipline to stay with a trade that lasted twice as long as the average winning trade? If you are not patient, this may be a difficult task, and you might miss out on a mega-trade.

Alternately, ask if the length of an average winning trade coincides with your trading horizon. If the length of the average trade it is too long or too short, test the system first over more data and then over other markets. If you are still not comfortable with this number, you should consider changing your trading system.

The maximum consecutive winners and losers data will vary with the test period. Maximum consecutive losers have a great influence on your drawdowns. You should carefully examine the period when the consecutive losers occur to understand under what conditions your trading system will produce large losses.

As a rough rule of thumb, ask yourself if you could tolerate twice the number of consecutive losers as the number reported for maximum consecutive losers. This will tell you how to set your money management guidelines to avoid serious drawdowns. Ask yourself also if you would hold a losing trade as long as the average losing trade number suggests.

The last block shows the maximum intraday drawdown. Ask yourself if you could tolerate a number twice as large. The account size and return on margin numbers are not very useful. The profit factor, as discussed above, should be greater than 1.

What the Performance Summary Does Not Show

The test summary leaves out some important information, highlighted below. You may wish to examine these factors in greater detail.

One simple ratio is the recovery factor (RF). RF is absolute value of the ratio of net profit to maximum intraday drawdown, and it measures how far you recovered from the depth of the drawdown. In Table 3.13 the recovery factor is approximately equal to 5.6 (155,675/27,881). This number should be greater than 2, and the higher the better. It tells whether the potential benefits over the long haul are worth the aggravations caused by the drawdowns.

Another useful value is the adjusted gross profit, in which the largest winning trade is deducted from the gross profit. To penalize the system, do not correspondingly deduct the largest losing trade. The rationale here is not to expect to get the periods with large profits, but that a period of losses comparable to the worst losses in the test period is likely. The profit factor is then recalculated to see if it is still greater than 1. For the data in Table 3.13, the adjusted gross profit is $155,675 − 40,769 = $114,906. The adjusted profit factor is then 114,906/111,244 = 1.03. This is a sharp reduction from the reported profit factor of 2.40. Thus, a more realistic assessment of this system is that it will produce a small net profit over time.

The summary also does not give a histogram of your trades. You may wish to export your data to a spreadsheet to look for the maximum favorable excursion and maximum adverse excursion. These quantities will be explained in Chapter 4 with the 65sma-3cc system.

The summary does not give you any feel for the variation in test results. It does not give a standard deviation of trade profits and losses for all trades. The variability is another important item you should calculate, using a spreadsheet if needed. The variation tells you what you can expect for volatility of returns.

You cannot get an idea of how a typical trade evolves in time from the test summary. For example, it does not tell you the average profit or maximum profit or loss on a day-in-trade basis. It does not show what happened on day 1 in the trade, or day 10 in the trade. A typical trade template, by Chande and Kroll, as discussed in *The New Technical Trader* (see bibliography), would help you understand the time-price evolution of a typical trade.

In addition, the test summary does not give a realistic impact of slippage. The software provides fills in a manner that may not be representative of fills in the real world. It is safer to assume that you will experience greater slippage than the model. In some instances, the software will give you a fill that you could not have obtained in practice. If this happened to be a big winner, you may overestimate trade profitability. Hence, you are better off using the average trade numbers to assess system performance, since they have averaged out the effects over many trades.

The performance summary also does not give any idea of how many successive *x*-month periods would have been profitable. For example, it is useful to know how many successive 6-month periods have been profitable over a 5-year period. You could use any time interval you like. This breakdown tells you how quickly you can expect to get out of drawdowns, and is a vital piece of information for your mental approach to trading the system.

The most important factor to recognize is that the test summary does not tell you how the system will perform in the future. Your test results are hostage to your data. You should look below the surface of the results to get a better understanding of your system tests.

Ideally, you should examine the results on a trade-by-trade basis on the charts to understand how your system rules worked. This will reinforce your trading beliefs, and give you a good feel for when the system does or does not work. A study of unprofitable trades often reveals flaws in your logic. Convince yourself that you want to follow this system because its rules make money under market conditions that are likely to repeat in the future. A trade-by-trade review may also strengthen your ability to use discretion in trade entries or exits.

Some Avoidable Pitfalls in System Testing

You can easily test a system with today's sophisticated software. However, this same software also allows you to arrive at impractical solutions. Ideally, the rules you find will work just as well in actual trading as they did in your tests. A number of factors can influence your actual trading results, so it is rare to get a "perfect" match between testing and trading. In many cases, you would be perfectly happy to come close to the hypothetical performance. Let us review some common pitfalls to avoid in system testing.

The starting point for any test is the length of the test period. The data series should be long enough to cover several trading ranges and trending periods, perhaps 3 years or more. Another choice is to have a test period long enough to generate 50 or more trades. In testing and optimizing for a single market, a common practice is to divide the entire data series into three parts. Use the middle piece of data to develop the system rules, and then use a portion of data at the beginning and the end of the test period to recheck the performance of the system. The middle portion of data used to develop the rules is called "in-sample" data. You need "out-of-sample" data to avoid overoptimization during testing.

The results you will get for the two in-sample and out-of-sample testing periods will depend on the particular time periods chosen by you. It is not critical that the profitability be identical in the two periods because the markets will have behaved differently. However, the other internal measures of your system should be essentially unchanged. The following quantities, which are not sensitive to returns, should be nearly the same in the in-sample and out-of-sample periods: average duration of winning and losing trades, maximum consecutive winners, maximum consecutive losing trades, worst losing trade, and average losing trade. The statistical criteria that are dependent on returns may or may not be similar due to what the markets did in a particular period. You should expect greater similarity in the in-sample and out-of-sample results as the lengths of the sample periods increase.

Consider an optimization exercise using a simple moving-average crossover system for the Eurodollar market. The first test period was from September 1, 1993 to December 31, 1996. The optimized lengths of the two moving

Table 3.14   Performance summary: In-sample period, optimized simple moving-average crossover lengths of 13 and 50.

```
Opt.Maxo   EurodollarGlbx(3Mth) 63/00-Daily    09/01/1993 - 12/31/1996

        Performance Summary:  All Trades

Total net profit          $   80575.00    Open position P/L      $    900.00
Gross profit              $   99075.00    Gross loss             $ -18500.00

Total # of trades                 14      Percent profitable            50%
Number winning trades              7      Number losing trades           7

Largest winning trade     $   30625.00    Largest losing trade   $  -4950.00
Average winning trade     $   14153.57    Average losing trade   $  -2642.86
Ratio avg win/avg loss          5.36      Avg trade(win & loss)  $   5755.36

Max consec. winners                3      Max consec. losers             3
Avg # bars in winners             88      Avg # bars in losers          25

Max intraday drawdown     $   -8875.00
Profit factor                   5.36      Max # contracts held          10
Account size required     $    8875.00    Return on account            908%
```

averages were 13 days and 50 days. The out-of-sample period was from January 2, 1997 to December 31, 1999. Note that the return-independent measures of performance, such as the duration of average winning and losing trades, and the consecutive winners and losers (see Table 3.14 and Table 3.15), were similar. This implies that the model traded the longer-term trends in a manner similar to the in-sample period. The performance-sensitive measures were different because the net profit was significantly lower in the out-of-sample period. The "optimal" moving-average combination for the out-of-sample period was 18-day and 30-day moving averages, suggesting that the Eurodollar market had long consolidations and shorter trends in the out-of-sample period.

How do you judge that a system is potentially unstable? An unstable system has typically been overfitted to the test data or poorly specified in some

Table 3.15   Performance summary: Out-of-sample period, optimized simple moving-average crossover lengths of 13 and 50.

```
Opt.Maxo   EurodollarGlbx(3Mth) 63/00-Daily    01/02/1997 - 12/31/1999

        Performance Summary:  All Trades

Total net profit          $    7725.00    Open position P/L      $   4700.00
Gross profit              $   44812.50    Gross loss             $ -37087.50

Total # of trades                 14      Percent profitable            36%
Number winning trades              5      Number losing trades           9

Largest winning trade     $   23925.00    Largest losing trade   $  -7300.00
Average winning trade     $    8962.50    Average losing trade   $  -4120.83
Ratio avg win/avg loss          2.17
Max consec. winners                2      Max consec. losers             5
Avg # bars in winners             91      Avg # bars in losers          25

Max intraday drawdown     $  -28700.00
Profit factor                   1.21      Max # contracts held          11
Account size required          28700.00   Return on account            27%
```

Table 3.16   Performance summary: In-sample period, nonoptimized volatility breakout system.

```
Opt.VolBo  EurodollarGlbx(3Mth) 63/00-Daily   09/01/1993 - 12/31/1996

   Performance Summary:  All Trades

Total net profit     $-161862.50        Open position P/L    $   1500.00
Gross profit         $ 181912.50        Gross loss           $-343775.00

Total # of trades          310          Percent profitable         30%
Number winning trades       93          Number losing trades       217

Largest winning trade $ 10000.00        Largest losing trade $  -3750.00
Average winning trade $  1956.05        Average losing trade $  -1584.22
Ratio avg win/avg loss     1.23         Avg trade(win & loss) $   -522.14

Max consec. winners          5          Max consec. losers          12
Avg # bars in winners        4          Avg # bars in losers         2

Max intraday drawdown $-161862.50
Profit factor              0.53         Max # contracts held        11
Account size required $ 161862.50       Return on account        -100%
```

subtle way. Two clues to look for are a high proportion of profitable trades (say, greater than 60 percent with less than 30 total trades) or a large number of consecutive losing trades. Tables 3.16 and 3.17 show the performance for the Eurodollar market using the same test periods as the moving-average crossover tests. We use a simple volatility breakout system using the recent range in price activity. Note the number of consecutive losing trades: 12 in the in-sample period and 16 in the out-of-sample period. The large number of consecutive losing trades implies that this is a poorly specified strategy for this market, which moves in smooth trends, as evidenced by the potential profitability of simple moving-average systems. The duration of the trades with the volatility system is 4 days, versus 88 to 91 days for the trend-following systems, indicating that the

Table 3.17   Performance summary: Out-of-sample period, nonoptimized volatility breakout system.

```
Opt.VolBo  EurodollarGlbx(3Mth) 63/00-Daily   01/02/1997 - 12/31/1999

   Performance Summary:  All Trades

Total net profit     $-235462.50        Open position P/L    $      0.00
Gross profit         $ 126800.00        Gross loss           $-362262.50

Total # of trades          274          Percent profitable         27%
Number winning trades       75          Number losing trades       199

Largest winning trade $  7600.00        Largest losing trade $  -5362.50
Average winning trade $  1690.67        Average losing trade $  -1820.41
Ratio avg win/avg loss     0.93
Max consec. winners          4          Max consec. losers          16
Avg # bars in winners        4          Avg # bars in losers         2

Max intraday drawdown $-237037.50
Profit factor              0.35         Max # contracts held        16
Account size required $ 237037.50       Return on account        -99%
```

98 Foundations of System Design

Table 3.18 A 10–20 moving-average system on coffee, with all profits from a single trade in 1996–1997.

```
Opt.Maxo  Coffee-CSCE 63/00-Daily   02/10/1994 - 07/27/2000

     Performance Summary:  All Trades

Total net profit       $4846275.00   Open position P/L      $ -11587.50
Gross profit           $4965225.00   Gross loss             $-118950.00

Total # of trades            66      Percent profitable           39%
Number winning trades        26      Number losing trades         40

Largest winning trade $4833812.50    Largest losing trade   $  -8668.75
Average winning trade $ 190970.19    Average losing trade   $  -2973.75
Ratio avg win/avg loss     64.22     Avg trade(win & loss)  $  73428.41

Max consec. winners           6      Max consec. losers            7
Avg # bars in winners        30      Avg # bars in losers         12

Max intraday drawdown $-274031.25
Profit factor              41.74     Max # contracts held        395
Account size required $ 274031.25    Return on account          1769%
```

specification of the short-term volatility breakout system is probably inappropriate for the Eurodollar market.

Other unusual situations to check for include when a single trade accounts for 40 percent or more of the net profits during a given test period, or the intraday drawdown exceeds the largest losing trade. A hugely profitable trade may not occur for another 3 to 10 years, or perhaps ever, and the benefits of trading that market with a particular system may be overestimated (see the situation for coffee in Table 3.18). Consider now the volatility system discussed previously traded on the Swiss government bond from January 4, 1999 through July 27, 2000. The largest winning trade of $100,928 is greater than the reported net profit of $67,284 (see Table 3.19). The largest intraday drawdown is shown at –$214,833, considerably greater than the largest losing trade of –$63,538. This implies that the trading strategy allowed for a large retracement against the position without exiting the market. Thus, a volatility breakout reversal strategy may be inappropriate for a bond market that often moves in long, smooth trends.

When testing a system you wish to trade over many markets, the system should be profitable on a minimum of ten unrelated markets. The broad sectors in the futures markets may be described as follows: agriculturals, currencies, energies, interest rates, metals, softs, and stocks. Hence, your system should be profitable on more than two markets in each sector. The stock indices as a group tend to trade idiosyncratically, and optimized systems on stock indices will typically have characteristics different from those profitable on the other sectors. A review of test results of the systems, presented later in this book, will show that their rules are robust because they are profitable over ten or more markets over different times. Note that there may be sector-specific systems that may use in-

Table 3.19   Testing the volatility breakout system on Swiss federated bonds.

```
Opt.VolBo  Swiss Gov Bnd(10Yr)- 63/00-Daily    01/04/1999 - 07/27/2000

         Performance Summary:  All Trades

Total net profit      $  67284.44    Open position P/L    $  18714.08
Gross profit          $ 423509.06    Gross loss           $-356224.63

Total # of trades            25      Percent profitable          44%
Number winning trades        11      Number losing trades         14

Largest winning trade $ 100928.09    Largest losing trade $ -63538.52
Average winning trade $  38500.82    Average losing trade $ -25444.62
Ratio avg win/avg loss      1.51      Avg trade(win & loss) $   2691.38

Max consec. winners           5       Max consec. losers            7
Avg # bars in winners        15       Avg # bars in losers         10

Max intraday drawdown $-214833.11
Profit factor               1.19      Max # contracts held         53
Account size required $ 214833.11     Return on account           31%
```

formation available about a particular sector, such as macro-economic data, commitment of trader's report, crop production data, or Organization of Petroleum Exporting Countries (OPEC) production quotas. Clearly, such systems cannot be expected to work across other sectors, but should be profitable on most of the markets in the sector.

Your computer may internally carry computations to more than 20 decimal places. Thus, when you optimize your system, the computer can suggest parameter values that pick up nuances in the data. For example, entering a single trade or avoiding a single trade can have a major influence on the profitability over a particular data set. The optimizing process will manipulate the rules to pick up or avoid the trade in question. However, such selectivity has little long-term value because the random market factors affecting that trade may never be replicated. For example, if you are using percent bands, the computer may suggest a width of, say, 1.73205087 percent around the 50-day moving average. However, you may be better off using "rounded" numbers, such as 2 percent or 1.75 percent, for parameters in your system. Using rounded numbers avoids overfitting because it is unlikely that the optimized width calculated over one time period will continue to be the best period at some other future period. The assumption behind rounding is that a major trend is just as likely to rise above the 1.75 percent, band as it is to rise above the 1.73205087 percent band or the 2 percent band. Rounding generalizes the solution to the design problem, and hence reduces dependence on the performance over the test data. Naturally, using 2 percent bands instead of 1 percent bands would reduce the trading frequency because the 1 percent bands will be penetrated more frequently than the 2 percent bands. This behavior is true across all markets, and can be postulated without massive testing and optimization. Thus, the structure of the system requires a certain move above the band before you enter a market, and that is more significant than the precise value of the band carried out to ten decimal places.

How can someone measure robustness? We define one system-market-year (SMY) as a unit related to a system being profitable on one market for one year. One minimum measure of robustness would be 30 SMY, in which a system is profitable over at least ten markets over a 3-year period. Another measure is that the largest losing trade is always less than a prespecified limit in all markets. However, one can also use qualitative assessments of the design features. Brittle systems have design flaws that are almost certain to cause repeated failures.

Consider a system that exits on the lowest low or highest high of the past 20 days. Assuming this is a trend-following system, a major reversal in any market will eventually take out the lowest low or highest high of the past 20 days. Such a system is robust because it will certainly exit on a strong move against the trend. Conversely, an exit strategy that requires a large one-day move to exit the trend, such as a retracement three times the 10-day average true range from the previous high or low, is fairly brittle because the market can make large net moves against the position over several days without a large move on any given day.

Now consider an entry strategy that enters with a limit order placed at a fixed dollar or volatility distance from today's high or low. It is possible for the market to trend up or down for a series of days, making moves just shy of the limit order this system has generated. For example, say you want to buy on weakness in an uptrend, and you specify that you want to buy with a limit order on a retracement to the 5-day simple moving average of the close. It is possible to have a sustained trend of 10 or more days without a retracement to the trailing 5-day simple moving average, and you would miss that move entirely. A modification of this approach, for which entry is with a stop order at or just above the high of the previous day, would allow more consistent entries into strong swing moves. Hence, when you design your system, look for brittle rules that can be easily thwarted by the market.

A Reality Check

This section sounds a note of warning before you proceed: Test results are not what they seem. You should recognize that trading systems are designed with the benefit of hindsight. This is true because you know, a priori, what the market has done in the past. Any trading system you design or optimize reflects your view of past market action. You may state your understanding in a generalized way that avoids the dangers of curve-fitting. However, it is worth recognizing that the influence of hindsight is difficult to eliminate.

It is also important to recognize that past price patterns may not repeat in precisely the same way. Hence, because the exact future sequence of trades is unpredictable, your system may not achieve profits or losses similar to the hypothetical system. It should be easy to conclude that past results are not indicative of future results because neither market action nor trader reaction is predictable.

There is another key problem area with simulated trades. Hypothetical trades from a trading system design exercise have not been entered in the markets and do not represent actual trading. They do not accurately reflect the effects of market liquidity, slippage, bad fills, overnight trading, or fast markets. They also do not reflect a trader's psychology accurately since each and every signal is assumed to be executed with identical simplifying assumptions.

You, the trader, are perhaps the most capricious variable in the trading system. Because system testing is performed in an emotional vacuum, there is no assurance that you will execute all signals from a trading system without deviation. Thus, the biggest slippage could occur not in the markets, but at the source if you fail to enter orders as required.

As you will see in Chapter 8 on data scrambling, it is possible to encounter market conditions that generate a long string of losing trades or one huge loss. Just because the probability that an event occurs is very small, this does not mean that it will not occur. The usual distribution of trades from a typical trading system has "fat" tails. This simply means that the probability that unusual market conditions will occur is much greater than you might expect from a normal distribution. Hence, system testing results will often underestimate market risks.

Thus, when you design trading systems, be aware that your hypothetical results do not accurately predict system performance in the future. In general, you should view any trading system results with all due caution.

Appendix to Chapter 3: Design Issues—Entry and Exit Strategies

There are at least as many entry and exit strategies as there are traders. An entry strategy is any process that leads to a buy or sell signal to initiate a trade. An exit strategy is any combination of rules that closes out an open position. Two broad combinations of entry and exit packages exist. One is always in the market, either long or short. The other broad category of systems can be long, short, or out of the market entirely (flat). The general discussion of entry and exit strategies and their strengths and weaknesses presented here provides an overview that may serve as a good introduction or as a useful reference.

Information about markets can be categorized as either technical or fundamental. Technical information is internal market information generated during the trading process, and includes such information as trading prices, volumes, open interest, and commitment of traders. Fundamental, or external, information is generated by the economic processes governing a market during the normal course of business, and usually includes information about production or consumption. Hence, the two broad categories of trading strategies are those relying on technical information and those based on information flows. Traders who use technical information believe that prices (and other internal data) reflect all information available to market participants and, more important, reflect the market's evaluation of all available data. Therefore, traders who use technical data are a step behind the market, being price takers rather than price (market) makers. Conversely, traders who use information flows believe they can take positions ahead of the markets, anticipating new trends before the markets complete their adjustment to new data. Discretionary or fundamental traders tend to be market makers rather than price takers. The emphasis in this discussion focuses on entry signals derived from technical data.

Design Issues for Entries

Technical entries are based on market-generated data, such as prices, volumes, open interest, or commitment of traders. Every entry strategy must meet one or more criteria to generate a buy or sell signal. For futures and stocks, prices must move in the direction of the trade for it to be profitable. For example, prices must rise beyond the entry price for long trades to be profitable. How, then, does one evaluate successful entry strategies? Four general design issues must be solved by each entry strategy: sensitivity, selectivity, susceptibility, and sustainability, referred to collectively as 4-S.

1. *Sensitivity.* The greater the sensitivity, the smaller the time delays between market action and the actual entry signal. For example, by design, an entry signal based on intraday data will be more sensitive than one based on monthly data.

2. *Selectivity.* The better the selectivity, the larger the profit factor of the system. The profit factor is the ratio of the gross profit to the gross loss. Selective systems tend to trade less frequently, as measured by the total number of trades over a test period. For example, breakout-style entries typically tend to be more selective than trend-following entries because they do not generate signals when prices are within a trading range.

3. *Susceptibility.* The more robust an entry strategy, the lower its susceptibility to noise and the greater the probability that it will work as intended. For example, a simple trend-following strategy is less likely to miss a major trend than a complex volatility-breakout strategy because prices may move higher or lower for several days without triggering a volatility-breakout entry signal.

4. *Sustainability.* The more sustainable a strategy, the broader the portfolio to which it can be applied, and the more easily profitability is main-

tained over time. For example, trend-following strategies can be applied profitably to more markets than antitrend strategies.

These criteria suggest that a well-designed entry strategy reacts promptly to market action, leads to profitable trades, is not likely to misfire at critical moments, and can be traded across a broadly diversified portfolio. Let us now analyze some common strategies and see how they compare.

Trend-Following Strategies

A trend-following (TF) strategy puts on positions in the direction of the observed trend. A system based on the moving average is a good example of a trend-following strategy. The simplest case uses two moving averages, such as 3-day and 12-day simple moving averages (see Figure 3.12). The type of moving average may vary, such as simple, exponential, or adaptive. A buy signal is generated when the shorter moving average crosses above the longer moving average. A sell signal is generated when the shorter moving average crosses under the longer moving average. Such systems are called reversal systems because they reverse from long to short and vice versa and always have a position in the market. A number of variations of this strategy can be derived, such as by using more than two moving averages or specifying more complex "penetration" conditions for recognizing a valid crossing of the averages or anticipating

Figure 3.12   An example of a simple trend-following system, a 3-day and 12-day simple moving-average crossover system, applied to New York Heating Oil futures. Moving-average systems lose money when prices are trapped in a trading range.

crossovers with oscillators. It is possible to design moving average systems with a neutral zone.

Advantages of Trend-Following Strategies Trend-following strategies react to, rather than anticipate, price movement. Hence, there is a built-in lag between market action and the positions taken in the direction of the measured trend. Using this strategy, it is unlikely that you will be short in rising markets or long in falling markets, assuming that you are comparing time frames correctly. For example, if you trade daily data, it may appear that you are going short in a market with a rising trend on weekly or monthly charts. Trend-following strategies work well when a market is trending smoothly or making swing moves (swing moves are smooth trends lasting 5 to 20 days). Trend-following strategies require orderly markets so that you can establish and liquidate positions without undue slippage or loss of open trade equity. These strategies are relatively early when getting into sustained trends, and can produce good risk-reward ratios when markets trend smoothly. Initial risk can be clearly defined with TF strategies, so they are easy to trade with good risk control.

Disadvantages of Trend-Following Strategies Trend-following strategies are susceptible to whipsaw losses when the market is in a trading range because a succession of crossovers and crossunders occur without meaningful price movement in either direction. If the trendless period lasts many months, the moving-average strategy will continue to be unprofitable. If prices make a large move very quickly, the moving averages may be slow in signaling the trend change. Hence, TF strategies may often seem slow to enter or exit at key turning points. Giving up a large portion of open trade equity before exiting is a particular weakness of long-term TF strategies. Because other market participants are also aware of key moving-average values, TF strategies can lead to extra slippage during entries or exits.

4-S Evaluation of Trend-Following Strategies

- *Sensitivity:* Can be varied by using different lengths or moving averages or type of data.
- *Selectivity:* Can be increased by increasing the lengths of moving averages.
- *Susceptibility:* Is generally low at all lengths; even randomly chosen lengths are unlikely to miss a major move.
- *Sustainability:* Can be applied to a diversified portfolio of markets.

Antitrend Strategies

Antitrend (AT) strategies are anticipatory strategies that seek to put on positions in anticipation of a new trend; these positions are typically against the prevailing trend. For example, short positions are considered after the market has made an up move of "large" amplitude, or long positions are considered after the market has sold off sharply for 5 days. The definition of what constitutes a "large" move during a market "correction" goes to the heart of the design of such systems. Some traders used oscillators to measure overbought or oversold conditions to define what they perceive to be unsustainable market extremes. Others may "fade" new highs (see Figure 3.13) or lows (i.e., sell new x-day highs or buy new y-day lows). Yet others look for momentum divergences, in which markets make new price extremes without corresponding extremes in momentum. For example, a market may make new lows in price, but the momentum oscillators may not (see Figure 3.14). Even pattern-based approaches, such as those identified using "Japanese Candlestick analysis," can be tried. The essence of this strategy is to identify points at which momentum is depleted in the direction of the existing trend.

Advantages of Antitrend Strategies   Antitrend strategies can produce spectacular risk/reward ratios if the market timing is accurate. It is relatively easy to trade in large size with good execution because the position is against

Figure 3.13   Antitrend strategy of selling new highs on the MEFF Ibex 35 Plus stock index in Spain.

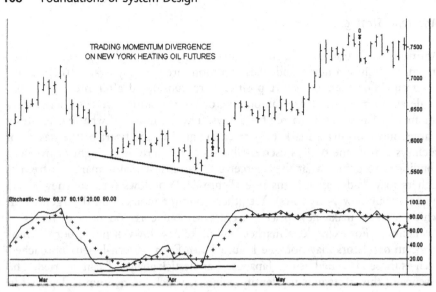

Figure 3.14 Putting on a long position in anticipation of rising prices following a momentum divergence in the New York Heating Oil futures contract. Prices made new lows, but the stochastic oscillator did not, producing a positive divergence.

the prevailing trend. Such approaches are particularly profitable at key turning points or within prolonged trading ranges. Antitrend strategies can be sensitive, particularly because there is little delay between the detection of extreme price action and the execution of the trade.

Disadvantages of Antitrend Strategies Antitrend strategies are vulnerable to large losses if market momentum is sufficient to push prices along the previous trend. Because market momentum can be powerful, one large losing trade can offset many winning trades. Antitrend strategies often require sensitive exits to preserve profits. The amplitude of trading ranges is usually smaller than the amplitudes of trending moves. Hence, the size of the average winning trade can be relatively small. Antitrend strategies need good execution and low transaction costs to be consistently profitable. Such strategies may not work well in all markets because the amplitude of the move against the trend may be small.

4-S Evaluation of Antitrend Strategies

- *Sensitivity*: Is generally high; can detect market extremes within a day of occurrence.

- *Selectivity*: Is generally low; varies widely from market to market and time period to time period.

- *Susceptibility*: Is generally high; key turning points are not easy to detect consistently.

- *Sustainability*: Is generally low; must be applied to a small number of markets.

Breakout-Style Strategies

Breakout-style strategies buy strength and sell weakness when prices move "decisively" beyond a predefined price barrier. Thus, these systems can be long, short, or flat. We assume that prices will continue to develop into a longer-lasting trend in the direction indicated by the near-term price breakout, so breakout (BO) strategies are a special type of trend-following strategy. Many variations of the BO style are possible, depending on one's definition of the price barrier and what constitutes a decisive move beyond the barrier. One simple approach is to define a price breakout as new highs or lows measured over a fixed period of many days or weeks, such as 20 to 80 days for futures or 52 weeks for stocks. Other, more complex definitions of price breakouts are possible, such as using volatility bands around moving averages. By design, BO strategies can avoid trading in an area of price congestion occurring within the time period used to measure new highs or lows. In addition, by design, prices have moved a considerable distance before making the new highs, and therefore may be perceived to be overbought or oversold. Hence, BO strategies are vulnerable to the simultaneous triggering of AT systems, producing "false" breakouts that move back into the region of price consolidation. Breakout entries can provide timely entries into new trends when markets have consolidated for many months, and will react more quickly than traditional TF systems.

Volatility breakout strategies are a variation of BO strategies in which the breakout is defined not over a time window, but by price excursion of a certain amplitude beyond a reference level. For example, entry is defined as a certain distance away from yesterday's high, low, or close, rather than the highest high or lowest low over a fixed time period, such as 20 days. The amplitude of the excursion is usually expressed as some multiple of recent price volatility, which can be measured in several ways. Volatility breakout strategies are a shorter-term, more sensitive variation of the standard BO-style approach.

Advantages of Breakout-Style Strategies   Breakout-style strategies are designed to overcome the limitations of TF strategies by avoiding trading in regions of price congestion while putting on positions in the direction of the trend with little or no delay in the signal. It is easy to define risk because the

Figure 3.15 A breakout-style strategy on New York Heating Oil futures showing the susceptibility of this approach to false breakouts.

entry point and exit point can be determined accurately before putting on the trade. This approach often provides timely entries into dynamic moves that can be most satisfying to trade. Breakout strategies have proved to be robust and reliable over a long time using a broadly diversified portfolio.

Disadvantages of Breakout-Style Strategies Breakout-style strategies are vulnerable to false breakouts, when new price highs or lows are followed by reversals into the region of prior price consolidation (see Figure 3.15). These strategies are vulnerable to slippage on entry because key breakout levels can be easily identified by other market players. A BO strategy applied to a portfolio is vulnerable to simultaneous BO failures across unrelated market sectors. Breakout strategies are psychologically difficult to trade because breakouts are preceded by large moves in the direction of the breakout. Hence, the entry may be perceived to be too slow if the breakout barrier is set too far from prices. Finally, the price action after the breakout may be weak or marred by insufficient followthrough, making the account vulnerable to choppy markets.

4-S Evaluation of Breakout-Style Strategies

- *Sensitivity:* Is generally high; can detect market extremes immediately.
- *Selectivity:* Can be increased by increasing the time period or using complex definitions.

- *Susceptibility:* Is generally moderate; false breakouts occur 30 to 70 percent of the time, depending on the time period.

- *Sustainability:* Is generally high; can be applied to a broadly diversified portfolio.

Pattern-Based Strategies

Pattern-based (PB) strategies use traditional or nontraditional "chart" analysis to identify groups of price bars with predictive capability. The pattern length may vary from 2 to 50 days, and one hopes that significant movement occurs after the completion of the pattern. Traditional price patterns include patterns such as double bottoms (see Figure 3.16) and triangles. Nontraditional patterns may include any pattern that the eye can see. Such patterns can be used to initiate trend-following, antitrend, or breakout-style entries. Many so-called seasonal trading strategies fall into this broad category. These systems also can be long, short, or flat.

Event-based strategies may also be classified into this broad category. An event-based strategy exploits market action before and after such scheduled events as the release of economic statistics or dividend distributions. For example, U.S. unemployment data are generally released on the first Friday of the each month, and bond and stock markets often eagerly anticipate such data.

Figure 3.16   Identifying potential double-bottom formations for trading Spain's MEFF Ibex index.

The reaction of the bond market to such data can be categorized into patterns and the market can be traded systematically.

Advantages of Pattern-Based Entries   By using pattern-based entries, one can create unique entries that cannot be easily deduced by the market. Hence, slippage at entry can be reduced, and correlation with TF and BO-type entries can be lowered. There is little or no delay in reacting to the pattern once it is completed. Risk and reward can be clearly defined, and some patterns are simple to test and validate. Many patterns may be the result of scheduled events (economic reports) or agricultural relationships (new crop/old crop). Hence, there may be a fundamental explanation for the occurrence of certain price patterns. Such strategies will generally have low correlation to TF strategies.

Disadvantages of Pattern-Based Entries   The entire pattern-based approach relies on identifying a pattern quickly and correctly, making it sensitive to errors in market data. Some patterns, such as triangles, may be difficult to identify conclusively in real-time trading because the trend lines defining the pattern may suffer many "false" violations, thus prompting a frequent redefinition of the pattern.

The frequency of occurrence of the patterns may be low, and hence an extensive library of patterns may be needed. Sometimes no logical explanation can be given for why patterns have produced profitable trades in the past. Hence, the future profitability may not be as reliable as testing may indicate. Further, it is not easy to decide when a pattern has failed and should therefore be discarded. Although some patterns can be shown to work on a diversified portfolio, or for all markets within a sector, others may be market specific. The limitation of market-specific patterns is that they may stop working without prior notice. The amplitude of the market's movement after each pattern often shows unusual variability. Thus, pattern-based systems may be subject to a large variability in risk/reward performance.

4-S Evaluation of Pattern-Based Strategies

- *Sensitivity:* Is generally high; can detect some patterns immediately.
- *Selectivity:* Is generally low to random; may not be altered systematically.
- *Susceptibility:* Is generally high; prone to random failures.
- *Sustainability:* Is generally low; generally applied to selected markets.

Table 3.20 Summary of the strengths and weaknesses of trend-following (TF), antitrend (AT), breakout-style (BO), and pattern-based (PB) entry strategies.

	Type of Entry Strategy			
Attribute	TF	AT	BO	PB
Sensitivity	Variable	High	High	High
Selectivity	Variable	Low	Variable	Low
Susceptibility	Low	High	Moderate	High
Sustainability	High	Low	High	Low
Style	L/S; L/S/F	L/S/F	L/S/F	L/S/F

Entry Strategy Characteristics

Table 3.20 summarizes the characteristics of different entry strategies. Style refers to the typical systems used with these strategies, with L meaning long entries; S, short entries; and F, flat position. Thus, L/S implies a system that is always in the market, long or short, and L/S/F is a system that can be long, short, or flat (out) with respect to a particular market over time.

Design Issues for Exits

Once you are in a trade and your money management algorithms are set, the next strategic issue is how and when to exit. The exact course of any given trade is, of course, unknown, because prices can evolve in myriad ways. Hence, we do not know when we will exit (time in trade) or the price at which we will exit. The strategic choices for exits are aimed at resolving one or both of these uncertainties (see Figure 3.17). Thus, you could try to specify a strategy for the time when you wish to exit or the price at which you would like to exit, but not both.

If you choose to specify a strategy for the time in the trade, then the exit price is usually unknown. An example of this strategy is to exit on the close of the third day in the trade, or to exit on the open of the second day in the trade. In both these instances, you are willing to accept the market price to exit at the specified time.

The second strategic option is to specify the price at which you would like to exit, but you are willing to stay with the position as long as needed to secure the desired price. In setting the exit price, you have two choices. One is to exit with a limit order at a predetermined profit target, and the other is to exit with a stop order on a trailing stop. The limit order requires you to pick highs or

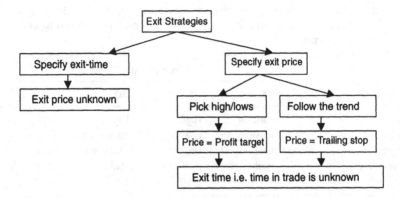

Figure 3.17 Decision tree for exit strategies. You can specify the exit time or the exit price, but not both.

lows. With the trailing stop, you are willing to follow the trend as long as necessary, and to wait for the market to take out the stop to close out the trade. The strategic choices are summarized in Table 3.21.

The purpose of this analysis is not to suggest that the two choices (time to exit and exit price) do not interact with one another. For example, by setting the trailing stop far away from prices, you can effectively increase the duration of the trade. Conversely, by setting a profit target close to the current price, you can shorten the trade duration. Thus, though the time/price dissection is a good device to understand exit strategies, remember that choosing one can influence the magnitude of the other.

Any trade-off you make in designing an exit strategy also has other costs associated with it, such as leakage, shrinkage, vibration, and robustness.

1. *Leakage:* The loss in open trade equity: the cost of exiting too slowly.

2. *Shrinkage:* The opportunity cost of exiting too soon.

3. *Vibration:* The amount of market volatility tolerated before exiting.

4. *Robustness:* The stability of the strategy in the face of changing market conditions.

Table 3.21 Summary of the strategic choices for exit strategies.

	Type of Exit Strategy	
	Specifty Time (Price Unknown)	**Specify Price (Time Unknown)**
Proactive	Time stop	Profit target
Reactive	Conditional time stop	Trailing stop

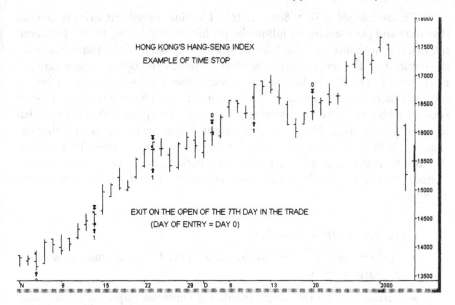

Figure 3.18   An example of a time stop: exiting at the open of the seventh day in the trade, with the entry day being counted at day zero.

Time-Based Exit Strategies

Time-based exits specify when to exit a trade, with or without regard to the profit or loss in the open trade. For example, one strategy would be to exit every trade after *n* days in the trade (see Figure 3.18). Another approach would be to exit on the open of the fifth day if the trade is unprofitable. In both cases, the time to exit is specified, and the trader is willing to accept the market price in order to secure the time of exit.

Advantages of Time-Based Exits   The time-based exit strategy is simple to implement because the clock starts ticking as soon as the trade is initiated. This strategy works best when the market is in a trading range or in a cyclic mode. Time-based exits also get you out of a trade in which the market is moving sideways. The capital can then be deployed into markets that are more active. For example, should a breakout fail, the market can slowly drift back into the price range of the previous consolidation. A time-based exit provides a good safety valve to exit this sideways market. This strategy can be implemented with minimal slippage by trading at times with good liquidity, such as the open or the close.

Disadvantages of Time-Based Exits   The time-based exit strategy dictates that time and price evolution follow the profile created by the trader. However, the markets are more likely to follow their own dynamics. The time chosen for the duration of the trade tends to be market-specific; no optimal trade duration exists for all markets. A likely scenario is that the trend will continue after we exit, and there may be significant lost opportunities. This exit strategy must be coupled with a sensitive entry strategy to permit reentry into a strong trend that is exited prematurely. The trade-sizing algorithm is critical to profitability because trade size will usually decrease during subsequent reentries. This strategy may not be effective on a broad portfolio of markets, and may have to be recalibrated for a given market over time, as the nature of market participants changes.

Assessment of Time-Based Exits

- *Leakage:* Relatively low loss in trade equity before exiting; vulnerable to sharp reversals.

- *Shrinkage:* Relatively high; trends can continue, requiring reentry and resizing.

- *Vibration:* Relatively low; exits before trends enter period of volatility preceding reversals.

- *Robustness:* Relatively low; usually market specific and may need recalibration.

Price-Based Exits: Profit Targets

Profit-target exits specify an exit price and hold a trade as long as necessary to achieve that price. The exit price is above the market for long positions and below the market for short positions. This trend-anticipatory approach tries to pick tops or bottoms. The further the profit target from the current price, the longer the market will take to get there. Time to exit can be reduced by placing the profit target relatively close to the current price. However, the exact duration of each trade is unknown. The profit target may be derived from historical testing or observations of chart patterns. The price target may be stated in terms of dollars or some other measure of market volatility. However, specifying the profit target can be a bit of an art; no optimal, universal profit target exists for all markets (see Figure 3.19).

Advantages of Profit Targets   Profit-target exits can produce a high percentage of profitable trades and a relatively smooth equity curve. Market liquid-

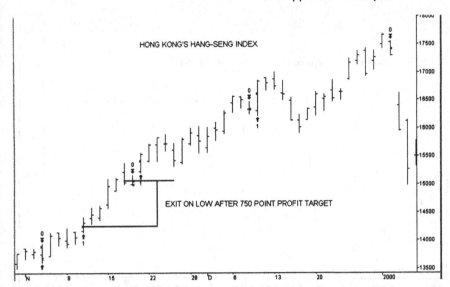

HONG KONG'S HANG-SENG INDEX

EXIT ON LOW AFTER 750 POINT PROFIT TARGET

Figure 3.19   Example of a profit-target trading strategy: exiting on the close after a gain of at least 750 points on the Hong Kong Hang Seng index.

ity determines slippage and the size that can be traded. These exits work well when the market is in a trading range or making swing moves.

Disadvantages of Profit Targets   The biggest limitation of profit-target exits is that the trend can continue after one has exited. Hence, reentry conditions and trade sizing have an important influence on overall performance. The profit target usually has to be a market-specific value and may need to be recalibrated frequently. Hence, sometimes a trend can end without ever reaching the profit target. You will need a good broker to use this strategy successfully.

Assessment of Profit-Target Exits

- *Leakage:* Relatively low loss in trade equity before exiting; vulnerable to poor execution.

- *Shrinkage:* Relatively high; trends can continue, requiring reentry and resizing.

- *Vibration:* Relatively low; exits before trends enter period of volatility preceding reversals.

- *Robustness:* Relatively low; usually market specific and may need recalibration.

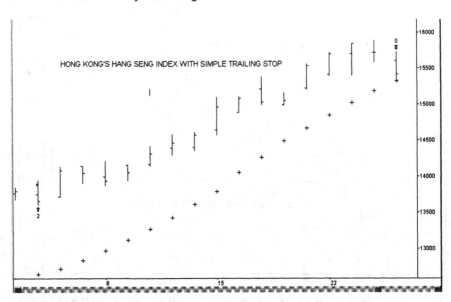

Figure 3.20   A simple trailing stop used on the Hong Kong Hang Seng index.

Price-Based Exits: Trailing Stops

The trailing-stop strategy specifies an exit price below the market for longs and above the market for shorts, and holds the trade as long as necessary. This is a trend-following approach that makes few assumptions about how the trade will evolve. The exit price can be chosen in many different ways, a few common approaches being a fixed dollar stop, a stop based on percentage of equity, a stop based on price channels, a stop based on chart patterns, a stop based on retracing a percentage of open trade equity, and exits based on volatility (see Figure 3.20).

Advantages of Trailing Stops   A trailing stop works best when markets make smooth, long-lasting trends. They can be designed to control risk and obtain a good risk/reward ratio. Because they make no assumptions about price evolution, these stops keep you aligned with the major trend in the market. When placed "far" away, they are good at absorbing market volatility without being shaken out of the trade. The time in the trade can be adjusted by adjusting the rate of advance of the stops or by shortening the time frame used in the analysis.

Disadvantages of Trailing Stops   Trailing stops may be slow to exit when markets make compressed moves, and they tend to give up a significant proportion of open trade equity before exiting. Because these exits must be placed as stop orders, floor traders may try to "gun" for stops by trying to push the market through key resistance or support levels visible on price charts. It takes great patience to sit through market corrections, some of which can continue on to new highs or lows. Hence, such exits can be difficult to deal with psychologically.

Assessment of Trailing Stops

- *Leakage:* Relatively high loss in trade equity before exiting; vulnerable to poor execution.

- *Shrinkage:* Relatively low; exits can occur after trend reversals are confirmed.

- *Vibration:* Relatively high; can absorb significant volatility without exiting position.

- *Robustness:* Relatively high; can be used across markets and over time.

Summary: Review of Entry and Exit Strategies

This conceptual design review gives an overview of the design philosophy of the major types of entry and exit strategies. Trade-offs can be made to balance the strengths and weaknesses of different choices for entries and exits. Countless variations can be adapted to the likes and dislikes of individual traders as they combine entry and exit strategies to develop unique trading systems.

Chapter

Developing New Trading Systems

Don't count your chickens until they are incubated.

Introduction

A trading system is only as good as your market intuition. You can formulate and test virtually any trading system you can imagine with today's software. The previous chapters studied the basic principles of system design. This chapter develops and tests several original trading systems to illustrate the application of those principles:

1. A simple trend-following system—the 65sma-3cc system.

2. A pattern-based system for long trades only—the CB-PB system.

3. A trend-seeking, strength-of-trend system—the ADX burst system.

4. An automatic mode-switching system—the trend-antitrend system.

5. Intermarket systems for correlated markets—the gold bond systems.

6. A system for picking bottoms—a bottom-fishing pattern.

7. A system for increasing bet size—the extraordinary opportunity model.

In this chapter, each case illustrates a different design philosophy. The 65sma-3cc system is examined in the greatest detail; the same principles can be applied to all other systems. Long-term test results with continuous contracts are shown for every system.

This is not a recommendation that you trade these systems. These systems have all the limitations of hypothetical test results. They are discussed here only as examples of the art of developing systems that suit your trading style.

The Assumptions behind Trend-Following Systems

The basic assumptions behind a simple trend-following system are as follows:

1. Markets trend smoothly up and down, and trends last a long time.

2. A close beyond a moving average signals a trend change.

3. Markets do not have large countertrend price swings.

4. Prices do not move too far away from an intermediate moving average.

5. Whipsaws are relatively few and do not cause large losses.

6. Significant price moves last many weeks or months.

7. Markets are predominantly in a trending mode.

The reality of a trend-following system is that:

1. Markets are often in ranging mode with choppy swing moves, so losses in trading ranges are significant.

2. There are large swings in trade equity, since the model "gives back" a large proportion of profits before signaling an opposite trend.

3. These systems need a relatively "loose" stop in order to avoid missing about 5 percent of trades that account for major profitable moves.

4. These systems often enter the market on strength or weakness, so that they can be stopped out during short but vicious countertrend moves.

The advantages of simple trend-following systems are:

1. They provide guaranteed entry in the directions of the major trend.

2. They are profitable over multiple markets and multiple time frames, as long as time frames are 6 months to 5 years in horizon.

3. These systems are usually robust.

4. These systems have well-defined risk-control parameters.

The 65sma-3cc Trend-Following System

This section discusses how to formulate and test a simple, nonoptimized, trend-following system that makes as few assumptions as possible about price action. It arbitrarily uses a 65-day simple moving average of the daily close to measure the trend. Sixty-five days is simply the daily equivalent of a 13-week SMA (13 × 5 = 65), representing one-quarter of the year. This is an intermediate length moving average that will consistently follow a market's major trend.

As shown in Figure 4.1, when the market is trending up, prices are above the 65-day SMA, and vice versa. In sideways markets, this SMA flattens out and prices fluctuate on either side. Clearly, the trading system picks up and sticks with the prevailing trend (see Figure 4.2).

There are many ways to make the decision that the trend has turned up. The usual way is to use a shorter moving average of, say, 10 days, and decide that the trend has changed when the shorter average crosses over or under the longer moving average. If you decide to use a short moving average, its "length" will be crucial to your results. Another weakness is that often prices will move faster than the shorter moving average, so that the entries can seem rather slow.

Hence, the 65sma-3cc system will require three consecutive closes (3cc) above or below the 65-day SMA (65sma) to determine that the trend has changed. For example, the trend will be said to have turned up after three

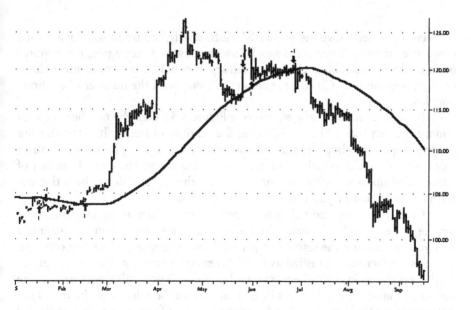

Figure 4.1 September 1995 Japanese yen contract showing the 65-day SMA and the signals generated by the system.

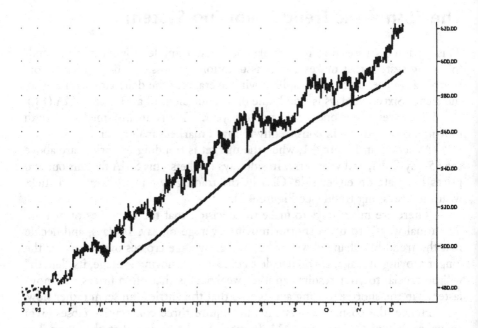

Figure 4.2 The 65sma-3cc system stayed long throughout this major uptrend in the S&P-500 index in 1995.

consecutive closes above the 65-day SMA. Similarly, the trend will have turned down after three consecutive closes below the 65sma. Once again, the requirement of three consecutive closes is arbitrary. It could be ten consecutive closes or any other number. Clearly, the results will vary with the number of confirming closes.

If you are afraid of false signals (see Figure 4.3), then the number of closes you use will act like a filter in reducing the number of trades. In a fast-moving market, requiring a large number of consecutive closes will give delayed entries (see Figure 4.4). Conversely, if a market is moving sluggishly, a small number of consecutive closes will give false signals. Thus, there is a trade-off here that determines how quickly you recognize a change in trend.

Once you recognize a change in trend, you still have to decide how to enter the trade. You should enter the trade on the next day's open, to guarantee that you can execute the signal and get a fill. For example, if the three consecutive closes criterion is satisfied as of this evening's close, you should buy at the market on the open of the next trading day. You will get a fill somewhere in the opening range the next day. It is likely that you will be filled near the top of the opening range for buy orders, and near the bottom of the opening range for sell orders. This slippage should be ignored, and just lumped into your $100 allowance for slippage and commissions. The main effect of this entry mechanism is

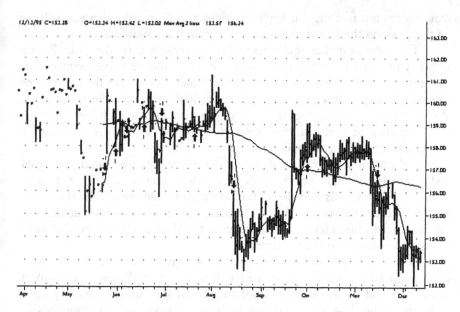

Figure 4.3   The choppy sideways action in December 1995 British Pound generated a string of whipsaw losses for the 65sma-3cc system.

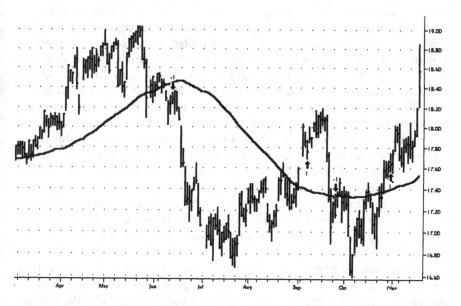

Figure 4.4   These swing moves in December 1995 crude oil produced many trades but small profits because the 65sma-3cc system does not have a specific exit strategy.

that you are not filtering out any entry signals, and ensuring that you will put on this position the first time the entry conditions are satisfied.

There are a number of choices on how to actually enter the trade. For example, you could enter the trade on the close of the third consecutive close above or below the 65sma. A second choice would be to enter the next day on a stop order beyond the previous, or a nearby, high or low. In effect, you would also filter out some entry signals, because you would not get a fill on every signal. This may be useful in situations where prices briefly spike beyond the 65sma during prolonged trends.

A third entry choice would be to delay entry for *x* days after the signal, and then enter beyond a nearby *n*-day high or low. This is another way to filter down the entry signals in order to find more profitable ones. Note that if you use a limit order for your entries, occasionally you may not be filled at all, missing the entry by just a few ticks. Hence, you should enter on the next day's open to assure an entry into the new trend.

Before we proceed, let us put this entry signal through a critical test to check if the 65sma-3cc entries are better than random. Following the approach of Le Beau and Lucas (see bibliography for details), let us test the entry signal with exit on the close of the *n*-th day, without any stops, and no deductions for slippage and commissions. For simplicity, only the effect of long entries are shown. The proportion of trades that are winners should consistently be more than 55 percent. The test includes the long entry over 21 markets, stretching from January 1, 1975, through July 10, 1995, using a continuous contract. Because not all markets were trading back in 1975, all available data are used.

Table 4.1 shows that, on average, 55 percent of the long entries were profitable, suggesting that the 65sma-3cc model probably does better than random. The result for short trades is similar, and you can be reasonably confident that this model provides robust entry signals. Your task is now to combine this model with risk control and exit methods that match your trading mentality.

To summarize this nonoptimized system, the actual trade entry is at the market on the open of the next trading day after the close of the day the signal is received. You will notice that there are no specific exit signals at this point, which means that the short entry signal is also the long exit signal, and vice versa. In practice this means that if you are long one contract, you will sell two contracts to go net short one contract, and vice versa.

Note that for the tests below we will add a condition to prevent back-to-back entries of the same type. This will allow an apples-to-apples comparison when studying the effect of adding stops or exits. You do not need this condition for actual trading.

To summarize what is not defined at this point: There are no specific risk-control rules in terms of an initial money management stop, nor any money-management rules to determine the number of contracts to trade. We will just trade one contract for simplicity without any risk-control stop. This is not a recommendation to trade without a risk control stop; the calculations are done

Table 4.1   Testing 65sma-3cc long entry for randomness over 21 markets using all available data between 1/1/75 and 7/10/95. Exit on the close of the *n*-th day.

Market	5 days	10 days	15 days	20 days	30 days	50 days
British pound	55	59	60	58	60	60
Coffee	54	57	56	54	50	51
Copper	51	49	50	52	50	46
Corn	53	55	56	57	59	55
Cotton	60	61	62	63	64	60
Crude oil	54	53	53	56	58	45
Deutsche mark	59	59	60	58	59	63
Eurodollar	59	59	61	62	63	62
Gold	54	55	54	49	53	47
Heating oil	53	55	58	56	51	51
Japanese yen	55	53	60	61	59	69
Live hogs	57	57	59	57	55	59
Orange juice	53	52	52	55	55	45
Silver	48	50	45	46	44	46
Soybeans	52	47	51	52	53	51
S&P-500	54	59	58	62	58	69
Sugar	56	56	55	58	57	52
Swiss franc	56	56	59	58	63	61
10-year T-note	57	59	59	58	58	56
U.S. bond	55	52	56	50	50	46
Wheat	52	52	51	51	51	51
Average	54.62	55	55.95	55.86	55.71	54.52

without any stops here to illustrate a point. Later, we will examine how to add risk control and study the effect of money management.

The 65sma-3cc system should make all its profits during strong trends. It should lose money in sideways or nontrending markets. And it should have between 20 and 50 percent profitable trades. We tested this model over 23 markets using 20 years of continuous contract data. If a contract was not traded for 20 years, then we used all available data from the starting date. The usual allowance of $100 per trade for slippage and commissions was made. Thus, this is a rigorous test for a nonoptimized system over a long test period, and across a large number of markets. The results are summarized in Table 4.2.

The results for this simple, nonoptimized trend-following system are encouraging. You could have made a paper profit of $1,386,747 by trading just one contract for each market, and been profitable on 19 of 23 widely diverging markets. The test sample generated 2,400 trades, so this is a highly significant

Table 4.2   Test results for 65sma-3cc trend-following system.

Market	Years	Paper Profit ($)	Total Trades	Winning Trades (%)	Average Win/ Loss	Average Trade ($)	Maximum Intraday Draw- down ($)
British pound	7/75–7/95	125,344	105	34	3.72	1,193	–25,431
Canadian dollar	6/77–7/95	–12,750	125	25	2.32	–102	–21,030
Cocoa	5/80–7/95	–15,370	101	28	1.80	–153	–2,219
Coffee	5/75–7/95	239,096	120	30	5.83	1,993	–36,956
Copper, high-grade	12/88–7/95	–7,890	49	34	1.48	–161	–17,355
Corn	5/75–7/95	26,081	106	38	2.98	246	–4,331
Cotton	5/75–7/95	112,490	110	38	4.26	1,023	–8,730
Crude oil	8/83–7/95	17,570	74	35	2.58	238	–11,690
Deutsche mark	7/75–7/95	68,575	102	38	2.90	673	–13,250
Eurodollar	6/82–7/95	34,175	60	25	3.16	569	–7,150
Gold, Comex	5/75–7/95	53,770	121	33	3.44	444	–28,440
Heating oil	7/79–7/95	56,198	103	32	3.89	545	–18,021
Japanese yen	12/76–7/95	143,425	87	47	3.80	1,649	–12,963
Live hogs	5/75–7/95	31,971	120	42	2.49	266	–5,863
Orange juice	5/75–7/95	13,018	120	27	3.05	109	–27,950
Silver	5/75–7/95	197,305	144	37	6.87	1,370	–51,040
Soybeans	5/75–7/95	62,406	114	38	2.86	547	–21,768
S&P-500	9/82–7/95	–7,260	101	24	3.13	–72	–97,470
Sugar	5/75–7/95	49,493	113	37	3.75	438	–10,806
Swiss franc	7/75–7/95	108,475	100	40	3.28	1,086	–11,638
10-year T-note	9/82–7/95	34,219	85	29	3.66	402	–13,743
U.S. bond	1/78–7/95	50,143	102	35	2.62	491	–38,819
Wheat	5/75–7/95	6,263	138	28	2.78	45	–19,663
Total		1,386,747	2,400				
Average		60,293.3	104	34	3.3	558	–22,014
Standard Deviation		66,698.1	22	6	1.17	583	20,342

test. Approximately 34 percent of all trades were profitable, a number typical of trend-following systems.

The ratio of average winning to average losing trades was excellent, at 3.3 averaged over the 2,400 trades. This number is useful for calculating the risk of ruin; a number above 2.0 is desirable, and anything over 3 is welcome news. The average trade made a profit of $558, an attractive amount, considering transaction and slippage costs. It is customary to seek a number over $250 for the average trade. The average profit per market was $60,293, approximately 2.74 times the average maximum intraday drawdown, of –$22,014. This is a healthy recovery factor, or coverage of the worst losing streak of the system.

In summary, a simple trend-following approach worked on many markets over a long time period with few assumptions and no optimization.

The results also point out some weaknesses of this system. The average profit per market is 90 percent of the standard deviation of the average profit. This means that profitability varied widely from market to market. The maximum intraday drawdown was 108 percent of its standard deviation, implying that the drawdowns also varied considerably among markets. The standard deviation of the average trade also implies that results can vary substantially over time or across markets. A further weakness is the relatively small number of profitable trades. Thus, we can summarize the principal weakness as a large variability in the results over time and across markets.

Combining the strengths and weaknesses, you would say that this is a sound trend-following system with good chance of being profitable over many markets over a long time period. But because of the large variability in results, you would have to trade this system relatively conservatively. You should allow a large equity cushion to absorb drawdowns.

A look under the hood of this trading system, so to speak, and a closer examination of the results of the analysis reveal further details of 65sma-3cc trades. A histogram of all 2,400 trades shows the distribution of trade profits and losses (see Figures 4.5 and 4.6). There are more large winners than large losers, and many small losers. Remember that these results were calculated without using an initial money management stop. Most of the trades are bunched between –$3,000 and $2,000, with the highest frequency near zero. There are few losing trades worse than –$5,000, balanced by even more trades with profits greater than $5,000. An initial money management stop will clean up the negative part of this histogram.

Thus, it should be obvious that most of the profits come from a relatively small number of trades. In Figure 4.6, 12.5 percent of the trades are seen to have closed-out profit greater than $3,000. Be aware that if you get out too soon, you are likely to miss one of 100 or so (4 percent) of the mega-trades that make trend-following worth the aggravation.

Many measurements follow what is called a standard normal distribution. For example, if you measured the diameter of ball bearings, the measurements will follow a normal distribution. The normal distribution is a bell-shaped probability distribution of the relative frequency of events. The standard normal is a special case of the normal distribution with a mean of zero and standard deviation equal to one. To compare the distribution of the 65sma-3cc trades to

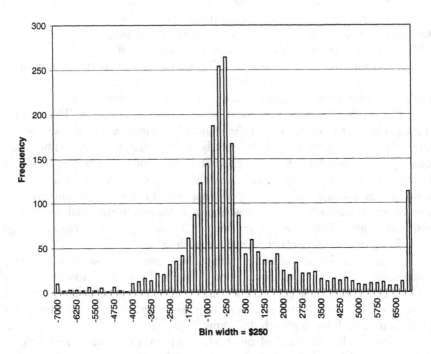

Figure 4.5   Histogram of all 2,400 trades for the 65sma-3cc trading system.

the standard normal distribution, we first have to "normalize" the bin sizes. The comparison is shown in Figure 4.7.

The 65sma-3cc curve is more sharply peaked than the standard normal curve. To generate a normal distribution that would fit our data, I used a Microsoft Excel® 5.0 spreadsheet and employed an iterative process of manually tweaking the values. The fitted normal curve, with a mean of –0.16 and standard deviation of 0.18 is shown in Figure 4.8. The fitted normal distribution shows that the actual 65sma-3cc distribution has "fat" tails. This simply means that there is a larger probability for the "big" trades than would be expected from the normal distribution. This chart shows that unusually large profits or losses are more likely than might normally be expected.

The modified normal distribution fits the observed curve nicely on the losing side, but the small positive trades fall off sharply. This implies that you will not get very many small positive trades with a trend-following model. Small trades will occur during broad consolidations, and these are not very common. Small losing trades are more likely during consolidations, as shown by the good fit on the left side of the peak.

Distribution of Trade P&L for 65sma-3cc: 2400 trades

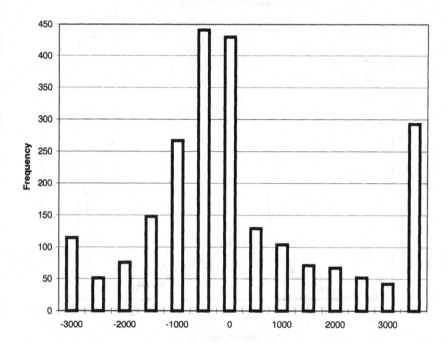

Figure 4.6   A histogram of the 65sma-3cc system over a narrower range of profits and losses. Notice that only a small number of trades show large profits.

The huge spike at the right-hand edge of the Figure 4.6 represents the 4 percent or so of mega-trades that make trend following worthwhile. The distribution shows you it is easy to miss these trades, and if you do, your portfolio performance will drop off quickly. You should try to develop such a frequency distribution curve for your own systems to get a better feel for model performance.

A closer look at losing trades reveals another weakness of the 65sma-3cc system. Figure 4.9 is a distribution of the maximum profit of each of the 1,565 trades that were closed out at a loss, called the maximum favorable excursion (MFE). The glaring weakness is that because there is no specific exit strategy, many trades with profits greater than $3,000 were eventually closed out at a loss. However, we have to be careful with our exit strategy, since only 4 percent of the trades were mega-winners. If we are not careful, we may lock in some profits from losing trades, but lose out on the truly big winners. Another way to use the information from the maximum favorable excursion plot is to select the profit point at which to move your trailing stop to break-even. For example,

Comparing frequency distribution of 65sma-3cc trades to standard normal distribution

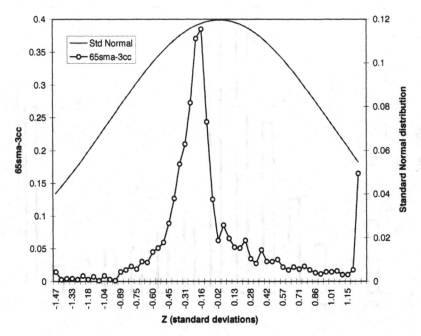

Figure 4.7   The distribution of 65sma-3cc is peaked more sharply than the standard normal distribution.

you can move your stop to break-even after a $2,000 profit and capture a significant proportion of losing trades.

You can also use the maximum adverse excursion plot to set profit targets for scaling out of large positions. For example, if you were trading ten contracts, you could sell some at each of the profit targets of $500, $1,000, $2,000 and $3,000. We continue our analysis by examining the maximum drawdown in 777 winning trades following John Sweeney (see bibliography for details). This drawdown is on an intraday basis. These trades show some loss, but were eventually closed out at a profit. The histogram (Figure 4.10) reveals several interesting insights. About 500 (64 percent) of the trades were immediately profitable, with a loss during the trade of less than –$250. Another 100 trades showed drawdowns of less than –$500.

Thus, almost 77 percent of the trades showed a loss of –$500 or less during their evolution. There were very few trades that showed losses greater than –$1,750 and then closed out at a profit. This suggests that we could set an initial stop at $1,000 and capture almost 88 percent of the winning trades. This is a

**Frequency distribution of 65sma-3cc trades compared to a
modified normal distribution**

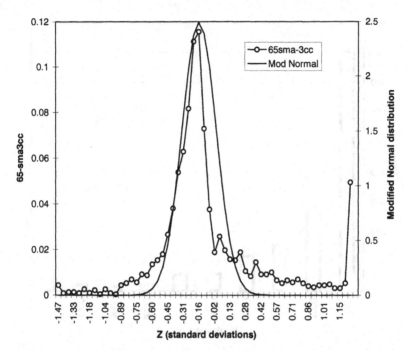

Figure 4.8 A fitted normal distribution shows that the 65sma-3cc trade distribution has "fat" tails, and falls off more quickly for small positive trades.

realistic way to pick the point at which a mechanical initial money management stop could be placed.

The same information can be viewed as a cumulative frequency chart to see how many trades achieved a certain profit target (see Figure 4.11). This type of chart shows what proportion of trades had a maximum favorable excursion of, say, $500. It shows, for example, that 50 percent of trades had reached a $1,000 profit target, and so on.

In summary, the 65sma-3cc system test over 20 years of data and 23 markets showed it is a robust and profitable system that makes money in trending periods. Since we tested the system without any initial money management stop, there were several trades with losses greater than –$3,000. We can try to clean this up by placing a stop at $1,000, as shown by the MAE plot. The detailed analysis showed several profitable trades that were closed out at a loss. We would like to minimize such trades. There were about 4 percent truly huge trades with profits in excess of $5,000. We must find an exit strategy that does not miss out on such mega-profits.

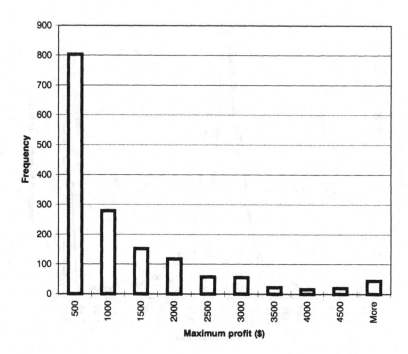

Figure 4.9 A histogram of maximum profit in 1,565 losing trades over 20 years and 23 markets from the 65sma-3cc system. This is a maximum favorable excursion plot.

Effect of Initial Money Management Stop

Since the initial test of the 65sma-3cc model was encouraging, we can now do more testing. The first item of business is to insert an initial money management stop into this model. Our detailed analysis of the MAE showed that we could safely set our stop at $1,000, or even as high as $1,750, and capture substantially all profitable trades.

However, we should insert another condition into the formulation of the model before testing for the effect of initial stops. If our stop is too "tight" during testing, we will be stopped out right after the first signal. Then, there may be a succession of trades, all in the same direction (all long or short signals), that will also result in losing trades, before one of them kicks into the major trend. Thus, the analysis would be distorted. What we want is to pick off exactly the same trades as we did without any initial stop. To achieve this goal, we must insert rules that do not allow successive trades of the same type, to ensure that we

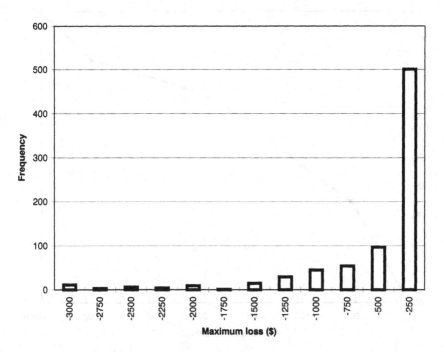

Maximum adverse excursion for 777 winning trades of 65sma-3cc system

Figure 4.10   Analysis of 777 winning trades: maximum loss in trades that were closed out at a profit. This is also known as the maximum adverse excursion plot.

will not have two back-to-back long or short trades if we get stopped out after the first signal. In effect, with this rule, if we get stopped out, we must wait for the opposing signal before getting in. Of course, you do not need this condition for actual trading.

Inserting an initial condition should have two effects. (1) It should reduce the maximum intraday drawdown, since some potentially large losing trades will be cut off. (2) It should also reduce the number of profitable trades and the total paper profit, since the same stop will also cut off some potentially profitable trades. Some calculations will show if we can verify these expectations.

The results of these calculations are shown in Table 4.3, which can be compared to the results in Table 4.2. The markets and test periods are identical in both tables. Adding a $1,000 stop reduces total paper profits by 21.5 percent, from $1,386,747 to $1,088,804. Similarly, the number of winning trades fell to 689 from 810, or by 17.6 percent. As expected, the average maximum draw-down and its standard deviation also decreased, showing the desired smoothing effect due to the initial stop. The reduction was about 18.5 percent in the draw-

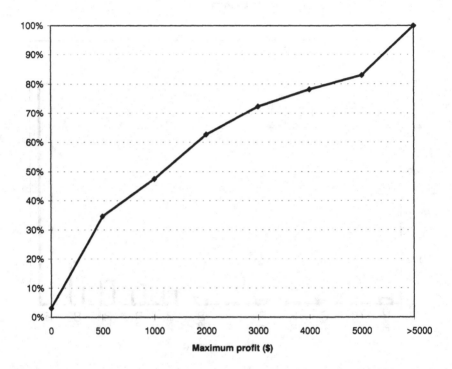

Cumulative Frequency of winning trades, 65sma-3cc system

Maximum profit ($)

Figure 4.11   Cumulative frequency of maximum favorable excursion of 65sma-3cc system. Note that horizontal scale is not linear.

down, and 40 percent in the standard deviation. Thus, adding a hard dollar initial money management stop had the desired effect of reducing drawdown and smoothing out the variation in system performance. There was also a resultant reduction in total returns.

We chose the $1,000 initial money management stop from the MFE plot. Calculations for a $500 stop result in an even greater reduction in profits, drawdown, and volatility.

We can continue this line of thought by looking at the U.S. bond and deutsche mark markets. Our analysis of 777 profitable trades showed that once the drawdown exceeded -$1,750, few trades ended with a profit. Hence, the initial stop is varied from $250 to $1,750 in the following tests to look at the effect on the total number of profitable trades. As the initial money management stop increases, the number of profitable trades increases and then levels off (see Figure 4.12). This shows that the initial stop acts as a filter, and as the stop widens, it allows more trades to pass through. Eventually, the filter is too big, and

Table 4.3   Effect of adding a $1,000 initial money management stop to the 65sma-3cc system.

Market	Paper Profit ($)	Winning Trades	Average Trade ($)	Maximum Intraday Drawdown ($)
British pound	121,325	28	1155	–18,100
Canadian dollar	–8,490	32	–68	–17,080
Cocoa	–9,670	29	–96	–17,110
Coffee	203,719	23	1698	–24,953
Copper, high-grade	478	17	10	–9,175
Corn	26,525	41	250	–4,175
Cotton	99,695	39	906	–7,810
Crude oil	8,290	24	113	–10,410
Deutsche mark	69,100	34	677	–6,675
Eurodollar	17,875	21	298	–5,225
Gold, Comex	36,850	37	305	–36,960
Heating oil	16,760	24	163	–22,328
Japanese yen	106,388	33	1222	–12,963
Live hogs	29,970	50	250	–5,609
Orange juice	20,435	32	170	–22,188
Silver	143,165	29	994	–47,710
Soybeans	47,281	38	415	–23,806
S&P-500	29,975	14	297	–47,295
Sugar	32,044	34	283	–8,582
Swiss franc	55,638	27	556	–14,975
10-year T-note	30,407	22	358	–8,606
U.S. bond	2,706	22	26	–22,700
Wheat	8,338	39	60	–18,331
Total	1,088,804	689		
Average	47,339	30	436	–17,946
Standard deviation	53,800	9	465	12,301

does not cut off any trades. This allows the number of profitable trades to level off.

We have so far placed our stop using a dollar figure without accounting for market volatility. However, whereas in the coffee market, a $1,000 stop may seem too tight, in the corn market it may seen too wide. Thus, in some markets, a given stop will work like a stop near the left edge of Figure 4.12, and, conversely, in other markets, the same dollar stop will work like a stop on the right side of the figure.

Number of trades increases and levels off.

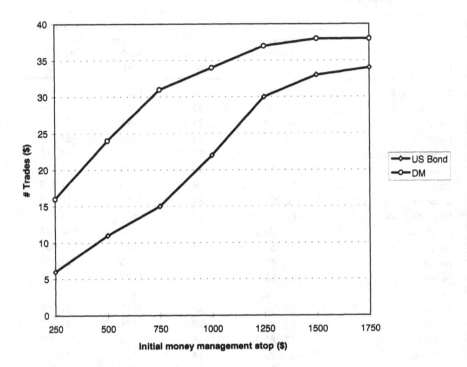

Figure 4.12 Effect of initial money management stop on number of profitable trades. As the stop tightens, fewer and fewer profitable trades survive. The upper line is for the deutsche mark and the lower line is for the U.S. bond market.

We can get around this problem by using a volatility-based initial money management stop. For our calculations, we can set an initial money management stop as a multiple of the 15-day SMA of the daily true range for measuring volatility. We use the same continuous contracts as in Table 4.2 to test the U.S. bond market with volatility-based stops ranging from 0.25 to 3.0 times the 15-day SMA of the daily true range.

Figure 4.13 shows that a stop set at less than 1.25 times the average volatility is too tight. Once the stop increases past 2.00, the paper profit increases and the drawdown increases. The drawdown is minimized at a 1.50 stop. This means there is a balance between being too tight or too loose. The same behavior can be seen very nicely in the live hogs market (see Figure 4.14).

As might be expected, when we increase the money-management stop, the largest losing trade will probably increase. This happens because our stop is farther and farther away from the entry price. The sugar market shows this nicely (see Figure 4.15) when tested over the same period as Table 4.1. Other

**Variation in profits and drawdown with volatility-based stop for US
Bond market**

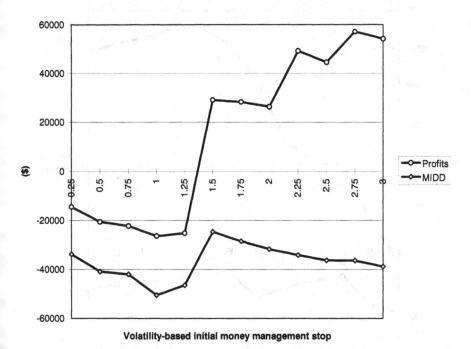

Figure 4.13   The profits (upper line) increase as the initial money management
stop is loosened. Eventually, the stop is too wide and profits begin to level off. The
lower line is the maximum intraday drawdown. Data are for the U.S. bond market.

calculations (not shown) show that the largest winning trade is affected only a
little by the initial stop, since these trades usually are profitable from the very
beginning. You may set a volatility-based stop or a hard-dollar stop with equivalent results. You may have to set a different dollar stop for each market, although
you could use the same volatility stop across all markets. Note that with a volatility stop, the actual dollar amount changes over time, and hence you must ensure that this stop is within your overall hard-dollar limits for risk control.

You should note some limits on how the initial money-management stop
can be tested. In most cases, the amount of the stop must be larger than the
daily trading range. The software cannot determine if your stop could have
been hit intraday if the stop is smaller than the daily trading range. Unless you
have intraday data, you cannot test the effect of, say, a $250 stop using daily
data.

In summary, adding an initial money-management stop is useful from a
risk-control point of view because it reduces the largest losing trade and the

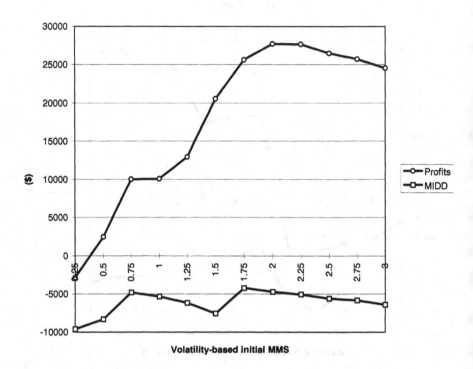

Profit and MIDD for LH as a function of initial MMS

Figure 4.14 The profits (upper line) increase as the initial money management stop is loosened. The lower line is the maximum intraday drawdown. Data are for the live hogs market.

maximum drawdown. But, it also cuts off some winning trades, and hence total profits are lower over the long term. You may add a dollar stop or a volatility-based stop, but both must follow sound guidelines.

Adding Filter to the 65sma-3cc System

So far, we have let the trading system generate pure signals without trying to filter the signals in any way. As we have seen, this system will generate many short-lived or "false" signals when a market is in a consolidation region. A filter is simply a set of rules that will try to refine the entry signals. By design, this system is always in the market. Remember that we do not have a specific exit strategy, and the long entry signal is also the short exit, and vice versa. At this stage, the goal of the filter is only to reduce some of the signals in a congestion area.

Largest losing trade increases as MMS increases

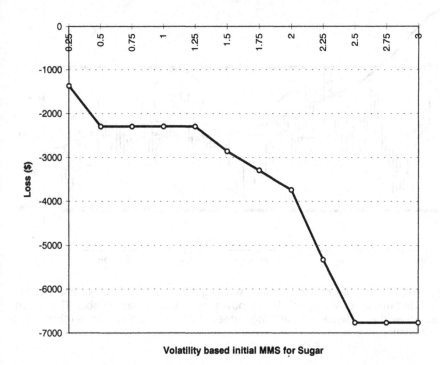

Figure 4.15   Largest losing trade for sugar using the 65sma-3cc trading system increases as the volatility-based initial money management stop increases.

You can design many types of filters. Here we use a momentum-based filter using the range action verification index discussed earlier. The RAVI is the absolute percentage difference between the 7-day and 65-day simple moving averages of the daily close. This means that when the market is in a congestion or consolidation phase, the short (7-day) and long (65-day) moving averages tend to be close together. Conversely, when the markets are trending, these averages are far apart.

You can also use Wilder's ADX (average directional index) as a filter for trending or nontrending markets. Specifically, if the ADX is declining, and/or below 20, then you can assume that the market is consolidating or entering a congestion phase. You could also use the x-day high-low range, or other momentum oscillators, to diagnose market conditions. Remember that any indicator you use, including the RAVI, will not work perfectly every time.

First, let us briefly review the performance of 65sma-3cc trading system in consolidating markets. As prices begin to trade in a narrow range, without a definite direction, the longer moving average (65sma) flattens out. Prices oscil-

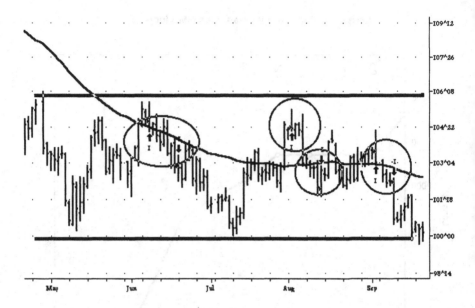

Figure 4.16   The 65sma-3cc trading system generated several entry signals as the U.S. bond market consolidated after its now-famous bear market tumble. The circled areas show the six signals—three long entries and three short entries—in this broad consolidation region.

late on either side of this average. Hence, you can get a succession of long and short signals as the market posts three consecutive closes above or below the 65sma.

In some sense, this becomes a self-correcting process, because the entry signals are not very far apart in price. Hence, even though you will have several losing trades in succession, the amount of the losses will be relatively small. You can imagine that in some cases the market will trade within a broad trading range, with sharp, but quick moves in both directions. The U.S. bond market has a tendency to form such consolidations. This is a worst-case scenario for the 65sma-3cc system because you will get short-lived entry signals but incur relatively large losses, since the market is making choppy moves that quickly span the trading range. Some examples of such market action follow.

Figure 4.16 shows the September 1994 U.S. bond contract consolidating after its now-famous bear market. Observe the six "false" signals from the system. Since the market was in a broad trading range, and prices were moving about on either side of the average, the false signals are inevitable given our definition of the trading system. This is a good illustration of a general principle: Whatever conditions you define, markets can always find ways to trigger false signals.

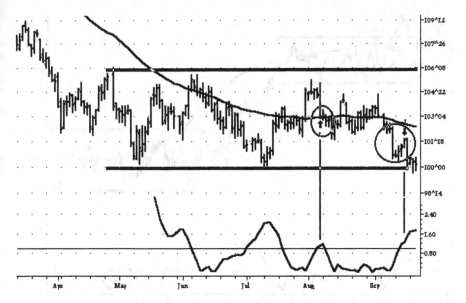

Figure 4.17   Adding a RAVI filter with barrier equal to 1.0 eliminates four of the six false trades in this broad congestion region. Notice that the 65sma-3cc model is fired only if RAVI is greater than 1 in both remaining instances.

Figure 4.17 shows the results of the same trading system with a filter. Now there are only two trades in the congestion region. The RAVI is plotted under the prices, so you can see that the signals occurred in regions where the RAVI was greater than 1. Since the model was already short coming into the picture, the first trade is a buy. The filtered model could generate a buy signal only if RAVI was greater than one and there were three consecutive closes above the 65sma.

A tight consolidation region developed immediately after the buy signal, dropping the RAVI below 1. Hence, this filtered out the next two signals, a sell and then a buy. Similarly, it also filtered out a buy signal and a sell signal in June. The last sell signal occurred when the RAVI climbed above 1 and there were three consecutive closes below the 65sma. Thus, we used the level of the RAVI to filter out some whipsaw signals.

What should be the barrier value for the RAVI to filter out signals? There is no perfect answer to this question; you will have to pick a value using one method or another. Raising the RAVI barrier to 1.5 from 1 will filter out even more trades. As Figure 4.18 shows, this model would have been short from the previous October 1993, all the way down and through two major consolidation areas, for a per contract profit of $13,696. Notice how the RAVI rose strongly

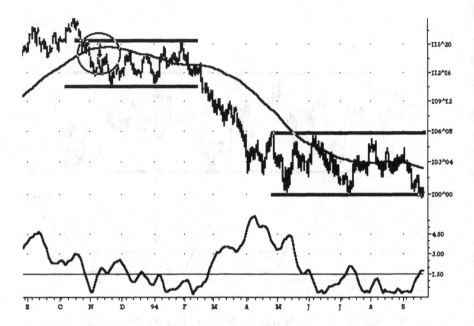

Figure 4.18   Increasing the RAVI filter barrier to 1.5 eliminates even more trades.

above 1 when the trend gathered strength, peaking just before the start of the lower consolidation phase.

These figures illustrate that you can use a filter to reduce the number of trades from a trend-following model. You can use different filters, and for a given filter you can use different barrier levels. Note that this system still is in the market at all times: either long or short.

By now, the effects of adding a filter should be clear: (1) We filter out some false signals; (2) we can reduce the maximum intraday drawdowns; (3) we can improve the profit factor of a system, i.e., the ratio of gross profit to gross loss over the test period; (4) the average trade usually increases; and (5) the length of the average winning trade increases. Our results will depend on how we choose the filter and its barrier level.

These comments can be supported with more data. Table 4.4 shows the results of calculations for adding a 0.5 percent RAVI filter to the 65sma-3cc model with a $1,000 initial stop and $100 deducted for slippage and commissions for 14 arbitrarily selected markets. These markets are a broad basket of softs, grains, metals, energies, currencies, and index and interest rate contracts. You can compare them to Table 4.2 for an estimate of their performance without stops or filters.

Table 4.4   Effect of adding a filter of RAVI = 0.5 to the 65sma-3cc system; filtering reduces the number of trades.

Market	Test Period	Paper Profit ($)	Number of Trades (Filtered)	Number of Winners (Filtered)	Number of Trades (No Filter)	Number of Winners (No Filter)
British pound	2/75–7/95	111,106	80	10	102	13
Corn	2/75–7/95	26,613	81	35	105	41
Crude oil	3/83–7/95	2,150	63	18	73	22
Deutsche mark	2/75–7/95	49,613	81	28	103	34
Eurodollar	2/82–7/95	11,775	14	3	60	20
Gold	2/75–7/95	36,690	95	30	120	38
Silver	2/75–7/95	152,585	107	23	143	28
S&P-500	4/82–7/95	59,310	80	10	102	13
Sugar	2/75–7/95	29,055	102	31	112	33
U.S. bond	8/77–7/95	31,588	71	19	102	22
10-year T-note	5/82–7/95	16,750	50	12	85	21
Wheat	2/75–7/95	–2,040	111	36	137	38

Table 4.5 shows the effect of the 0.5 percent RAVI filter on the dollar value of the average trade. The filtered system has a higher average trade, reflecting the improved quality of the entries.

Tables 4.4 and 4.5 show that as you filter a trading system, the number of trades decreases, the average trade increases, and the profit factor improves. These results are sensitive to the filtering rules. You can choose to filter a system many different ways. For example, you can use the ADX instead of the RAVI. Again, you have to make trade-offs in every choice you make.

In summary, we took the 65sma-3cc trend following system and tested its performance over 20 years of data and 23 markets. Then, we analyzed the winning and losing trades to select an initial money management stop. We filtered the system to reduce the number of signals. We used a "one-way" model, which does not allow back-to-back long or short trades. The main advantage of using a one-way model for testing is that it allows an apples-to-apples comparison of changes in trading strategy. You do not need this restriction for actual trading.

We have not tried to manage the equity curve in each of our analyses; the system was allowed to run to maximize profits. However, this system was always in the market. If we add a neutral zone, the system will not be always in the market. We can also consider adding one or more exit rules to get a smoother equity curve. With a bit of luck, the exit strategy will also create a neutral zone.

Table 4.5 Adding a filter increases the average trade.

Market	Average Trade (No Filter) ($)	Average Trade (Filtered) ($)
British pound	1,269	1,543
Corn	231	329
Coffee	2,783	3,488
Crude oil	−66	34
Deutsche mark	699	613
Eurodollar	221	841
Gold, Comex	323	389
Silver	1,014	1,426
S&P-500	406	741
Sugar	253	284
U.S. bond	56	449

Adding Exit Rules to the 65sma-3cc System

Selecting general and powerful exit rules is a difficult challenge in system design because the markets exhibit many different price patterns. One form of exit that is particularly easy to implement is the initial money-management stop. If the stop is hit, you exit the trade, no questions asked. However, taking profits is another matter, since you must design reentry rules should the trade continue on after meeting your exit criteria.

In the 65sma-3cc system, the approach of using entry rules as exit rules does catch long trends, but at the cost of wide swings in account equity. Hence, including exit rules tends to smooth out the equity curve. If possible, you should trade multiple contracts in each market, assigning one or more contracts to each exit rule. This allows you the luxury of not having only one "best" exit strategy.

As an alternative to the entry-triggers-exits approach, you can consider many exit strategies. One simple rule is to use a fixed-dollar trailing stop. In this case, you will set a stop, say, $1,500 away from the point of highest equity in the trade. Instead of a fixed-dollar stop, you can use a volatility-based stop, which sets a stop some multiple of the true-range away from the point of highest trade equity. Yet another exit strategy is to use a time-based stop, such as the price extremes of the last n-days. Another effective exit strategy is to exit on the close of the n-th day in the trade. For example, you could exit on the close of the fifth day in the trade. This approach works nicely if you can trade multiple contracts, and arrange to close trade from say the fifth through the twenty-fifth day in the trade.

Table 4.6   Effect of adding an exit on number of days in the market.

Market	Profit ($)	Maximum Intraday Drawdown ($)	Days in Market, All Trades (With Exit)	Days in Market, All Trades (No Exit)
British pound	38,788	–12,350	1,070	2,609
Coffee	227,610	–29,500	880	1,692
Corn	8,125	–$4,544	2,086	4,790
Crude oil	8,250	–$7,680	1,446	2,718
Deutsche mark	25,887	–$7,275	1,851	3,863
Eurodollar	–2,450	–$7,874	335	2,000
Gold, Comex	24,130	–$7,080	2,034	4,170
Silver	44,970	–32,410	1,506	3,459
S&P-500	2,490	–29,640	460	1,290
Sugar	10,386	–$7,854	1,991	4,591
U.S. bond	17,925	–20,887	1,218	1,689
Averages	36,919	–15,190	1,352	2,988

If you use exit strategies without an effective reentry strategy, you will miss significant moves. Hence, it makes little sense to use a trend-following strategy and then to cut off trades with a sensitive exit strategy. Exit strategies offer many opportunities for discretionary approaches. Hence, if you wish to use discretion, exit strategies are a good place to focus your attention.

An example of the effect of adding a 14-day exit to our 65sma-3cc model run with a 0.5 percent RAVI filter and a $1,000 initial money-management stop is shown in Table 4.6. The trailing exit closes out a trade if prices exceed the previous 14-day range. For example, if long, we would exit a trade tomorrow on the open if today's close is lower than the lowest low of the last 14 days. This is a trend-following exit that should get you out near the end of a major trend, with the criterion being a 14-day reversal in prices.

Adding an exit condition decreased the days in market by 45 percent on average. At the same time, you can confirm that the profitability and maximum drawdown decreased also. Any investments you make in money market instruments during the time that the system is out of the market will add to your total return. Thus, as you make the model more restrictive, the overall profitability is restricted also. Your choice in this case is governed by your preference for a smooth equity curve versus growth in equity.

Channel Breakout–Pullback Pattern

This section discusses a trading system based on a pattern observed in mature markets, that is, markets with a large volume of institutional activity. In these markets, the big players have a tendency to fade market moves. Thus, they will resist advances and support declines. For example, when a market makes a new 20-day high, many big players will short it heavily, and push the market back into the previous consolidation. If the fundamental forces underlying the market are strong, the up trend will resume after a brief consolidation. A trading system that trades the long side only, by going long during the pullback after new 20-day highs, is called the channel breakout–pullback (CB-PB) system.

We begin with a few examples of how the CB-PB system works, and show the actual code used for the tests. Next, we test the basic CB-PB entry strategy across 22 markets to illustrate the general validity of the idea. Then, we discuss three different exit strategies to show how you can convert the same entry strategy into vastly different trading systems. These systems vary from a short-term system, which is in the market for 7 to 9 days, to a long-term trend-following system. We will also explore the effect of using a $1,500 "close" initial stop versus a $5,000 "wide" stop. The analysis focuses on the following mature markets: coffee, Eurodollar, Japanese yen, Swiss franc, S&P-500, 10-year T-Note, and the U.S. bond.

The channel breakout–pullback pattern is for long trades only. The assumptions underlying this system are:

1. The market will begin an uptrend after the consolidation ends, because it has recently made a new 20-day high.

2. The entry during the consolidation is a low-risk entry point.

3. Exits could be placed at the nearby 20-day high, by using trailing stops, or by exiting after x-days in the trade.

The reality is that markets may have an extended consolidation after making a new 20-day high, or could even make new 20-day lows. Hence, a bias to the long side may be correct only 50 to 70 percent of the time. It is also difficult to find consistent exits, since the markets do not follow the same script every time. Hence, another difficulty with the CB-PB system is finding a consistent exit strategy. A third area of difficulty is where to place the initial stop. If the market rolls over and starts a new downtrend, then an initial stop is critical for risk management and loss control, whether it is a simple-dollar stop or a volatility-based stop.

The first example of the CB-PB pattern uses the March 1995 deutsche mark contract. Figure 4.19 shows the daily bars and, superimposed on the bars, the 20-bar trading range. The 20-day range lines have a 13-tick barrier added to both the lines to filter out some false breakouts. The chart shows that the deutsche mark broke above its 20-day range in December 1995 and then consolidated for 7 days before moving higher. Upon moving higher, it made a higher high, and consolidated again.

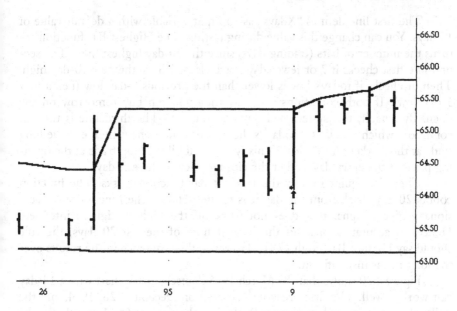

Figure 4.19   The deutsche mark pulls back after making a new 20-day high. The goal is to buy after the pullback. The 20-day price channel is shown for visual reference.

Ideally, we would like to buy some time during the pullback, but we do not know how long the pullback will last. Hence, the problem is how to specify that a pullback has occurred. During the pullback, markets often also make new 5-day lows. Hence, we can define this breakout and pullback long entry rule as follows: the market must make a new 20-day high, and then define a 5-day low in the next 7 days. Once it forms a 5-day low, buy on the open the next trading day. These choices are arbitrary, and you can experiment with these numbers. For example, we can buy on the close instead of on the open after the market forms a 5-day low following a 20-day high.

We now need an exit condition to evaluate this entry rule. To keep it simple, we will exit on the close of the n-th day in the trade, with $n=5$ for short-term systems and $n=50$ for intermediate systems. Again, these numerical values are arbitrary. You may try other values, such as a 3-day low instead of a 5-day low.

Using the Omega Research TradeStation Power Editor™, the rule appears, in part, as:

```
Input: Xdays (14);
If Highest Bar(High,20)[1] < 7 and Low < Lowest
   (Low,5)[1]
then buy tomorrow on the open;
If BarsSinceEntry = Xdays then exitlong at the close;
```

The first line defines "Xdays" as an input-variable with a default value of 14 days. You can change this value during testing. The Highest Bar function returns the number of bars (trading days) since the 20-day highest high. The second line first checks if 7 or fewer days have elapsed since the new 20-day high. Then, it checks if today's low is lower than the previous 5-day low (i.e., a new 5-day low). If both conditions are true, then you can buy tomorrow on the open. By default, this system will buy one contract. The third line is the exit condition, which says that if today is the x-th day since entry, then exit the long trade at the market on the close. This system will fill the long trade at the opening price of the entry day, and at the closing price of the exit day.

There is a quirk in how the Highest Bar function works. The function counts 20 days back from the day it is testing. Hence, the function will occasionally give a signal that does not work off the highest high as intended. Hence, to accurately pick off the highest high of the last 20 days, the rule should say Highest Bar(High,27)[1]. However, the difference in the results over the long run is insignificant.

Figure 4.20 shows that the March 1995 deutsche mark chart with a 14-day exit worked well. The first breakout occurred on December 28, 1994, and the pullback entry occurred on January 9, 1995, at the open of 64.11, which was the exact low of the ensuing 14 days. The exit was on the close of January 30, 1995, at 66.52, for a profit of $2,913, after allowing $100 for slippage and commis-

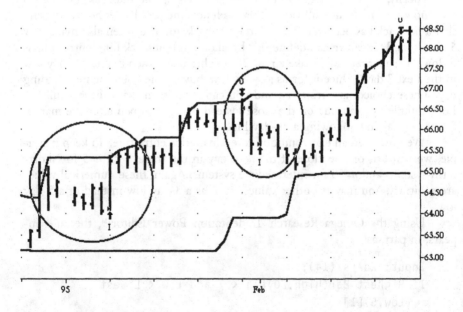

Figure 4.20   The CP-PB strategy gave good trades with low-risk entry points.

sions. The next entry occurred on February 1, 1995, on the open at 65.65. The low of the trade occurred four days later at 65.07, for a 58-tick risk of $725. The exit was on the close of February 23, 1995, at 68.19. The nominal profit was $3,075.

Thus, the CB-PB system generated low-risk entries into an emerging up trend in the March 1995 deutsche mark contract. The exit on the 14th day was a lucky choice for this chart. You could use a number based on your individual preference just as well.

Note here that we specified a generic entry pattern with no specific assumptions about DM price patterns. The exit was again arbitrary. Of course, if you had exited on the fifth-day close instead of the fourteenth-day close, the profits would have been smaller. Note that the CB-PB pattern offers a relatively low-risk entry method. You can use it as a short-term system or a long-term system by simply varying the exit strategy.

So far, the exit strategy has been trend-following in nature, with some variation based on the actual day of the exit. For example, we could vary the exit from 5 days to 50 days and get completely different results. However, we will never make the "perfect" choice of x days. We can anticipate market action in a different way that does not use time as the exit signal. Instead, we will use a price we already know. Since we are buying a pullback, it is plausible to assume that the market will retest the recent 20-day high. Hence, we can write an exit signal that buys the pullback and exits the retest of the recent high. Here is how we would write the new system variation in TradeStation™:

```
If Highest Bar(High,20)[1] < 7 and Low < Lowest
   (Low,5)[1]
then buy tomorrow on the open;
Exitlong at highest(h,20)[1] limit;
```

The first line of the CB-PB rule is exactly the same as before. The second line specifies a long exit for tomorrow with a limit order at the most recent 20-day high. This turned out to be the "perfect" model for the December 1995 S&P-500 contract. There were 12 winning trades in a row, with a total profit of $50,000 (see Figure 4.21).

The noteworthy feature here is that we started with the DM contract, using very general price patterns, and arrived at an intriguing short-term system, which performs particularly well in choppy up-trends. We made no contract-specific assumptions, and captured a general market behavior that we can expect to see in every market in the future. The CB-PB entry with an exit at a recent high works well in consolidations.

Another exit strategy involves a trailing stop, but one that will not cut off long trends prematurely. Hence, we will exit at the lowest low of the last 40 days. This will convert CB-PB into a long-term trend-following system.

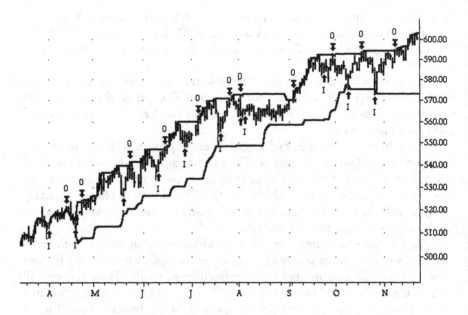

Figure 4.21 The CP-PB model with exit at the recent 20-day high using limit orders produced 12 winning trades in a row for a nominal profit of $50,000.

```
If Highest Bar(High,20)[1] < 7 and Low < Lowest
    (Low,5)[1]
then buy tomorrow on the open;
exitlong at lowest(low, 40)[1] - 1 point stop;
```

The CB-PB entry rule remains intact. The second line exits on a stop set one tick below the trailing 40-bar (trading days) low. You can see that this will become a trend-following exit. Our initial stop will close out our trade should the market head lower. The trailing stop at the 40-bar low will keep us in the trade through minor consolidations.

Notice how we took an intuitive understanding of a market pattern and adapted it to three different exit philosophies to meet specific trading preferences. Remember you could use it as a short term system by exiting at the recent high. You could exit on the close of the n-th day in the trade, for short- or intermediate-term trading. Or you could use a trailing stop. Each exit produces a trading system with different characteristics off the same entry signal. These are the types of modifications you should consider as you look at trading systems. Figure 4.22 from the March 1995 U.S. bond market will help you visualize the three exit strategies.

Now let us take a closer look at the entry signal, to see if it is any better than a random entry system. Following the suggestion of Le Beau and Lucas (see bibliography), we will try to isolate the effect of this CB-PB entry signal.

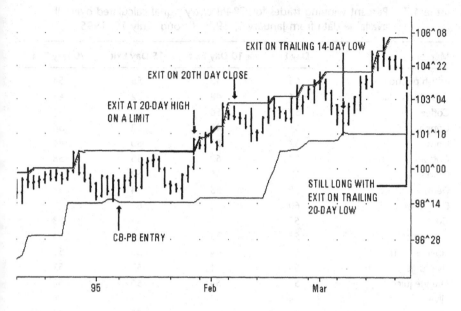

Figure 4.22   The CB-PB gave a low risk entry into the new trend for the March 1995 U.S. bond contract.

We test the CB-PB entry signal with exit on the close of the n-th day (n=5, 10, 15, and 20), without stops and assuming no slippage or commission costs. Le Beau and Lucas suggest that if the entry signal is performing better than a random system, it should result in at least 55 percent profitable trades over a range of markets. They tested only 6 years of data and 6 markets to measure a signal's ability to perform better than random. Here we use 22 markets and continuous contracts using all available data from January 1, 1975, through July 10, 1995. This should be a severe test of this entry signal, and our goal is to check if it is consistently profitable more than 55 percent of the time.

Table 4.7 shows that about 55 percent of all CB-PB entries were profitable. Hence, you can be reasonably confident that the CB-PB entry signal provides better than random entries. You can now marry this entry signal to a variety of risk control and exit strategies to fashion a trading system that fits your trading mentality.

The first exit strategy is simply to exit on the close of the n-th day in the trade. You are making the working assumption that the market is going to trend after the entry signal. Hence, consider now the CB-PB entry using continuous contracts, $1,500 initial stop, and allowing $100 for commissions and slippage. As discussed at the beginning of this section, we are focusing on "mature" markets. Let us consider the case when we exit the long trade on the close of the fifth day. The test uses all available data from January 1, 1975, through July 10, 1995.

Table 4.7   Percent winning trades for CB-PB entry signal calculated over all available data from January 1, 1975, through July 10, 1995.

Market	5-Day Exit	10-Day Exit	15-Day Exit	20-Day Exit
British pound	55	52	55	54
Canadian dollar	54	48	52	45
Coffee	52	56	45	46
Copper	51	48	52	56
Corn	57	52	50	46
Cotton	57	62	55	58
Crude oil	57	55	62	58
Deutsche mark	55	55	54	55
Eurodollar	60	58	60	60
Gold	55	52	53	53
Heating oil	52	53	55	54
Japanese yen	56	49	50	55
Live hogs	56	51	53	51
Orange juice	54	54	50	50
Silver	54	53	56	48
Soybeans	56	58	53	46
S&P-500	64	54	56	61
Sugar	57	53	57	48
Swiss franc	48	50	52	53
10-year T-note	63	57	60	57
U.S. bond	56	53	52	52
Wheat	63	52	51	47
Average	56	54	54	53

The results of exiting on the fifth day of the trade are not impressive (see Table 4.8). Since we are buying the markets during a consolidation, most of them have not done much in the 5 days after entry. Hence, we should consider holding on to the long trade for a little while longer.

Consider what happens if we hold the long position for 50 days, exiting on the close. The conditions for the test are identical to those for Table 4.8. Table 4.9 shows there is a dramatic improvement in performance with $n = 50$ days. The average profit per market has increased three-fold, and the profit factor is up 46 percent. Thus, our basic assumption that the market will trend after the consolidation seems to work well about 39 percent of the time on these markets. Thus, we have converted our anemic short-term system into an interesting intermediate term system by exiting on the close of the fiftieth day.

We have previously stated that the initial stop should depend on market volatility. For example, the $1,500 stop may be "too close" given the volatility of the S&P-500 market. For the CB-PB system with exit on the 50th day using

Table 4.8   CB-PB long trades with exit on the 5th day using $1,500 initial stop, tested on all available data from January 1, 1975, through July 10, 1995.

Market	Profit ($)	Number of Trades	Percentage of Wins	Average Trade ($)	Maximum Intraday Drawdown ($)	Profit Factor
Eurodollar	6,050	99	54	61	–4,350	1.27
Japanese yen	27,450	96	51	286	–9,863	1.63
Coffee	–11,273	122	54	–94	–23,500	0.86
S&P-500	69,330	185	42	375	–19,640	1.42
Swiss franc	–4,988	120	45	–42	–17,913	0.94
10-year T-note	18,831	122	58	154	–8,756	1.39
U.S. bond	27,306	126	52	217	–13,219	1.45
Average	18,958	124	51	280	–13,892	1.28

a $5,000 initial stop instead of the $1,500 initial stop, the profits dropped for all markets in Table 4.9 except S&P-500. Profits for S&P-500 increased to $141,840 on just 55 trades with 56 percent winners, a $2,579 average trade. The maximum drawdown was -$24,795, with the profit factor increasing to 2.29 from 1.62. Hence, the initial stop will influence overall system performance.

Table 4.9   CB-PB long trades with exit on the fiftieth day, using $1,500 initial stop, tested on all available data from January 1, 1975, through July 10, 1995.

Market	Profit ($)	Number of Trades	Percentage of Wins	Average Trade ($)	Maximum Intraday Drawdown ($)	Profit Factor
Eurodollar	21,875	45	56	485	–8525	1.74
Japanese yen	76,613	52	46	1,473	–11,525	2.69
Coffee	27,434	71	27	387	–18,719	1.33
S&P-500	86,085	102	22	781	–26,475	1.62
Swiss franc	52,889	63	37	839	–13,900	1.81
10-year T-note	49,799	58	47	831	–9,575	1.98
U.S. bond	63,094	66	37	923	–14,169	1.95
Average	53,970	65	39	817	–14,698	1.87

Table 4.10 CB-PB long trades with exit on a trailing stop at the 40-day low, using $1,500 initial stop, tested on all available data from January 1, 1975, through July 10, 1995.

Market	Profit ($)	Number of Trades	Percentage of Wins	Average Trade ($)	Maximum Intraday Drawdown ($)	Profit Factor
Eurodollar	32,200	37	35	870	−3,375	3.65
Japanese yen	70,419	34	38	2,063	−7,112	4.39
coffee	53,928	59	14	914	−24,020	2.00
S&P-500	85,200	70	14	510	−25,480	1.41
Swiss franc	55,200	59	20	936	−11,550	2.42
10-year T-note	57,250	51	28	1,123	−8,038	3.39
U.S. bond	62,513	54	24	1,158	−11,475	2.13
Average	59,530	52	25	1,082	−13,007	2.77

We can continue to explore the long-term nature of this entry by using a trailing stop. We know from Table 4.9 that we should use a trailing stop that will allow trends to develop. Hence, let us arbitrarily specify an exit on the lowest low of the last 40 days; this should convert the intermediate system into a long-term trading system. As before, we will use $1,500 initial stop and allow $100 slippage and commissions.

Table 4.10 shows the long-term performance of this entry with a profit factor of nearly 3 and an average trade of $1,082. The ratio of net profits to drawdown is more than 4.5. These numbers suggest that you can take the same entry and make it into a strong long-term trend-following system.

Let us now take the CB-PB entry and attach it to an exit at the recent 20-day high. It is reasonable to assume that the market will retest the recent 20-day highs as part of the backing and filling during the consolidation. Table 4.11 summarizes the test results using a $1,500 initial stop and a $100 allowance for slippage and commissions.

The CB-PB system with an exit at the recent 20-day high was interesting only on the Eurodollar, S&P-500, 10-year T-note, and U.S. bond markets. The large proportion of winning trades makes this exit particularly attractive. Notice that the length of the average winning trade was only 9 days.

You can develop other variations of this strategy. For example, one of the design features of the CB-PB system is that we want a low risk entry point into long trades. Hence, you can use a multicontract trading strategy to improve performance. Another approach would be to add a filter to reduce the number of trades.

Thus, the CB-PB system has a flexible entry to suit many trading styles. The CB-PB strategy is more profitable with an intermediate to long-term

Table 4.11 CB-PB long trades with exit at the recent 20-day highs on a limit, using $1,500 initial stop, tested on all available data from January 1, 1975, through July 10, 1995.

Market	Profit ($)	Number of Trades	Percentage of Wins	Average Trade ($)	Maximum Intraday Drawdown ($)	Number of Days in Wins	Profit Factor
Eurodollar	7,250	98	72	74	−8,750	9	1.24
Japanese yen	17,200	93	54	185	−11,225	13	1.30
Coffee	−7,751	117	43	−66	−24,463	11	0.93
S&P-500	48,860	185	36	264	−25,070	6	1.25
Swiss franc	−5,963	116	50	−51	−16,625	7	0.97
10-year T-note	26,781	120	65	223	−8,388	9	1.42
U.S. bond	37,306	126	60	296	−10,856	8	1.47
Average	17,669	122	54	132	−17,377	9	1.22

trading strategy. A short-term approach worked on a few active markets. Note also how we can develop different systems from the same entry signal by changing the exit strategy.

An ADX Burst Trend-Seeking System

We have assumed that the market was about to trend in both the 65sma-3cc and the CB-PB systems, although we did not actually verify that the market was trending because it is difficult to measure trendiness consistently. As was shown in the discussion in Chapter 3 on the range action verification index, market momentum is often a good measure of trendiness. Unfortunately, a certain amount of smoothing is essential to minimize noise in the indicator, and this smoothing usually causes undesirable lags in indicator response.

Figure 4.23 shows the March 1993 U.S. T-bond contract trending upward nicely from December 1992 through March 1993. The indicator under the daily bars is the 18-day average directional index. ADX measures the amount of activity outside the previous bar over a given period; a strong trend usually leads to a rising ADX line. An ADX reading above 20 is considered to indicate a trend, but the ADX is a lagging indicator, and there is little significance to any particular indicator value.

ADX is closely related to double-smoothed absolute momentum, and hence will often have quirky lags. The ADX will often seem to be late in signaling a trend, and choppy markets will not follow through in the original direc-

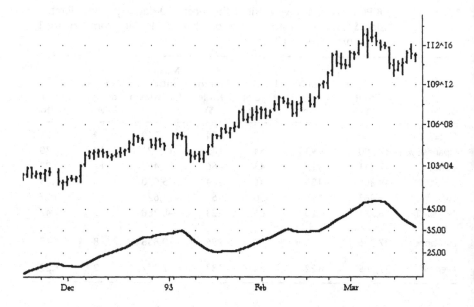

Figure 4.23   A rising 18-day ADX can be a good indicator of a trending market.

tion that caused the ADX to rise. In fact, the market can reverse strongly, and the ADX will keep on rising.

During a strong trend, as markets make big daily moves in the direction of the trend, the daily ADX momentum can "pop" over 1.0 point, an ADX "burst." Figure 4.24 shows the March 1993 U.S. bond contract with the histogram of the ADX burst superimposed on the 18-day ADX line. As the trend accelerates, the daily ADX changes are more than 1, and you can see relatively large bars associated with this ADX burst activity. Now you can build a trading system using this idea as shown in Figure 4.25, where the entries are circled.

Obviously, the ADX burst indicates accelerating momentum. So, here the design philosophy has changed to begin with a check that increases the odds of success of a trend-following strategy. Notice that the ADX burst is itself triggering the trade, and that the ADX is not acting as a filter. For reference, you can look up a similar system in Lucas and Le Beau (see bibliography for reference). Our goal is to take the trade in the direction of the short-term trend. If the 3-day SMA is greater than the 12-day SMA, then the trend is up, and vice versa. Table 4.12 shows the results using a simple 20-day exit strategy and allowing $100 for slippage and commissions, over all available data from Janury 1, 1975, through July 10, 1995.

The rather large profit factor suggests that the entries are effective in identifying profitable trades, so that an ADX burst is a good entry into strong trends. The profit factor is overestimated here to some degree because we are

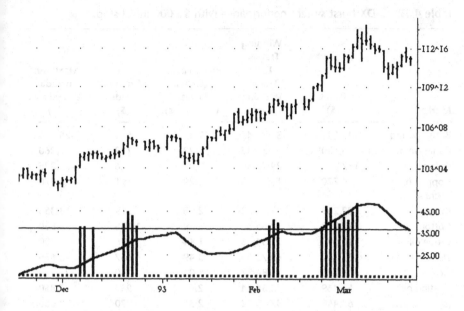

Figure 4.24   The histogram of ADX burst momentum shows daily changes greater than 1.

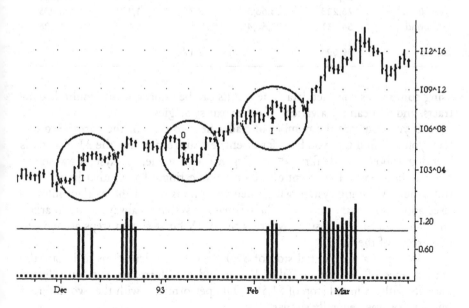

Figure 4.25   A trading system triggered by ADX burst with daily momentum changes more than 1.

Table 4.12   ADX burst system performance with $5,000 initial stop.

Market	Profit ($)	Winning Trades; Total Trades; Winning Percentage	Profit Factor (Gross Profit/ Gross Loss)	Average Trade ($)	Maximum Intraday Drawdown ($)
British pound	40,531	34;75;45	1.39	540	−25,113
Canadian dollar	6,830	20;56;36	1.28	122	−7,060
Coffee	137,014	29;75;39	3.86	1826	−21,225
Copper, high-grade	4,770	15;25;60	1.29	191	−5,970
Corn	22,269	37;70;53	2.58	319	−3,356
Cotton	72,770	32;64;50	3.49	1,138	−4,860
Crude oil	10,590	21;54;38	1.44	196	−13,400
Deutsche mark	63,300	40;73;55	3.49	867	−8,675
Gold	4,770	31;84;37	1.04	30	−27,450
Heating oil	52,469	30;56;54	2.61	937	−7,850
Japanese yen	63,450	37;69;54	2.35	920	−18,050
Live hogs	20,080	36;75;48	1.65	268	−6,140
Orange juice	25,013	29;80;36	1.63	313	−12,692
Soybeans	38,606	31;73;42	1.81	529	−10,713
S&P-500	−28,650	20;55;36	0.79	−520	−65,815
Swiss franc	76,238	35;68;51	2.75	1,121	−8,075
U.S. bond	54,531	27;60;45	2.56	909	−11,306
Average	39,093		2.12		

using continuous contract data. The results can be improved with multiple contracts, and you can try a variety of other exit strategies.

   If you compare the number of trades here to that for the 65sma-3cc system, you will find that you have fewer entries, suggesting that the ADX burst is working as both a trade filter and a trigger. For example, this system was in the market about 35 to 45 percent of the time, indicating it has a rather large "neutral zone." A trading system with a neutral zone is out of the market unless it rises above stiff entry barriers. The 65sma-3cc system is always in the market, and is a reversal-type system, whereas the ADX burst system steps aside 55 to 65 percent of the time.

   We used a wide initial stop of $5,000 in these calculations to isolate the performance of the system. Table 4.13 includes performance data on selected markets with an initial stop of $1,500. The performance with the two different initial stops was generally similar.

   One of the quirks of the ADX burst system is that it will often get in late, near the tops or bottoms of short but swift moves (see Figure 4.26). Such moves

Table 4.13   ADX burst system performance with a $1,500 initial stop.

Market	Profit ($)	Number of Trades	Percentage of Wins	Average Trade ($)	Maximum Intraday Drawdown ($)	Profit Factor
British pound	64,438	82	39	744	–18,719	.1.82
Coffee	148,584	85	33	1,749	–13,851	3.07
Cotton	66,800	66	48	1,012	–6,015	2.95
Crude oil	6,070	55	38	110	–13,440	1.24
Deutsche mark	62,088	73	55	851	–8,457	3.34
S&P-500	19,160	68	25	282	–33,675	1.24
Swiss franc	61,575	72	44	855	–9,125	2.88
U.S. bond	40,556	66	36	615	–12,944	1.74

fire its entry signals, but the capricious market fails to follow through with a trend in the advertised direction. Hence, you should always trade a system such as this one with a preplaced stop loss order.

In summary, the ADX burst system provides entries into strong trends. It tests well across many markets and over long time periods. The system has a

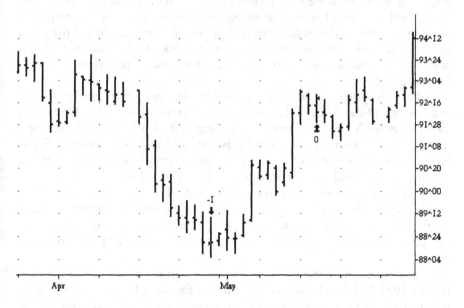

Figure 4.26   The June 1990 U.S. bond contract sells off beyond a trading range to make a new low with good momentum. The system kicks in with a short. The bond market soon reverses, to get back into the prior consolidation region.

large neutral zone, so it is in the market only 35 to 45 percent of the time. It differs from the 65sma-3cc system, which is always in the market, and does not have a trend filter. You can use it to enter trades or increase the position in those markets. You can derive other variations using different values of the ADX burst, the look-back period for the burst calculations, and other exit strategies.

A Trend-Antitrend Trading System

In this section we explore the trend-antitrend (T-AT) system, designed to switch automatically between an antitrend mode and a trend-following mode. You will like this system if you aggressively like to fade the market, but do not mind reversing into a with-the-trend position if needed. This system shows you that trend following is not the only way to trade the markets. Many institutions and money managers, with their deep pockets, big positions, excellent execution, and low costs, usually assume the market is ranging. These sophisticated souls will be selling new highs and buying new lows. Of course, the difference is in the trading time frames: They are in and out a dozen times, before most of us are warming up to the trade.

The challenge in this type of system is to find a consistent basis to define when to trade with the trend and when to fade it. Markets will often make new 25-day highs or lows, but without strong momentum. This can be interpreted to mean that the market is likely to reverse, so we should try to sell the highs and buy the lows. However, if the market then goes on to make news highs or lows with increasing momentum, we must immediately reverse into a trend-following position.

For this system, we will use the 18-day ADX to measure market trendiness, and an 18-day SMA of the ADX as the reference. If the ADX is above its own 18-day SMA, then the market is trending, and we will buy new highs, and sell new lows. Conversely, if the ADX is below its 18-day SMA, we will sell new highs, and buy new lows. Since we will be going against the short-term trend, we must use an initial risk control stop, or the losses will be unbearable.

We must also decide how to enter the trade. For simplicity, we will enter on the open of the next trading day. We can use the usual 20-day exit to check on the trend-following aspects. Again, for simplicity, we will test this system without specific exits, so that the entries also serve as the exit for the opposite position.

You can see how this trading system works in Figure 4.27 from the September 1993 U.S. bond contract. The market formed a base during a congestion phase, and then rallied strongly, experiencing one brief sideways period. Observe how the model readily fades new highs, and then quickly reverses in the direction of the trend. This system picked off the top and bottom cleanly during the consolidation in April and May. It was long coming into the rally off

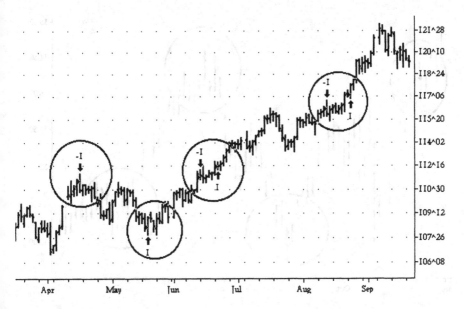

Figure 4.27   The trend-antitrend system in action on the September 1993 U.S. bond contract. Notice how it picked off turning points nicely during the consolidation. It detected two turning points during the uptrend, but quickly reversed to follow the up move.

the May bottom. It hiccuped twice, in June and August, but quickly returned to the underlying long trend.

As Figure 4.27 shows, the T-AT system caught some turning points very well. This system will also see turning points that turn out to be insignificant, and, of course, there will be some turning points that it will not notice at all. The drawback of the T-AT system is the potential for significant loss as it switches fruitlessly between its anti-trend and trend-following modes.

The usual T-AT system worked beautifully on the December 1985 deutsche mark contract (see Figure 4.28). The DM was defining a broad consolidation region after a down trend. Note how the T-AT system quickly reversed to long in September after a premature short signal. The subsequent market turns were timed flawlessly. This is quite remarkable for a mechanical system using a single trend-checking rule.

You must use good risk control with this system, since the market could move against the position in a vicious countermove. The June 1995 deutsche mark contract provides a good illustration of this (see Figure 4.29). The T-AT system signaled a perfect short trade within a day of the actual contract high. Then, it correctly picked off the bottom of the quick sell off. However, it rolled over to short during the brief congestion and then was short through the

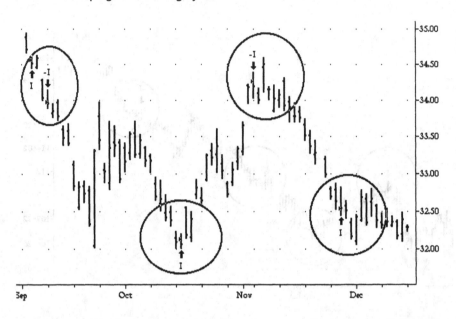

Figure 4.28 The T-AT system picked off turning points flawlessly in this December 1985 deutsche mark contract. Notice how it quickly returned to a trend-following mode in September, as the market drifted lower.

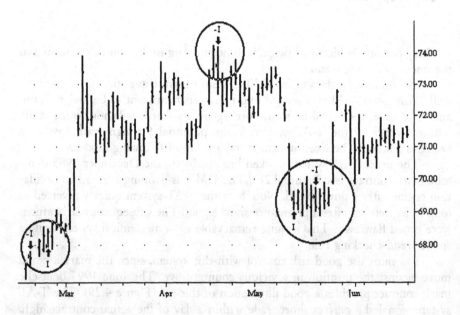

Figure 4.29 The June 1995 deutsche mark contract illustrates how the T-AT system can get trapped by a volatile countermove.

volatile countermove in late May. Trend-antitrend trading requires great faith in the system and rigid risk control, with the added benefit that the risk/reward ratio can be excellent.

The June 1995 deutsche mark contract also illustrates the difficulty of using a heavily smoothed ADX indicator in volatile markets. The same smoothing that desensitizes ADX works against it if the market is choppy and thin.

Another quirk of the T-AT system is that it will often be slow in signaling a countermove if the market is drifting slowly, as the December 1993 cotton contract was doing near the summer top. T-AT logic correctly picked the first low (see Figure 4.30), but had to sit through the ensuing double bottom in November before the trend turned up. Once again, we have the hiccup at the start of the trend, with the system quickly reversing into the intermediate trend.

Let us briefly explore how this system was actually written, using the Power Editor from Omega Research's TradeStation™ software. There is only one input variable, the length of the breakout period, currently set to 25 bars (days). The antitrend entry at a new 25-day high is written as follows: if today's high was the highest high of the previous 25 days, but the 18-day ADX was below its 18-day SMA, then sell tomorrow at the market on the open. The countertrend buy signal is also similar.

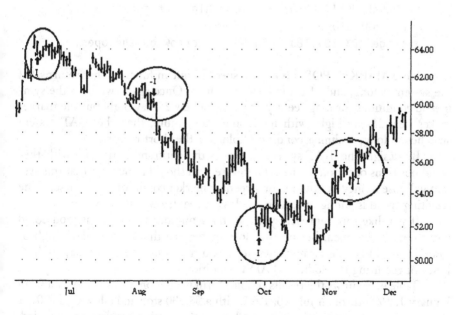

Figure 4.30   The T-AT system was slow to respond to the market drift in the summer for the December 1993 cotton contract. It correctly picked the first dip of the eventual double bottom.

```
If high > highest (H,25)[1] and ADX(18) < average
   (adx(18),18) then sell
tomorrow on the open.
```

```
If low < lowest (L,25)[1] and ADX(18) < average
   (adx(18),18) then buy
tomorrow on the open.
```

This approach gives a symmetric long and short sell order on an antitrend basis. Let us assume you have a long position near a potential bottom. However, the market bounces up for a few days, and then reverses to begin a strong downtrend. In this situation, you want the system to switch to a short trend-following position only if it is long to begin with. Similarly, a new 25-day high with rising momentum is your signal to switch to a long position if you were short to begin with. Thus, the trend-following entries are similar to the antitrend entries, but you should first test if the system is short or long.

```
If MARKETPOSITION(0) = 1 and low < lowest(L,25)[1] and
   ADX(18) >
average(ADX(18),18) then sell tomorrow on the open.
```

```
If MARKETPOSITION(0) = -1 and high > highest(H,25)[1]
   and ADX(18) >
average(ADX(18),18) then buy tomorrow on the open.
```

Here MARKETPOSITION is a special built-in function that returns 1 if the system is long, and –1 if the system is short. Once again, we have the symmetric conditions for long reentry. If we sell a new 25-day high, but the market makes new 25-day highs with increasing momentum, then the T-AT system switches to long. A similar condition holds for the short reentry.

By design, the T-AT system first tries the antitrend entry, and with-the-trend positions occur on reentry. Therefore, you should remember that this system will lose money as it hunts for a reentry market condition. Of course, if the resulting trend is a long one, then the loss at reentry will seem minor.

If you like this approach, you can try a number of variations. You could enter not on the open, but on the close or beyond the previous day's high or low. You could also use a more sensitive reentry, as just a new 25-day high or low, not requiring the additional ADX conditions.

Table 4.14 shows the results of long-term testing on all available data from January 1, 1975 through July 10, 1995 with a $5,000 stop and allowing $100 for slippage and commissions. Only markets with positive results are included, since this strategy requires active markets.

Table 4.14 points out the strengths and weaknesses of the T-AT system. First, it does not work on all markets, and second, it generates a lot of trades. Hence, this is an expensive system to run, as shown by the drawdown numbers. The initial stop had to be rather wide, at $5,000, to allow a cushion for the antitrend component to work. However, the profit factor is healthy, as is the average trade. Hence, on mature and active markets, the T-AT system seems to work quite well. The strategy requires excellent risk control and good discipline to implement. You can now develop other variations of this system, adapting it to your trading preferences.

Figure 4.31 presents a frequency distribution of 1,311 trades generated by the T-AT system. This distribution is broader than the distribution for the 65sma-3cc system (see Figure 4.5). It also shows a spike near the $5,000 initial stop. Like the 65sma-3cc distribution, it also shows a spike for trades with big profits. Figure 4.32 shows this distribution normalized and compared to a fitted normal distribution. It is immediately clear that the T-AT trade distribution has "fat" tails compared to the normal distribution. Thus, the probability of a trade far from the center is much greater than the corresponding normal distribution. The tail on the profits side is fatter than on the losing side, suggesting that the entries are working well. Observe how the initial stop cuts off losing trades. However, there is no such cutoff on the profit side, as seen by the spike at the right edge of the distribution. This is the TOPS COLA principle introduced in Chapter 1 applied to a trading system in practice.

In summary, the T-AT system illustrates how to develop a system that automatically adjusts to market conditions. It differs from the 65sma-3cc system in that its initial stance is to take an antitrend position; the 65sma-3cc system always takes a position with the trend. A reversal condition switches the T-AT

Table 4.14   Long-term performance of T-AT system over all available data from January 1, 1975 through July 10, 1995 with $5,000 stop and $100 for slippage and commissions.

Market	Profit ($)	Total Trades	Profit Factor	Maximum Intraday Drawdown ($)	Average Trade ($)
British pound	46,956	207	1.17	–42,163	226
Coffee	29,005	203	1.08	–101,753	145
Copper, high-grade	17,563	57	1.55	–7,333	308
Cotton	91,585	194	1.77	–12,300	467
Crude	26,260	103	1.45	–17,310	255
Deutsche mark	69,775	175	1.53	–11,975	399
Gold	22,060	168	1.16	–19,050	131
S&P-500	92,435	141	1.34	–56,030	656
Swiss franc	103,850	188	1.58	–16,475	552
U.S. bond	106,269	172	1.68	–20,281	617

Frequency Distribution of 1311 T-AT Trades

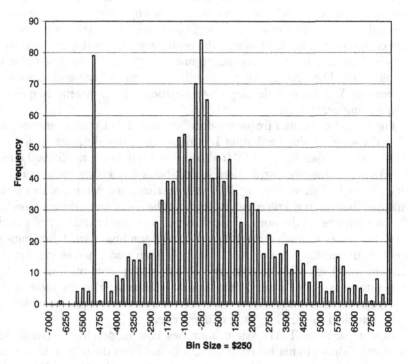

Figure 4.31 Frequency distribution of T-AT trades showing a spike at the $5,000 initial stop and at trades with profit greater than $8,000.

system from antitrend to a trend-following mode. The objective reversal condition assures entry in the direction of a major trend, thus allowing you to take advantage of all market conditions.

Gold-Bond Intermarket System

This section develops intermarket trading systems for trading negatively or positively correlated markets. We begin with a quick review of the difficulties of formulating intermarket models. The gold-bond system is illustrated for negatively correlated markets and tested on other market combinations also. An example of using three markets for intermarket analysis is then given. Lastly, the gold-bond system is modified for positively correlated markets. This section will convince you that it is possible to develop interesting intermarket systems. You may have greater confidence in such systems because they contain a weak

T-AT Closed trades Frequency Distribution (N = 1311)

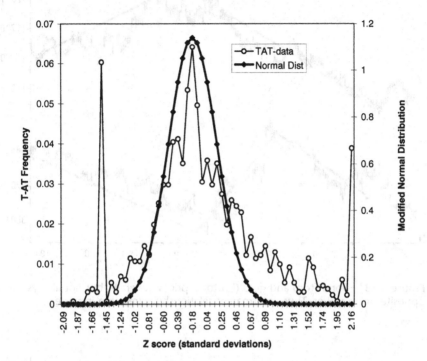

Figure 4.32   T-AT frequency distribution normalized and compared to a fitted normal distribution.

form of cause-and-effect relationships. Hence, they are often a good addition to your analytical tool set.

Many analysts have recognized intermarket relationships, which imply some form of weak cause-and-effect relationship. For example, bond prices decline when inflation is rising, and rising gold prices suggest potentially higher inflation. Therefore, we expect gold prices and bond prices to move in opposite directions (see Figure 4.33). You can also measure inflation with the prices of industrial metals such copper or aluminum. The idea is that increasing economic activity will raise the price of copper, and herald a rise in inflation. Therefore, we expect copper prices and bond prices to move in opposite directions (see Figure 4.34).

Other intermarket relationships occur with positive correlation. This means that the prices of some commodities rise and fall together. For example, rising crude oil prices suggest potential inflation, and we should expect gold prices to rise. You can use the currency markets as another good example of

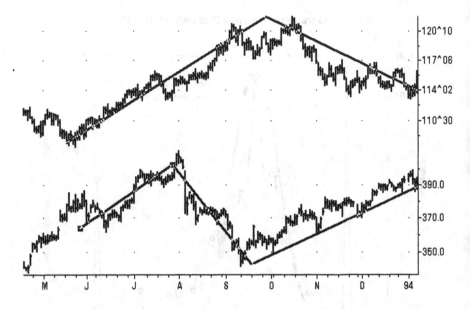

Figure 4.33   Bond (top) and gold (bottom) prices generally, but not always, move opposite one another. Thus, intermarket relationships are often imperfect.

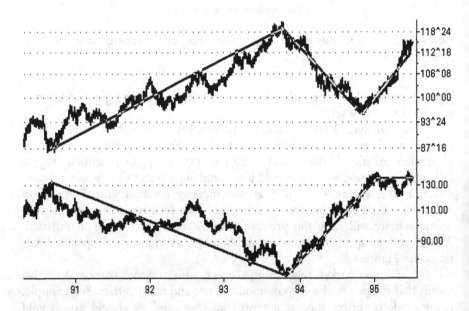

Figure 4.34   The general inverse relationship between weekly bond (top) and copper (bottom) prices.

correlated markets. Exchange rates reflect long-term fundamental forces in the economy such as inflation and interest rates. Thus, we expect the U.S. dollar to decline at approximately the same time against other foreign currencies such as the Japanese yen and the deutsche mark. Thus, we should expect that Japanese yen and deutsche mark prices are correlated, and we should be able to generate buy or sell signals for one market from the other.

There are several difficulties involved with exploiting intermarket relationships. First, weak intermarket cause-and-effect relationships have time lags. Thus, the price of copper may rise for several months before bond prices begin to fall. This difference in the timing of peaks and troughs among related markets is called a time lag. The problem is that the time lags are neither constant nor consistent.

A second difficulty is that each market has its supply and demand forces, which will often distort the usual intermarket relationships. For example, we would expect copper and gold prices to move up or down at about the same time. However, there have been periods when gold and copper prices have moved in opposite directions (Figure 4.35). Thus, any systems built on intermarket forces will not be correct all the time.

A third problem is the internal technical condition of each market. Each market can become "overbought" or "oversold" at different times. The usual intermarket trends are broad trends, which could unfold over many months. Hence very short term trends in the markets can move opposite the cause-and-

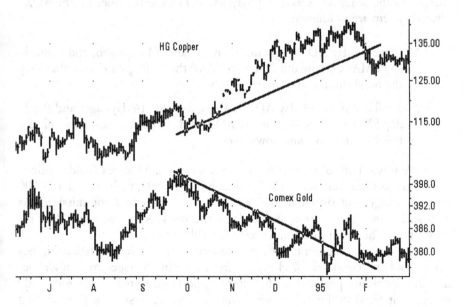

Figure 4.35   An example of copper and gold prices moving in opposite directions in late 1994-early 1995.

effect relationship. Such movements can complicate your entry signals because they can trigger a risk control exit without changing the underlying trend.

All these issues influence the precise form of relationship you select for your system. You must also decide if you want to relate two markets or more than two markets.

The gold-bond system, which assumes that bond prices move in the opposite direction of gold prices, is a simple but effective example of how to construct an intermarket trading system. The system assumes that rising gold prices signal potential inflation and thus influence the bond market. We will use a dual moving-average crossover system, using arbitrary 10-day and 50-day simple moving averages to build the system. Here are the rules:

1. If the 10-day SMA of gold crosses above the 50-day SMA, then sell the T-bond futures tomorrow on the open.

2. Conversely, if the 10-day SMA gold crosses under the 50-day SMA, then buy the T-bond futures tomorrow on the open.

These rules say that an upside crossover of the moving averages signals rising gold prices and therefore predicts falling bond prices. Here we have not used any filters for the emerging trend in the gold market, but you could certainly use the ADX indicator. To use the ADX filter, simply require that the 14-day ADX be rising, and determine the direction of the short-term trend by comparing the 3-day SMA to the 20-day SMA. The specific rules for the ADX-filtered system are as follows:

1. If the 14-day ADX is greater than its value 14 days ago, and if the 3-day SMA is below the 20-day SMA of the daily gold closes, then buy the bond futures on tomorrow's open.

2. Similarly, if the 14-day ADX is above its value 14 days ago, and the 3-day SMA is above the 20-day SMA of daily gold closes, then sell the bond futures on tomorrow's open.

We tested both of these models on U.S. bond and Comex Gold continuous contracts from August 23, 1977, through July 1, 1995, with an initial $5,000 money management stop and $100 allowed for slippage and commissions. As discussed above, the short-term trends in the markets can be a problem for trade entry. The results are summarized in Table 4.15.

These results suggest that there is indeed a broad inverse relationship between gold and bond prices. However, from a trading perspective, only about half the signals are profitable. The filtered gold-bond system was significantly more profitable than the dual moving average crossover system, with about half the maximum drawdown. The gold-bond system could function as a filter to check whether the "trading environment" favors rising bond prices.

Table 4.15   Results of testing the gold-bond systems, August 21, 1977 through July 10, 1995.

	Dual MA Gold-Bond System	ADX Gold-Bond System
Net profit ($)	38,675	92,488
Profit factor (gross profit/gross loss)	1.24	1.62
Total number of trades	122	152
Percentage of winning trades	48	52
Ratio: average win/loss	1.37	1.50
Average trade ($)	317	608
Maximum intraday drawdown ($)	−34,724	−16,506

We know that there are lags between the price movements among markets. Since a hint of inflation can move many other markets, we should check out the basic gold-bond system on other market combinations, such as the soybeans-bond, copper-bond and deutsche mark–bond combinations. The grain markets often signal inflation, and the soybeans market is used as a proxy for those markets. The copper market follows strength in the industrial sector and is a leading indicator of inflation. Lastly, interest rates signal broad forces in the economy that also influence the currency markets, such as the deutsche mark. We used the gold-bond system for negatively correlated markets with the same $5,000 initial stop, one contract per trade, and $100 for slippage and commissions, and tried to generate buy and sell signals for the bond market from the markets indicating inflation.

The data in Table 4.16 confirm that changing trends in markets heralding inflation can be used to trade the bond market. Of all the combinations tested, the copper market seems to provide the best indication. In every case, only about half of the signals were profitable. Thus, these systems follow the well-known principle of economic forecasting: if you must forecast, forecast often.

So far, we have used only one market to develop trading signals for bonds. However, you could use more than one market to derive trading signals. We tested the use of two markets, gold and soybeans, to develop trading signals for bonds. We chose these two markets because they seemed to have unrelated supply-demand forces. We also tested the gold, copper, and bond combination for completeness.

We extended the basic gold-bond system to three markets by specifying that both gold and soybeans must be trending up or trending down at the same time to generate the opposite signal for bonds. For example, if the 10-day SMA of the daily close was below the 50-day SMA for both gold and soybeans, then that would trigger a buy signal for bonds. The results of the historical tests for the combined gold-soybeans-bond system were better than either the gold-

Table 4.16 Results of testing the gold-bond system on other market combinations.

	Soybeans-Bond	Copper-Bond	Deutsche Mark–Bond
Test period	8/21/77 – 7/10/95	7/28/88 – 7/10/95	8/21/77 – 7/10/95
Net profit ($)	34,556	41,269	42,950
Profit factor (gross profit/gross loss)	1.23	2.27	1.39
Total number of trades	122	42	88
Percentage of winning trades	52	57	53
Ratio: average win/loss	1.15	1.70	1.21
Average trade ($)	282	983	488
Maximum intraday drawdown ($)	–16,100	–12,694	–28,006

bond or soybeans-bond systems. As usual, we used a $5,000 initial stop and allowed $100 for slippage and commissions .

The test results in Table 4.17 show that using three markets reduced the total number of trades, as you would expect. For example, the gold-bond tests and soybeans-bond tests produced 122 trades, whereas the gold-soybeans-bond trio produced only 77 trades. The profit factor also improves with three markets, as you would expect from improved filtering. For example, the gold-copper-bond trio had an impressive profit factor of 2.53, and produced essentially the same profits as the copper-bond combination with 35 percent fewer trades. These tests show that you could try to improve the effectiveness of intermarket

Table 4.17 The gold-bond system extended to three markets.

	Gold-Bond System Extended to Three Markets: Gold, Soybeans, and Bond	Gold-Bond System Extended to Three Markets: Gold, Copper, and Bond
Test period	01/02/75 – 07/10/95	07/28/88 – 07/10/95
Net profit	69,706	42,206
Profit factor (gross profit/gross loss)	1.56	2.53
Total number of trades	77	27
Percentage of winners	47	56
Ratio: average win/loss	1.78	2.02
Average trade ($)	905	1,563
Maximum intraday drawdown ($)	–30,600	–12,388

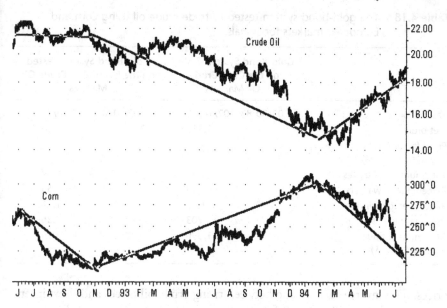

Figure 4.36 The approximate inverse price relationship between crude oil and corn.

systems by using three or more markets to filter out the signals. Note that as you add more markets, the effectiveness often decreases because of random noise among markets.

The basic gold-bond system tries to capture the weak negative correlation between the gold and bond markets. Such correlations also exist among other markets. Most trend-following systems have tested out poorly on the crude oil market, losing more than –$40,000. A negative correlation exists between crude oil and corn (Figure 4.36), and between crude oil and short-term interest rates. The Eurodollar market can be used as a proxy for short-term interest rates. Results of tests of the gold-bond system as developed on the corn–crude oil and Eurodollar–crude oil combinations are shown in Table 4.18. These tests use trend change signals from the corn and Eurodollar markets to trade crude oil.

The results show that the gold-bond system could be used to make a small profit on the crude oil markets, if we derive our signals from the corn market or the Eurodollar market. This is a big improvement over the results for typical trend-following systems.

Thus, these results show that you can use the gold-bond system to trade weak negative correlations among markets. The negative correlation between crude oil and corn is not obvious; it may have to do with the rising costs of international shipments—as crude oil prices increase, transportation costs increase, and U.S. corn producers must pay for the higher costs by lowering corn

Table 4.18 The gold-bond system tested to trade crude oil using corn and Eurodollar markets for signals.

	Gold-Bond System Tested on the Corn-Crude Oil Markets	Gold-Bond System Tested on the Eurodollar-Crude Oil Markets
Test period	03/30/83 – 07/10/95	02/01/82 – 07/10/95
Net profit	11,550	16,320
Profit factor (gross profit/gross loss)	1.25	1.36
Total number of trades	57	57
Percentage of winners	53	53
Ratio: average win/loss	1.13	1.22
Average trade ($)	203	286
Maximum intraday drawdown ($)	–11,390	–20,020

prices. The inverse relationship between rising crude oil prices and short interest rates is through the fear of future inflation.

So far, all the intermarket systems we have discussed exploited the negative or inverse price relationships between markets. You could certainly extend these ideas to trade positively correlated markets, in which a rising trend in one market would be a buy signal in the other market. The Japanese yen–deutsche

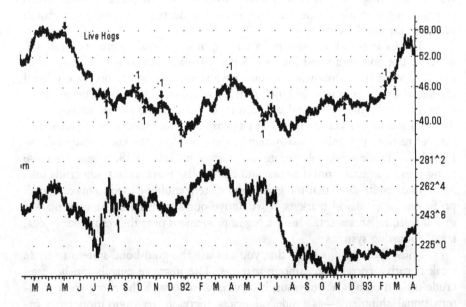

Figure 4.37 The relationship between corn prices and live hog prices.

Table 4.19   Gold Bond system extended to correlated markets, such as JY-DM and C-LH.

	Gold-Bond System for Correlated Markets: Japanese Yen–Deutsche Mark	Gold-Bond System for Correlated Markets: Corn–Live Hogs
Test period	02/13/75 – 07/10/95	01/02/75 – 07/10/95
Net profit ($)	51,188	34,052
Profit factor (gross profit/gross loss)	1.53	1.64
Total number of trades	99	105
Percentage of winners	46	44
Ratio: average win/loss	1.77	2.11
Average trade ($)	517	324
Maximum intraday drawdown ($)	–12,800	–12,184

mark combination uses trend change signals in the Japanese yen market to produce signals for the deutsche mark. The corn–live hogs combination uses trend changes in corn to generate signals for live hogs. Since corn is fed to hogs, rising corn prices could increase the production costs for hogs (see Figure 4.37). To test the gold-bond system in these correlated markets, we use a $5,000 initial stop for the currency markets, but only a $1,000 initial stop for the live hog market due to its relatively low volatility. As usual, we deduct $100 for slippage and commissions (see Table 4.19).

In summary, these results show that you can successfully use correlated markets to generate trading signals. You may feel more comfortable with the signals from intermarket systems because there are weak cause-and-effect relationships that have stood the test of time. At a minimum, you could use intermarket analysis to develop "background" information that could be used as input into your money-management algorithm. For example, an intermarket system signal could be used to increase the size of existing positions or put on new ones. You could also use an intermarket signal as an exit strategy for conventional single-market systems.

A Pattern for Bottom-Fishing

Market-specific systems work best on a particular market because they capture some unusual feature of that market. It is difficult to speculate why certain markets show signature patterns. We should take extra care when developing such systems because the market mechanics driving such patterns could change abruptly.

The S&P-500 futures contract can be used to illustrate a pattern-based approach. For instance, we consider a continuous contract from April 21, 1982 through July 10, 1995, and test the standard simple moving average crossover system with 10-day and 11-day simple moving averages. We use a relatively loose $2,000 initial stop, which will absorb random price fluctuations, and allow $100 for slippage and commissions.

The 10- and 11-day dual crossover system lost $181,005 on paper, with 530 trades. Only 34 percent or 178 trades, were profitable, with a maximum intraday drawdown of $189,370. One interesting feature was that virtually all the loss ($185,545) was on short trades. This makes sense if we recognize that the market has been generally moving up since 1982. However, it is striking that this simple trend-following system fared poorly in spite of the prolonged uptrend. So the S&P-500 futures market is not a trend-follower's delight.

Because all of the losses were on the short side in the previous test, it makes sense to try the simple moving crossover system in the antitrend mode. The antitrend rules are as follows:

1. Buy if the 10-day SMA crosses below the 11-day SMA on the close.

2. Sell if the 10-day SMA crosses above the 11-day SMA on the close.

Using the same test period, initial stop, and allowance for slippage and commissions as the previous test, the turnaround in profits with the antitrend rules was remarkable. This antitrend 10- and 11-day system netted $55,920 for a swing of $240,925 on 531 trades. Fully 48 percent, or 254 trades, were profitable, with a maximum intraday drawdown of $32,735.

The results of the antitrend approach are not spectacular. However, they do highlight the unusual nature of the S&P-500 market. They suggest that you could find market-specific systems that would test poorly on other markets. For example, the 10/11 antitrend strategy lost $56,775 when tested on the Swiss franc continuous contract over the same period, but the 10/11 trend-following strategy lost just $13,088 over the same period.

The following is a glaring example of how "hindsight" influences system design. There were many "V" bottoms on the daily bar-charts of the S&P-500 market, so a bottom-fishing strategy that tries to pick bottoms was attempted. Theoretically, it should test well since this is an antitrend approach. The rules for the S&P-500 "bottom fishing" pattern are as follows:

1. A 20-day low has formed within the last 5 days.

2. Today's high-low range > X; $X = 4$ for conservative trades; $X = 1$ for aggressive trades (each point is not one tick, but one full S&P index point = $500)

3. Today's closing-opening range > Y; $Y = 3$ for conservative trades; $Y = 0$ for aggressive trades.

Table 4.20 Performance of bottom-fishing system with $2,000 initial stop and exit on the close of the twentieth day in the trade using actual S&P-500 data with rollover.

Pattern	Test Period	Net Profit ($)	Number of Trades; Percentage of Wins	Ratio: Average Win/ Loss	Average Trade ($)	Maximum Intraday Drawdown ($)	Profit Factor
X=4, Y=3	9/82–2/88	40,900	18; 44	3.80	2,272	–6,300	3.04
X=4, Y=3	2/88–7/95	60,650	46; 39	3.25	1,319	–13,675	2.09
X=1, Y=0	9/82–2/88	58,625	57; 45	2.45	1,029	–11,425	2.06
X=1, Y=0	2/88–7/95	70,600	93; 35	2.81	759	–27,125	1.54

4. If rules 1, 2, and 3 are true, then buy tomorrow on the close.

5. Exit on the close of the twentieth day in the trade.

6. Initial money management stop = $2,000 per contract.

Note that we can fully automate the bottom-fishing pattern. We have no difficulty getting entries, because if we get a signal today, we can buy on tomorrow's close. So it is easy to implement using a mechanical system. For example, the analysis can be done after market hours, and the order entered before trading begins.

This system has a conservative entry combination and an aggressive entry combination. The conservative approach generates fewer trades. You can modify this pattern in many ways. The most obvious change is the exit strategy. For example, you could set an exit target at the most recent 20-day high.

The system was tested using System Writer Plus™ and actual S&P-500 contracts. The rollover date was the twentieth day of the month before expiration. The results are in two blocks in Table 4.20 because System Writer can process only 30 contracts at a time. You can treat either the conservative or the aggressive set of X and Y values as an unoptimized set. Both combinations were profitable on both blocks of data.

The equity curves for both options are shown in Figures 4.38 and 4.39. The equity curve for the conservative option is smoother than the aggressive option. Also, the aggressive option can produce larger drawdowns than the conservative values.

Data using the March, 1995 S&P-500 contract yield Figure 4.40, for X = 4 and Y = 3, and Figure 4.41 is for X = 1 and Y = 0. This system picked off the bottoms very accurately. Entry and reduced slippage are assured by entering and exiting on the close. Thus, a pattern-based, antitrend, bottom-fishing approach works nicely on the S&P-500 market.

You can try a variety of exit strategies. Instead of an exit on the close of the twentieth day (case 1), use a trailing stop on the 5-day low after a $1,000 profit on the trade (case 2). Case 2 with $X = 4$, $Y = 3$, a $2,000 initial stop, and $100 for slippage and commissions from February 12, 1988 through July 10, 1995, had a profit of $59,025 over 44 trades (45 percent winners) with a drawdown of –$7,625. You can compare these data to the second row in Table 4.20 (case 1). Thus, the new exit strategy produced approximately the same profits, but with a smaller drawdown and more winners. The equity curves for case 1 and case 2 are shown in Figure 4.42. You can see that case 2 has shallower drawdowns than case 1.

To check the basic validity of the bottom-fishing pattern on other markets, we must modify the pattern slightly to make it more general. Values of $X = 0.1$ and $Y = 0$ are chosen in order to test across many markets. A trend-following exit, at the lowest low of the last 20 days, was chosen because not all markets are as dynamic as the S&P-500 market. The entry is switched to above the high of the signal day, instead of buying at the next day's close, to reduce the number of entries in downtrends. The initial money management stop is $2,000, and as usual, $100 is deducted for slippage and commissions. The pattern uses all

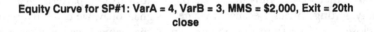

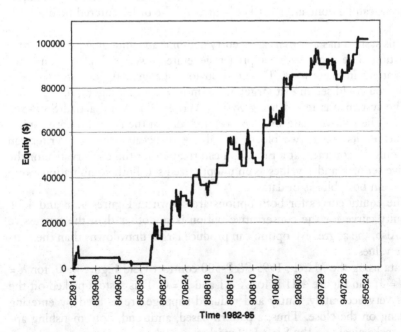

Figure 4.38 Equity curve for bottom-fishing pattern (9/82-7/95) with $X = 4$ and $Y = 3$ (conservative trades) for S&P-500 data with rollovers. Initial money management stop was $2,000 per contract.

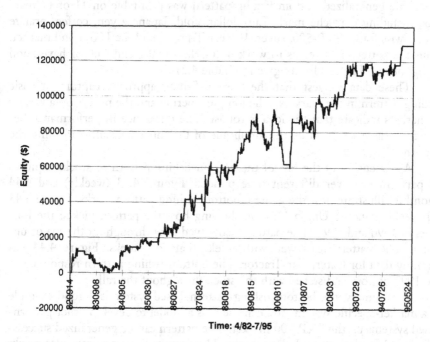

Figure 4.39   Equity curve for bottom-fishing pattern (9/82–7/95) with X = 1 and Y = 0 (aggressive trades) for S&P-500 data with rollovers. Initial money management stop was $2,000.

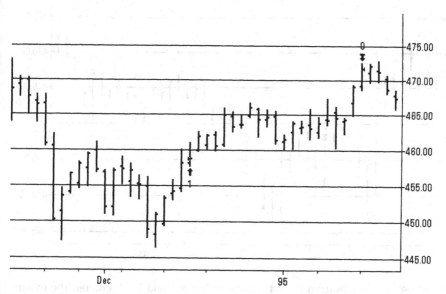

Figure 4.40   The bottom-fishing pattern with X = 4 and Y = 3 picked off the important December 1994 bottom.

available data from January 1975 through July 1995 using continuous contracts on 17 markets. The results are for trading one contract at a time.

The generalized bottom-fishing pattern was profitable on 11 of 17 markets, including deutsche mark, Eurodollar, gold, Japanese yen, coffee, orange juice, Swiss franc, S&P-500, silver, 10-year T-notes, and the U.S. bond market. Thus the pattern also seems to work on markets that trend well or have good swing moves. The results are given in Table 4.21.

These data suggest that the bottom-fishing approach captures a basic trading pattern in the markets. The long test period and the profits on a variety of markets indicate that the idea is robust. The difference in performance between markets seems to be the amplitude of the movement after forming the pattern.

An extension of the test of the bottom-fishing pattern to stocks explores its performance over different time periods. Figures 4.43 (weekly) and 4.44 (monthly) illustrate how the generic bottom-fishing pattern works. Figure 4.43 has weekly data for Union Carbide showing how the pattern picked the bottoms in 1990 and 1991. The pattern also stayed long throughout the major uptrend. The pattern tests well with weekly data on stocks. Figure 4.44 has monthly data for Caterpillar Tractor. The bottom-fishing pattern responded to the 1992 bottom and stayed with the stock throughout the rally.

In summary, the bottom-fishing pattern-based system is a good example of a market-specific system. You can use it as a model to develop other pattern-based systems on the S&P-500 market. The pattern can be generalized successfully to other markets, including stocks. The bottom-fishing pattern also works

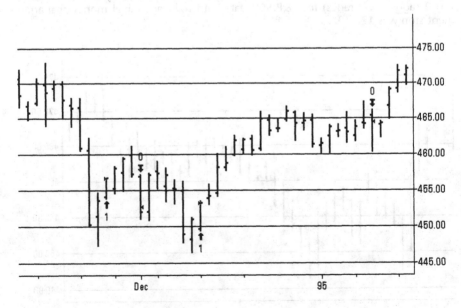

Figure 4.41   The bottom-fishing pattern with $X = 1$ and $Y = 0$ entered the market closer to the December 1994 bottom.

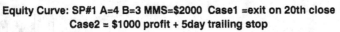

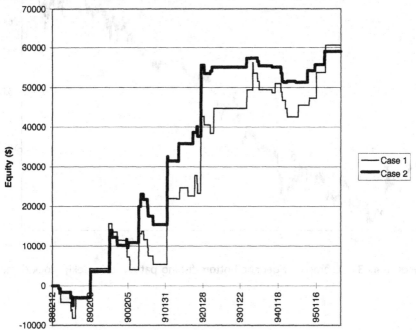

Figure 4.42   Equity curve for case 1 and case 2.

Table 4.21   Results of testing the generic bottom-fishing pattern on other markets.

Market	Profit ($)	Number of Trades	Percentage of Wins	Maximum Intraday Drawdown ($)	Profit Factor
British pound	–17,694	195	21	–6,403	0.92
Coffee	86,740	200	20	–62,251	1.36
Crude oil	–35,660	117	22	–38,000	1.43
Eurodollar	20,650	45	36	–5,825	1.71
Gold	7,510	187	25	–40,000	1.06
Heating oil	–19,687	158	23	–50,124	0.88
Japanese yen	98,513	138	30	–15,188	1.95
Live hogs	–17,853	201	22	–22,176	0.83
Orange juice	12,653	194	21	–11,978	1.16
Silver	121,970	189	23	–54,550	1.81
Soybeans	–17,869	193	25	–35,719	0.86
S&P-500	127,925	111	30	–43,065	1.64
Sugar	–23,660	175	25	–34,166	0.75
Swiss franc	64,450	162	27	–28,387	1.48

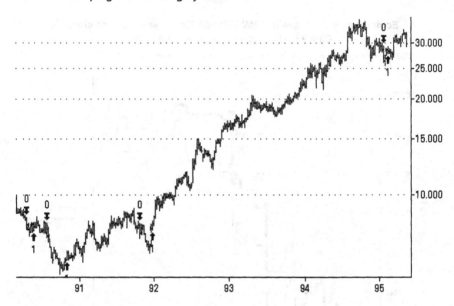

Figure 4.43   Example of generic bottom-fishing pattern on weekly stock data.

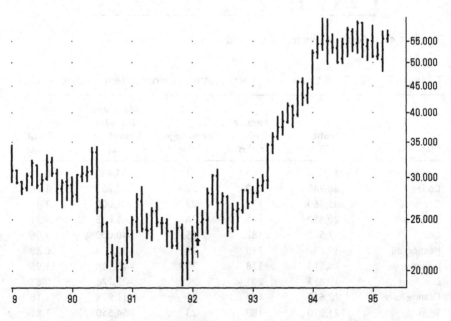

Figure 4.44   Example of generic bottom-fishing pattern on monthly stock data.

across time periods such as daily, weekly, or monthly. Thus, the bottom-fishing pattern captures a fundamental pattern of price evolution.

Identifying Extraordinary Opportunities

Once or twice a year, the futures markets provide extraordinary opportunities for exceptional profits, and if you can take advantage of these opportunities, your account performance will improve significantly. Ideally, you should try to increase position size in markets that present extraordinary opportunities. You can use a fixed formula or discretion in arriving at the increased exposure.

Figure 4.45 of the September 1995, Japanese yen contract illustrates such an extraordinary opportunity. If you had tripled your exposure to the Japanese yen during these two awesome moves, you would have made an extra $40,000 with only moderate extra risk. These are the situations when you need "the courage to be a pig," as one famous money manager has said.

The challenge for system design is to find a consistent definition of an extraordinary opportunity. Once you have a consistent definition, you can use it any way you wish. In particular, you can use discretionary trading to adjust your exposure to the markets to exploit these situations.

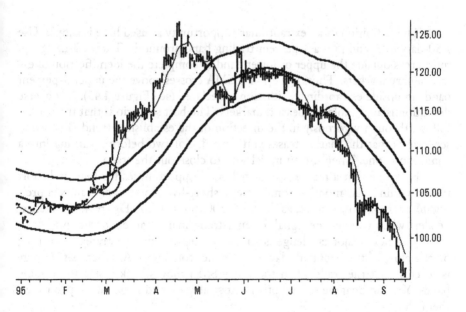

Figure 4.45   Extraordinary market opportunity identified by the 7-day SMA crossing beyond the 3 percent band around the 50-day SMA.

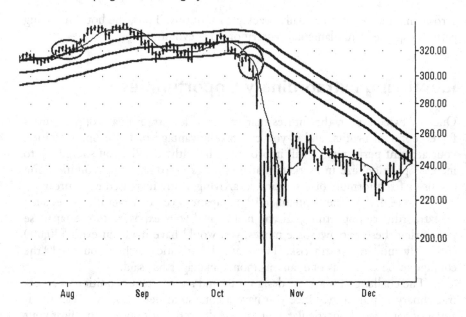

Figure 4.46   A market can signal extraordinary opportunities on the long and short side within a short period.

The definition of an extraordinary opportunity as used here is simple. Use a 50-day SMA and plot a 3-percent trading band around it. Then a 7-day SMA must cross outside the upper or lower band to complete the identification of extraordinary markets. Thus, if the 7-day SMA crosses above the upper 3-percent band, an upside extraordinary situation is declared (see Figure 4.45). A converse definition is applicable for bearish markets. The best scenario is that the market follows through vigorously in the direction of the established trend. The worst scenario is that the market teases you for a day or two before returning into a congestion zone. Then use an initial stop to close out the trade.

Be aware that a market can signal good opportunities for long and short trades within a few months. Some times a short-lived long signal can be a prelude to a strong down move, as the S&P-500 did in 1987 (Figure 4.46). Hence, be alert when you get the signal for an extraordinary market condition.

The next major challenge is an exit strategy. A simple strategy of exiting on the close of the twentieth day in the trade works well. Another exit strategy is to close out the trade when the 7-day SMA moves back inside the trading bands. You can imagine several other exit strategies, and I encourage you to test them all.

Table 4.22 summarizes a test for the extraordinary opportunity idea on all available data for several markets from January 1, 1975, through June 30, 1995. These calculations combined the usual 20-day channel breakout with the rules

Table 4.22 Performance summary with 3-percent trading band, exit on close of twentieth day in trade.

Market	Profit ($)	Winners; Total Trades	Percen-tage of Winners	Ratio: Average Win/ Loss	Profit Factor	Maximum Intraday Drawdown ($)
British pound	38,125	37; 62	60	1.08	1.60	–11,756
Coffee	122,273	69; 157	44	1.94	1.52	–34,683
Cotton	48,255	66; 123	54	1.33	1.55	–11,505
Crude oil	12,610	40; 73	55	1.08	1.31	–7,800
Deutsche mark	9,963	36; 71	51	1.15	1.19	–10,688
Gold	46,310	42; 85	49	1.75	1.71	–21,520
Heating oil	19,220	59; 117	50	1.18	1.20	–17,822
Japanese yen	18,225	34; 71	48	1.42	1.31	–16,638
Live hogs	10,805	82; 149	55	0.94	1.15	–11,832
Soybeans	25,756	49; 107	46	1.50	1.26	–25,675
S&P-500	28,040	22; 58	38	2.08	1.27	–27,932
Swiss Franc	19,187	44; 85	52	1.14	1.22	–15,050
10-year T-Note	3,918	88; 18	44	1.53	1.23	–7,506
U.S. bond	3,468	34; 65	54	0.89	1.04	–27,932
Average	29,011		50	1.36	1.33	–17,739

for declaring an extraordinary market opportunity. The long entry rule requires that the 7-day SMA be beyond 1.03 times the 50-day SMA in order to purchase just above the highest high of the last 20 days. The opposite conditions are needed for the short trades. The exit was on the close of the twentieth day, and as usual, a $3,000 stop and $100 for slippage and commissions were used, to allow for a more accurate test.

The long test period (20 years in some cases), the wide diversity of markets, and the relatively high proportion of winning trades suggests this strategy is a valid approach toward identifying extraordinary market opportunities. The MIDD numbers suggest that the exit strategy is critical to the success of this system. As an example, the results of adding a trailing stop and narrowing the bands are shown in Table 4.23.

In our discussion of risk of ruin, we assumed the following constant parameters: probability of winning, payoff ratio, and fraction committed to trading. However, in actual trading, the probability of winning and payoff ratio change with time. Hence, you should consider changing your fraction of capital risked on a trade, especially if an extraordinary market opportunity is recognized.

Table 4.23 Performance results with 1 percent trading band and trailing 20-day stop.

Market	Profit ($)	Winners; Total Trades	Percent-age of Winners	Ratio: Average Win/ Loss	Profit Factor	Maximum Intraday Drawdown ($)
British pound	146,544	47; 93	51	2.39	2.44	–17,319
Coffee	242,119	47; 118	40	3.84	2.49	–26,970
Cotton	58,135	46; 100	46	2.21	1.56	–19,160
Crude oil	4,740	28; 69	39	0.73	1.11	–8,020
Deutsche mark	69,526	48; 94	51	1.90	1.98	–10,425
Gold	29,360	41; 112	37	2.29	1.32	–27,170
Heating oil	44,177	42; 101	42	2.11	1.50	–26,879
Japanese yen	99,400	46; 87	53	2.32	2.60	–11,338
Live hogs	53,768	57; 108	53	1.88	2.10	–9,376
Soybeans	45,688	44; 116	38	2.58	1.57	–19,275
S&P-500	–25,955	25; 105	23	2.44	0.73	–79,710
Swiss franc	80,338	50; 101	50	1.97	1.93	–9,188
10-year T-note	37,768	22; 58	38	2.60	1.65	–5,206
U.S. bond	57,100	35; 90	39	2.28	1.5	–16,075
Average	67,336		43	2.25	1.75	–20,437

The test results in this chapter are with just one contract; this is an opportunity to use discretion and increase your exposure to the markets. Hence, the potential impact on returns can be quite significant with multiple contracts, based on the one-contract results shown here. You also have the option of using discretionary exits, or other exits based on shorter term data, such as an hourly chart.

Remember that you can check fundamental developments to confirm the presence of extraordinary market conditions. For example, there may be an unusual weather pattern, a political development, or a crop failure, to name just a few of the types of events you can read about in the financial press. In a purely technical sense, you do not need the confirmation from fundamental analysis. However, if unusual fundamental conditions exist, that may give you clues as to the probable duration and potential amplitude of possible market movements, and help you determine how you could adjust the size of your position.

Performance Update: 65sma-3cc System

A retest of the 65sma-3cc was performed on a globally diversified portfolio from January 1995 through July 2000 using a $5,000 initial risk, variable-contract

Table 4.24   Globally diversified portfolio for the 65sma-3cc system.

Energy	Grains	Short Rates	Stock Indices
Heating Oil	CBT Corn	Canadian Banker's Accpt	Aussie All Ordinaries
IPE Brent Crude	CBT Wheat	Eurodollars	CAC-40 Index
IPE Gas Oil	Kansas Wheat	Euro Swiss Franc	DAX Index
NY Crude Oil	Soybean Meal	LIFFE Euribor	FTSE-100 Index
NY Natural Gas	Soybean Oil	NZ Bank Bills	Hang Seng index
Unleaded Gasoline	Soybeans	Short sterling	Ibex 35
	Tokyo Red Beans	SIMEX EuroYen	MIB-30 Index
	WCE Rapeseed		SIMEX Nikkei 225
			SOM OMX Index
			Swiss Market Index
IMM Currencies	Metals	Long Bonds	Softs
Aussie Dollar	Gold Comex	Australian 10-yr Bond	Orange Juice
British Pound	Hi Grade Copper	Australian 3-yr Bond	NY Cotton
Canadian Dollar	NY Silver	Canadian Govt Bond	Sugar #11
D-Mark/Euro	Tokyo Palladium	Eurex BOBL	Tokyo Rubber
Japanese Yen		Eurex Bund	
Mexican Peso		Long Gilts	
Swiss Franc	Meats	Matif Notional	
	Live Cattle	Simex JGB	
	Live Hogs	Spanish Govt Bond	
		Swiss Fed Bond	
		US 30-yr T-Bonds	
		US 5yr Note	

trade sizing using the 50-day average true range and allowing $100 for slippage and commissions. This is a long-term trend-following system that should bene-fit from portfolio diversification. The portfolio is shown in Table 4.24.

This model is currently in the midst of a drawdown that started in Sep-tember 1998 (see Figure 4.47). In addition, the current leverage is probably too high, with a monthly standard deviation of about 14 percent before interest and fees. However, the return efficiency is a respectable 0.25, in line with bench-marks discussed later in this book. The average monthly return before fees and interest was 3.45 percent, implying raw annual returns in the 50 percent range. The worst theoretical drawdown was 43 percent, in line with recent stock mar-ket declines, and about three times the standard deviation of monthly returns, also in line with the discussion to follow in Chapter 7. The calculations confirm the validity of the original model and the robust nature of basic trend-following systems that use few parameters and can be traded on a broadly diversified port-folio without changing parameters.

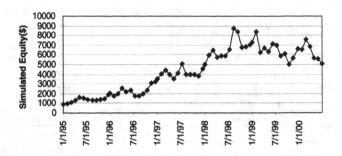

Figure 4.47   True out-of-sample equity curve for the 65sma-3cc system.

The 22-month length of the current drawdown has exceeded the length of all previous drawdowns but is below the theoretical projection of 33 months. It still raises concerns about the level of portfolio diversification and the slow exits of the model. The best one can hope for is a strong recovery because it is unusual to have such a long drawdown in a diversified portfolio.

ATR-Band Breakout Model

We can extend the idea of the extraordinary opportunity system by devising volatility-based bands. The simplest definition of a band breakout model is the use of breakout levels a fixed percentage above and below an intermediate to long-term moving average. These types of bands were the basis of the extraordinary opportunity system. The idea of bands can be interpreted to mean a moving barrier that can be based on any imaginable criterion. One class of such bands is that of volatility bands, in which the volatility can be measured with average true range (ATR) or the standard deviation of prices. The principal benefit of this extension is to make the bands adaptive, that is, responsive to market volatility. When the volatility is low, the breakout barrier is closer to the moving average. Conversely, near the tops and bottoms of trends, volatility is relatively higher, and the bands are farther apart.

Band breakout models share all of the benefits of breakout-style systems with the additional advantage that they adapt to the market. Such systems can be applied easily to a global portfolio. The bands can be based on any measure of price change that adapts to market action. Let us now examine bands based on average true range. We use a 50-day moving average for convenience, and build bands by averaging the daily true range over the last 50 days (ATR50). Thus, the bands are located one ATR50 range above and below the 50-day simple moving average. The long and short exits are at the 25-day simple moving

Figure 4.48   Equity curve for a volatility-band system, which is an extension of the extraordinary opportunity system. Note the vertical axis is drawn to show the growth in the value of a $1,000, instead of a $1,000,000, account.

average of the close because we want to avoid trading in congestions. We use two times the ATR50 and $5,000 risk to trade multiple contracts. The portfolio is composed of the major liquid markets in North America, Europe, and the Pacific Rim, covering the major sectors, such as stock indices, long and short interest rates, energies, currencies, agriculturals, and softs. Thus, we are testing a nonoptimized, prespecified system on a broadly diversified portfolio.

The simulated equity curve with a $100 allowance for slippage and commission is shown in Figure 4.48. The average monthly return, without fees or interest, is 2.9 percent, and the standard deviation of monthly returns is 8.9 percent. This works out to a return efficiency of approximately 0.33, with a maximum drawdown of just under 20 percent (~2.25 sigma). There were 11 drawdown streaks since January 1, 1995, the average drawdown being 4 months. However, a fit of the exponential distribution to the drawdown streaks suggests a potential "worst" case drawdown length of 22 months.

These calculations show the strengths and weaknesses of breakout-style systems. These systems are robust, and many markets can be traded with the same parameters. They are vulnerable to false breakouts, and their primary resistance to drawdowns comes from portfolio diversity. However, should the correlations between markets shift, or should the major groups not have sustained trends, a prolonged drawdown will result.

Trading Stocks

All of the ideas developed so far in this chapter can be used to trade stocks. In this section, we develop and test the trend-following model on futures and stocks. We begin by discussing the strategic differences between futures and stocks as they relate to portfolio design and trading systems.

The simplest stock-trading approach is a multiyear, long only, buy-and-hold strategy. In general, it is difficult to beat a buy-and-hold strategy on stocks that are in a secular uptrend because the buy-and-hold strategy is a trend-following model without trailing stops. Thus, the buy-and-hold strategy can withstand large percentage retracements as well as long-lasting retracements (that last 12 months or more) without exiting the position. This strategy is always in the market, so you are unlikely to miss sudden, large moves in a stock you own. Note further that the buy-and-hold strategy has low transaction costs and is a tax-efficient strategy because there are no tax consequences to holding a stock with unrealized gains. One can approach the buy-and-hold stocks strategy with futures by using very slow exit strategies that will hold a position for 65 trading days of longer. However, almost by definition, a buy-and-hold strategy is impossible to execute using futures contracts because, unlike stocks, futures contracts expire according to a prespecified schedule. Thus, a buy-and-hold strategy using futures has large transaction costs and tax consequences.

Another key difference between futures and stocks is the leverage implicit in the approach. The buy-and-hold strategy is typically an unleveraged strategy, so the effect of volatility is muted when compared to futures trading. The leverage in futures necessitates profit-taking strategies (i.e., exits) that will lock in gains in a position. When any profit-taking approach is applied to trading stocks, we immediately have tax consequences, and we will often be late entering and exiting moves. Thus, for a stock-trading strategy to be successful, the choice of the stocks being traded is critical.

The trade sizing algorithms are also significantly different for futures and stocks because of the varying contract sizes and available leverage. The equity in one's account will limit the quantity and number of stocks that can be traded. In futures, there is an extra factor: one's account equity and the desired leverage determine the size of positions. However, the amount of cash actually required to put on positions is much larger in trading stocks. Thus, it may be easier to purchase 1,000 instead of, say, 50,000 shares of a stock because of the equity in the portfolio and liquidity considerations.

The duration of the average trade will depend on the time frames used for analysis. Monthly, weekly, and daily data can be used with stocks to follow the long-term trend. The essential choice for stocks is between weekly and daily data, with trade durations being approximately five times longer with weekly data. The more volatile a stock, the shorter the needed time frame of analysis. Hence, for technology stocks, daily data may be more relevant than weekly data. You will be closer to a buy-and-hold strategy with weekly data than with daily data because of the longer time frame for analysis.

A variety of stock selection screens can be developed to identify stocks that are in favor. It is best to trade stocks that are in leading industry groups. The new highs list, the most actives list, and the holdings of leading mutual funds are good places to find stocks that may be worth trading. *Investor's Business Daily* prints a number of proprietary performance measures and offers graphical chart reviews to help identify leading stocks. Over time, different groups come into favor and go out of favor, as the "story" changes. Hence, reading the financial press will help isolate popular investment themes. The results of your trading using the same system on all stocks will be highly dependent on the stocks you choose to include in your portfolio.

The following momentum-based model uses a long-term trend-following approach on stocks in well-defined uptrends. Using this model, we want to buy when the stock is in a definable uptrend and makes new 20-day highs in price accompanied by strong momentum, as measured by the ADX indicator. We use daily prices and the 65-day simple moving average (SMA65) as references, and assume that the trend is up if the current close is above the SMA65 and the highest high of the past 20 days is also above the SMA65. We then add a condition that confirms that the stock is indeed trending higher. We use the average directional index (ADX) indicator and require that the current value of the 18-day ADX be above 20. The choice of the ADX indicator and its reference level is based on a "general rule" from futures trading. If both conditions are satisfied, then we set the entry price two-ticks above the highest 20-day high. Now a single tick is the minimum increment in which the stock trades, which may be, say, one-hundredth of a currency unit or some other value based on the exchange on which the stock is traded.

The trade sizing algorithm uses a retracement distance ("Dist") or risk of three times the average 40-day true range (ATR40). The true range is measure of the "effective" daily price range that is popular with futures traders, and allows for gaps in prices. The true range is the difference between the true high (today's high or yesterday's close, whichever is higher) and the true low (today's low or yesterday's close, whichever is lower). The true range is a measure of the range of price action or "volatility"; the higher the ATR40, the greater the market volatility at that point in time. We convert the ATR40 into dollars (or any other currency unit) by multiplying the ATR40 by the value of 1 full point change (the so-called "BigPointValue") in the value of the stock, usually $1 or 1 currency unit. Note that the BigPointValue can vary widely among futures contracts. We then calculate position size by dividing the equity at risk, in this case $5,000, by the dollar value of the ATR40. Note how the size varies inversely as the volatility. When prices have consolidated, volatility is relatively low and the size of the position is relatively high.

Our exit strategy is very simple: merely the trailing SMA65. This fulfills the requirement that we stay with the trending stock as long as possible. If one uses daily data, the SMA65 is relatively far away from prices and can absorb a fair amount of adverse price movement without being shaken out of position. The ability to absorb adverse movements is considerably greater with weekly data. The ADX condition tries to protect us from the scenario in which the stock is trading choppily, and the 20-day highest high is not too far from the SMA65, so that the stock repeatedly makes new 20-day highs and then retraces down to the SMA65. Thus, a secondary benefit of the ADX indicator is to protect account equity in choppy markets. The actual Omega Research TradeStation™ software code is:

```
{--- Code for Omega Research TradeStation ---}
{--- Momentum Trend System for Stocks and Futures ---}
{--- © 2000 Tushar Chande ---}
    Inputs:  Eqty(5000);
    Vars   : NumLong(0), Dist(0) ;

{---- Contract calculations ---}

    Dist = 3*Average(Truerange, 40);
    {-- convert to currency units --}
    Dist = Dist*BigPointValue ;
    {-- protect division by zero --}
    If Dist > 0 then
            NumLong = intPortion( Eqty / Dist)
    Else        NumLong = 0 ;

{--- Entry Signals ---}

    if c > average(C,65) and highest(h,20)[1] >
    average(C,65) and adx(18) > 20 then buy NumLong
    contracts at highest(h,20) + 2 points stop;

{---- Exit Signals ---}

    Exitlong at average(C,65) stop ;

{--- End of Code ---}
```

Let us now see how this system works on stocks and futures. Figure 4.49 shows an entry into Veritas Software Corp (VRTS) stock in August 1999. Notice that the close was above the SMA65 (crosses) as was the 20-day highest high. The 18-day ADX was above its reference level of 20. Thus, VRTS met our entry conditions, and the system opened a long position at a new 20-day high in late August with a suggested size of 1,088 shares. Figure 4.50 shows how the trade evolved into 2000. The rally in technology stocks in late 1999-early 2000 carried VRTS substantially higher. The strength of the trend kept the 18-day ADX above the reference level throughout the rally. The correction in technology stocks in March 2000 caught up with VRTS, and it crashed through its SMA65, triggering an exit.

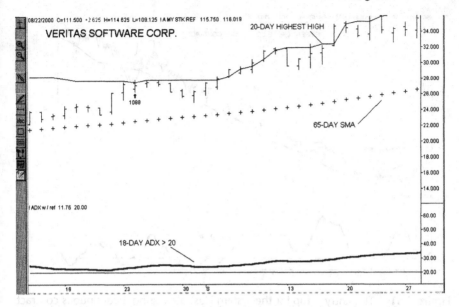

Figure 4.49 A daily chart for Veritas Software Corporation stock showing the building blocks of the system. The entry conditions are satisfied when the 18-day ADX indicator is greater than 20 and the daily close and the 20-day highest high price are both above the 65-day SMA of the close. The entry price is two-ticks above the 20-day high.

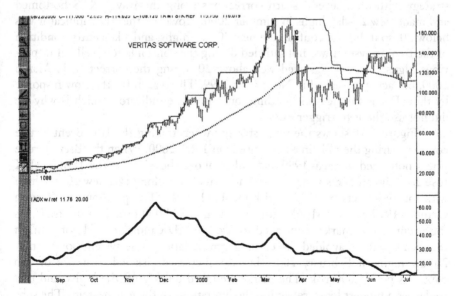

Figure 4.50 The system exits Veritas stock at the 65-day SMA of the close, shown here by the dotted line. The trend was exceptionally strong because the 18-day ADX stayed above 20 for the duration of the move.

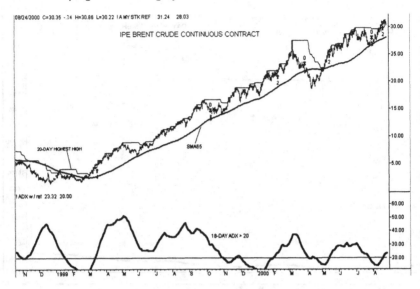

08/24/2000 C=30.35 -.34 H=30.86 L=30.22 I A MY STK REF   31.24   28.03

Figure 4.51   The entry setup for the system illustrated using a continuous contract of the London IPE Brent Crude futures contract. The entries work similarly on stocks and futures—buying strength in a rising market with confirmation of trend strength.

Note how the relatively slow exit strategy did give up a significant portion of open trade equity before actually closing the position. However, this same strategy withstood several sharp corrections along the way. VRTS bottomed and made new 20-day highs in summer 2000. However, the ADX indicator was below 20, so it did not confirm the new 20-day highs, and a key entry condition of the trading system was not satisfied during the consolidation well below previous highs. The ADX stayed well above 20 during the correction in March 2000, but actually peaked in November 1999. The reason for the slow response by the ADX is the heavy smoothing built into the indicator, which is why we did not use the it to trigger exits.

Figure 4.51 shows the same strategy when trading the IPE Brent Crude contract during the rally in energy prices in 1999–2000. When the Brent Crude prices bottomed in early 1999 and rallied above the SMA65, the 18-day ADX rose also, signaling a strong trend. The system went long at a new 20-day high with four contracts per $5,000 risk in March 1999. The position was close in October 1999 at the SMA65 with more than a $32,000 profit on the trade. As the Brent Crude market continued to rise, the ADX indicator did not confirm the trend, and we avoided the ensuing consolidation. The system bought new 20-day highs in February 2000, but the increased risk led to a size of two contracts per $5,000 risk. The market retraced quickly off the highs, and that trade was a modest loser, reflecting the limitations of the exit strategy. The subsequent sell-off helped the ADX to adjust to rising prices, so that it signaled a strong rally in May 2000. Notice how the SMA65 can absorb considerable ad-

Figure 4.52   The system applied to a continuous contract of the Paris MATIF Notional Bond futures contract showing that the entry conditions can be satisfied by a stock or market without significant follow through, causing trading losses.

verse price action in futures, just as it does in stocks, but needs smooth trends to lock in substantial profits. The Brent Crude example illustrates the similarity of trends in stocks and futures, and how the same technical rules can be used on both, producing similar responses during trends. Naturally, if the markets do not trend smoothly, or retrace rapidly off new highs, then this system will be unprofitable because it is not designed to react to those scenarios.

Figure 4.52 illustrates the scenario in which the market satisfies the entry conditions of the system but does not follow through sufficiently to be profitable. We examine the Paris MATIF Notional Bond as it rallied after a long downtrend and then continued to consolidate after putting in a bottom. Note that the ADX will often behave like a coincident indicator rather than a leading indicator because it is also derived from closing prices. Hence, a "high" value of ADX is not sufficient to signal a strong trend that persists for many weeks or months.

This system can be used to trade mutual funds using daily data in the same manner as any other stock. Figure 4.53 shows the results of trading the Janus Twenty mutual fund. The length of the average trade was 98 days; there were just ten trades from September 15, 1993, through August 1, 2000; and the trading profits would be $193,436, assuming "zero" transaction costs. However, this would have paled in comparison to the buy-and-hold gains over the same period because the fund was in a multiyear uptrend, increasing some 16-fold over the period. The capital outlay for this trading strategy would also have been substantial, varying from $80,000 to more than $150,000. Hence, the po-

Figure 4.53 The system applied to a diversified portfolio of stocks, represented here by the Janus Twenty mutual fund.

tential benefits of trading mutual funds should be carefully analyzed, given the broad correlation between funds.

What is a good size for a portfolio of stocks? It is difficult to find a consensus on this issue, and there are too many subjective issues to permit a fully objective answer; however, a number between 30 and 50 seems to be reasonable. Some support for this range is evident in industry practice, as shown by the following examples. The instantly recognizable Dow Jones Industrial Average has 30 stocks. Several mutual fund families offer portfolios concentrated in 20 to 50 stocks, with the Janus Twenty fund embedding this concept in its name. Many so-called "diversified" billion-dollar plus mutual funds have 80 to 120 stocks, with 15 to 40 percent of the fund concentrated in 10 stocks. Over half the value of the NASDAQ index is concentrated in the top 30 stocks. Hence, a number between 30 and 50 seems to be a good guess for the size of a "well-diversified" portfolio. The same size constraint can also be applied to futures portfolios.

For completeness, we tested the stocks system on a diversified portfolio futures market. A simulated equity curve for a constant $1,000,000 account with $5,000 risked per trade is shown in Figure 4.54. The monthly standard deviation was 4.6 percent, and the average hypothetical monthly return was 1.2 percent, yielding a return efficiency of 0.26. The length of the average trade was 75 days, the longest drawdown streak was 13 months, and 61 percent of the months had positive returns. The overall performance of the system was quite respectable for a simple trend-following system, and illustrates that it is possible to build simple systems that can work on both stocks and futures.

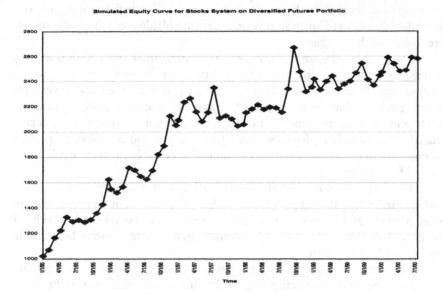

Figure 4.54   The equity curve of the system applied to diversified futures portfolio.

Summary

In this chapter we examined seven major systems, each exploring a different philosophy. The 65sma-3cc system is a simple trend-following system that offers solid performance. We examined this system in great detail. You should perform such a detailed analysis of your systems. We used many important ideas such as maximum favorable and adverse excursions, frequency distribution of trades, and the effect of a volatility-based initial stop. You should endeavor to understand these ideas and use them often. In summary, the 65sma-3cc system was a robust and profitable system that makes money in trending periods. About 4 percent of the trades were mega-trades, and you should pick your exit strategies carefully so as not to cut off such trades prematurely.

The channel breakout-pullback (CB-PB) system was our first pattern-based system for long trades. The system gives reliable long entries; it was profitable about 55 percent of the time without stops or exits over many markets. Our tests with different exit strategies found that the CB-PB system provides low-risk entries and can be easily adapted to many trading styles. CB-PB does well in short- to intermediate-term systems on active markets. In summary, we showed how we can develop very different systems of the same entry signal.

The ADX burst trend-seeking system uses a filter based on the strength of the trend. It successfully provides entries into strong trends. The system has a large neutral zone so it is in the market only 35 to 45 percent of the time.

We next looked at the trend-antitrend (T-AT) system, which automatically switches between antitrend and trend-following modes. This system often picks tops and bottoms with surprising accuracy. It is essential to use good risk control with a system such as this because the volatility can trap you on the wrong side of the market.

The gold-bond system allows us to use intermarket analysis on positively or negatively correlated markets. This system tries to capture weak intermarket relationships. It can be used with or without a trend filter. We found several interesting relationships between the U.S. bond market and the gold, copper, soybeans, and currency markets. We extended the gold bond system to look at correlated markets such as deutsche mark–Japanese yen and corn–live hogs. At a minimum, you can use this system to evaluate a favorable or unfavorable background for your trading.

The bottom-fishing pattern started off as a market-specific system for trading the S&P-500 futures. We found that the pattern can be generalized to other markets, as well as to stocks. The pattern also works on daily, weekly, or monthly data. Thus, we captured a fundamental feature of price behavior in markets with this pattern.

The extraordinary opportunity system is primarily a flag to vary bet size during trading. It is an effective trend-following system in its own right. It assumes that during major moves, a significant portion of the move will be outside 1-percent or 3-percent trading bands drawn around a 50-day SMA.

The true out-of-sample calculations for the 65sma-3cc system show that this is a robust system with respectable risk-adjusted performance. They also show that drawdowns can last a long time unless a majority of the markets has sustained trends. The ATR band system is similar to the extraordinary opportunity system and shows how to create robust, unoptimized systems that can be specified a priori, before testing any individual markets. Thus, the ideas presented in this section can be used to trade stocks and futures by testing the same system on both types of instruments.

You will notice that we did not follow the usual practice of dividing the test period into two or more subintervals, "perfecting" our system on one interval, and then testing it on the remaining data. This procedure exposes the system to new data, and its performance on such "out-of-sample" data is used to determine how well it might work in the future. If you do test many combinations of parameters, try to find the most "stable" combination. Stability means that the system is profitable across most of the test data, and results do not change suddenly for small variations in test conditions. A detailed discussion of this approach is found in Babcock, Chande and Kroll, Pardo, and Schwager among others (see bibliography).

Instead of relying on testing alone, here we have focused on the ideas driving the trading strategy. We tested these systems on all available data over 20 years without optimization. Thus, we stressed our systems to check if they were based on valid market dynamics that can be tapped for future trading profits. These systems are examples of the art of building new strategies around a particular market intuition. In the next chapter we examine how you can modify well-known, proven ideas to create useful variations for your collection of trading systems.

Appendix to Chapter 4: Additional Performance Updates

This performance update was completed at the end of December 2000, well after an initial updates for the second edition discussed in detail in the text. In the interest of brevity and simplicity, we used a smaller portfolio (of 30 futures markets around the world representing all subsectors), a single trend-following exit strategy (exiting on high or low of the past 20 days), and an initial risk of $50,000 (or 5 percent per million) to generate trades even in high-volatility markets such as the S&P-500 index futures.

The CB-PB system (Channel Breakout Pullback) barely broke even on the original portfolio of six markets, but was unprofitable on the diversified portfolio because a majority of those markets were not trending higher over the test period. It probably needs additional filtering to make it more successful.

The ADX-Burst system tested well on the portfolio of 30 markets, with an average annual return since January 1995 of approximately 33 percent, a monthly standard deviation of 12.4 percent, and a worst peak-to-valley drawdown of 35 percent, just three times the monthly standard deviation. The equity curve peaked in September 1998, along with other trend-followers, and has rebounded smartly to within 13 percent of the 1998 high at the end of 2000. The return efficiency was a respectable 0.19, in line with other trend-following systems.

The T-AT (Trend-Antitrend) system tested poorly on the diversified 30 market portfolio, barely breaking even. It had a relatively low correlation to trend-following systems as one might expect, at 0.43. However, that was not sufficient compensation to trade this system on a highly diversified portfolio.

The Gold-Bond system was profitable over the last six years. The idea behind this system is to be short the U.S. long bond futures when gold prices were trending up strongly (and vice versa) because rising gold prices are supposed to be signaling the start of an inflationary period. The test period was from January 1, 1995 through December 21, 2000, providing an overlap of approximately 7 months over the data set used in the first edition. We used $50,000 as the initial risk to generate trades of sufficient size for all signals. This reversal system was profitable, reporting profits of $229,669 over 42 trades and a profit factor of 1.39, as shown in Table 4.25. Thus, this true out-of-sample test confirms the premise of the tests from the first edition.

This S&P-500 bottom-fishing pattern seeks to trade the V-Bottoms often seen in the S&P-500 index with a trend-following exit. We tested the S&P-500 from January 1, 1995 through December 21, 2000, using a $50,000 initial risk. With an exit on the close of the twentieth day, the tests reported a profit of $668,150 with 62 trades and a profit factor of 1.57. Thus, the retest on a true

Table 4.25   Performance table for Gold-Bond system (01/01/1995 through 12/21/2000).

Net Profit	$229,669	Open position P/L	$11,500
Gross Profit	$816,200	Gross loss	($586,531)
Total number of trades	42	Percent profitable	48%
Number of winning trades	20	Number of losing trades	22
Largest winning trade	$137,700	Largest losing trade	($52,369)
Average winning trade	$40,810	Average losing trade	($26,661)
Ratio average win/ average loss	1.53	Average trade	$5,468
Maximum consecutive winners	3	Maximum consecutive losers	4
Average number of bars in winners	50	Average number of bars in losers	15
Maximum intraday drawdown	($195,975)		
Profit Factor	1.39	Maximum number of contracts	20
Account size required	$195,975	Return on account	117%

Table 4.26   Performance for S&P-500 bottom-fishing system (01/01/1995 through 12/21/2000.

Net Profit	$668,150	Open position P/L	$0
Gross Profit	$1,843,025	Gross loss	($1,174,875)
Total number of trades	62	Percent profitable	37%
Number of winning trades	23	Number of losing trades	39
Largest winning trade	$282,975	Largest losing trade	($50,400)
Average winning trade	$80,132	Average losing trade	($30,125)
Ratio average win/ average loss	2.66	Average trade	$10,776
Maximum consecutive winners	3	Maximum consecutive losers	9
Average number of bars in winners	20	Average number of bars in losers	6
Maximum intraday drawdown	($286,025)		
Profit Factor	1.57	Maximum number of contracts	21
Account size required	$286,025	Return on account	234%

out-of-sample data validates the premise of the system discussed in the first edition. The test results are summarized in Table 4.26.

We retested the extraordinary opportunity system on the 30 market global futures portfolio using a 1 percent band around the 50-day moving average and exits on the 20-day high and low. The 1 percent band was tested to get more trades than the 3 percent band. Note that even the 1 percent band was too wide to generate any trades in the Eurodollar and Euribor contracts, two markets that generally favor long-term trend-following models. The average annual return from January 1995 through December 2000 was approximately 31 percent, with a monthly standard deviation of 11.3 percent, and a worst drawdown of 66 percent. The relatively large drawdown and the prolonged flat period implies that the portfolio is not sufficiently diversified. It would be better to use volatility bands, as discussed earlier in this chapter, because the specification of a band at 1 percent is arbitrary and not related to the underlying volatility.

Chapter

Developing Trading System Variations

Even change is never the same.

Introduction

This chapter explores how you can take existing ideas and then develop variations that suit your trading style. In this way, you can build a large collection of trading systems that meet different objectives. Every trader has different beliefs, time horizons, equity limitations, profit objectives, and confidence levels. Hence, few traders are executing precisely the same strategy. Thus you can trade even well-known systems without much difficulty. However, you can gain an edge by developing your variations of well-known ideas. As usual, this is not a recommendation of specific ideas for trading, but an attempt to stimulate your creativity. The focus should be on how each variation changes the structure of the trading system and its response to market data.

We first consider the 20-day or 4-week breakout system, perhaps one of the oldest mechanical trading systems in the business. We set the stage by looking at the results of a 20-bar breakout on the close using two different exit strategies. One exit strategy is a simple x-day trailing exit, but the other is a more complex volatility-based exit. The first variation is using a fixed barrier above the 20-day range. The next step, after a fixed barrier, is to consider systems with a variable or volatility-based barrier.

In an interesting twist, instead of adding, we will deduct a volatility-based "barrier" from the 20-day channel, and examine the statistical significance of these channel breakout variations. All these variations should convince you that it is possible to take a proven idea and then adapt it to your needs or trading style.

We then look at two models based on the ADX indicator. The average directional index measures the strength of price trends. You will see that the heavily smoothed ADX reduces trades without missing major trends. We first test the effects of using a fixed ADX level to trigger the trades, and next, impose the restriction that the ADX be rising. You will see that the absolute level of the ADX is not as significant as its trend.

You may have heard this bit of trading advice, "Buy on a pullback into support." This advice by itself is not sufficient to build a trading system, but we will discuss a pullback system that works in uptrends as well as downtrends.

This chapter ends with a pattern-based system for long entries only. The deep pass in football inspired the "long bomb" system. With this system you can gather useful patterns off your favorite charts.

We will test these systems without optimization. Model values are chosen at random, before any testing, so that the test results do not bias the selection. The systems are tested on the same data set so you can understand the subtle interactions between system rules and market action. You should try to develop your variations of well-known ideas to find the particular combinations that best suit your trading style and meet your goals.

We chose the markets in Table 5.1 for testing simply because they represent a diverse group that had shown strong trends, periods of volatility, and many consolidations. The tests used an initial stop of $1,500 and allowed $100 for slippage and commissions.

Table 5.1 Summary of markets and test periods used in this chapter.

Market	Test Period
British pound	2/75–7/95
Coffee	1/75–7/95
Crude oil	1/83–7/95
Cotton	1/75–7/95
Deutsche mark	2/75–7/95
Eurodollar	2/82–7/95
Gold	1/75–7/95
Japanese yen	8/76–7/95
U.S. bond	8/77–7/95
Wheat	1/75–7/95

Channel Breakout on Close with Trailing Stops

We begin by examining the effect of adding a trailing stop to the usual channel breakout system. Our purpose is to convert the channel breakout logic into a short-term trading system. The logic of the channel breakout on close is probably familiar to you. The symmetrical long and short entry rules are as follows:

1. If today's close is higher than the highest high of the last 20 days, then buy on the close.

2. If today's close is lower than the lowest low of the last 20 days, then sell on the close.

The exit condition is a simple trailing stop placed at the highest high or lowest low of the last few days. In our case, we want to use a 5-day trailing stop. The exit conditions are as follows:

3. Exit the long trade at the lowest low of the last 5 days on a stop.

4. Exit the short trade at the highest high of the last 5 days on a stop.

We assume that the market will make quick, decisive moves once it breaks out of the 20-day channel. The implication is that we can use a relatively tight trailing stop to protect most of the profits. A close stop works well in markets that make swing moves. Conversely, this close trailing stop will exit too soon during prolonged trends. You may see more than one trade during long-trending periods because the system will generate a new trade on a fresh breakout beyond the barrier. Table 5.2 gives the results of the historical tests using a $1,500 initial stop, trading one contract per signal, and allowing $100 for slippage and commissions.

The basic 20-bar breakout system is a typical trend-following system, with 36 percent profitable trades and an average win-loss ratio greater than 2. Sixty-three percent of the profits are from just one market, coffee. The average profit factor (the ratio of gross profit to gross loss) is 1.19, so the system produces slightly more profits than losses. The average trade at $112 is barely acceptable, partly the result of staying in the trade for only a short time.

The 2,195 total trades suggest that trading costs and slippage are a significant factor in overall performance. Losses in four of the ten markets tested are a bit worrisome. The average profit is not much greater than the average maximum drawdown, which is another concern.

These tests used an exit on the highest high or lowest low of the last 5 days. The 5-day high or low exit strategy assumes that the market will make a strong move after making new 20-day highs. The following two cases show how this exit works in practice. In the case of wheat (see Figure 5.1), the market was in a choppy uptrend. A choppy uptrend is weak, because the market consolidates after making new highs. Our exit on the 5-day high or low closes out the

Table 5.2   Historical results for 20-bar breakout on the close with exit on the 5-day high or low.

Market	Profit ($)	Number of Trades	Percent-age of Wins	Win/Loss Ratio	Average Trade ($)	Maximum Intraday Draw-down ($)	Profit Factor
British pound	38,869	259	34	2.35	150	–21338	1.21
Coffee	177,438	255	38	3.26	696	–24,414	2.03
Cotton	–1,300	260	35	1.81	–5	–23,275	0.99
Crude oil	–43,230	157	29	1.10	–275	–44,230	0.44
Deutsche mark	38,575	229	43	1.86	168	–12,800	1.42
Eurodollar	14,225	142	45	1.71	100	–5,175	1.40
Gold	19,180	222	31	2.67	86	–36,870	1.18
Japanese yen	64,913	201	44	2.01	323	–11,388	1.56
U.S. bond	–5,013	222	36	1.71	–23	–35,994	0.96
Wheat	–24,169	248	29	1.61	–97	–32,475	0.67
Total	279,488	2,195					
Average	27,949	220	36	2.01	112	–24,796	1.19

trade in the consolidation region following new highs. Hence, in the choppy uptrend of the wheat market, there is a string of short-lived trades.

The next case (see Figure 5.2), presents the ideal trade for the current exit strategy. The coffee market made a strong move upward once it broke out of the 20-day price range. The first significant correction triggered the trailing stop on the 5-day low. Comparing the two cases, we see that the trailing exit works best with swing moves. If you wish to use discretion, you should remember this exit strategy in swing markets.

The limitation of having to specify the number of days to "look back" to set the trailing stop is not ideal. In the next section we discuss how a volatility-based exit overcomes this limitation.

Channel Breakout on Close with Volatility Exit

Sometimes there is a big move against the established trend when a consolidation is at hand. A volatility criterion can pick off the "big" move against the trend. We want a trailing exit for which we do not have to specify the x-day look back period. In effect, we will create a volatility-based trailing stop.

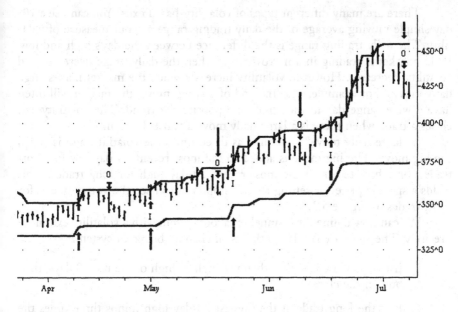

Figure 5.1   The close on the 5-day high or low gives frequent exits in a choppy uptrend in the wheat market.

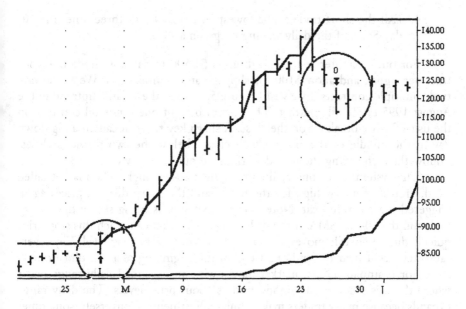

Figure 5.2   The coffee perpetual contract shows ideal market action for the 5-day trailing exit, which works best with markets that move quickly after a breakout.

There are many different types of volatility-based exits. You can use a 10-day simple moving average of the daily trading range as your measure of volatility. The daily trading range is the difference between the day's high and low. If the market is trading in a narrow range, then the daily range decreases and volatility decreases. However, volatility increases when the market makes large daily moves. For example, near the end of a swing move, the market will often have a wide range day in the direction opposite the trend. The volatility exit closes a trade when there is a large daily move against the trend.

A "large daily move" is defined as three times the volatility, and is called the big move. The big move is added to the most recent 20-day low for short trades, or subtracted from the most recent 20-day high for long trades. This yields a specific price for setting an exit stop. You can see the volatility exit for short trades in Figure 5.3.

We can now define the channel breakout system with a volatility exit more precisely. The rules are similar to the usual channel breakout system.

1. If today's close is higher than the highest high of the last 20 days, then buy on the close.

2. Exit the long trade at the highest 20-day high minus three times the 10-day SMA of the daily trading range on a stop.

3. If today's close is lower than the lowest low of the last 20 days, then sell on the close.

4. Exit the short trade at the lowest 20-day low plus three times the 10-day SMA of the daily trading range on a stop.

For our computer tests, we will use a $1,500 initial stop, trade one contract per signal, and allow $100 for slippage and commissions. We can always trade multiple contracts if we wish. Figure 5.4 shows the volatile uptrend in the August 1995 crude oil contract. The system bought one crude oil contract on the usual 20-bar breakout on the close. A sharp key reversal caused a big down day in the middle of the chart, which closed below the two previous closes. Follow-through selling the next day triggered our volatility exit.

The system went long again after a new 20-bar high. The market failed on the retest of a new high for the move, and the sharp drop in prices again triggered the volatility exit. Note that the exit stop is being set by the 20-day high and the 10-day SMA of the daily range. A market can reach this stop price quickly during volatile moves, or slowly drift down to the stop level. Key reversals often occur near the end of a trend or the beginning of a consolidation.

For example, sudden market moves with an expanded daily range occur where there is a consensus among traders about price levels. The daily range expands because many traders make similar adjustments. Conversely, sometimes there is no news or information to drive the market. Prices can then drift in small increments toward the exit stop. The main advantage of a volatility-based

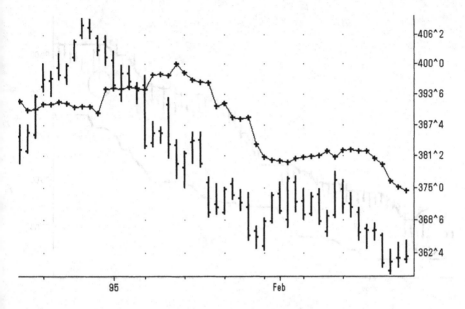

Figure 5.3   The volatility exit for short trades trails prices until a big move or reversal closes out the trade.

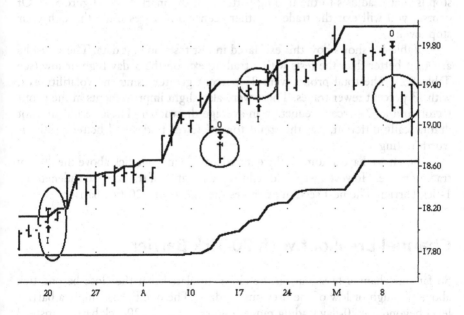

Figure 5.4   Volatility-based exit closes long trades after two big reversals in this crude oil market.

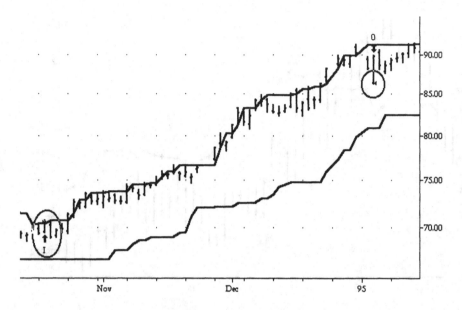

Figure 5.5 The volatility exit often catches long trends, as in the cotton market.

stop is that it adjusts to the trading patterns of the market (see Figure 5.5). Of course, you will exit the trade in either scenario if prices trade through your stop level.

Table 5.3 shows how this exit fared in our tests on past data. These results are a bit better than the tests with a trailing exit on the 5-day high or low (see Table 5.2). The total profits were 25 percent greater using the volatility exit, with 13 percent fewer trades. There were also slight improvements in the profit factor, and a 12 percent reduction in average drawdown. These results are not dramatically different, but the trend toward fewer trades and better profits is worth noting.

So far we have automatically entered a trade just one tick above the 20-day trading range. However, we could reduce the number of trades if we widened the 1-tick barrier. The next section examines the effects of a 20-tick barrier.

Channel Breakout with 20-Tick Barrier

So far our channel breakout on the close stipulated that the close be one tick above the high or low of the previous 20 days. The one tick is simply a barrier level beyond the 20-day trading range. Figure 5.6 uses a 20-tick barrier, instead of the 1-tick barrier. This number is arbitrary; you could certainly test other values. In this case, the decisive close above the barrier led to a strong rally.

Table 5.3   Results for 20-bar channel breakout with volatility exit.

Market	Profit ($)	Number of Trades	Percent- age of Wins	Win/ Loss Ratio	Average Trade ($)	Maximum Intraday Draw- down ($)	Profit Factor
British pound	29,650	242	40	1.75	123	–27,331	1.17
Coffee	187,210	222	38	3.15	843	–21,405	2.02
Cotton	27,565	194	35	2.28	143	–18,690	1.23
Crude oil	–45,210	158	32	0.99	–286	–44,970	0.46
Deutsche mark	51,275	201	45	1.89	255	–9,813	1.56
Eurodollar	20,925	115	41	2.42	182	–4,775	1.67
Gold	31,170	199	33	2.66	157	–31,430	1.29
Japanese yen	59,350	209	43	2.06	284	–12,500	1.53
U.S. bond	–1,669	182	33	2.01	–10	–28,838	0.99
Wheat	–12,069	187	30	2.00	–54	–19,306	0.85
Total	348,197	1909					
Average	34,820	191	37	2.12	164	–21,906	1.28

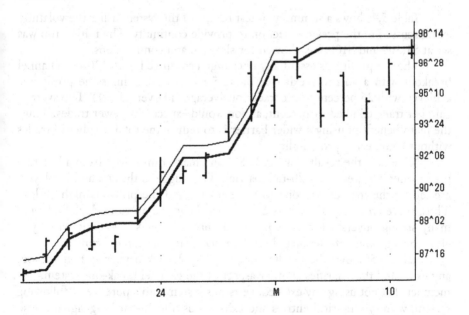

Figure 5.6   The 20-tick barrier for the March 1986 U.S. bond market contract. The thick line is the 20-day high. The narrow line is the 20-tick barrier.

Table 5.4   Results for the 20-bar channel with a 20-tick barrier and volatility exit.

Market	Profit ($)	Number of Trades	Percent-age of Wins	Win/ Loss Ratio	Average Trade ($)	Maximum Intraday Draw-down ($)	Profit Factor
British pound	24,588	222	41	1.69	110	–26,888	1.15
Coffee	175,631	213	39	3.04	825	–22,605	1.98
Cotton	27,430	178	35	2.28	154	–18,595	1.25
Crude oil	–40,630	111	28	1.04	–366	–42,130	0.40
D-Mark	33,275	152	39	2.23	219	–7,813	1.46
Eurodollar	2,250	17	41	1.92	132	–2,900	1.34
Gold	31,610	142	32	2.87	222	–25,640	1.38
Japanese yen	53,950	161	43	2.08	335	–9,550	1.60
U.S. bond	29,925	77	38	2.46	388	–20,113	1.49
Wheat	–5,250	137	29	2.17	–38	–15,650	0.89
Total	332,779	1,410					
Average	33,278	141	37	2.18	198	–19,188	1.29

Table 5.4 shows a summary of test results of the system using the volatility exit discussed in the previous section to provide continuity. The initial stop was set at $1,500 and $100 was allowed for slippage and commissions.

The net profit was essentially unchanged compared to the 20-day channel breakout with a volatility exit (see Table 5.3). However, this same profit was achieved with 26 percent fewer trades on average (141 versus 191). The average gain per trade climbed 21 percent, as you would expect with fewer trades. Thus, the main benefit of using a wider barrier is to reduce the total number of trades without hammering profitability.

Note how the results for the U.S. bond market improved from a loss to a profit when we went to a 20-tick barrier. This suggests that many big players are fading the market, say one to ten ticks beyond the previous high or low. Thus, there are many big sellers a few ticks above the previous day's high, and many strong buyers a few ticks below the previous day's low. Only when you clear through this interference does the price change become significant.

Table 5.5 shows the results of testing the 20-tick barrier system without any exits, and thus clarifies another aspect of the channel break-out system. Remember that not using any exits converts this system into a pure trend-following system, with symmetrical entries and exits. Thus, the 20-bar long signal is also the 20-bar short trade exit and vice versa.

Table 5.5   Results for the 20-bar channel with a 20-tick barrier and no exit.

Market	Profit ($)	Number of Trades	Percent-age of Wins	Win/ Loss Ratio	Average Trade ($)	Maximum Intraday Draw-down ($)	Profit Factor
British pound	101,644	135	31	3.75	753	–25,544	1.69
Coffee	220,100	144	30	5.46	1,508	–25,224	2.37
Cotton	43,345	114	37	2.94	380	–15,310	1.41
Crude oil	–17,320	55	33	1.40	–315	–29,020	0.68
Deutsche mark	49,900	89	38	2.66	561	–10,163	1.64
Eurodollar	2,150	10	30	2.78	215	–7,225	1.19
Gold	–6,320	100	30	2.14	–83	–56,940	0.92
Japanese yen	74,575	95	35	3.40	785	–12,813	1.81
U.S. bond	44,400	55	27	4.50	800	–19,825	1.69
Wheat	–12,581	88	30	1.87	–143	–29,494	0.79
Total	499,893	885					
Average	49,989	89	32	3.09	446	–23,156	1.42

The net profits with a barrier but without exits are 50 percent higher with 37 percent fewer trades than with an exit (compare Table 5.4). Surely the basic trend-following system is quite attractive. So it is fair to ask why we should have any exits with the channel breakout. The answer lies in the number of days the systems are in the market, and by implication in the potential risk exposure. If we do not use any exits, the 20-bar breakout system is always in the market. If we add an exit strategy, the system is out of the market some portion of the time. You can expect a reduction in exposure to market risk if the system is often out of the market.

Table 5.6 summarizes the number of days the 20-day channel breakout is in the market with and without an exit. Adding the volatility exit reduces the number of days the system is in the market by 58 percent on average. Thus, there is a significant reduction in potential risk when we add an exit to the channel breakout system. Your account could be earning interest when you are out of the market. Your interest income will also help to smooth out account equity.

Note that the average maximum intraday drawdown was $19,188 with the volatility exit, versus $23,156 without any exits. Thus, there was also a 17-percent reduction in average drawdown by adding the exit strategy, but this could have occurred purely by chance. Thus, the primary benefit of expanding the barrier is to reduce the number of days the system is in the market.

Table 5.6   Adding an exit decreases the number of days a system is in the market.

Market	Days in Market, No Exits	Days in Market, Volatility Exit	Percentage Difference
British Pound	4,028	2,322	–42
Coffee	2,945	1,932	–34
Cotton	4,568	2,948	–35
Crude oil	2,732	883	–68
Deutsche mark	4,605	1,904	–59
Eurodollar	1,643	279	–83
Gold	4,110	1,713	–83
Japanese yen	3,838	1,645	–58
U.S. bond	3,005	1,196	–57
Wheat	4,816	2,287	–60
Average	3,629	1,711	–58

Ideally, you should base the width of the barrier on market volatility. A fixed barrier may be too far away to trigger trades within the usual range of daily volatility. For example, the 20-tick barrier is too wide for the Eurodollar market. A volatility-based barrier will respond to market action and provide a more consistent barrier across all markets. The next section discusses the effect of using a volatility-based variable barrier instead of a fixed barrier.

Channel Breakout System with Inside Volatility Barrier

In the previous section we saw the effects of a 20-tick barrier that was outside the 20-day price range. The barrier widened the 20-day price range, and helped to filter out some trades. In the case of the Eurodollar market, the 20-tick barrier was much wider than the normal volatility of that market. Hence, the 20-tick barrier allowed only ten trades to pass through, reducing profits and trading opportunities.

This section will show you how to set up a volatility-based barrier. In an interesting twist, we will set the barrier inside the 20-day price channel (see Figure 5.7). We will have more trading opportunities because the channel will be narrower. The width of the barrier acts as a filter that cuts off trades. You should understand the interaction between volatility and channel width very clearly. If the volatility is low, then the relative channel width will widen. How-

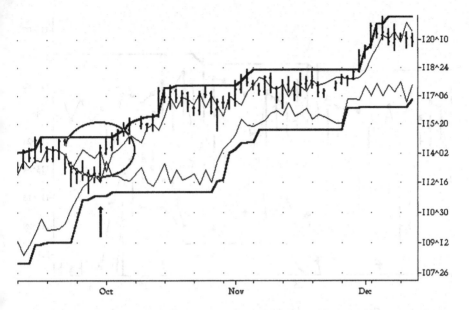

Figure 5.7   The inside volatility barrier superimposed on the 20-day channel shows a long trade in the December 1995 U.S. bond market.

ever, if the volatility is high, the actual channel width will be narrower. As volatility increases this system will trade more frequently.

Volatility is defined here as the 10-day SMA of the daily trading range. The daily trading range is simply the difference between today's high and low. Thus, the upper inside barrier is the highest 20-day high minus the volatility. Similarly, the lower inside barrier is the lowest 20-day low plus the volatility. We will go long on the close if it is above the upper inside barrier, and sell on the close if the market closes below the lower inside barrier. The volatility exit is at three times the 10-day SMA of the daily trading range.

Figure 5.8 shows a more detailed view of how the inside barrier works. The actual width of the barrier is narrower, but the width changes every day. The number of trades increases with an inside barrier because the width is narrower than the 20-day channel. Figure 5.8 shows that during narrow consolidations the inside barriers can come close together, or even cross each other. As the inside barriers come close together, the number of trades increases. Thus, the inside barrier system can produce several whipsaw trades in a region of price consolidation.

You may dislike the increased frequency in consolidations caused by an inside barrier system. One of the strengths of the usual channel breakout system is that it tends to produce fewer trades during price congestions. Hence, the inside barrier system will not appeal to all traders.

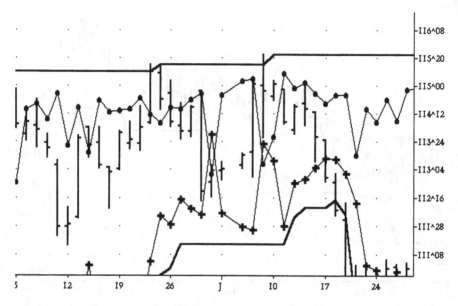

Figure 5.8 The inside volatility barriers come close together during consolidations, increasing trading frequency.

Table 5.7 shows a summary of testing over previous market data. You will notice that the total profits are up 35 percent versus the fixed 20-tick barrier with volatility exit (compare Table 5.4). The total number of trades has more than doubled to 294 over the fixed 20-tick barrier. The higher trading frequency may be attractive to you if your trading costs are low.

Statistical Significance of Channel Breakout Variations

One of the key questions you must ask when you see system variations is whether the differences in the performance are statistically significant. There are many ways to differentiate systems other than comparing their net profits. For example, one system may produce fewer trades. Another system may produce a smaller drawdown. Some systems may have a higher percentage of profitable trades. A variation may be useful precisely because it suits your trading style.

A paired t-test compares the means of two system variables measured on the same data sets. This test will tell you if the means of the two series being compared are truly different in a statistically significant sense. You can find a detailed discussion of the t-test in any book on statistics. For our purpose, the

Table 5.7   Results for 20-day channel breakout system with inside volatility barrier and volatility exit.

Market	Profit ($)	Number of Trades	Percentage of Wins	Win/ Loss Ratio	Average Trade ($)	Maximum Intraday Drawdown ($)	Profit Factor
British pound	49,394	356	37	2.01	139	–27,719	1.20
Coffee	235,774	355	33	2.58	664	–29,451	1.79
Cotton	21,050	281	33	2.31	153	–18,395	1.13
Crude oil	–57,300	249	32	1.11	–230	–57,720	0.52
Deutsche mark	48,700	318	39	2.12	153	–14,213	1.34
Eurodollar	26,975	184	41	2.25	147	–6,600	1.55
Gold	47,900	323	32	2.91	148	–23,620	1.34
Japanese yen	63,588	329	35	2.56	148	–19,550	1.36
U.S. bond	28,875	265	34	2.19	109	–22,875	1.15
Wheat	–17,638	279	32	1.73	–63	–30,719	0.81
Total	447,318						
Average	44,732	294	35	2.18	137	–25,086	1.22

test gives two numbers: a t-statistic for the data and an appropriate reference value (t-critical). If our t-statistic is greater than t-critical, then the difference in performance is statistically significant. The Microsoft Excel® 5.0 spreadsheet has a built-in t-test in the Tools menu under Data analysis.

We need a reference or standard system for comparison before we can use the t-test. Here we use a 20-day channel breakout system without any exits as the reference system. If you do not use any specific exits, you have a system in which long entries are short exits and vice versa. Thus, the effects of adding exit strategies should be easy to measure against this reference system. Table 5.8 summarizes the results of testing the 20-day channel breakout system without any exits on the previous data. As usual, there is a $1,500 initial stop and $100 allowance for slippage and commissions.

Let us examine the effects of adding the 5-day high-low trailing stop to the reference system (see Table 5.2). In comparing the net profits from each system, the t-statistic was 2.224 and the t-critical value was 2.262 with 9 degrees of freedom. Thus, the t-statistic was smaller than the reference t-critical value. The average profit for the reference system is $51,368 versus $27,949 with the trailing exit. At the 5-percent level, this difference barely missed being significant. Hence, adding the exit probably significantly reduced average profits. The spreadsheet calculations are given in Table 5.9.

Table 5.8   Historical results for 20-bar breakout on the close without any exits.

Market	Profit ($)	Number of Trades	Percent-age of Wins	Win/ Loss Ratio	Average Trade ($)	Maximum Intraday Draw-down ($)	Profit Factor
British pound	92,494	149	30	3.76	621	−29,250	1.58
Coffee	222,042	152	30	5.21	1,461	−26,083	2.34
Cotton	35,870	77	31	1.55	276	−20,270	1.29
Crude oil	−12,740	130	34	2.91	−165	−27,400	0.70
Deutsche mark	72,000	109	44	2.44	661	−9,975	1.92
Eurodollar	25,825	63	44	2.16	410	−10,275	1.73
Gold	29,920	124	35	2.36	241	−39,520	1.30
Japanese yen	64,388	121	38	2.61	532	−17,563	1.60
U.S. bond	−1,956	133	30	2.29	−15	−32,629	0.99
Wheat	−11,463	125	33	1.73	−92	−27,775	0.85
Total	516,380	1183					
Average	51,638	118	35	2.70	393	−24,074	1.43

Table 5.9   A summary of the t-test comparing the reference system to the CHBOC with 5-day trailing stop.

t-Test: Paired Two Sample for Means

	Reference System	5-Day Exit
Mean	51,638	27,948.8
Variance	4.85×10^8	3.77×10^9
Observations	10	10
Pearson correlation	0.875	
Hypothesized mean difference	0	
df	9	
t Stat	2.224	
P(T<=t) one-tail	0.027	
t Critical one-tail	1.833	
P(T<=t) two-tail	0.053	
t Critical two-tail	2.262	

Table 5.10 T-test comparing number of trades from reference system and with 5-day exit.

t-Test: Paired Two Sample for Means

	5-Day Exit	Reference System
Mean	220	118.
Variance	1736.72	818.455
Observations	1	1
Pearson correlation	0.410	
Hypothesized mean difference		
df		
t Stat	8.055	
P(T<=t) one-tail	1.05	
t Critical one-tail	1.833	
P(T<=t) two-tail	2.10	
t Critical two-tail	2.262	

Table 5.10 compares the number of trades from each system. The average number of trades was 220 with the trailing exit (see Table 5.2), and 118 with the reference system (see Table 5.8). The t-statistic for the number of trades was 8.05. The t-critical value is 2.262, confirming that there is a statistically significant increase in the number of trades. Therefore, the total number of trades increases significantly when we add a trailing exit.

You can now combine the results from these two comparisons. Those results say that adding a trailing exit at the 5-day high-low significantly reduced profits by 30 percent while increasing the number of trades by 76 percent. Now you have to decide if these changes suit your trading style.

Next we examine the effects of adding the volatility exit to the reference system (see Table 5.3). There is a statistically significant (t-statistic: 2.54 > t-critical: 2.26) reduction in average profits from $51,638 to $34,820. Thus, the 33-percent reduction in profits occurs with a significant 61-percent increase in the total number of trades (t-statistic: 8.82 > t-critical: 2.26). Thus, the volatility exit reduces profits and increases trading frequency. Of course, it introduces a neutral zone, and should reduce your overall market exposure. You may like this exit because it responds to a particular exit pattern, such as a large countertrend move. Some traders may prefer the equity curve produced by this exit to the equity curve of the reference system. Others may like the higher trading frequency because it means they will get many opportunities to trade.

The effect of using the 20-tick barrier did not produce a statistically significant reduction in net profits when tested without any exits (see Table 5.5). The average profit per market was $51,638 with the reference system, and $49,989 with the 20-tick barrier. Thus, adding the barrier did not reduce profits significantly. However, it did reduce the number of trades by about 25 percent, which was statistically significant (t-statistic 4.71, t-critical = 2.62), suggesting that the barrier acted as a filter.

The effect of adding a volatility exit to the 20-tick barrier (Table 5.4) also produced no statistically significant difference in net profits. However, the number of trades was significantly higher. You will have to examine the equity curves to decide if you like the effects of adding the exit.

There was no significant difference in performance between the reference system and the breakout with the inside volatility barrier (Table 5.7). For example, the average profits with the 20-tick barrier are $51,638 versus $44,732 with the inside volatility barrier. However, the number of trades was 60 percent smaller without the inside volatility barrier. The inside volatility barrier produces a statistically significant increase in the trading frequency. Thus, the inside barrier will whet your appetite for frequent trading without a large performance penalty.

The analysis of this section shows that you should use a statistical test to verify that the differences in performance are statistically significant. You can use a spreadsheet for your statistical analysis, or you may use specialized software. You should carefully note how changing exit strategies changed the profits, trading frequency, and drawdowns. Thus, you can easily match an entry signal to your trading needs.

Two ADX Variations

The average directional index is a widely used measure of trendiness. A test of two small variations of an ADX system showed that the absolute value of the ADX has no particular significance. The test used a $1,500 stop and allowed $100 for slippage and commissions on the following markets: British pound, coffee, cotton, crude oil, deutsche mark, Eurodollar, gold, Japanese yen, U.S. bond, and wheat. All available data from January 1, 1975, through July 10, 1995, were used.

The first system tested entered long or short when the 14-day ADX value crossed over 30. A crossover occurs when yesterday's value is less than 30 and today's value is more than 30 for the ADX. If the 3-day SMA of the close is greater than the 20-day exponential moving average, then the system buys on the next day's open. Conversely, if the 3-day SMA of the close is less than 20-day exponential moving average, then the system sells on the next day's open. The initial stop is at $1,500 and there is a $100 allowance for slippage and commissions. The exit signal was a trailing stop at the highest high or lowest low of the past 20 days.

The second variation does not rely on the absolute value of the ADX; it requires only that the ADX be rising. The ADX was assumed to be rising if it was higher than its value 28 days ago. Otherwise, the rules of the two variations

Table 5.11   Results for ADX > 30 trading system.

Market	Profit ($)	Number of Trades	Percent- age of Wins	Win/ Loss Ratio	Average Trade ($)	Maximum Intraday Draw- down ($)	Profit Factor
British pound	66,188	51	41	3.72	1,298	–8,869	2.61
Coffee	112,531	64	33	5.76	1,758	–13,065	2.81
Cotton	68,795	50	50	4.09	1,376	–8,355	4.09
Crude oil	17,780	22	50	2.93	808	–3,550	2.93
Deutsche mark	21,338	57	44	2.00	374	–7,238	1.56
Eurodollar	18,675	36	53	2.13	519	–3,350	2.38
Gold	-1,860	50	34	1.85	-37	–25,180	0.95
Japanese yen	42,125	47	47	2.56	896	–9,887	2.25
U.S. bond	2,525	56	34	2.05	–45	–14,588	1.05
Wheat	5,675	48	44	1.65	118	–6,950	1.28
Total	355,632						
Average	43,745	47	43	2.87	323	–10,103	2.19

are identical. The results are summarized in Tables 5.11 and 5.12. The rising ADX system seems to be more profitable than the ADX > 30 system. A t-test determined that the difference was indeed statistically significant, since t-statistic was 2.76, greater than the t-critical value of 2.26.

These results show that the trend of the ADX is more useful than the absolute value of the ADX. However, using a value such as ADX > 30 is a restrictive condition that reduces the number of trades significantly. You will find that the ADX > 30 system is in the market for only 40 to 45 percent of the time spent by the rising ADX system. Therefore, the losses and drawdowns are smaller for the ADX > 30 system. Thus, both approaches have their strengths and weaknesses, and your choice will reflect your trading preferences.

Figure 5.9 and Figure 5.10 will help you visualize how the two systems work. Figure 5.9 shows the entry due to an ADX rising system in the November 1995 orange juice contract. The ADX indicator along with the reference level of 30 appear in the lower half of the figure. It may appear that the ADX has turned down, but it is rising on a longer time frame of 28 days. Figure 5.10 shows the entry after ADX has crossed over the 30 level. The entry signal from the ADX>30 system came 3 months after the signal from the ADX rising system. You should expect such delayed entries because the ADX is a heavily

Table 5.12   Results for ADX rising trading system.

Market	Profit ($)	Number of Trades	Percent-age of Wins	Win/ Loss Ratio	Average Trade ($)	Maximum Intraday Draw-down ($)	Profit Factor
British pound	131,469	180	35	3.43	730	–24,850	1.85
Coffee	217,465	213	28	5.28	1,021	–19,824	2.08
Cotton	57,495	173	35	2.90	332	–17,745	1.54
Crude oil	-1,590	121	32	2.05	–13	–14,620	0.97
Deutsche mark	74,888	141	49	2.07	531	–10,475	1.99
Eurodollar	38,600	96	43	3.45	402	–4,000	2.57
Gold	33,150	182	35	2.46	182	–24,120	1.33
Japanese yen	71,850	164	36	2.94	438	–16,763	1.65
U.S. bond	60,163	164	37	2.52	367	–12,188	1.49
Wheat	5,105	151	52	1.98	15	–24,131	1.04
Total	690,185						
Average	85,635	159	37	2.91	323	–16,872	1.65

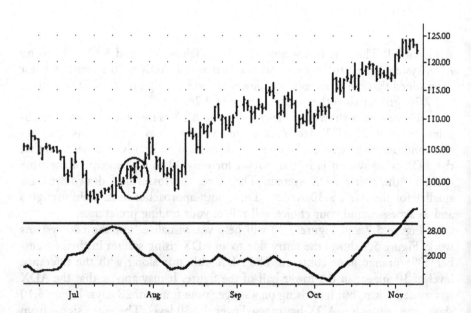

Figure 5.9   The entry point derived from a rising ADX entry system for the November 1995 orange juice contract.

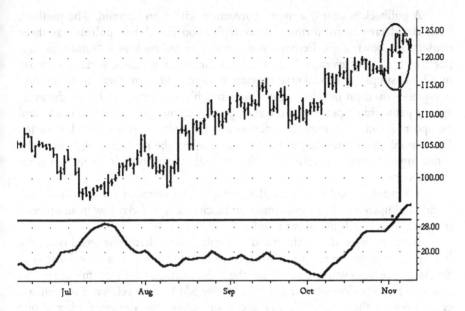

Figure 5.10   Note how the ADX > 30 entry occurs almost 3 months after the rising ADX entry in Figure 5.9.

smoothed indicator. Clearly, trading styles and preferences will govern which entry method you prefer.

The ADX logic assumes you are trying to confirm the presence of a strong trend. These entries could occur after prices have made a small move, since the heavily smoothed ADX takes several days to react to changing prices. Many traders do not like to buy on strength or sell on weakness. These traders prefer to lower risk at entry by buying a pullback or selling a small bounce in prices. In the next section we review a variation that tries to trade the "pullback" in prices.

The Pullback System

An old market maxim says, "Buy on a pullback into support." Many traders like to trade the pullback because it often provides an entry point with relatively low risk. Contrast this philosophy with trading the ADX systems, which buy on strength or sell on weakness. The pullback maxim, however, is not a precise statement of a trading system. We have to define what we mean by pullback and what represents support. This system is a variation of the CB-PB system examined in Chapter 4. Here the pullback is defined relative to a moving average rather than after a 20-day breakout.

A pullback is simply a minor correction within an uptrend. The pullback itself could take many forms. For example, you can define pullback as three consecutive down days. Perhaps you can define pullback as a "return to support" by a moving average. You can pick a variety of averages, such as a 20-day or 50-day simple or exponential moving average. The term "return to support" is vague—you must decide if prices must touch the average, go below the average, or get within 1 percent of the average. Once you agree what "pullback" and "support" mean, you must then decide at what point to place your buy order. For example, you could buy at the next day's open, the next day's high, or at the 5-day high. Picking a precise definition will allow you to build many variations of this system.

We want to build a system that recognizes a retracement in both downtrends and uptrends. We will define a pullback as a new 5-day low in an uptrend or a new 5-day high in a downtrend.

Next, we must define the trend. We will assume that if the trend is up, the low remains above the d-day SMA when the market makes a new 5-day low. Similarly, the high will remain below the d-day average when the market makes a new 5-day high. We arbitrarily pick a 50-day SMA as the reference moving average because the prices will stay above or below this average during strong trends. Thus, the trend is defined as up when the market makes a new 5-day low but the low remains above the 50-day SMA (see Figure 5.11). The matching

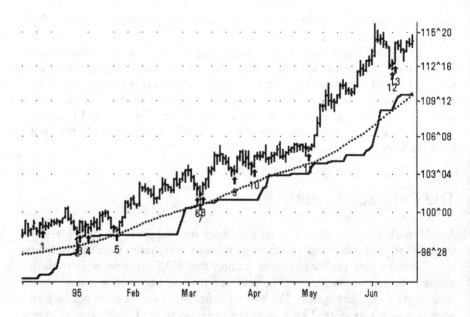

Figure 5.11 The pullback system had many entry points into the strong uptrend in the June 1995 U.S. bond market. The solid line is the trailing 20-day low. The 50-day SMA is shown by crosses.

Table 5.13   Results for pullback system: new 5 day low above 50-day SMA or new 5-day high below 50-day SMA; exit on trailing 20-day high or low; $1,500 initial stop, $100 S&C.

Market	Profit ($)	Number of Trades	Percent- age of Wins	Win/ Loss Ratio	Average Trade ($)	Maximum Intraday Draw- down ($)	Profit Factor
British pound	122,269	149	28	5.62	821	−16,569	2.21
Coffee	205,035	174	21	9.34	1178	−26,063	2.52
Cotton	46,630	132	30	3.96	353	−10,360	1.72
Crude oil	1,840	90	32	2.21	20	−12,070	1.05
Deutsche mark	30,725	129	34	2.82	238	−14,963	1.46
Eurodollar	16,575	82	29	4.01	302	−4,200	1.66
Gold	34,320	139	27	4.04	247	−25,430	1.47
Japanese yen	27,575	135	31	3.03	204	−14,925	1.37
U.S. bond	35,850	129	31	3.84	278	−15,400	1.43
Wheat	−7,588	134	24	2.70	−56	−21,131	0.85
Total	513,231						
Average	57,869	129	29	4.16	359	−16,111	1.65

condition for the downtrend is that the new 5-day high remains below the 50-day SMA.

You can imagine other variations of this system. For example, you can add a trend filter, using the ADX as suggested by Connors and Raschke (see bibliography for reference). They suggest using a 14-day ADX value greater than 30 and using a 20-day exponential moving average. Another option is to use a 14-day RSI or stochastic oscillator and to look for reversals. For example, you could look for the stochastic to fall below 20 and then rise above 20 to define the buying point.

The results of tests of the pullback systems using the same data sets as for all other systems in this chapter are shown in Table 5.13. We again used a $1,500 initial stop and allowed $100 for slippage and commissions. The entry was on the open after a new 5-day low above the 50-day SMA and vice versa. The exit was on the trailing 20-day high or low. The basic idea of the pullback system seems valid when you consider its profitability over a wide range of markets. The 20-year test period also confirms that the pullback system will find profitable trades in the future.

The percentage of profitable trades is relatively low, about 20 to 30 percent. However, the low win ratio is offset by the high average win-loss ratio.

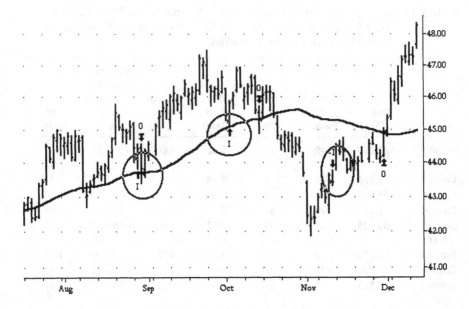

Figure 5.12 The choppy trend in live hogs triggered the system entries but did not generate significant profits. This is a common problem in choppy markets, and your exit strategy becomes even more important.

The drawdowns are moderate compared to other systems we have studied. The pullback system seems to work best in markets that have regular corrections within choppy trends. The pullback system also likes markets that make swing moves. Note, for example, the small loss in crude oil and the small profit in the U.S. bond market. The other trend-following systems discussed in this book have tested poorly on these markets, which often have choppy trends.

In keeping with its design philosophy, the maximum drawdown figure is substantially smaller than in other trend-following systems. However, the results in Table 5.13 are not as attractive as some of the trend-following systems we have seen. The reason is obvious in the live hogs chart shown in Figure 5.12. The market did not make profitable swing moves after retreating to the 50-day average. Your exit strategy is more important in such markets that bounce weakly off the 50-day average. You can experiment with your favorite exits, or use discretion.

So far we have not taken advantage of a key design feature. Since we are buying or selling after a pullback, we hope to get a low-risk entry point. A low-risk entry point is ideal for using a variable-contract money-management strategy. If you can risk $10,000 per position signaled by the pullback system, then trade up to a maximum of ten contracts using the 5-day high-low range as the measure of volatility. In Table 5.14, we traded a new 5-day high or low beyond

Table 5.14   Results for pullback system with a maximum of ten contracts.

Market	Profit ($)	Number of Trades	Percent- age of Wins	Win/ Loss Ratio	Average Trade ($)	Maximum Intraday Draw- down ($)	Profit Factor
British pound	871,719	126	32	5.89	6,919	−67,419	2.74
Coffee	794,998	155	24	6.68	5,039	−174,653	2.11
Cotton	406,250	134	28	4.63	3,031	−100,755	1.83
Crude oil	33,360	91	24	3.54	367	−68,100	1.13
Deutsche mark	297,975	135	29	3.79	2,207	−126,825	1.54
Eurodollar	237,850	68	38	3.79	3,498	−35,750	2.34
Gold	129,290	135	24	3.99	958	−226,310	1.24
Japanese yen	86,288	128	26	3.26	674	−135,263	1.10
U.S. bond	316,050	140	22	4.82	2,258	−133,200	1.65
Wheat	19,419	126	23	3.22	154	−162,260	1.06
Total	3,193,199						
Average	352,642	122	27	4.36	2,511	−123,054	1.74

the 50-day average. The exit was placed at the 20-day trailing high or low, and we used a $1,500 initial stop, and charged $100 for slippage and commissions.

There is a striking difference in performance among a one-contract strategy and a variable-contract strategy with a ten-contract limit. The profits of the latter strategy were more than six times greater. However, the drawdown increased almost eight times on average, so the gains come at a price. Note that the drawdowns are still smaller than always trading ten contracts. Thus, the variable-contracts strategy could be better than trading the equivalent number of fixed contracts. You can test other variable-contract approaches with this entry strategy to match your preferences.

In summary, the basic idea behind the pullback system is valid. It has relatively high win-loss ratio and average trade. You could try to add filters to improve system performance. You should consider a variable-contracts money-management approach to exploit the low-risk entry points.

The Long Bomb—A Pattern-Based System

Many a football team has lived, and died, by the "long bomb." In American football, this is a pass play designed to gain big yardage by going deep down the playing field. A successful long bomb can rekindle enthusiasm in your team, demoralize the opposition, and even get a quick score when little time remains. It is a gutsy play, but not without some risk. This section discusses a pattern-based system inspired by the philosophy of the long bomb. Pattern-based systems allow you to react immediately. However, the patterns do not repeat frequently, and the market does not have to follow through on the pattern each time. You must also be careful when you test the pattern to use a sufficiently large data set.

The long bomb is a 5-bar, bottom-picking pattern. It is related to market action near double bottoms. The usual sequence is that a market probes for a bottom. As big players sense a bottom, they buy in "bulk" and produce a sharp rally. Other traders feel this may be an opportunity to short, and the smart-money–led rally is thwarted by short-sellers late to the party. As a result, the market retests the prior bottom. If there is no significant selling on the retest, the market is ready to resume an upward move, and does so with a strong surge. The strategy here is to get in during the upsurge—a simple enough idea. As it bursts out of the base, the market closes above the highs made over the past few days. If the following conditions are satisfied, buy tomorrow just above today's high:

1. Today's close is greater than the high of 2 days ago

2. Yesterday's close is greater than the high of 3 days ago

3. The close 2 days ago is greater than the high of 4 days ago

This relationship is perfectly general with no market-specific assumptions. In addition, there is no need to optimize the system. The following twist makes this system interesting. Suppose you buy multiple contracts, betting $10,000 per trade. You can use the difference between today's close and the 5-day low, convert this "range" into dollars, and calculate the number of contracts. Thus, if the "range" is $2,000, you will buy five contracts and use a $10,000 hard-stop on the position. Here is another twist. You will exit at the trailing 50-day low to get a long-term system.

By now you should understand why the name of the system is the long bomb. By buying multiple contracts and using a very slow exit, we are following the TOPS COLA strategy, and, in football parlance, going deep.

The Power Editor code for Omega Research's TradeStation™ software is:

```
input : dx (50) ;
Vars: Numc(0);
if C - lowest(low,5) <> 0 then
Num C = intportion(10000/((C-lowest(low,5))*Big
    Pointvalue)) else NumC = 1;
Condition1 = c > h[2] ;
Condition2 = c[1] > h[3];
```

```
Condition3 = c[2] > h[4];
If Condition1 and Condition2 and condition3 then buy
  ("123 Signal") NumC
contracts at high + 1 point stop;
ExitLong at Lowest(low,dx)[1] - 1 point stop;
```

An input, *dx*, which is the number of days in the exit, allows us to experiment with the exit strategy. Just before we calculate the number of contracts, we should double check that today's close is above the 5-day low to avoid division by zero. The three conditions specifying the pattern are entered as inequalities. If the entry conditions are satisfied today, we will enter tomorrow just above today's high on a buy stop. Hence, we could see some slippage if the market opens beyond our stop, but this barrier entry condition acts as a filter and reduces the number of trades.

Figure 5.13 shows how this entry condition looks on a real bar chart, using the March 1995 Eurodollar contract just after a significant market low. The long-bomb pattern went long just after the retest of the low, after the first bounce. Notice that there was no retracement after entry: like the long bomb, it was up, up, and away. A similar pattern is shown in Figure 5.14 for the December 1995 heating oil contract.

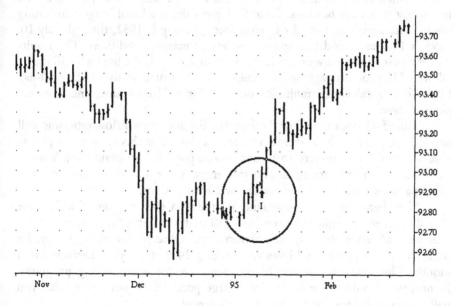

Figure 5.13 The long-bomb pattern enters as the Eurodollar accelerates out of its major bottom.

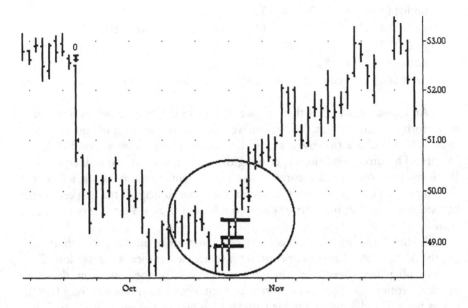

Figure 5.14   The long-bomb pattern in the December 1995 heating oil contract. The entry point saw good followthrough with little retracement.

Strange as it may seem, you will find that the long-bomb pattern occurs frequently at market bottoms. Table 5.15 gives the results of long-term testing over 10 markets. The period chosen is from January 1, 1982, through July 10. 1995, a 14-year period that spans a variety of market conditions. The results would be even better if we included a longer test period. We used a $1,500 stop, allowed $100 for slippage and commissions, and exited at the trailing 50-day low. We also calculated multiple contracts for a $10,000 investment, as explained above.

Table 5.15 does not show the fact that the average win/loss ratio was well above 3 for most of the markets. The results show that this system was profitable with multiple contracts, with considerable potential for drawdown. You can test a variety of exit strategies with this entry. You could also derive and test other patterns, such as a 3-bar pattern or 20-bar pattern.

Note here that we have around 30 trades in each market. If we assume that all markets are equivalent, we have 330 trades in Table 5.15, giving us reasonable confidence about system performance. Observe that these 330 trades occurred over a period of 14 years, averaging 24 trades a year, perhaps two a month. This may be a relatively low frequency for most trading programs. Hence, you should strive to develop a large portfolio of patterns, so that you will generate perhaps ten or more trades a month.

Testing patterns can be interesting, but must be done carefully. For example, there are a large number of candlestick patterns with tantalizing names and

Table 5.15   Long-term results for long-bomb trading system.

Market	Profit ($)	Profit Factor (Gross Profit/ Gross Loss)	Number of Wins; Total Trades; Percentage Profitable	Maximum Number of Contracts	Maximum Intraday Drawdown ($)
British pound	114,313	1.54	12;35;34	9	−96,407
Coffee	417,770	3.03	9;34;26	5	−49,660
Cotton	222,590	1.98	10;31;32	25	−136,040
Deutsche mark	234,263	2.17	10;31;32	22	−60,725
Eurodollar	142,825	1.76	12;29;41	57	−72,200
Heating oil	25,544	1.07	12;45;27	22	−135,565
Japanese yen	779,324	5.93	11;24;46	17	−38,000
Soybeans	62,018	1.20	11;42;26	28	−120,695
Swiss franc	256,453	2.70	10;26;38	15	−42,310
U.S. bond	272,363	2.41	12;33;36	9	−63,400

exciting descriptions. However, they often do not withstand thorough testing. The long-bomb pattern shows that you do not need complexity to achieve your means—just a particular market intuition.

Summary

In this chapter we saw how you can develop variations on a theme. We saw how the profit, trading frequency, and drawdown change with different exit strategies using the channel breakout system. Once you find a variation you like, you can use statistical tests to verify that the changes in performance are significant. We explored two variations on the ADX idea. The tests showed that the trend in the ADX is more useful than a fixed value, such as 30, in designing trading systems. We then saw a variation of the CB-PB system for long and short trades. In this case the pullback was referenced to a moving average rather than to the 20-bar channel. Lastly, we looked at a bottom pattern that is a variation of the usual double bottom formation. That example illustrates how you can take widely recognized patterns to form your own variations.

In this chapter we explored how you can easily develop variations of well-known ideas. Once you know that the results are statistically significant, you can evaluate how well they fit your trading style. In this way you can develop a large collection of systems for trading.

Chapter

Equity Curve Analysis

The holy grail of trading system design is the perfectly smooth equity curve.

Introduction

Only the equity curve provides a complete and continuous picture of your system's performance over time. The usual test summary tells you little about how your design trade-offs alter performance on a day-to-day basis. Hence your system development is not complete until you understand the impact of your decisions on the evolution of account equity.

In this chapter we take a detailed look at how to measure the smoothness of the equity curve using the standard error (SE) from linear regression analysis—the larger the SE, the rougher the equity curve. Then we see how the equity curve for the 65sma-3cc system changes with different exit strategies at the contract level. You will get a feel for how your design choices translate into equity changes.

Next, we discover how SE changes when you combine two systems trading the same market. A common belief is that trading many different markets gives a smoother equity curve. We explore this belief by combining two markets that have some positive covariance.

We then explore the monthly changes in equity curves, examining the performance of the 65sma-3cc system trading the deutsche mark over monthly intervals of different lengths. These quantities are termed the interval equity changes. Our goal here is to see how a system does over all 1-month, 3-month or 6-month intervals in the test period. These measures help in understanding the effects of adding a trailing stop or changing exit strategies.

These tests show that exit strategies alone do not improve equity curve smoothness (that is, reduce standard error); we look at changing a system's design. Filtering the usual channel breakout system gives a smoother equity curve.

The usual performance summary reveals none of this information, so the new insights from this analysis make it well worth the effort. After reading this chapter you can:

1. Measure the smoothness of an equity curve.

2. Understand the impact of system design on changes in the equity curve.

3. Grasp the effect of diversification on equity curves.

4. Recognize the benefits of using filters in system design.

Measuring the "Smoothness" of the Equity Curve

This section shows how to use linear regression analysis to measure the smoothness of an equity curve. We will use contrived data to perform actual calculations. You will understand how to use standard error and how to calculate the risk reward ratio. In later sections of this chapter we apply these ideas to market data and trading system calculations. The main advantage of using linear regression analysis is that it provides a consistent framework to analyze every equity curve.

The equity curve of your trading account or system is simply its daily equity. The daily equity is the sum of your starting account balance, plus the profit or loss of all closed trades, plus the profit or loss of all open trades. Ideally, we want an equity curve that rises steadily in time, as shown for the hypothetical data in Figure 6.1. The slope of this equity line is $100 per day, all the points lie exactly on a straight line through zero, and the standard error is zero. This line shows an account whose equity increases exactly $100 each day.

Since we all have some trades that lose money, the equity curve is never a perfectly straight line. As you begin to compare the equity curves of different trading systems, you need a way to measure their "smoothness." If you compare two systems with similar performance, the one with the smoother equity curve is preferred. We assume here that you are comparing system performance over the same time unit (days) and similar length (months or years). You could compare systems over other time units and length, but you must recognize that sometimes you may not be comparing these systems on a consistent basis.

We will use linear regression analysis to determine smoothness. One of the outputs of linear regression analysis is the residual sum squares (RSS). The

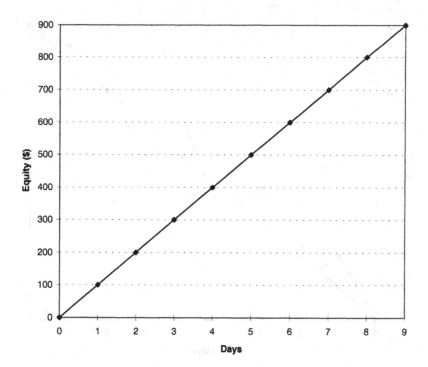

Figure 6.1 The perfectly smooth equity curve.

RSS is the sum of the squared vertical distance between the actual data and the fitted regression line at each point. The next step is to divide the RSS by the number of data points minus two, and then to take the square root, to calculate the standard error. The standard error measures the smoothness. If all the points fall exactly on the best fit linear regression line, then RSS is automatically zero, and the standard error is also zero, for the ultimate smoothness in an equity curve.

The curve in Figure 6.2 shows more hypothetical data. The slope of the best-fit linear regression line through zero is again $100. However, the points are scattered on either side of the best fit line. The standard error for these data is $82. If you measured the vertical distance between the actual equity value and the best fit line every day, on average, this absolute, average vertical distance is $82. Thus, the standard error tells you typically how far a point is from the best-fit line.

In Figure 6.3, which uses even more hypothetical data, the slope of the best-fit equity curve is still $100, but there is a lot more scatter in the data on

Hypothetical Equity Curve: Slope $100, SE = $82

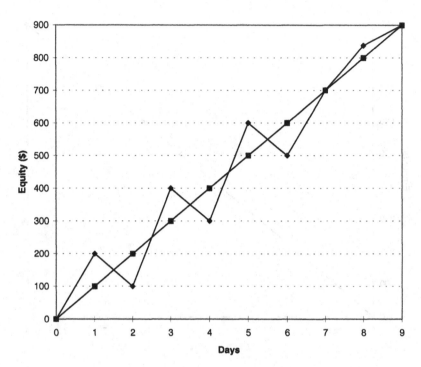

Figure 6.2   These hypothetical data have a slope of $100, and the scatter about the regression line increases the standard error to $82.

either side of the best-fit line. As expected, the SE is almost four times bigger, at $318.

You can get a better feel for what standard error means by looking at Figure 6.4, which contains the data in Figure 6.3 plus two lines one standard error away from the best-fit line. The data points are inside, or close to, the standard error lines. Remember we find the standard error by squaring the vertical distance between the actual point and the best-fit line, summing this up, and dividing by the number of points less two. Hence, the standard error is the average "offset" on either side of the best-fit line, and the data clearly lie inside or close to the "offset" or standard error.

Thus, the standard error from linear regression analysis is a good measure of the smoothness of the equity curve. Note that the linear regression method can be applied to any number of time periods and to any equity curve. The standard error offers a general, consistent, and powerful method to measure smoothness.

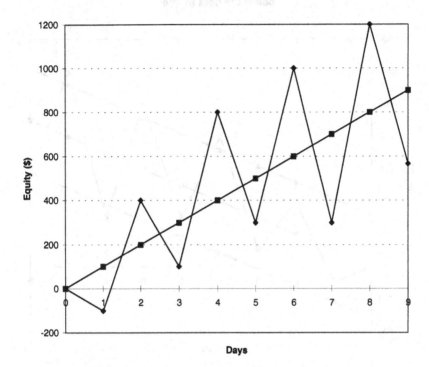

Figure 6.3   These data have a $100 slope, but the large scatter about the linear regression line increases the standard error to $318.

The combined SE of two or more equity curves will be smaller than the SE of the individual curves only if the curves are negatively correlated. Negative correlation means that when one increases, the other decreases. For a data set that is exactly negatively correlated to the data in Figure 6.3, the combined equity curve is a perfect straight line with zero standard error (see Figure 6.5).

Lowering SE is one of the arguments for diversification, usually interpreted as trading many markets within a single portfolio. If the markets are negatively correlated at least some of the time, then the joint equity curve of the combined portfolio will be smoother. Note that the slope of the joint equity curve will be just the algebraic sum of the slopes of the individual equity curves. This simply means that the slope of the line through the origin will change to accommodate all profits made over a given period.

You can expand the diversification theme to include different systems on the same market. Again, the equity curve will be smoother only if the systems are negatively correlated. If the systems have positive covariance, then the overall standard error will increase. Of course, if all systems are profitable then the

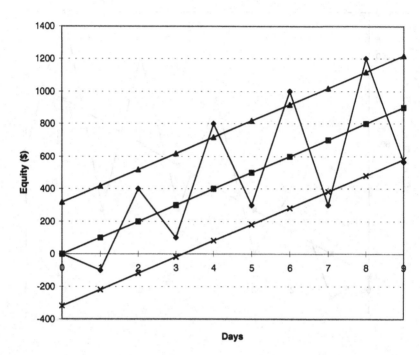

Hypothetical data with lines one standard error above and below the best fit line

Figure 6.4   The same data as in Figure 6.3 with lines on either side of the best-fit line one standard error away.

slope will increase as well. Remember that slope and roughness are independent. Thus, increasing the slope does not translate into a smoother equity curve.

We can extend the linear regression–based analysis to calculate the risk-reward ratio of a particular system by taking the ratio of the slope to the standard error. This is a quick and reliable way to compare different systems tested over the same data sets. This calculation assumes we are using daily data and looking at system paper profits.

RRR (risk reward ratio) = slope / standard error.

In the three hypothetical cases, the RRR approaches infinity for the first system because its SE is equal to zero. For the second system it would be 1.21 (100/82) and for the third 0.31 (100/318). There is little doubt we would all prefer the first system if one ever existed. You can use a spreadsheet such as Microsoft Excel® for linear regression calculations. For example, in Excel you can

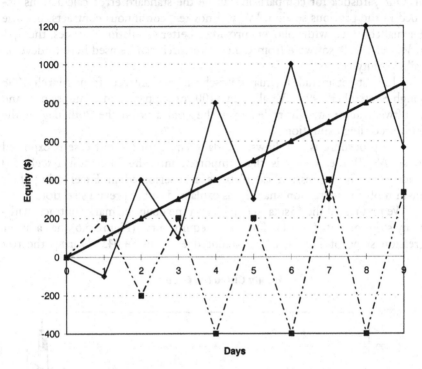

Figure 6.5 Hypothetical equity curves that are perfectly negatively correlated; combining them reduces the SE to zero in this contrived example, because the resultant equity curve is a perfect straight line.

use the built-in tools to find all relevant regression data by just filling out a template (pick Tools, then Data Analysis, then Regression, and fill out the template). Otherwise, you could use one of the many easily available packages for statistical analysis.

In the following sections we use SE to measure equity curve smoothness. Remember that increasing the slope does not automatically increase smoothness (that is, reduce SE). We will examine how different system designs affect portfolio level equity curves.

Effect of Exits and Portfolio Strategies on Equity Curves

All the decisions you make about entries, exits, and stops show up in the slope and smoothness of the equity curve. In this section we will explore the equity curves of the 65sma-3cc model using a deutsche mark actual contract with rollovers. We will study how the equity curve responds to changes in system design. Our yardstick for comparison will be the standard error calculations described in the previous section. We will not test continuous contracts, because the actual contracts with rollovers provide a better simulation. Besides, the System Writer Plus™ software from Omega Research can be used here to develop detailed equity curves.

The test set includes actual deutsche mark contracts from March 1988 through September 1995. We allowed $100 for slippage and commissions, and the software automatically rolled over the contracts on the 20th day of the month preceding expiration.

The procedure is as follows: the daily equity of the test case is exported into an ASCII file, which is then imported into the Microsoft Excel® 5.0 spreadsheet. The regression calculations are perfomed in Excel using their built-in tools for regression analysis, as explained in the previous section.

We first tested the 65sma-3cc model on the deutsche mark contracts without any stops or exits (case 1). The case 1 equity curve (Figure 6.6), has a linear regression slope of $17.54, and a standard error of $4,043. During the test

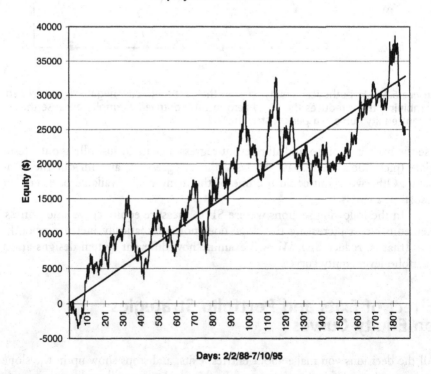

Figure 6.6   Case 1, the 65sma-3cc model without any stops or exits, on actual deutsche mark data with rollovers.

Equity Curve DM Case 2

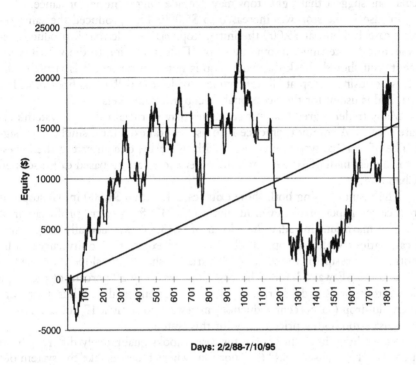

Days: 2/2/88-7/10/95

Figure 6.7   Case 2, the deutsche mark contracts and 65sma-3cc system with $1,500 initial stop.

period, the 65sma-3cc model produced paper profits of $24,288, with a profit factor of 1.34 and a maximum intraday drawdown of –$11,938, trading one contract at time. The equity curve for case 1 is rather jagged, with a significant retracement in 1992, and is typical of trend-following systems without any exits. Note how many trades gave up significant profits before being closed. Also, if the market enters an extended sideways period, this model will suffer drawdowns, and you can go a long time before new equity highs.

Case 2 is the same system with a $1,500 hard stop. The equity curve (Figure 6.7) shows that adding this stop decreased profits and reduced smoothness compared to case 1. The net paper profit dropped sharply from $24,288 to just $6,913, for a meager profit factor of 1.10. The maximum intraday drawdown almost doubled, to –$20,225, suggesting that a $1,500 stop is too tight. The equity curve (see Figure 6.7) shows the lower profit and higher drawdown. Note that the slope has halved from case 1, to $8.24, and the standard error has increased to $7,517. Hence, when you set your stop, compare the hard dollar amount to the market's volatility, and ensure you are safely outside its zone of random movements. Many traders seem to favor tight or close stops, and these calculations suggest that tight stops may degrade long term performance.

In case 3, the stop was increased to $5,000. This produced the same results as case 1. Thus, at $5,000 the initial stop was so wide that it produced results identical to testing without any stops. Thus, returning to the volatility argument, you should check that your stop is not so wide that it is virtually the same as not using a stop at all. Of course, a wide stop will act as firewall of last resort, and is useful for the occasional hiccup in the markets.

Many traders agree that exit strategies play a crucial role in a system's ultimate success. A common practice is to use several exits for a single entry signal. The 65sma-3cc system was tested with two exits, one an exit at the lowest low or highest high of 10 days, and the other the volatility-based exit discussed in Chapter 5.

The result of using both these exits (case 4) with a $5,000 initial stop was to reduce the paper profits even further, to $3,737, for a paltry profit factor of 1.07. The maximum intraday drawdown of -$13,337 was actually larger than the calculations with no stops at all. You would expect the equity curve to be smoother as a result of the exits. As Figure 6.8 shows, the slope decreased to $5.08 and the SE was $3,368. The new slope was only 29 percent of the slope without stops, but standard error was only 17 percent smaller. Thus, there was a sevenfold drop (85 percent reduction) in reward for only a 17 percent reduction in risk—too high a price to pay for this system.

Notice how the equity curve for case 4 looks qualitatively different from that for case 1, because it has "flat" portions where the exits take the system out of the market. Case 4 neatly illustrates one of the trade-offs in system design: you can go for higher profits or a smoother equity curve. Your choice may depend on many factors, including your personal preferences for risk and equity fluctuations.

We next consider a delayed 20-bar breakout system with a $5,000 initial stop and a trailing stop at the 14-day high or low (case 5). The DM contracts over the same period for this case yielded a slope of $8.36, with a SE = $1,960. Case 5 had a clipped equity curve (see Figure 6.9) with many flat portions when the model was out of the market. The equity shows that this approach successfully caught some of the trends, and avoided most of the sideways markets.

You must be careful not to judge the relative smoothness of an equity curve simply by inspecting it visually. For example, consider case 6, the equity curve obtained by adding those for case 1 and case 5. This equity curve (Figure 6.10) seems smoother to the eye than the equity curve for case 1. Besides, we are adding an equity curve to case 1 that has just half of its SE. A regression calculation shows that the slope of the joint equity curve is $25.90 and the SE = $5,263, bigger than either curve. You may find this easier to believe if you grasp that the profitable periods coincide, increasing the amplitude of the movement during these overlapping periods. The result is an equity curve with larger

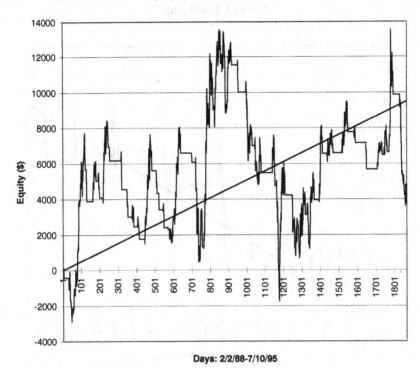

Figure 6.8 The 65sma-3cc system on DM with trailing stop, volatility stop, and $5,000 exit.

standard error. Thus, you should check the regression numbers when you combine multiple systems on the same market.

Note that due to its greater slope, the composite equity curve (case 6) has a higher reward/risk ratio (25.90/5263 = 0.00492) then the original case 1 (17.54/4043 = 0.00434). Thus, we could improve the risk/reward ratio by combining systems using different logic to trade the same market.

You should not underestimate the potential difficulties caused by positive covariance. Figure 6.11 shows the effect of combining two DM systems with positive covariance. The usual rules for combining variance of two independent systems predicted a standard error of $5,430. The actual calculated SE was $6,935, about 28 percent greater. The two systems have positive covariance because they tend to make (or lose) money at the same time, at least some of the time. Figure 6.11 shows lines one standard error on either side of the best fit line. These SE lines include most, but not all, of the points of the joint equity curves. The points that lie outside the SE bands occur when both systems

Equity curve for DM Delayed Breakout model with 14-day high-low exit, $5000 stop

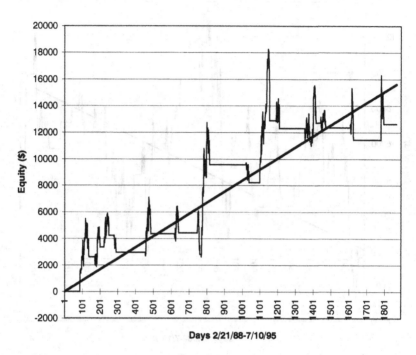

Days 2/21/88-7/10/95

Figure 6.9   Equity curve for a delayed breakout model with $5,000 stop and 14-day high-low trailing stop (case 5).

"reinforce" each other, when they make money at the same time. Thus, combining systems with positive covariance will increase SE and reduce smoothness. Now add the complication that we do not know how covariances will change in the future. Therefore, improvements in smoothness may not result from simply adding different systems trading the same market.

One popular prescription for smoothing the equity curve is diversification through trading multiple markets. The equity curve for the cotton (CT) market, using the 65sma-3cc system from February 22, 1988, through June 20, 1995, with a $5,000 stop is shown in Figure 6.12. The system reported a profit of $28,720, with a profit factor of 1.64, and a maximum intraday drawdown of –$7,120. As usual, $100 was allowed for slippage and commissions in these calculations. Regression calculations showed a slope of 11.65 and a SE of $3,184. The 65sma-3cc calculations for DM for the same period and conditions as the CT calculations yielded profits of $24,900 with a profit factor of 1.34 and a maximum intraday drawdown of –$11,687.

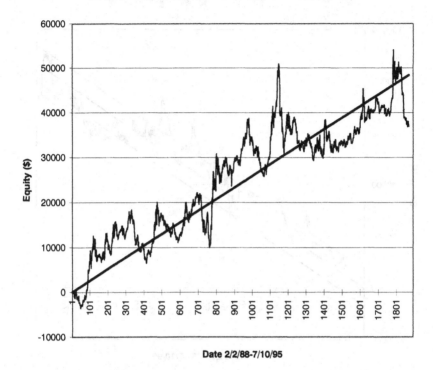

Figure 6.10   Case 6 combined equity curve for case 1 plus case 5.

The CT and DM equity curves to test for increased smoothness. The assumption here is that the CT and DM markets are not dependent on each other. The regression analysis of the joint CT plus DM equity curve (Figure 6.13) showed a slope of $29.34 and a SE of $5,265. The increase in slope is understandable, since adding the two markets roughly doubled the profits over the same period. The joint slope for CT and DM is the sum of their individual slopes ($29.34 = $11.65 + $17.69). The rules for combining variance suggest that if the two markets were independent, then their variances (squared standard error) would just add up linearly. This indicates that the expected value of the standard error for the joint CT + DM equity curve is $5,098. However, we see that the actual value is slightly higher, at $5,264, implying some positive covariance. Thus, we could not have reduced equity curve roughness by combining these two markets. We can show that adding more markets to a portfolio does not increase smoothness (reduce SE) unless the two markets are negatively correlated. Usually, there is some weak correlation between markets due to

Joint equity for two DM systems with positive covariance

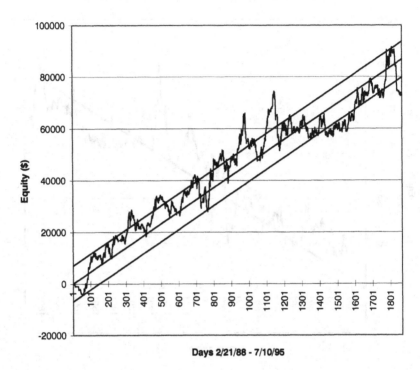

Figure 6.11   Trading two systems on the DM market with strong positive covariance increases SE and equity curve roughness. The lines above and below the best fit line are one standard error away.

random or fundamental factors, and markets rarely move exactly opposite to each other. Hence, we should expect roughness (or SE) to increase as we combine the equity curves from different markets.

In summary, the SE of the equity does not automatically decrease when you change exit strategies, combine different systems on the same markets, or combine different markets on the same system. However, changing entry strategies can change SE significantly. This conclusion goes a bit against the popular wisdom that "diversification" gives a smoother equity curve. Diversification in this context means trading many different markets with the same system, or the same market with many systems. Of course, we are measuring the smoothness using the standard error from linear regression analysis. We saw in the previous section that increasing the slope does not reduce the SE.

You should use the information in this section to understand how system design and portfolio strategies can affect the smoothness of your equity curve.

Equity Curve for CT using 65sma-3cc model, $5000 stop

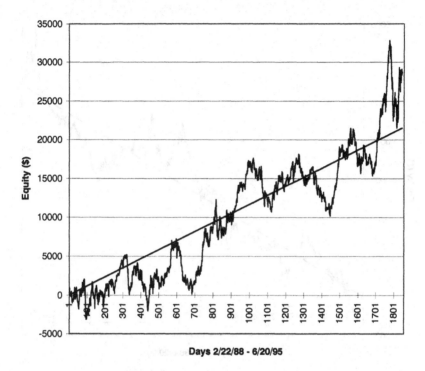

Days 2/22/88 - 6/20/95

Figure 6.12   Equity curve for CT using the 65sma-3cc system.

In this section we examined the daily equity curve for individual markets or systems. In the next section we look at the monthly equity curve and how it changes with money-management rules.

Analysis of Monthly Equity Changes

The impact of a given system on your equity curve will depend on system design and money-management decisions. In this section we look at the monthly equity curve, to understand month-to-month performance. We follow standard accounting procedures and look at the profit and loss figures at the end of each month. You may wish to look at the equity curves on a weekly basis, but the random noise in the market often complicates the analysis of such detailed data.

We saw in the previous section that the standard error of the linear regression provides an excellent measure of the roughness of the equity curve.

Equity for joint CT + DM using 65sma-3cc and $5000 stop

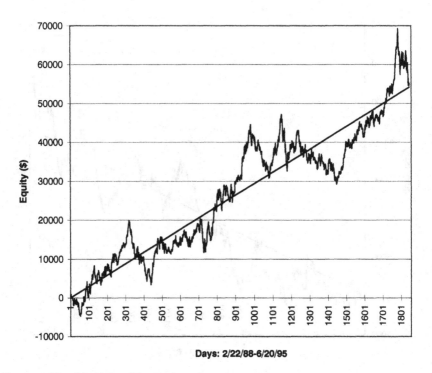

Figure 6.13   The joint CT + DM equity curve.

However, the linear regression approach does not show how much money the system lost over a 1-, 2-, or 3-month period, nor does it reveal the maximum cumulative loss. We also would like to know what percentage of the months showed profitable returns, and whether the curve becomes smoother when we add certain markets or change the portfolio mix. Another useful bit of information is how quickly the system recovers from a losing streak, measured in months between new highs.

You must remember that this analysis reflects past data, not how the system will do in the future. However, if you use average numbers and standard deviations, you can get a fair estimate of future performance. You can then decide how to capitalize the system, by quantifying the equity swings you can tolerate. Thus, analyzing the equity curve on a portfolio basis gives a deeper understanding of system performance, and you can better prepare for future equity swings in real-time trading.

Most of this analysis was done in a spreadsheet, since the popular system testing software does not provide this information. We first used Omega

Research's System Writer Plus™ software to generate the daily equity curve using real contract data with rollovers, because we found that continuous contracts were not giving reliable results. We then used Tom Berry's Portfolio Analyzer™ software to summarize these data into monthly performance numbers. You can do the same using a spreadsheet, or you can write a simple program.

Once in the spreadsheet, we calculated the actual dollar changes in equity over 1, 2, 3, 4, 5, 6, and 12 months. We could then quickly calculate the best performance, the worst performance (drawdown) and standard deviation of profits over each period. The advantage of making the dollar equity change calculations was that we could clearly see the effects of a particular exit strategy or of combining different markets in a portfolio. Some sample calculations will give you a feel for analyzing equity curves at a portfolio level.

We used actual DM contracts from automatic rollover on the 20th day of the month preceding expiration. The test period was February 1988 through June 1995. We allowed $100 for slippage and commissions and used the 65sma-3cc system with one-way entries to test different exit strategies. A one-way model does not allow back-to-back entries of the same type, so that you will not see two consecutive long or short trades. Thus, the number of entries over a data set is constant, allowing an apples-to-apples comparison.

Figure 6.14 is the monthly equity curve for the 65sma-3cc system with a $5,000 initial stop and no other exits. Thus, the long entry was also the short exit signal, and vice versa. The large stop makes it a better test of the inherent robustness of the entry signals. The system reported a paper profit of $24,900 from February 22, 1988 through June 20, 1995, with a profit factor of 1.34, 35 of 70 profitable trades, and a drawdown of –$11,687.

The monthly equity curve (see Figure 6.14) shows the overall rising trend with many sharp equity retracements, which occurred during trading range markets following a strong trend. Interestingly, rolling over the contract captured most of the profits in an uptrend, better than most exits. However, the system gave up most of the profits in the consolidation that followed the uptrend, suggesting that filtering this model should smooth out the equity curve. You could have deduced this information by studying the charts of each contract tested. However, the equity curve clearly shows a need to check those charts if you had not checked them already.

Our usual summary does not tell us what the equity changes are over periods of 1, 2, 3, 4, 5, 6, or 12 months. Yet we need this type of information to understand the impact of the trading strategy on account equity. So, let us review how the 65sma-3cc system did over different time intervals. Figure 6.15 is a plot of the worst drawdown over any consecutive periods of 1, 2, 3, 4, 5, 6, or 12 months. The drawdowns were in the range of –$9,000 to –$13,000. This is the maximum peak-to-valley reduction in equity over the monthly period of interest.

You will recognize that such a drawdown is meaningful only in the context of your account equity. Thus, if you traded this system with a $25,000 account,

Equity Curve DM 65sma-3cc

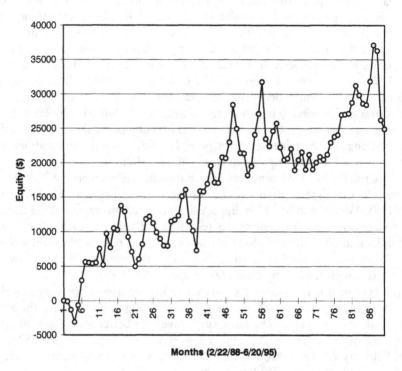

Months (2/22/88-6/20/95)

Figure 6.14 Monthly equity curve for deutsche mark calculations with rollover contracts.

it would suffer drawdowns greater than 20 percent, suggesting you should trade this system with $50,000 or more of equity per contract traded.

Another important piece of information we can gather from the equity analysis is the percentage of intervals that were profitable. This will show what percentages of consecutive months were profitable on a monthly basis, a useful measure of system performance. Figure 6.16 shows these data for the DM test with 65sma-3cc. More than 50 percent of the 90 monthly intervals from February 1988 through June 1995 were profitable. The proportion of winning intervals increases as the period increases. This could be interpreted as the longer you are in a drawdown mode, the more likely you are to come out it.

You should take a good look at the proportion of profitable intervals for each market when you combine different markets hoping to increase the proportion of profitable intervals. A good measure of your successful diversification processes is upward changes in the proportion of profitable intervals. Here diversification includes multiple markets, multiple trading systems, and different money-management strategies.

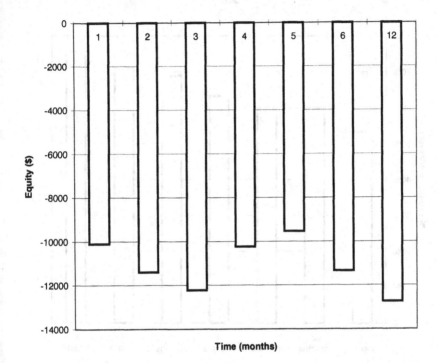

Figure 6.15   Maximum losses in DM over fixed monthly intervals from February 1988 through June 1995. Data are for 1- to 12-month intervals.

You should also look at the standard deviation of monthly equity changes. You can use it to project drawdowns for this system. This idea is explored in the next section. For now, we will test the effect of adding a $1,500 trailing stop to the 65sma-3cc model using actual DM contracts with rollovers and a $5,000 initial stop. As usual, we allow $100 for slippage and commissions. The $1,500 stop trails from the point of highest equity for long and short trades. The net paper profit was $7,500, with a profit factor of 1.12, and a drawdown of –$15,515. These results were somewhat worse than not using a trailing stop at all. However, the net profit analysis does not provide the additional insight sketched below.

Figure 6.17 compares the average monthly equity changes with and without a trailing stop for the 65sma-3cc system. There is little doubt that the trailing stop significantly reduces average monthly performance. You should expect the drop in monthly performance since the net profit with the trailing stop was $7,500 versus $24,900 without the trailing stop. A key point not evident from the profit summary, but clearly visible in Figure 6.17 is the performance at the 12-month level, which strongly favors not using a trailing stop.

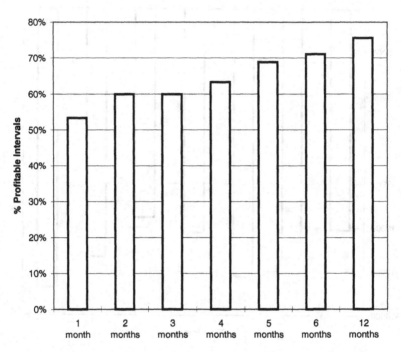

Percentage of profitable intervals (90 total) for DM using 65sma-3cc

Figure 6.16   Proportion of profitable intervals shows that this system tends to have fewer unprofitable intervals as the length of the interval increases.

Unfortunately, the trailing stop also had the effect of reducing the proportion of profitable intervals. The trailing stop did little to improve the smoothness of the equity curve. For example, the standard error with the trailing stop was 3 percent higher, at $4,087, even though profits plummeted nearly 70 percent.

Deleting the trailing stop and adding an exit on the twentieth day of entry increased the reported profit to $14,950 (versus $7,500 with the trailing stop) with a profit factor of 1.27, and drawdown of –$11,325. These data are virtually the same as those with a $5,000 initial stop. Hence, there should be little change in portfolio level performance as a result of adding this exit.

The new SE was 10 percent smaller, at $3,781, but the performance over the intervals was comparable to tests without the stop. Hence, adding this exit produced little improvement, but cost a 40-percent drop from $24,000 in potential profits. Although not shown here, the proportion of profitable intervals dropped about 10 percent, another strike against this exit strategy.

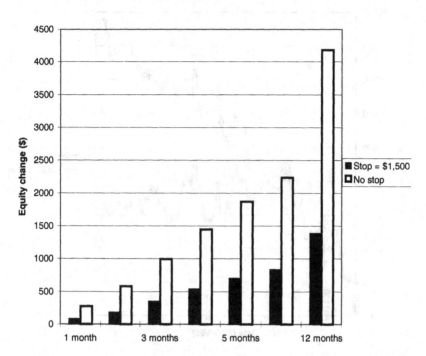

Average interval equity change for 65sma-3cc with and without a trailing stop

Figure 6.17   The average profit over each monthly interval was substantially better without the trailing stop, suggesting that many trades were cut off prematurely. The unmarked bars are for 2 months, 4 months, and 6 months.

A number of other exit strategies yielded similar results: none improved smoothness of the equity curve by more than 10 percent, a few worsened it, and most had a heavy profit penalty. Changing exit strategies often seems to degrade month-to-month performance. Hence, in the next section we will try to get a smoother equity curve by changing system design.

Effect of Filtering on the Equity Curve

Filtering is a way to reduce the number of trades and provide better entries into the trade. Filtering can also produce a smoother equity curve. We saw that we could not improve smoothness (reduce standard error) with exits alone. Of course, you can argue that there might be other exits that work better, and you can check them all if you like.

Equity curves for filtered and unfiltered CHBO systems for DM

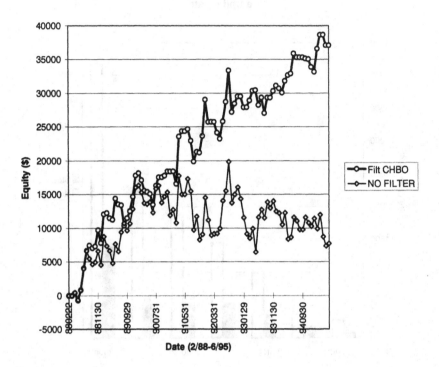

Figure 6.18   Equity curve for a 20-day channel system on DM with (upper line) and without (lower line) filter. Calculations are with rollovers on actual daily contract data.

In order to get a smoother equity curve, we will try changing the system design by introducing a filter. Because losses come from entries during consolidations, the primary benefit of filtering would be to eliminate some of the unprofitable entries. The penalty would be late entry into trends, resulting in lost profits. In some cases, the late entries would be near intermediate tops or bottoms, with the market reversing into the previous consolidation region. Such trades would trigger the initial stop loss orders. We explored how to use the RAVI filter with the 65sma-3cc system in Chapter 3. You can use momentum-based filters or invent other filtering schemes.

We tested a breakout system because breakout systems inherently do not produce entries during small consolidations. For example, a narrow consolidation will not produce new 20-day highs or lows. Therefore, entries from the 65sma-3cc system in these areas would be eliminated. We used a simple filter based on the directional movement index (DMI) because it is a bit more sensitive

Equity curves of 65sma-3cc and filtered channel breakout

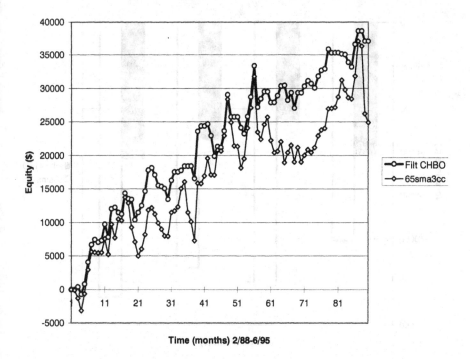

Time (months) 2/88-6/95

Figure 6.19   The filtered breakout system (upper line) had a smoother curve compared to the 65sma-3cc system without initial stop or exits (case 1; lower line).

than the average directional index, or ADX. The purpose of the filter is just to reduce false breakouts, since breakouts during wide consolidations will occur without strong market momentum. The filter merely stipulates that the 14-day DMI be greater than an arbitrarily chosen level such as 50. For details on the construction of the DMI please refer to Wilder's book (see bibliography for reference).

We tested the system on DM data from March 1988 through June 1995 with rollovers on the twentieth day of the month before expiration, a $1,500 initial stop, and $100 allowed for slippage and commissions. The equity curves for the filtered and unfiltered system are shown in Figure 6.18.

Filtering also produced an equity curve (see Figure 6.19) that is smoother than for the unfiltered 65sma-3cc system, described in this chapter as case 1. Note that the case 1 equity curve has been converted from daily to monthly data. The SE for case 1 was $3,776, versus $2,507 for the filtered equity curve,

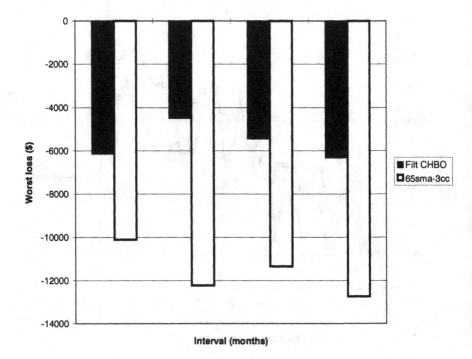

Worst interval drawdown for 65sma-3cc and filtered CHBO

Figure 6.20   The filtered breakout system produced smaller drawdowns than the 65sma-3cc system without initial stop or exits (case 1). Data are for 1-, 3-, 6-, and 12-month intervals (from left to right).

a difference of 50 percent. The interval drawdowns were also smaller, confirming the smoother equity changes (see Figure 6.20).

We then compared the performance of the channel breakout system with and without filtering. The average interval equity change over 1, 3, 6, and 12 months was greater for the filtered system, as shown in Figure 6.21. Thus, the filtered system produced more consistent results for DM. For example, standard deviation of interval returns was greater for the unfiltered system (see Figure 6.22), confirming its uneven performance.

As expected, a linear regression analysis showed the standard error for the filtered system to be $2,507 versus $3,937 for the unfiltered system. Thus, filtering produced a smoother equity curve, since the standard error decreased by 36 percent. A brief comparison of the filtered and unfiltered system is shown in Table 6.1.

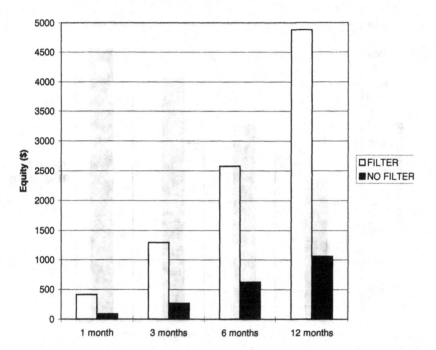

Figure 6.21   The interval equity changes were greater for the filtered deutsche mark system.

The data in Table 6.1 show that filtering reduced the number of trades, and improved profitability and the profit factor in this instance. These calculations suggest that filtering can produce a smoother equity curve. Hence, you should also evaluate the effects of changing entry strategies at the portfolio level.

Table 6.1   Comparison of DM systems.

	Unfiltered DM System	Filtered DM System
Net profit ($)	6,863	37,125
Total number of trades	105	64
Percentage of winners	38	50
Ratio: average wins/losses	1.75	1.74
Average trade ($)	65	580
Maximum drawdown ($)	−11,338	−5,688
Profit factor	1.08	1.74

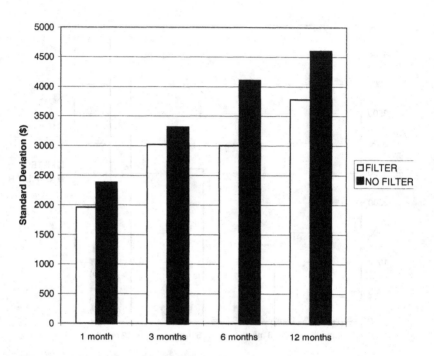

Standard deviation for interval equity change, filtered vs. unfiltered DM system

Figure 6.22   The unfiltered channel breakout system had larger standard deviation of interval equity changes.

Modeling CTA Returns

Where do commodity trading advisor (CTA) returns come from? Can the origin of returns explain variations in correlation among managers? The returns on the track record of a CTA can be explained by returns on subsectors of the futures markets. One can thus try to synthesize the equity curve of a manager by "correctly" combining subsector returns using simple trading systems. Synthesizing an equity curve requires some knowledge of the manager's trading philosophy and approach, but such information is not easily available. For example, it should be relatively easy to synthesize the returns of trend-following CTAs because trend followers, as a group, should be long or short a market at about the same time during major trends. Of course, the details of entries, exits, and trade sizing are unknown and can vary widely.

We examine this issue by using a simple 80-channel breakout system to generate hypothetical returns on the major sectors on the futures markets, namely agricultural and soft commodities (AG), currencies (CR), energies (EN),

Table 6.2   Correlation between composite CTA returns and portfolios of subsector returns. The degree of diversification of the portfolios increases from left to right.

	Portfolio #1 LR & SR & CR	Portfolio #2 LR & SR & CR & EN	Portfolio #3 LR & CR & SR & ST	Portfolio #4 LR & CR & SR & ST & EN & MT	Portfolio #5 LR & CR & SR & ST & EN & MT & AG
CTA-20	0.52	0.60	0.58	0.67	0.73
CTA-21	0.56	0.54	0.35	0.46	0.40
CTA-22	0.66	0.66	0.48	0.54	0.59
CTA-23	0.71	0.67	0.50	0.56	0.57
CTA-24	0.54	0.50	0.40	0.50	0.45
CTA-25	0.76	0.70	0.59	0.67	0.65
CTA-26	0.35	0.34	0.15	0.23	0.40
CTA-27	0.69	0.70	0.51	0.58	0.64
CTA-28	0.44	0.49	0.42	0.49	0.59
CTA-29	0.63	0.54	0.27	0.42	0.42
CTA-30	0.56	0.61	0.46	0.55	0.56
CTA-31	0.76	0.78	0.60	0.64	0.64
Average	0.60	0.59	0.44	0.53	0.55

short rates (SR), long rates (LR), metals (MT), and stock indexes (ST). Included are all of the major liquid markets in North America, Europe, and the Pacific Rim that are traded by the top CTAs. For comparison purposes, we use a random sample of a dozen top CTAs who together manage more than $6 billion. Table 6.2 summarizes sector-by-sector correlation of the composite returns for each CTA without regard to fees or interest, assuming $100 for slippage and commissions per trade. The table shows the correlation of the actual returns to the theoretical returns of the long-term channel breakout system. The calculations cover a period from January 1996 to December 1999. A correlation less than 0.30 may be considered a weak relationship, and a correlation greater than 0.60 may be considered a strong suggestion that the manager uses long-term trend-following strategies on a portfolio comprising those subsectors. The correlations for the simple long-term model vary from as low as 0.15 to as high as 0.78, showing that the model does have some explanatory power.

Of interest is a comparison of CTA-20 and CTA-31, who manage close to $1 billion between them. The correlation between the actual track records of CTA-20 and CTA-31 is 0.59, implying that there a moderately strong similarity, but the strategies are not "identical." With respect to Portfolio #1, long and short rates and currencies, the two seem to have quite different strategies (see Table 6.2, column 1). However, comparing CTA-20 on a diversified portfolio (column 5) with CTA-31 on a portfolio with interest rates and currencies (column 1), we see that their correlation to a long-term trend-following system rises to the low to mid-seventies, implying they seem to have similar trading strategies. Thus, the similarity between the strategies of CTA-31 and CTA-20 are not apparent unless we break down the performance on a sector basis. Indeed, CTA-20, CTA-23, CTA-27, and CTA-31 all seem to favor long-term trend-following strategies, and the portfolio differences seem to be the leading explanation for differences in correlation among them.

We now extend the analysis by using multiple linear regression analysis of CTA-25's results and subsector returns. We can explain at least 60 percent of the variation in the returns of this CTA with a statistically significant regression using the sector returns of long bonds and currencies (see Table 6.3). The actual equity curve and the curve estimated from the linear regression model are shown in Figure 6.23. Thus, subsector analysis may provide clues into the "black-box" that is the trading strategy of a CTA. A "high" value of correlation (greater than 0.60) implies a good explanation of the source of CTA returns. A test of the returns of very short term CTAs, whose returns should have nothing to do with long-term trend-following returns, showed correlations to interest rate subsectors in the 0.2 to 0.3 range, but a linear regression analysis did not

Table 6.3   A summary of the statistically significant linear regression calculations from a spreadsheet showing that a substantial percentage of the variation in this CTA-25's returns could be explained by the returns of a long-term trend-following system trading long bonds and currencies.

SUMMARY OUTPUT

Regression Statistics	
Multiple R	0.7861
R Square	0.6179
Adjusted R Square	0.6010
Standard Error	0.0407
Observations	48

ANOVA

	df	SS	MS	F	Significance F
Regression	2	0.1207	0.0603	36.3927	0.0000
Residual	45	0.0746	0.0017		
Total	47	0.1953			

	Coefficients	Standard Error	t Stat	P-value
Intercept	0.0115	0.0060	1.9092	0.0626
LT Bonds	0.0082	0.0011	7.6891	0.0000
Currency	0.0072	0.0024	2.9677	0.0048

Returns from Interest Rates and Currency explain
CTA-25 Returns

Figure 6.23   The returns of CTA-25 can be modeled quite closely by the returns of a long-term trend-following system trading long bonds and currencies using the linear regression parameters calculated in Table 6.3.

show statistically significant relationships, as we would expect. Thus, correlations less than 0.3 could imply that the correlation is possibly spurious.

Our analysis in this section indicates that understanding correlations among CTAs also requires detailed information about their portfolios. In the absence of such information, we can use simple trend-following systems to derive subsector returns. Such returns can be synthesized into statistically significant models of CTA returns. This information can be used to build more robust and efficient portfolios.

Stabilized Money Manager Rankings

There is considerable interest in deriving a stable ranking procedure for the performance of return generation processes (RGPs). Such rankings could potentially be used to construct efficient portfolios and achieve greater returns. Unfortunately, the problem is more difficult than may first appear because past performance seems to bear little relationship to future performance. As a first step, we must define what we mean by performance. Performance can be measured on an absolute basis (percent return over the period), on a risk-adjusted basis (such as average monthly return divided by standard deviation of monthly returns) or on a relative basis (such as rankings compared to a group of other RGPs). The relative rankings themselves may be derived from a comparison of absolute or risk-adjusted performance versus the peer group.

For the purposes of the current effort, we will use commodity trading advisor performance for analysis, with each CTA considered as a separate RGP. A small body of work suggests that CTA rankings based on past performance have limited predictive value (see Irwin et al., Schwager, 1996). These studies from academia and industry compared a large number of CTAs over different periods and concluded that little can be said about absolute returns in a subsequent period. These studies did conclude that the rankings based on the standard deviation of monthly returns was relatively consistent, so highly volatile CTAs tended to retain their high volatility over subsequent periods.

Let us consider why past performance will vary over future periods for even a single CTA. We assume here that the CTA does not change the leverage employed in trading. If the RGP and portfolio remain unchanged, absolute performance will vary from year to year simply because the markets in the portfolio performed differently over time. These variations in market performance will be reflected in variations in risk-adjusted performance over time. Because most CTAs continually research new trading ideas, the portfolio and RGP typically vary over time—slowly for some CTAs and more rapidly for others. This further complicates performance comparisons over time. Furthermore, performance will show even greater variations if the CTA chooses to systematically vary the leverage. Hence, even if we used just a single CTA, performance measures will vary over time.

Now we consider the problem of comparing CTAs without regard to their RGP, portfolio, or average account size. In this situation, we may compare short-term traders with long-term traders, and specialized currency traders with those trading diversified portfolios without regard to market conditions over the period under review. The size of the accounts traded also has a significant impact on relative performance, with CTAs trading larger sizes likely to show performance that is more consistent. For example, trend-following models may all indicate that the accounts should be long the Japanese Government Bond (JGB). However, for some CTAs, the accounts may be too small to permit trading this market. Hence, even with diversified portfolios, account size can be a significant determinant of relative performance. Thus, there is little reason, a priori, to expect stability in relative, absolute, or risk-adjusted performance within a randomly selected basket of CTAs because the factors influencing their performance are so diverse.

Can we expect performance measures to show any stability at all? The answer is a resounding "maybe" if we select our sample carefully. First, we should compare apples to apples by selecting CTAs trading similar strategies and portfolios. For example, we can select trend-following CTAs all trading diversified portfolios. Even though there are many trend-following strategies, we expect the CTAs as a group to be long when the market is in a major uptrend and short in a major downtrend. Differences in strategy will be reflected in different entry and exit points. In any group that we pick, we can assume that the CTAs will not drastically change the leverage used over time. Even grouping by portfolios is problematic because most CTAs do not provide sufficient details on the markets traded and the relative weights for each. It would be an oversimplification to assume that all CTAs are trading all markets with the same relative weights. For example, two "diversified" trend followers may trade the currency markets with different weights within their portfolios. Hence, there will be differences in performance that cannot be completely accounted for.

Second, we can use overlapped samples to provide internal smoothing for changes in trading strategies used by the CTAs over time. For example, we use the latest two years of data when analyzing performance on December 31 of successive calendar years. A strong case can be made for using overlapped time intervals for performance comparison, even though previous studies have used nonoverlapping time intervals for comparison. The statistical theory of sampling allows for systematic rotation within the selected sample, as long as 50 percent or more of the sample has fresh data (see Jessen, 1978). In our case, we test the ideas by using two different overlapping strategies: using 2 years of data with 12 old and 12 new monthly data points (50 percent replacement), or using 21 months of data, with 9 old and 12 new data points (57 percent replacement).

Third, we can compare relative performance based on risk-adjusted returns by using return efficiency, defined as the ratio of average monthly returns to the standard deviation of those returns. For example, the CTA with the highest return efficiency will be ranked number 1, and the others will be assigned higher ranks in descending order of return efficiency. Comparison of absolute returns is corrupted by variations in leverage used by CTAs. The comparison of relative risk-adjusted performance assumes that structural differences in the design of RGPs will persist so that superior designs will perform better than inferior designs. Thus, we expect relatively stable relative risk-adjusted performance rankings among CTAs with similar trading strategies and similar portfolios. We also expect some changes in relative rankings as CTAs change their RGPs because of continuing research.

The statistical test used is similar to that used in prior studies. We first calculate the return efficiency over a 24-month period ending December 31, and rank the CTA based on return efficiency. Next, we advance the date by 12 months, to the end of the next calendar year, and use the latest 24-month data. This creates an overlapped sample with 12 data points carried over from the first 24-month sample. We then rank the CTAs by return efficiency in the second sample. The statistical test is the nonparametric Spearman's rank correlation test or Spearman's correlation coefficient, which is equivalent to running a linear regression between the two sets of ranks and calculating the correlation between them. If the two sets are correlated, then lower-ranked CTAs will continue to carry a low ranking in the second set, and higher-ranked CTAs will carry their high rankings into the second set.

International Traders Research's (of La Jolla, California) database was the source of the data for 17 CTAs, who report that they use a trend-following trading strategy on diversified portfolios. Their names have been replaced to maintain anonymity. The dataset spans 1995 to 1999 to allow comparison among all 17 managers, so we have four overlapped 2-year intervals. The relative rankings and correlations are summarized in Table 6.4. The correlation in ranks over the three periods is significant at the 1 percent level. The rankings

Table 6.4   CTA rank based on return efficiencies over 2-year overlapped samples calculated on December 31.

CTA	1995–96	1996–97	1997–98	1998–99
CTA-1	17	17	16	8
CTA-2	13	12	9	16
CTA-3	8	10	15	10
CTA-4	7	4	4	5
CTA-5	11	9	5	3
CTA-6	3	2	1	1
CTA-7	6	5	6	14
CTA-8	5	3	12	13
CTA-9	15	16	17	15
CTA-10	14	13	10	17
CTA-11	9	7	11	12
CTA-12	10	14	14	9
CTA-13	4	8	13	11
CTA-14	16	15	7	6
CTA-15	1	1	2	4
CTA-16	2	6	3	2
CTA-17	12	11	8	7
Correlation		0.90	0.67	0.63

have interesting implications for portfolio construction. Table 6.5 shows the portfolio comprising the five top CTAs at the end of each two-year period. The starting portfolio for each period is the same as the ending portfolio of the previous period. The rankings would have rotated the portfolio toward the best-performing CTAs on a risk-adjusted basis over the test period.

The results are similar if we use a different rule to construct the overlapped intervals. We now use a rule in which we use 21 months of data, with 12

Table 6.5   Portfolio rotation based on rankings at year-end using 24-month overlapped data.

Starting Portfolio		CTA-15	CTA-15	CTA-6
		CTA-16	CTA-6	CTA-15
		CTA-6	CTA-8	CTA-16
		CTA-13	CTA-4	CTA-4
		CTA-8	CTA-7	CTA-5
Ending Portfolio	CTA-15	CTA-15	CTA-6	CTA-6
	CTA-16	CTA-6	CTA-15	CTA-16
	CTA-6	CTA-8	CTA-16	CTA-5
	CTA-13	CTA-4	CTA-4	CTA-15
	CTA-8	CTA-7	CTA-5	CTA-4

Table 6.6   CTA ranks based on 21-month intervals with 57 percent replacement of data.

CTA	1995–96	1996–97	1997–98	1998–99
CTA-1	17	17	15	6
CTA-2	13	7	17	17
CTA-3	8	12	6	10
CTA-4	7	4	3	5
CTA-5	11	14	4	4
CTA-6	3	1	1	1
CTA-7	6	3	5	12
CTA-8	5	5	11	16
CTA-9	15	13	16	14
CTA-10	14	9	14	15
CTA-11	9	10	12	13
CTA-12	10	11	8	8
CTA-13	4	8	13	11
CTA-14	16	16	7	9
CTA-15	1	2	2	3
CTA-16	2	6	9	2
CTA-17	12	15	10	7
		0.81	0.43	0.70

new data points and 9 old data points from the previous interval. We again rank the CTAs based on return efficiency and measure rank correlation (see Table 6.6). These rankings are statistically significant at the 1 percent level for 1996–97 and 1998–99, and at the 10 percent level for 1997–98. Thus, as the amount of overlap decreases, we see the results continue to be stable. The portfolio rotation results change slightly, but not enormously, as shown in Table 6.7.

Table 6.7   Portfolio rotation based on analysis of 21 months of data.

		CTA-15	CTA-6	CTA-6
		CTA-16	CTA-15	CTA-15
		CTA-6	CTA-7	CTA-16
		CTA-13	CTA-4	CTA-5
		CTA-8	CTA-8	CTA-7
Ending Portfolio	CTA-15	CTA-6	CTA-6	CTA-6
	CTA-16	CTA-15	CTA-15	CTA-16
	CTA-6	CTA-7	CTA-16	CTA-15
	CTA-13	CTA-4	CTA-5	CTA-5
	CTA-8	CTA-8	CTA-7	CTA-4

These data suggest that using overlapped data on CTAs trading similar RGPs and portfolios could provide stable relative rankings, with important implications for portfolio rotation. The rankings themselves are not a guarantee of superior performance. A CTA ranked highly at the end of one year may drop out of the top five in the subsequent year. Conversely, a CTA not ranked in the top five at the end of the year may zoom to the top of the list at the end of the subsequent year. Thus, there will be a lag in the rankings because of the smoothing process used to develop them. Note that we use return efficiency, a risk-adjusted measure of performance, to create these rankings. Return efficiency makes sense because the leverage can be adjusted to arrive at the desired risk/reward ratio. However, the rankings would be different if different criteria were used to rank the managers.

Mirror, Mirror on the Wall . . .

"Mirror, Mirror on the Wall! Who has the smoothest equity curve of all?" This is a question of much interest. The evaluation of past performance, whether actual or simulated, is an essential part of portfolio design and system development. The analysis usually focuses on the equity curve of a return generation process or trading manager using monthly data, but daily data can be equally valuable. You can adopt a quantitative, qualitative, or mixed strategy to evaluate the equity curve, with the challenge being to achieve an apples-to-apples comparison.

A qualitative approach compares two or more managers over periods characterized by unique market events. For example, you may analyze a 3-month period in which interest rate contracts rallied vigorously and then experienced a sharp retracement. Alternatively, you could compare the risk-control strategies of two equity managers during the week in which the NASDAQ index dipped about 25 percent in April 2000. A qualitative approach would examine how each RGP handled the sharp retracement.

A quantitative approach compares two or more RGPs over the same period by using a number of separate quantitative criteria. The difficulty with this approach lies in interpreting whether meaningful differences exist between RGPs using numerical criteria. First, the user must be careful to identify whether the selected criterion is sensitive or insensitive to the actual sequence of returns in the equity curve. The actual sequence of returns is certainly relevant to calculating compounded returns. However, the average return and standard deviation are not sensitive to the actual order in which returns were realized. Second, the effects of leverage also influence the absolute values of many numerical criteria. For example, as the leverage used by a manager increases, absolute returns, drawdowns, average monthly return, and standard deviation all increase. Hence, it is often meaningless to compare managers or RGPs without accounting for differences in leverage used in obtaining those returns. A third problem with using quantitative criteria is selecting the actual criteria used to make comparisons. These criteria may not have significant predictive value for even a single RGP. For example, absolute returns over a fixed calendar period, such as 12 months, have so much variability that reliable projections about future returns are difficult to make.

A hybrid approach allows you to combine desirable features of both the qualitative and quantitative strategies. For example, you can use risk-adjusted quantitative measures over selected months to compare RGPs. This focuses the discussion, allowing a direct apples-to-apples comparison.

Normalizing Returns

Imagine you are comparing two RGPs or managers at the end of a month of strong positive performance. You want to decide if one or other is doing better than expected during the strong month. For example, even though one manager is actually reporting a larger absolute return than the other, that manager may be underperforming, given the level of leverage used by the managers. A second issue you want to resolve is whether the return over the past quarter is consistent with the leverage used, and a third issue is whether the returns are consistent with the pattern of prior returns. For example, one manager may have predominantly upside volatility (i.e., large positive returns and small negative returns), and the other may have about equal upside and downside volatility. Your qualitative assessment of the strong months would be quite different if you had a prior expectation for returns based on the pattern of prior performance.

We need a yardstick to measure the performance in the most recent month (or the month under study). We arbitrarily choose the standard deviation of monthly returns over the trailing 24 months (Std24), not including the most recent month or the month under study, as the basis for normalizing returns. You could make a case for using the prior 12 months, or the prior 36 months, or any other interval. We arrived at 24 months as a compromise between being too short or too long, but remember that the results of the normalization will change as you change the yardstick.

Table 6.8 shows the actual performance data for eight commodity trading advisors from December 1989 through December 1991. December 1991 was a strong positive month for this group of CTAs, and we wish to determine which CTAs turned in the best performance that month. Table 6.9 shows the CTAs ranked by absolute returns. CTA-3 had the highest absolute returns, at 44.6 percent. However, CTA-7, with a 32.3 percent absolute return turned in the best risk-adjusted return, at 3.81 times the trailing 24-month standard deviation of monthly returns. CTA-3 had a return that was 2.98 times the trailing 24-month standard deviation. The magnitude of Std24 is related to the amount of leverage used by the CTA and the number of markets traded. All other parameters being equal, as leverage is increased, the dollar gains (and losses) also

Table 6.8 Actual monthly performance data for a random sample of eight CTAs.

Date	CTA-1	CTA-2	CTA-3	CTA-4	CTA-5	CTA-6	CTA-7	CTA-8
Dec-89	28.56%	10.24%	36.00%	5.00%	7.93%	17.01%	18.20%	29.50%
Jan-90	0.49	5.63	5.30	16.90	4.13	1.89	5.50	−1.40
Feb-90	3.37	2.45	0.50	27.90	4.21	7.76	3.50	6.10
Mar-90	8.62	5.68	36.40	10.70	2.99	12.16	5.60	13.90
Apr-90	4.37	8.34	39.60	5.90	2.40	16.71	5.60	23.40
May-90	−4.61	−12.09	−15.90	−15.10	−5.66	−13.61	−8.10	−20.60
Jun-90	1.77	4.55	18.00	3.10	3.51	9.50	4.80	3.80
Jul-90	6.25	4.32	11.50	5.30	16.05	16.06	7.40	23.90
Aug-90	15.15	8.98	16.70	12.00	3.39	21.80	15.00	36.80
Sep-90	0.60	0.72	9.40	8.20	2.67	10.40	12.80	8.80
Oct-90	1.86	2.13	2.90	−6.90	7.65	4.87	−3.70	3.20
Nov-90	−0.25	0.07	0.20	−0.30	3.00	2.51	−4.80	1.00
Dec-90	0.11	−0.82	−2.00	−2.30	0.24	−2.45	−6.10	−4.30
Jan-91	−1.29	−7.59	−7.30	−1.30	−5.32	−7.43	−14.10	−8.60
Feb-91	4.84	−2.58	−11.60	7.10	1.40	−7.75	4.40	−1.50
Mar-91	2.32	16.04	0.20	−4.90	2.60	2.26	12.00	8.60
Apr-91	−2.80	−1.66	−4.60	3.80	−0.09	−5.58	1.80	−10.00
May-91	0.27	2.66	−3.20	2.50	−1.13	−1.17	1.60	−7.40
Jun-91	−1.25	5.43	1.10	1.60	1.63	3.32	6.40	6.90
Jul-91	−1.75	−8.54	−11.30	−16.80	−4.02	−8.12	−14.00	−10.30
Aug-91	−3.32	−2.92	−1.80	0.40	−6.09	−2.93	−8.10	2.10
Sep-91	4.39	2.11	13.40	18.20	0.91	2.43	−0.80	5.60
Oct-91	4.21	0.31	−2.80	0.20	−0.30	0.66	2.80	−2.20
Nov-91	−4.68	−2.09	−2.60	1.90	0.10	−0.27	−3.30	1.10
Dec-91	12.08	16.01	44.60	28.20	16.35	22.14	32.30	30.40
Std24	7.05%	6.24%	14.99%	9.77%	4.76%	9.12%	8.47%	13.40%
Dec/Std24	1.71	2.56	2.98	2.89	3.43	2.43	3.81%	2.27

	CTA-1	CTA-2	CTA-3	CTA-4	CTA-5	CTA-6	CTA-7	CTA-8
1991YTD	12.51%	14.86%	3.66%	40.45%	4.44%	−5.69%	13.97%	8.62%
Ann. Std. Dev.	24.41%	21.62%	51.93%	33.86%	16.49%	31.58%	29.43%	46.43%
1991YTD/ Ann. Std. Dev.	0.51	0.69	0.07	1.19	0.27	−0.18	0.48	0.19

Std24 is the standard deviation of monthly returns (Dec'89–Nov'91). Dec/Std24 means returns for December 1991 are normalized using Std24.

Table 6.9   CTAs ranked by normalized and actual December 1991 returns.

CTA	Dec/Std24	CTA	Actual Return
CTA-7	3.81	CTA-3	44.60%
CTA-5	3.43	CTA-7	32.30%
CTA-3	2.98	CTA-8	30.40%
CTA-4	2.89	CTA-4	28.20%
CTA-2	2.56	CTA-6	22.14%
CTA-6	2.43	CTA-5	16.35%
CTA-8	2.27	CTA-2	16.01%
CTA-1	1.71	CTA-1	12.08%

increase, although the increase may be slightly nonlinear due to the effect of trading costs and performance fees. Because leverage can be used to increase absolute returns, normalization is used to identify which CTAs are using leverage efficiently. The difference in returns between CTA-3 and CTA-7 can at least partly be explained by the difference in leverage used by the two CTAs (Std24 is 14.99 percent for CTA-3 versus 8.47 percent for CTA-7), so had the two been traded with equal leverage, an investor would have made more money with CTA-7 than with CTA-3. Thus, Table 6.9 shows that CTA-7 and CTA-5 are making more efficient use of leverage than CTA-3, even though their absolute returns are proportionately lower because of using lower leverage.

This idea can be extended to normalize returns over periods longer than 1 month. Thus, you could normalize year-to-date returns by a yardstick based on volatility measured over a representative historical interval. For example, we can annualize the Std24 by multiplying it by the square root of 12 (3.4641). In Table 6.8, the trailing 24-month standard deviation of 7.05 percent annualizes to 24.42 percent, allowing for rounding error. The calendar year 1991 return of 12.51 percent is then divided by 24.42 percent to obtain the normalized 1991 year-to-date return. CTA-4 clearly led the others, based on normalized calendar 1991 returns.

There is a tendency to rank CTAs by returns alone, without regard to the leverage used by the CTA, as reflected in higher or lower monthly standard deviations. However, it may be more meaningful to compare CTAs based on normalized returns because it is easy to place CTAs on an equal footing by adjusting leverage to equalize the standard deviation of monthly returns calculated over a specified period.

Risk-Adjusted Measures of Performance

One category of measures of quantitative performance calculates risk-adjusted returns. The design strategy is to devise a ratio in which the numerator measures returns and the denominator measures risk. For example, the Sharpe ratio

(SR) is a popular measure of risk-adjusted performance. This ratio is defined as the excess annualized return over the risk free rate, divided by the annualized standard deviation:

$$SR = \frac{(R - r)}{\Sigma},$$ (6.1)

where SR is the Sharpe ratio, R is the expected annual return (%), r is the annual risk-free rate (%), and Σ is the annualized standard deviation of returns (%). The expected annual return is often the average annual return over the duration of the track record, and the risk-free rate is the 1-year U.S. Treasury bill interest rate. The calculation is obviously sensitive to how R, r, and Σ are specified and the period over which they are computed. The general design of SR is similar to the form of the standardized normal random variable Z from the definition of the normal distribution, $Z = (X - \mu)/\sigma$, where μ and σ are the parameters of the normal distribution, and X is a particular random sample drawn from that distribution. By analogy, if annual returns were drawn from a normal distribution with $\mu = r$ (the risk-free rate) and standard deviation Σ, then any particular realization of returns, R, would be normalized as $Z = (R - r)/\Sigma$, the definition of the Sharpe ratio. Note, however, that the true distribution of SR is not known.

The Sharpe ratio has been criticized as an imperfect measure of risk-adjusted performance, particularly for analyzing the returns of a futures trading program. A good summary of these criticisms can be found in Schwager (1996). Criticisms centering on the definition include sensitivity to manipulation by increasing leverage, the ambiguity in interpreting negative values, and the bias in favor of steady returns. For example, because the numerator contains the deduction of the risk-free rate that does not depend on the leverage used in trading, the Sharpe ratio can be increased by increasing leverage. The return R can be expressed as a multiple of Σ, so doubling Σ can double R, thus increasing the Sharpe ratio. Therefore, comparing programs based solely on the Sharpe ratio can mask the effect of differences in the leverage used by those programs. Continuing our analysis, reducing Σ by half would reduce R by half, and may even yield a negative SR. What is unclear is whether the negative SR would have resulted from using insufficient leverage or inferior returns alone.

Another peculiarity arises because the standard deviation, by definition, is more responsive to extreme values and less sensitive to values close to the average. Thus, if the annualized standard deviation increases, it is not clear if the increase results from extreme values on both sides of the average or just one side of the average, namely, on the positive side. Hence, the Sharpe ratio favors steady returns over time rather than a program in which the gains occur in spurts (i.e., a program with high upside volatility). Another result of using the standard deviation in building the Sharpe ratio is that, because the standard deviation computation is not sensitive to the chronological order in which returns are realized, the Sharpe ratio cannot distinguish between intermittent and consecutive losses.

A significant limitation of the Sharpe ratio arises from using the difference between expected returns and risk-free returns in the numerator. Because financial return series are mathematically described as Martingales, the "best" predictor for the return in the next period is the return in the latest period. This means that the numerator is not designed to "forecast" returns over an extended period, and hence the ratio has limited predictive potential. A final problem with the SR that its distribution is unknown; as calculated, it is a point estimate, and for actual performance data, the SR value changes when calculated over rolling time intervals.

Researchers have developed other alternatives to the Sharpe ratio to overcome some of its limitations. One approach focuses on the numerator and seeks a way to eliminate the risk-free rate. A theoretical justification for this change is that investors or traders in managed futures can margin their account with a Treasury bill and will collect all the interest earned on account balances. Hence, their annualized return can be written as $R = T_r + r$, where T_r is the expect return due to trading and r is the risk-free rate. Hence, the numerator in the Sharpe ratio would be $((T_r + r) - r)$, or just T_r, which is equivalent eliminating the risk-free rate.

An alternative formulation makes the argument that investors in a futures program are not risk averse and thus do not consider the risk-free rate in their investment decisions. This is the equivalent of setting the risk free rate to zero, and has the same effect as the previous argument. This approach to modifying the Sharpe ratio can be written as

$$SR* = \frac{R}{\Sigma}, \tag{6.2}$$

where SR^* is the modified Sharpe ratio, R is the annualized return, and Σ is the annualized standard deviation. Many authors use this definition interchangeably with the basic definition of Sharpe ratio and do not use any special notation to denote the difference. Although no consistent naming convention exists for this change, it should be obvious that the modified Sharpe ratio is not sensitive as the original Sharpe ratio to changes in leverage because the numerator and denominator will change linearly in most situations. Some nonlinearities due to "frictions," such as trading costs and advisory fees may exist, but the changes are linear for most practical purposes.

One interesting feature of the modified Sharpe ratio is that it can be interpreted and constructed slightly differently when computed on a monthly basis. The difference depends on whether we use arithmetic or geometric average returns in the numerator. Consider, for example, the "monthly" Sharpe ratio with the risk-free rate equal to zero. Note that we cannot derive equation (6.3) simply by rewriting R and Σ using monthly returns and the standard deviation.

Rather, we "create" this equation by copying the structure of SR* with monthly average return and monthly standard deviation. When computed on a monthly basis, SR* can be viewed as return efficiency ρ, where

$$\rho = \mu/\sigma. \tag{6.3}$$

Here μ is the average monthly return and σ is the standard deviation of monthly returns. The length of the data series is typically 36 months, but could be longer or shorter if necessary. Return efficiency combines the risk preferences of the investor, where the risk (read volatility) preference is quantified by the standard deviation, and the effectiveness of the RGP is measured by the average monthly return μ. Return efficiency can be interpreted as the fraction of the risk tolerance of the investor that is converted into returns. Return efficiency using arithmetic average return is easy to compute because performance data are easily available in monthly form, and easy to interpret as the fraction of the volatility tolerance that is converted to returns.

Let us clarify two technical issues. The numerator can be defined as the arithmetic or geometric return over a given time period. The arithmetic average return is not sensitive to the order in which the returns are realized, but the geometric return is. When the average monthly return is compounded to measure annualized returns, the precise method of calculating μ, whether arithmetic or geometric, will make a small, but perhaps significant, difference. The arithmetic average is better in calculating return efficiency because its statistical properties are well known: it is normally distributed with a standard deviation of σ√n, where n is the number of months in the data series. Few generalized statements can be made about the distribution of geometric returns.

When the return efficiency is computed on an annualized basis, it can be viewed as a gain/pain ratio, where the numerator is the expected annual gain, and the denominator is representative of the expected *future* "worst case" drawdowns (see Chapter 7). The gain/pain ratio is not sensitive to leverage, and it allows one to manage expectations on the upside (returns) as well as the downside (drawdowns). This interpretation serves to address the criticism that the denominator of the Sharpe ratio does not measure risk as viewed by the typical investor. To this end, Schwager (1996) has proposed the return retracement ratio (RRR),

$$RRR = \frac{R}{AMR}, \tag{6.4}$$

where the numerator R is the average annual compounded return, and AMR is the average maximum retracement for each data point. The AMR, in turn, is the average of the maximum retracement from a prior equity peak or maximum retracement to a subsequent low. The AMR tries to average the retracement up to and beyond each data point and does not arbitrarily restrict drawdown data to calendar-year intervals. The RRR is sensitive to the actual order in which returns were realized in both its numerator and denominator, and smoother curves will lead to a higher RRR. This sensitivity reduces its usefulness as a predictor of future performance. The AMR calculation, besides being complicated, can lead to quirky situations because the future drawdown is unknown. For example, when a market is making new equity highs, the maximum retracement from a prior equity peak and maximum retracement to a subsequent low are both zero. This can lead to distortions when the equity makes a series of new highs. Most investors are likely to experience drawdowns substantially different from the AMR because the magnitude of future drawdowns is impossible to predict precisely.

A couple of new approaches are suggested by the preceding discussion. One approach is to extend the idea of return efficiency by calculating it using rolling 3-month returns instead of monthly returns. The rolling 3-month return efficiency, R3RE, then becomes

$$R3RE = \rho_3 = \frac{\mu_3}{\sigma_3}, \tag{6.5}$$

where μ_3 is the average rolling 3-month return, and σ_3 is the standard deviation of rolling 3-month returns. One advantage of using a rolling 3-month return is that it reflects quarterly performance, allowing sustained gains and drawdowns to be reflected more accurately.

The other approach is to calculate a "double" modified Sharpe ratio, that is, a modified Sharpe ratio of the modified Sharpe ratio, assuming the first SR* calculation occurs over rolling periods of, say, 24 or 36 months. The logic here is that if the returns are steady, without sharp gains or losses, then the standard deviation of SR* will be small, and the double SR* will be proportionately larger. In equation form,

$$(SR*)^2 = SR*(SR*) = \frac{\mu_{SR*}}{\sigma_{SR*}}, \tag{6.6}$$

where it is clear that the calculation of R3RE would be far simpler than that of $(SR*)^2$.

Comparison of Risk-Adjusted Performance Measures

We now compare and contrast the measures of risk-adjusted performance discussed previously. We use a specially contrived set of hypothetical data for our analysis (see Tables 6.10 and 6.11). The equity curves are 24 months long, and each has nominally the same starting and ending points (see Figures 6.24 through 6.27), with the 2-year return being approximately 12.7 percent. These contrived data allow us to compare different quantitative measures of performance on an apples-to-apples basis.

Table 6.10   Specially contrived equity curves to illustrate performance analysis (returns over 24 months nominally 12.7% for all curves).

Upside V	Lo-Rho	Med-Rho	Hi-Rho	Mgr E	Mgr F
0.50%	5.10%	3.10%	1.30%	2.12%	–1.06%
0.45	5.20	2.50	2.20	–1.04	–1.07
–0.50	–3.50	–0.50	–0.40	2.10	–1.08
0.60	–6.10	0.50	0.80	–1.03	–1.09
–0.50	8.50	0.60	0.70	2.08	–1.11
5.00	3.10	1.20	1.00	–1.02	–1.12
–0.50	0.20	–0.60	0.50	2.05	–1.13
–0.50	–0.50	–0.30	5.00	–1.01	–1.14
0.40	3.50	1.80	1.10	2.03	–1.16
0.40	4.20	–0.80	–0.50	–1.00	–1.17
0.40	–3.00	–0.30	–0.40	2.01	–1.19
0.37	–9.17	–1.10	–0.30	–0.99	–1.20
–0.40	–3.00	–1.60	–1.50	1.99	2.43
–0.40	3.30	–1.20	–0.90	–0.98	2.37
0.30	6.50	2.50	2.00	1.97	2.32
0.50	3.30	2.30	2.10	–0.97	2.26
0.50	2.10	1.10	1.20	1.95	2.21
0.50	–1.50	1.70	1.30	–0.96	2.16
–0.50	–0.65	–1.00	–0.50	1.93	2.12
–0.40	2.35	–0.50	–0.40	–0.95	2.08
0.40	–4.30	1.30	1.20	1.92	2.03
–0.40	–2.00	2.20	1.80	–0.94	1.99
–0.38	6.00	–2.00	–0.30	1.90	1.95
6.48	–5.26	1.35	0.12	–0.93	1.92

Upside V: Volatility concentrated in months with positive returns

Lo-Rho: Low return efficiency (ρ); volatility distributed over positive and negative months; ($\rho = \mu/\sigma$; μ = average monthly return, σ = standard deviation of monthly returns)

Med-Rho: Medium return efficiency

Hi-Rho: High return efficiency

Mgr E: Manager E from Schwager (1996): alternate up/down months; positive month dollar gains twice dollar losses in down months

Mgr F: Manager F from Schwager (1996): 12 consecutive down months, 12 consecutive up months; positive month dollar gains twice dollar losses in down months

Figures 6.24 through 6.27 show that equity curves for Lo-Rho and Manager F are the most "choppy," and Manager E has the steadiest equity curve. The Upside V curve is relatively flat with only 2 months with sharp gains. The Med-Rho and Hi-Rho curves are similar to the Lo-Rho curve, but with less volatility. They are "smoother" than for Lo-Rho, but not as steady as for Manager E. Let us now see how the numerical computations shake out.

Table 6.11 Specially contrived equity curves to illustrate performance analysis (derived from Table 6.10 by compounding monthly returns).

Upside V	Lo-Rho	Med-Rho	Hi-Rho	Mgr E	Mgr F
1000.00	1000.00	1000.00	1000.00	1000.00	1000.00
1005.00	1051.00	1031.00	1013.00	1021.19	989.40
1009.52	1105.65	1056.78	1035.29	1010.59	978.81
1004.47	1066.95	1051.49	1031.14	1031.78	968.21
1010.50	1001.87	1056.75	1039.39	1021.19	957.61
1005.45	1087.03	1063.09	1046.67	1042.38	947.02
1055.72	1120.73	1075.85	1057.14	1031.78	936.42
1050.44	1122.97	1069.39	1062.42	1052.97	925.82
1045.19	1117.35	1066.18	1062.42	1042.37	915.23
1049.37	1156.46	1085.37	1074.11	1063.56	904.63
1053.57	1205.03	1076.69	1068.74	1052.97	894.03
1057.78	1168.88	1073.46	1064.46	1074.16	883.44
1061.70	1061.69	1061.65	1061.27	1063.56	872.84
1057.45	1029.84	1044.67	1045.35	1084.75	894.03
1053.22	1063.83	1032.13	1035.94	1074.15	915.22
1056.38	1132.98	1057.93	1056.66	1095.34	936.41
1061.66	1170.37	1082.27	1078.85	1084.75	957.60
1066.97	1194.94	1094.17	1091.80	1105.94	978.79
1072.31	1177.02	1112.77	1105.99	1095.34	999.98
1066.94	1169.96	1101.64	1100.46	1116.53	1021.17
1062.68	1196.87	1096.14	1096.06	1105.93	1042.36
1066.93	1145.40	1110.39	1109.21	1127.12	1063.55
1062.66	1122.49	1134.81	1129.18	1116.53	1084.74
1058.62	1189.84	1112.12	1125.79	1137.72	1105.93
1127.22	1127.26	1127.13	1127.14	1127.12	1127.12

We begin by calculating RRR following Schwager (1996). A sample calculation for the Med-Rho data from Table 6.10 is shown in Table 6.12. The table first converts monthly returns into an equity curve, assuming that we start with $1,000, to find the equity E(I) at each point. The next two columns calculate the peak equity through the end of month I, PE(I), and the maximum retracement from a prior equity peak at point I, MRPP(I). The detailed formula is shown in the footnotes accompanying Table 6.12. The following two columns find the minimum month-end equity on or subsequent to any month, Min E(I), and the maximum retracement to a subsequent low, MRSL(I). For example, at the end of Month 1, the lowest retracement is 1,031, but from month 2 through month 14, it is 1,032.131. The last column in Table 6.12 finds the maximum MRPP or MRSL at each month end, MR(I). The average compounded return

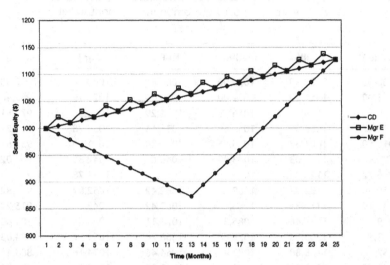

Figure 6.24   Contrived equity curves for comparing quantitative measures of performance. Manager E (Mgr E) from Schwager (1996) has alternate winning and losing months, whereas Manager F (Mgr F) has consecutive losing and winning months. The goal is to derive a measure of risk-adjusted performance to distinguish between these two extreme situations.

Figure 6.25   Contrived equity curves, as described in Figure 6.24. The Upside V equity curve has all its volatile moves on the up (or winning) side. The Lo-Rho curve has about equal volatility on both the upside and the downside.

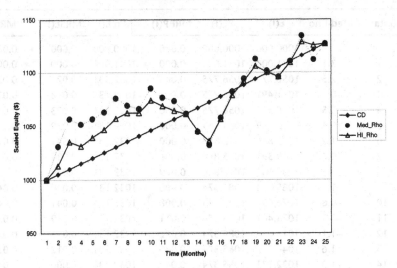

Figure 6.26   Contrived equity curves with low to medium volatility.

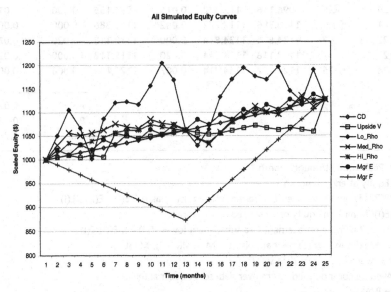

Figure 6.27   Contrived equity curves used to compare quantitative measures of risk-adjusted performance. The goal is to find risk-adjusted performance criteria that can distinguish between steady returns, volatile returns, and curves with infrequent or consecutive losses.

Table 6.12 Sample calculation of Schwager's RRR for Med-Rho data.

Data	Med-Rho	E(I)	PE(I)	MRPP(I)	Min E(I)	MRSL(I)	MR(I)
		1000.000	1000.000	0.000	1000.000	0.000	0.0000
1	3.1	1031.000	1031.000	0.000	1031.000	0.000	0.0000
2	2.5	1056.775	1056.775	0.000	1032.131	0.023	0.0233
3	−0.5	1051.491	1056.775	0.005	1032.131	0.018	0.0184
4	0.5	1056.749	1056.775	0.000	1032.131	0.023	0.0233
5	0.6	1063.089	1063.089	0.000	1032.131	0.029	0.0291
6	1.2	1075.846	1075.846	0.000	1032.131	0.041	0.0406
7	−0.6	1069.391	1075.846	0.006	1032.131	0.035	0.0348
8	−0.3	1066.183	1075.846	0.009	1032.131	0.032	0.0319
9	1.8	1085.374	1085.374	0.000	1032.131	0.049	0.0491
10	−0.8	1076.691	1085.374	0.008	1032.131	0.041	0.0414
11	−0.3	1073.461	1085.374	0.011	1032.131	0.039	0.0385
12	−1.1	1061.653	1085.374	0.022	1032.131	0.028	0.0278
13	−1.6	1044.667	1085.374	0.038	1032.131	0.012	0.0375
14	−1.2	1032.131	1085.374	0.049	1032.131	0.000	0.0491
15	2.5	1057.934	1085.374	0.025	1057.934	0.000	0.0253
16	2.3	1082.266	1085.374	0.003	1082.266	0.000	0.0029
17	1.1	1094.171	1094.171	0.000	1094.171	0.000	0.0000
18	1.7	1112.772	1112.772	0.000	1096.136	0.015	0.0150
19	−1	1101.644	1112.772	0.010	1096.136	0.005	0.0100
20	−0.5	1096.136	1112.772	0.015	1096.136	0.000	0.0150
21	1.3	1110.386	1112.772	0.002	1110.386	0.000	0.0021
22	2.2	1134.814	1134.814	0.000	1112.118	0.020	0.0200
23	−2	1112.118	1134.814	0.020	1112.118	0.000	0.0200
24	1.35	1127.132	1134.814	0.007	1127.132	0.000	0.0068

					AMR	0.0225
					R	0.0617
					RRR	2.7439

PE(I): Peak equity through month 1
E(I): Equity at end of month 1
MRPP(I): Maximum retracement from a prior equity peak = (PE(I) − E(I))/PE(I)
Min E(I): Minimum equity on or subsequent to month 1
MRSL(I): Maximum retracement to a subsequent low = (E(I) − ME(I))/E(I)
MR(I): Maximum retracement at point 1 = Max(MRPP(I), MRSL(I))
AMR = Average MR over data set
R = Average compounded return over data set in decimal terms
RRR = R/AMR

is simple to calculate in this case because there are only 2 years of data. The RRR is the average compounded return divided by the AMR, and is 2.7439 for the Med-Rho data.

The completed calculations are as follows (with RRR values in parentheses): Upside V (10.11), Manager E (6.54), Hi-Rho (4.85), Med-Rho (2.74), Manager F (0.96), and Lo-Rho (0.82). The RRR calculations clearly do not penalize upside volatility, and favor steady returns, explaining the high rankings for Upside V and Manager E. The relatively low-volatility Hi-Rho and Med-Rho managers are in the middle of the pack. The RRR clearly penalizes a string of consecutive losses, but likes volatile equity curves even less, explaining the low rankings for Manager F and Lo-Rho. These rankings are generally in agreement with our visual assessment, with the exception that Manager E ranked lower than Upside V, who had little downside volatility.

We have also computed the Sharpe ratio, modified Sharpe ratio, return efficiency, and R3RE for the data set to observe their ranking behavior (see Tables 6.13 and 6.14). Because all the series have nominally the same return, ranking using SR is equivalent to ranking by the inverse order of the monthly standard deviation. Table 6.15 shows that SR, SR*, and return efficiency produce essentially the same ranking order, which does not distinguish between upside and downside volatility. Hence, the Hi-Rho and Med-Rho curves are ranked ahead of the Upside V curve. The Upside V curve moves up to third when ranked using R3RE, showing that the R3RE approach is moving toward the RRR model with a simpler calculation. Note that the Lo-Rho curve, with its "big" upside and downside volatility, ranked last in all calculations.

To further test the relative performance of the different risk-adjusted measures, we tested data on the eight CTAs from Table 6.8; the results of the calculations are summarized in Table 6.16. For the purposes of comparison, we looked at just the return retracement ratio, RRR; the return efficiency, ρ; and the rolling 3-month return efficiency, R3RE = ρ_3. All three approaches ranked CTA-1 as the best performer and CTA-7 as the worst performer. The top three CTAs were identical for RRR and return efficiency, which also had the same four CTAs at the bottom half of the table. Similarly, RRR and ρ_3 picked the same four CTAs in the top half, but in different order. In summary, the rankings produced by the methods are similar, but the key difference is how they account for upside and downside volatility. The return efficiency and R3RE are easier to compute than RRR, and they do not have some of the computational quirks of the RRR. Hence, the rolling 3-month return efficiency may be a useful measure of risk-adjusted performance.

The key issue raised by these calculations is whether CTAs truly have different volatility on the upside versus the downside. If we assume that volatility will be "symmetric," volatility on the upside caused by favorable markets can also be seen on the downside during unfavorable markets. Under the assumption of symmetric volatility, measures such as the Sharpe ratio or its variants (return efficiency or R3RE) will provide more accurate measures of risk-adjusted

Table 6.13 Return efficiency, Sharpe ratio, and gain/pain ratio calculations for contrived data.

	Upside V	Lo-Rho	Med-Rho	Hi-Rho	Mgr E	Mgr F
	0.5	5.1	3.1	1.3	2.12	−1.06
	0.45	5.2	2.5	2.2	−1.04	−1.07
	−0.5	−3.5	−0.5	−0.4	2.10	−1.08
	0.6	−6.1	0.5	0.8	−1.03	−1.09
	−0.5	8.5	0.6	0.7	2.08	−1.11
	5	3.1	1.2	1	−1.02	−1.12
	−0.5	0.2	−0.6	0.5	2.05	−1.13
	−0.5	−0.5	−0.3	0	−1.01	−1.14
	0.4	3.5	1.8	1.1	2.03	−1.16
	0.4	4.2	−0.8	−0.5	−1.00	−1.17
	0.4	−3	−0.3	−0.4	2.01	−1.19
	0.37	−9.17	−1.1	−0.3	−0.99	−1.20
	−0.4	−3	−1.6	−1.5	1.99	2.43
	−0.4	3.3	−1.2	−0.9	−0.98	2.37
	0.3	6.5	2.5	2	1.97	2.32
	0.5	3.3	2.3	2.1	−0.97	2.26
	0.5	2.1	1.1	1.2	1.95	2.21
	0.5	−1.5	1.7	1.3	−0.96	2.16
	−0.5	−0.6	−1	−0.5	1.93	2.12
	−0.4	2.3	−0.5	−0.4	−0.95	2.08
	0.4	−4.3	1.3	1.2	1.92	2.03
	−0.4	−2	2.2	1.8	−0.94	1.99
	−0.38	6	−2	−0.3	1.90	1.95
	6.48	−5.26	1.35	0.12	−0.93	1.92
μ	0.513	0.599	0.510	0.505	0.511	0.513
σ	1.683	4.523	1.486	1.031	1.527	1.680
ρ = μ/σ	0.305	0.132	0.344	0.490	0.335	0.306

	Upside V	Lo-Rho	Med-Rho	Hi-Rho	Mgr E	Mgr F
R = Avg. Ann. Return (%)	6.337	7.426	6.300	6.231	6.307	6.337
Σ = Ann. Std. Dev. (%)	5.829	15.668	5.147	3.572	5.289	5.819
Sharpe (r=5%)	0.229	0.155	0.253	0.345	0.247	0.230
SR* = R/Σ = Sharpe (r=0) = Gain/Pain	1.087	0.474	1.224	1.744	1.192	1.089

μ = Average monthy return (%)

σ = Standard deviation of monthly returns (%)

ρ = μ/σ: Return efficiency, can be viewed as the monthly Sharpe ratio with risk-free rate = 0

R = Avg. Ann. Return (%): Average annual return (%) obtained by compounding μ over 12 months

Σ = Ann. Std. Dev. (%): Annualized standard deviation (%); $\Sigma = (\sqrt{12})\sigma / 3.46$; can be interpreted as expected future "worst case" drawdown

Sharpe (r=5%): Sharpe ratio with r = 5%

SR* = R/Σ = Gain/Pain = R/Σ; return adjusted by expected "worst case" drawdown (r = 0)

Table 6.14   Rolling 3-month returns, return efficiency, Sharpe ratio, and Gain/Pain ratio calculations.

Data	Upside V	Lo-Rho	Med-Rho	Hi-Rho	Mgr E	Mgr F
1						
2						
3	0.447	6.695	5.149	3.114	3.178	−3.179
4	0.547	−4.675	2.497	2.606	0.000	−3.213
5	−0.403	−1.684	0.597	1.100	3.145	−3.248
6	5.102	5.040	2.316	2.521	0.000	−3.283
7	3.953	12.087	1.196	2.216	3.112	−3.320
8	3.953	2.790	0.291	1.505	0.000	−3.357
9	−0.601	3.188	0.886	1.605	3.080	−3.395
10	0.298	7.308	0.683	0.594	0.000	−3.434
11	1.205	4.612	0.683	0.192	3.049	−3.473
12	1.175	−8.194	−2.186	−1.195	0.000	−3.514
13	0.368	−14.538	−2.974	−2.188	3.018	0.000
14	−0.431	−8.987	−3.850	−2.679	0.000	3.598
15	−0.501	6.714	−0.350	−0.434	2.988	7.283
16	0.398	13.645	3.599	3.205	0.000	7.111
17	1.306	12.325	6.011	5.392	2.959	6.946
18	1.508	3.887	5.184	4.668	0.000	6.789
19	0.497	−0.035	1.791	2.003	2.930	6.638
20	−0.402	0.161	0.180	0.390	0.000	6.495
21	−0.502	−2.686	−0.214	0.291	2.902	6.357
22	−0.402	−4.057	3.011	2.610	0.000	6.225
23	−0.382	−0.587	1.458	2.713	2.874	6.099
24	5.651	−1.584	1.508	1.616	0.000	5.977
μ_3	1.036	1.428	1.248	1.447	1.511	1.641
σ_3	1.893	7.148	2.476	1.998	1.548	4.888
$\rho_3 = \mu_3/\sigma_3$	0.547	0.200	0.504	0.724	0.976	0.336

μ_3 = Average return over rolling 3-month intervals (%)
σ_3 = Standard deviation of rolling 3-month returns (%)
$\rho_3 = \mu_3/\sigma_3$: Return efficiency, can be be viewed as the monthly Sharpe ration with risk-free rate = 0

performance. Empirical research of CTA and hedge fund track records shows that worst-case drawdowns measured on a monthly basis are usually less than four times the standard deviation of monthly returns (see Chapter 7). These data support the assumption of symmetric volatility. Note that typical CTA risk-control procedures cut off losing trades at a predetermined loss level; however, profitable trades are not always liquidated at a profit target, but usually allowed to proceed as long as possible. Thus, it is possible that under favorable market

Table 6.15   Ranking equity curves based on different risk-adjusted measures of performance.

SR	ρ	SR*	ρ_3(R3RE)	RRR
Hi-Rho	Hi-Rho	Hi-Rho	Mgr E	Upside V
Med-Rho	Med-Rho	Med-Rho	Hi-Rho	Mgr E
Mgr E	Mgr E	Mgr E	Upside V	Hi-Rho
Mgr F	Mgr F	Mgr F	Med-Rho	Med-Rho
Upside V	Upside V	Upside V	Mgr F	Mgr F
Lo-Rho	Lo-Rho	Lo-Rho	Lo-Rho	Lo-Rho

conditions you could have a prolonged performance period lasting 3 to 5 years in which the volatility is predominantly on the upside. This produces a distribution of returns skewed to the left. However, CTA performance in 1999 suggests that volatility on the upside will eventually be matched by volatility on the downside.

Control Charts for Future Performance

Analysis of past performance data can help distinguish performance of competing RGPs or managers, but it says little about future performance. We find it difficult to forecast the future with precision, but we can make some estimates about the range of future outcomes. Such range forecasts, instead of point forecasts, can be useful for devising trading or investment strategies.

We resort to the central limit theorem (CLT) from statistics, which applies to a simple random sample drawn from an infinite population of finite mean μ and standard deviation σ. The CLT says that if the sample size is sufficiently large, then the average of the sample is normally distributed with mean μ and standard deviation $\sigma \sqrt{n}$. The distribution of RGP returns may be nonnormal, but returns certainly have a finite mean and variance, given by μ and σ^2, respectively. In this instance, the sample mean statistic, $\overline{X}$ is approximately normally distributed for sufficiently large n (say, n > 25), with a mean μ and standard deviation $\sigma \sqrt{n}$, provided the population is infinite. This means that we can use the properties of the normal distribution to place limits on the range of values obtained for the rolling 12-, 24-, or 36-month average returns obtained over, say, the next 12 months. For example, we can calculate the rolling 24-month average monthly returns and the standard deviation of those returns. Then, we can say that in the next 12 months, there is a 68 percent chance that rolling 24-month average returns will be within an interval $\mu \pm \sigma \sqrt{24}$ calculated at the end of the current year.

Figure 6.28 shows rolling 24-month returns using actual CTA performance data. Also shown are the upper and lower bounds for the rolling 24-month

Table 6.16   Risk-adjusted performance measures for CTA data from Table 6.8.

Date	CTA-1	CTA-2	CTA-3	CTA-4	CTA-5	CTA-6	CTA-7	CTA-8
Jan-90	0.49%	5.63%	5.30%	16.90%	4.13%	1.89%	5.50%	−1.40%
Feb-90	3.37	2.45	0.50	27.90	4.21	7.76	3.50	6.10
Mar-90	8.62	5.68	36.40	10.70	2.99	12.16	5.60	13.90
Apr-90	4.37	8.34	39.60	5.90	2.40	16.71	5.60	23.40
May-90	−4.61	−12.09	−15.90	−15.10	−5.66	−13.61	−8.10	−20.60
Jun-90	1.77	4.55	18.00	3.10	3.51	9.50	4.80	3.80
Jul-90	6.25	4.32	11.50	5.30	16.05	16.06	7.40	23.90
Aug-90	15.15	8.98	16.70	12.00	3.39	21.80	15.00	36.80
Sep-90	0.60	0.72	9.40	8.20	2.67	10.40	12.80	8.80
Oct-90	1.86	2.13	2.90	−6.90	7.65	4.87	−3.70	3.20
Nov-90	−0.25	0.07	0.20	−0.30	3.00	2.51	−4.80	1.00
Dec-90	0.11	−0.82	−2.00	−2.30	0.24	−2.45	−6.10	−4.30
Jan-91	−1.29	−7.59	−7.30	−1.30	−5.32	−7.43	−14.10	−8.60
Feb-91	4.84	−2.58	−11.60	7.10	1.40	−7.75	4.40	−1.50
Mar-91	2.32	16.04	0.20	−4.90	2.60	2.26	12.00	8.60
Apr-91	−2.80	−1.66	−4.60	3.80	−0.09	−5.58	1.80	−10.00
May-91	0.27	2.66	−3.20	2.50	−1.13	−1.17	1.60	−7.40
Jun-91	−1.25	5.43	1.10	1.60	1.63	3.32	6.40	6.90
Jul-91	−1.75	−8.54	−11.30	−16.80	−4.02	−8.12	−14.00	−10.30
Aug-91	−3.32	−2.92	−1.80	0.40	−6.09	−2.93	−8.10	2.10
Sep-91	4.39	2.11	13.40	18.20	0.91	2.43	−0.80	5.60
Oct-91	4.21	0.31	−2.80	0.20	−0.30	0.66	2.80	−2.20
Nov-91	−4.68	−2.09	−2.60	1.90	0.10	−0.27	−3.30	1.10
Dec-91	12.08	16.01	44.60	28.20	16.35	22.14	32.30	30.40
μ	2.11%	1.96%	5.70%	4.43%	2.11%	3.55%	2.44%	4.55%
σ	4.91%	6.68%	15.83%	11.00%	5.49%	9.50%	10.00%	13.48%
$\rho = \mu/\sigma$	0.431	0.294	0.360	0.403	0.384	0.373	0.244	0.338
ρ_3	0.699	0.462	0.506	0.467	0.510	0.459	0.277	0.451
RRR	7.704	3.146	3.613	5.891	4.529	2.911	1.830	3.610

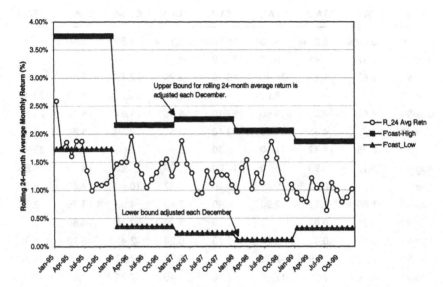

Control Chart: Rolling 24-Month Return and Forecast Upper and Lower Bounds from
Prior Year End Using Actual CTA Monthly Returns

Figure 6.28 A control chart for CTA performance showing the expected upper and lower bounds for the rolling 24-month average return.

returns obtained using the equation $\mu_{24} \pm \sigma_{24} / \sqrt{24}$, where μ_{24} is the average return over the 24 months ending December of the prior year, and σ_{24} is the standard deviation of those returns ending the prior December. Thus, for calendar year 1999, the values used are those calculated at the end of December 1998. For example, the average monthly return at the end of December 1998 for the prior 24 months was 1.10 percent, with a standard deviation of 3.77 percent, giving upper and lower bounds of 1.87 percent and 0.33 percent for calendar year 1999. What does this mean? If the rolling 24-month return was exactly 1.10 percent at the end of December 1999, then the return over the prior 24-month period would be approximated by compounding the average return as follows: $100((1+0.11)^{24} - 1) = 30$ percent (approximately). The upper bound of the expected 24-month returns ending December 1999 was $100((1+.0187)^{24}-1)$ = 56 percent (approximately). Similarly, the lower bound estimate for the 2-year period ending December 1999 was 8.2 percent (approximately). As it turned out, the actual December 1999 average 24-month return was 1.02 percent, with an estimated 2-year return of 27.5 percent; the actual 24-month return was 26.5 percent. The forecasting error was partly because we are compounding the arithmetic average return instead of the geometric average return. Nevertheless, the error in the forecast is acceptable because it gives us a graphical method of tracking expected and actual returns.

As Figure 6.28 shows, we can use the control chart with well-defined bounds for future performance to track performance as it evolves in the new year. In 1995, for example, the CTA returns fell outside the $\mu \pm \sigma / \sqrt{24}$ bands, and we had plenty of warning of that event. In 1996, the forecast bands shifted downward, to accommodate the new reality, and the performance rebounded strongly toward the upper end of expected performance. For 1997 through 1999, the bands did not shift very much, and performance has generally been in the middle of the expected range at year end. Thus, we can develop control charts using past performance data to make a range forecast for expected returns smoothed over a 24- or 36-month period. A 12-month smoothing period can also be used, but the forecast bands must be set wider apart to allow for greater variability in the shorter time frame.

Summary

In this chapter we saw that the standard error from regression analysis is a good measure of the roughness of the equity curve. A smoother equity curve has a smaller value for the standard error.

We saw that the usual prescriptions for producing "smooth" equity curves do not work every time. Most exit strategies tested did not reduce the SE by more than 20 percent, but had a substantial profit penalty. Diversification over different markets or systems also increased standard error. We also examined monthly equity changes to confirm these findings. Only a change in entry rules gave a smoother equity curve.

We modeled CTA returns and showed that they can be explained by returns on simple trend-following models on subsectors of the futures markets. This approach provides a deeper understanding of correlation relationships among CTAs and helps build robust portfolios. The process of assembling portfolios will be further assisted by the procedure for developing stabilized money-manager rankings, a key improvement over existing approaches in this area. Risk-adjusted measures may help you narrow the choices as you build portfolios, and hence this chapter presented a detailed discussion of competing measures of risk-adjusted performance accompanied by an apples-to-apples comparison of those measures. The rolling 3-month return efficiency was shown to be a simpler and effective alternative measure of risk-adjusted performance to the return retracement ratio. We ended the chapter with an application illustrating how control charts can be developed to monitor the performance of money managers.

This chapter showed that analyzing equity curves provides valuable insight into system design not available from the performance summary. Hence, no system development effort can be complete without examining equity curves.

Chapter

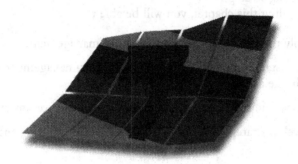

Ideas for Money Management

Bad money management will crush a good system.

Introduction

A big variable affecting the future performance of any system is money management. It is a major factor in properly implementing any trading system. There are many excellent books devoted just to this subject.

We begin by calculating the risk of ruin for the values you will meet during system testing. The data in the literature do not extend down to the range covered here. The risk-of-ruin calculations assume that your probability of winning and payoff ratio are constant. Since these values change from time to time, the risk-of-ruin calculations are simply for guidance.

We then study an example of the interaction between system design and money-management rules, and the effects of using fixed or variable contracts with a typical breakout system. We then expand on the theme of projecting drawdowns using the standard deviation of monthly equity changes. An out of sample test will convince you that it is reasonable to project future drawdowns with this method. It is very useful to have a reasonable projection of future drawdowns because it helps you pick a suitable equity level for a system.

Lastly, we will see how changing bet size affects the equity curve. For a given system, you can change the smoothness of the equity curve by how you alter your betting strategy.

After reading this chapter, you will be able to:

1. Apply the risk-of-ruin ideas for money management.

2. Understand how system design and money-management rules interact with one another.

3. Project the range of possible future drawdowns for any system.

4. Develop strategies for changing bet size after winning and losing periods.

The Risk of Ruin

The mathematical calculations of the risk of ruin are the heart of your money-management rules. These statistical calculations assume that you play the game thousands of times with precisely the same odds. However, your trading situation does not fit this ideal in the real world. Nevertheless, you can best understand the hazards of leverage by studying the risk of ruin.

Using certain simplifying assumptions, the risk of ruin estimates the probability of losing all your equity. The goal of money management is to reduce your risk of ruin to, say, less than 1 percent. Here we follow the general approach used by Nauzer Balsara (see bibliography for reference; refer to this excellent book for more details).

There are three variables that influence the risk of ruin: (1) the probability of winning, (2) the payoff ratio (ratio of average winning to average losing trade), and (3) the fraction of capital exposed to trading. Your trading system design governs the first two quantities; your money-management guidelines control the third. The risk of ruin decreases as the payoff ratio increases or the probability of winning increases. It is obvious that the larger the fraction of capital risked on each trade, the higher the risk of ruin.

The estimates here follow Balsara's general simulation strategy to estimate the risk of ruin, except that we used a total of only 1,000 simulations (rather than 100,000 simulations) to estimate the probabilities. If you can go broke in just 1,000 simulations, you probably would not survive 100,000 simulations.

Table 7.1 summarizes the risk of ruin if 1 percent of capital is at risk on each trade with a hard dollar stop. We looked at winning percentages ranging from 25 to 50 percent, and payoff ranging from 1 to 3. Most trading systems will show about 25 to 50 percent profitable trades.

Table 7.1 Risk of ruin with 1 percent of capital at risk. A 0 probability means the total loss of equity is unlikely, but not impossible.

Probability of Winning(%)	Payoff Ratio				
	1	1.5	2	2.5	3.0
25	100	100	100	73	3.1
30	100	100	46.9	0.20	0
35	100	74.6	0.1	0	0
40	99.8	0.5	0	0	0
45	52.4	0	0	0	0
50	0	0	0	0	0

This range of values is what you would typically see in testing. The 25 percent lower limit for profitable trades is a personal choice. The upper limit was chosen because the risk of ruin decreases substantially as the winning percentage goes beyond 50 percent. Similarly, it is relatively rare to get a payoff ratio greater than 3 when you test one contract per market. Conversely, there is little benefit to trading a system with a payoff ratio less than 1 unless it is very accurate and your transaction costs are small. The smaller bet size of testing (1 percent) is likely to be interesting because Balsara's book does not show risk of ruin for less than 10 percent risked per trade. The results generally agree with his calculations.

These theoretical calculations show that it is not attractive to trade a system with a payoff ratio near 1 unless it has a winning percentage greater than 50 percent. Similarly, the calculations show that if you have a payoff ratio greater than 2.5, then a winning percentage greater than 35 percent should reduce your risk to acceptable levels.

Tables 7.2 and 7.3 are for 1.5 and 2 percent of capital risked on each trade, respectively. Note how the risk of ruin increases as the amount risked increases, and decreases as the probability of winning increases or payoff ratio increases. These tables show why many traders recommend risking 2 percent per trade with a hard stop.

These calculations assume that the payoff ratio and probability of winning are constant. In reality, these numbers keep changing in time, and any estimates you have today will probably change in a few months. Thus, it is better to consider a range of payoff ratios and winning percentages when you consider your risk of ruin.

Looking at the problem from a different point of view, what would be the "magic" payoff ratios for a 1 percent risk per trade if your winning percentages ranged from 25 to 50 percent? The data in Table 7.4, which you can use as a quick reference when you evaluate system testing results, help to answer this

Table 7.2   Risk of ruin with 1.5 percent of capital at risk. A 0 probability means the total loss of equity is unlikely, but not impossible.

Probability of Winning(%)	Payoff Ratio				
	1	1.5	2	2.5	3.0
25	100	100	100	88.9	12
30	100	100	78.4	1.0	0
35	100	94.5	0.8	0	0
40	100	4.5	0	0	0
45	84.2	0	0	0	0
50	1.4	0	0	0	0

question. For example, if the system had a winning percentage of 40 percent, then a payoff ratio above 1.75 would reduce your risk of ruin to manageable levels.

Note the nonlinear nature of these relationships. For example, consider a payoff ratio of 1.5 and winning percentage of 40 percent. If you now change your risk per trade from 1 percent to 2 percent, the risk of ruin increases disproportionately from 0.5 to 9.2 percent (see Tables 7.1 and 7.3). Hence, there is little incentive to overleverage an account and consistently bet much more than 2 percent per trade. You should also notice the benefits of modifying system design to improve the payoff ratio, or probability of winning, or both. The main advantage is that you can then increase the fraction of capital allocated to the system without unduly increasing risk.

These calculations do not mean you cannot vary bet size from trade to trade based on other information. For example, as Table 7.4 shows, if your probability of winning is greater than 50 percent and the payoff ratio is greater

Table 7.3   Risk of ruin with 2 percent of capital at risk. A 0 probability means the total loss of equity is unlikely, but not impossible.

Probability of Winning(%)	Payoff Ratio				
	1	1.5	2	2.5	3.0
25	100	100	100	94.3	19.7
30	100	100	87.4	3	0
35	100	98.7	16	0	0
40	100	9.2	0	0	0
45	93.6	0	0	0	0
50	5.4	0	0	0	0

Table 7.4   Payoff ratio needed for negligible risk of ruin with a 1 percent hard stop.

Probability of Winning (%)	Payoff Ratio	Risk of Ruin (%)
25	3.25	0
30	2.75	0
35	2.25	0
40	1.75	0
45	1.5	0
50	1	0

than 1, then the risk of ruin is very small. Thus, if you can find a mechanism to identify extraordinary opportunities, you can vary bet size. Such variations could significantly improve your overall results. See the section on identifying extraordinary opportunities in Chapter 4.

In summary, the risk-of-ruin calculations show that there is little incentive to overtrade an account by regularly betting, say, 10 percent or more of account equity. A bet size of 1 to 2 percent of account equity is a more prudent choice. However, because the risk of ruin calculations assume that the probability of winning and payoff ratio are constants, and in actual trading, the probability of winning and payoff ratio vary from trade to trade, these risk-of-ruin results should be used only as general guidelines. They can be used to increase exposure for extraordinary opportunities.

Interaction: System Design and Money Management

This section examines the effects of two different money management strategies on portfolio performance. First we examine the effects of trading a system with a fixed or variable number of contracts. Then we see how portfolio performance differs for the two strategies. Finally, we check if our interval equity changes are useful for projecting worst-case drawdowns.

Your goal is to take care of the downside, and let the market take care of the upside. You would like to maximize the rate of growth of account equity while managing the extent of cumulative losses. Money management involves all the decisions specifying amount of capital risked per trade. This, in turn, determines the number of contracts traded. The contracts traded impact the percentage of account equity allocated to margin dollars. Of course, you must also choose the markets traded in each account. You can use relatively simple rules or relatively complex rules to make each of these choices, but your choice can significantly alter account equity evolution. You can also trade the same system with different money-management limits to produce significantly different results. This section briefly discusses common rules and shows their effects, but you should also review other books devoted just to this one subject.

The simplest risk control tool is an initial risk or money-management stop. This is usually a hard-dollar stop, with the dollar amount being usually less than 6 percent of your total equity. A hard-dollar stop is simply the amount of capital at risk per trade, usually implemented with a stop-loss order. Thus, you will exit the trade if the loss on all contracts approaches the hard-dollar stops. For example, we saw in the previous section that the usual choice is to risk 1 to 2 percent of your total equity on every position. Then, if your risk per contract is smaller than the total risk, you could trade more than one contract.

You are making a trade-off between the rate at which you want your equity to grow and the drawdown you are capable of absorbing. Theories such as optimal-f use more complex formulas to increase equity growth beyond the one-contract-per-market approach. However, when you trade multiple contracts, the drawdown tends to increase, and hence money management becomes even more important.

We can examine the interaction between system design and money management by using a channel breakout system on the deustche mark using actual contract data with rollovers. The monthly equity curve for the system trading one contract with $100 allowed for slippage and commission is shown in Figure 7.1. This system had a steady increase in equity with several significant retracements. We imported the monthly equity curve into a spreadsheet and analyzed the interval change in equity over 1, 3, 6, and 12 months. Those data appear in Table 7.5.

Some simple calculations will show the usefulness of Table 7.5. Assume that the monthly average return is zero and that monthly equity changes are normally distributed. Most trend-following systems have losing streaks lasting six months or less. Hence, to estimate downside potential, let us look at the worst loss over the 6-month interval. The maximum loss over six months was –$5,263, which is 3.5 times the monthly standard deviation of $1,471, rounded up to $1,500. We will use the 3.5 figure as a guideline, and round it up to 4. Thus, we will plan for a drawdown of four times the standard deviation of monthly equity changes. We know from statistical theory that the probability of getting a number larger than four times the standard deviation is quite small, about 6 in 100,000.

Now for a $50,000 account trading one deutsche mark contract for this system, our projected "worst" drawdown is 12 percent (= ($1,500 × 4) / $50,000). Using the same estimate for the upside, our "best" upside annual performance would be 12 percent. Thus, our most likely performance band will be ±12 percent. We can make this "linear" assumption because we are trading just one contract per market. Let us see how the system performed on an annual basis, assuming the account was reset to $50,000 at the beginning of each year.

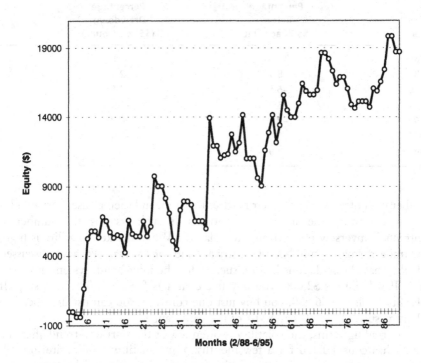

Figure 7.1   Monthly equity curve for deutsche mark trading one contract.

Table 7.6 shows that the performance band of ±12 percent was generally a good estimate. The 10.5 percent drawdown trading just one contract (1990) is worrisome. To cut the figure in half, trade this system with an account equity of $100,000. However, doubling the equity will halve your return, and you will have to decide your comfort level between returns and drawdowns.

Now that you have some feel for how to deal with a single contract, let us consider the impact of trading multiple contracts. One method of selecting the

Table 7.5   Interval equity change analysis for the deutsche mark over 90 months (2/88–6/95).

Interval Analysis	1 Month	3 Months	6 Months	12 Months
Maximum gain ($)	7,963	7,413	7,213	7,650
Maximum loss ($)	–3,137	–3,925	–5,263	–3,889
Average ($)	208	651	1,297	2,111
Standard Deviation ($)	1,471	2,263	2,667	2,928

Table 7.6   Annual return for DM system, $50,000 equity at start of year.

Year	Percentage Return ($50K account)	Percentage Drawdown ($50K account)
1988	11.5	–1.9
1989	8.1	–2.5
1990	–6.5	–10.5
1991	15.3	–5.0
1992	–2.1	–10.2
1993	5.6	–2.4
1994	–2.9	–5.4

number of contracts is to fix your hard-dollar stop, and then to use market volatility to determine the number of contracts. In such systems, the number of contracts is inversely proportional to volatility. When market volatility is high, you trade a smaller number of contracts, and vice versa. We have discussed volatility-based calculations before, such as for the long-bomb system in Chapter 5. If volatility is $2,000, you buy five contracts for a $10,000 hard stop. If volatility triples to $6,000, you buy just one contract. You can use any measure volatility, such as the 10-day SMA of the daily range.

In trading terms, the volatility is often low at the start of a trend after the market has consolidated for a few months. Your volatility-based criterion will trade more contracts, giving you a big boost if a dynamic trend occurs. Conversely, near the end of a trend, the volatility is usually higher, and you will buy fewer contracts. Thus, any false signals near the end of a trend will have a proportionately smaller impact.

If the volatility-based logic worked perfectly, you would have greater exposure during trends and smaller exposure during consolidations. Thus, your overall results should improve "nonlinearly" with variable contracts versus trading a fixed number of contracts each time. For example, trading, say, eight contracts using a volatility-based entry criterion may be better than just trading a fixed number of eight contracts at every signal. You hope to achieve greater returns with smaller drawdowns (higher profit factor) using the volatility-based contract calculations. Figure 7.2 shows the effects of using a volatility-based multiple contract system using the breakout system for the deutsche mark. Compare this equity curve to the curve in Figure 7.1 for one contract.

The annual returns for the multiple-contract strategy are shown in Table 7.7. The multiple-contract system made more than five times the profit of the single-contract system. The system traded a maximum of eight contracts, and an average of three contracts. The drawdowns were, on average, only three times higher. Thus, there was a significant improvement in performance by going to a

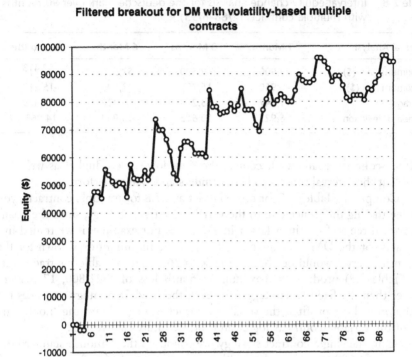

Figure 7.2   Equity curve for deutsche mark system with multiple contracts.

Table 7.7   Annual return for deutsche mark system, $50,000 equity at start of year, multiple contracts.

Year	Percentage Return ($50K Account)	Percentage Drawdown ($50K Account)
1988	102.8	−4.0
1989	44.5	−5.9
1990	−24.7	−43.6
1991	−15.1	−11.8
1992	−6.2	−30.5
1993	20.6	−6.0
1994	−15.7	−23.4

Table 7.8 Interval equity change analysis for the deutsche mark over 90 months with multiple contracts (2/88–6/95).

Interval Analysis	1 Month	3 Months	6 Months	12 Months
Maximum gain ($)	28,900	49,500	57,575	52,413
Maximum loss ($)	–7,950	–15,700	–21,800	–15,213
Average ($)	1,047	3,238	6,432	9,479
Standard deviation ($)	5,923	10,613	13,944	14,963

multiple-contract strategy. Of course, the drawdowns were higher as well. Let us look at the interval returns to better understand system performance.

Comparing Tables 7.5 for one contract and 7.8 for multiple contracts, you will see the big difference due to the variable contract strategy, since the quantities are three to four times larger in Table 7.8. For example, if we traded five contracts for the DM system from Table 7.5, the maximum drawdown for the 6-month interval would be –$26,315 (5 × $5,263). The variable-contract strategy (Table 7.8) produces a maximum 6-month loss of –$21,800, 17 percent smaller than the fixed 5× strategy. However, the fixed 5× strategy produces the same nominal net profit as the variable contract strategy. Thus, the "nonlinearity" of the variable-contracts logic can produce interesting results.

As in the single contract strategy, we round up the 1-month standard deviation to $6,000 and use a 4× multiple, to estimate –$24,000 as the "worst" drawdown. Thus, for a $50,000 account this would be a performance band of 48 percent. It should be immediately obvious that we are practically overleveraging a $50,000 account with this multiple-contract system. Comparing Table 7.6 for single contracts with Table 7.7 for multiple contracts, observe that in 1991, the 1-contract system made a 15.3-percent profit, versus a 15.1-percent loss for the multiple-contract system. It is not recommended that you trade an account with so much leverage, and these calculations emphasize this point.

When you increase the amount of account equity, it reduces the fluctuations in equity on a percentage basis. Hence, when you calculate a linear regression on the percentage changes in equity, then you get a smoother curve by using a smaller leverage. This is only natural, since the equity in the account acts like a buffer to absorb small fluctuations when you reduce leverage. You can see this pattern clearly in Table 7.9, which shows the standard error for account sizes of $50,000, $75,000, and $100,000 for the data shown in Table 7.5.

A decrease in the standard error means the equity curve is smoother. As the size of the account increases, the percentage fluctuations decrease. Note that our estimated performance band was a good guess about drawdowns. Thus, the 1-month standard deviation of equity returns times four may be a good starting point to estimate downside risk. You can then deduce the account size to maintain a low level of drawdowns. Say you trade six markets, and want to limit the "worst" drawdown to 3 percent. Then you would trade the multiple

Table 7.9 Smaller leverage gives a smoother equity curve on a percentage basis.

Account Size	Standard Error of Monthly Changes (%)
$50,000	2.94
$75,000	1.96
$100,000	1.47

contract system with an account equity of $800,000. This is very different from the $50,000 account.

The results and discussion of this section should convince you that money management strategies can significantly alter portfolio performance. As stated previously, as a design philosophy, you should try to protect the downside and let the market take care of the upside. In the next section we examine if it is possible to estimate future drawdowns using our interval analysis of the equity curve.

Projecting Drawdowns

A key money-management goal is to protect the downside using rigid risk control. We would therefore like to make reasonable projections about potential drawdowns. We have to rely on past analyses to forecast the future, so we should try to err on the side of caution, and bias our forecasts toward the high side. It is better to plan for a larger drawdown than a smaller one.

The previous section suggested that the standard deviation of monthly equity changes for a system is a reasonable tool to project the magnitude of future losses. We first developed the daily equity curve, then converted it into a monthly equity curve, and then calculated the monthly changes in equity. Using spreadsheet software, we can also calculate the standard deviation of monthly equity changes. Let us call this quantity σ_1 for convenience. A conservative forecast for future drawdowns is $4\sigma_1$ for any system. However, this is only an estimate, and you could consider other nearby values such as $5\sigma_1$ or even $3\sigma_1$.

To test this forecasting technique, we used continuous contracts from January 1, 1985, through December 31, 1990, for these seven arbitrarily selected markets: cotton, Eurodollar, gold, heating oil, Japanese yen, Swiss franc, and U.S. bond. We tested three arbitrary, nonoptimized systems: the 65sma-3cc, a 20-bar breakout on close (CHBOC) with a 10-tick barrier, and a volatility-based system (VOL). The rules for this last system are described in detail in Chapter 8 on data scrambling. We used a $2,500 initial stop and an exit on trailing 10-day high or low, and allowed $100 for slippage and commissions. These choices were all made arbitrarily, without any idea of how the systems will perform and without looking at the data.

The logic for entering the markets is quite different for each system, although they have the same exit strategy. Hence, being trend-following in nature, they should all be profitable in trending markets. It is their response to sideways markets that will differentiate system performance. The 65sma-3cc system will probably show smaller losses, since it tends to be self-correcting during trading ranges. The CHBOC 20-bar breakout will stay out of narrow trading ranges, but will suffer false breakouts during broad trading range markets. The volatility system will be vulnerable to sharp moves within the trading range.

By examining overall system profits and maximum intraday losses, you can better appreciate the analysis of monthly equity changes. Tables 7.10 and 7.11 show that there were wide differences in overall profitability and drawdowns for the three systems over the seven markets.

The 65sma-3cc system produced the smallest total drawdown, followed by the CHBOC system. Note the large drawdowns produced by the volatility system in heating oil from 1985 to 1990. Gold, heating oil and U.S. bonds were difficult to trade with these systems. Note also the large fluctuations in profits and losses over the test periods. You should focus on relative differences in system performance.

We would like to see if this interval analysis can project future drawdowns. Hence, we exported the daily equity curves, converted them into monthly curves, and used a spreadsheet to develop information on changes in equity over 1, 3, 6, 7, 8, 9, and 12 months.

In most systems tested, the periods of drawdown usually last less than 9 months. Hence, we paid greater attention to the 6- to 9-month range. We calculated the standard deviation of the monthly equity changes, and then determined the worst performance over any of the above intervals, hoping that the

Table 7.10   Simulated profits and drawdowns for the 1985–1990 period (Max P = net profit, MIDD = maximum intraday drawdown).

Market	CHBOC Max P ($)	CHBOC MIDD ($)	VOL. Max P ($)	VOL. MIDD ($)	65sma-3cc Max P ($)	65sma-3cc MIDD ($)
Cotton	5,245	−16,005	27,165	−7,330	20,675	−5,815
Eurodollar	13,950	−1,750	9,475	−8,725	9,675	−4,275
Gold	−10,330	−16,200	−1,170	−12,790	−4,280	−10,280
Heating oil	15,382	−20,751	−32,825	−50,571	21,761	−13,380
Japanese yen	38,663	−11,513	59,913	−8,938	13,475	−11,113
Swiss franc	1,450	−18,663	35,075	−18,750	12,350	−11,400
U.S. bond	17,513	−10,400	49,413	−9,125	−17,025	−28,438
Totals	81,873	−95,282	147,046	−116,229	56,631	−84,701

Table 7.11 Simulated profits and draw downs for the 1991–95 period (Max P = net profit, MIDD = maximum intraday draw down).

Market	CHBOC Max P ($)	CHBOC MIDD ($)	VOL. Max P ($)	VOL. MIDD ($)	65sma-3cc Max P ($)	65sma-3cc MIDD ($)
Cotton	18,430	–5,265	9,195	–11,425	33,060	–8,940
Eurodollar	3,850	–2,200	350	–4,675	1,525	–2,225
Gold	–12,630	–12,630	–17,750	–18,660	–870	–2,510
Heating oil	–7,080	–15,813	–24,330	–25,296	–5,113	–10,261
Japanese yen	19,563	–11,200	27,463	–13,925	44,500	–3,538
Swiss franc	17,925	–9,000	18,700	–10,850	5,750	–12,313
U.S. bond	–7,531	–19,756	–1,288	–9,556	–4,538	–10,706
Totals	32,527	–75,864	12,340	–94,387	74,314	–50,493

ratio of the worst interval performance to the standard deviation of monthly equity changes would be 5 or less.

The equity calculations were repeated for the next block of data, from January 1, 1991, through June 30, 1995, without changing the system. The new test period was an "out of sample" test to check stability. We then did the interval equity change calculations in a bid to see if the forecast for the worst drawdown based on the data from 1985 to 1990 had held up on the data from 1991 to 1995. Ideally, the standard deviation of monthly equity changes would be roughly comparable in the two periods, to reinforce our confidence in this approach.

Table 7.12 shows the standard deviation of monthly equity changes and maximum drawdown for the three systems over each period. The monthly standard deviation was quite stable. The ratio of the average loss was approximately four times the monthly standard deviation over both time periods. This is encouraging, since we did an "out of sample" test without optimization using arbitrarily selected systems and markets. These data show that it is reasonable to project future drawdowns by using the standard deviation of monthly equity changes, assuming a potential loss of four to five times the monthly standard deviation.

Once you know the projected loss, you can immediately gauge a possible equity level to trade the system or portfolio. Let us say you wanted to keep the drawdowns below 20 percent. To be safe, let us use a target of 15 percent, with a 5-percent cushion for future uncertainties. Hence, if you had a calculated standard deviation of $6,000, then a 5× forecast would be a drawdown of –$30,000. Since we want to keep projected drawdowns at the 15-percent level, the approximate equity level is $200,000 for trading this system or portfolio.

Table 7.12 Comparison of standard deviation and theoretical losses for three systems over two different time periods using monthly changes in equity.

System	Monthly Standard Deviation (1985–1990) ($)	Worst Drawdown (1985–1990) ($)	Ratio of Worst Drawdown to Standard Deviation (1985–1990)	Monthly Standard Deviation (1991–1995) ($)	Worst Drawdown (1991–1995) ($)	Ratio of Worst Drawdown to Standard Deviation (1985–90)
CHBOC	6,879	–21,977	3.2×	5,944	–28,587	4.2×
VOL	4,229	–21,729	5.2×	4,739	–11,277	2.7×
65sma-3cc	6,080	–25,550	4.2×	5,804	–23,072	3.8×
Average	5,729	–23,085	4.0×	5,496	–20,979	3.7×

Remember that our projections are only approximations of what might happen, and no guarantee that losses will remain at or near this level. However, the method discussed in this section does provide an objective tool to plan for reasonable equity losses. You must rigidly enforce the risk control mechanism incorporated into the system tests, otherwise these forecasts are meaningless. Ideally, once we have protected the downside, the design of our system and future market action will take care of performance on the upside.

Changing Bet Size After Winning or Losing

One of the key money-management decisions you have to make is how you will change your bet size as your account equity evolves in time. Your trade-off is between equity growth and smoothness of the equity curve. This section presents some common "betting" strategies and their impact on the equity curve.

Two references will fill in the background on betting strategies. Bruce Babcock's book on trading systems examines different betting strategies. Jack D. Schwager's interviews with market wizards shows that many indicated that they reduced the size of their trades during losing periods. These references (see bibliography for details) should convince you that changing bet size can be as important as your system design.

The premise behind changing bet size is that you can use the outcome of the last trade to predict the outcome of the next trade. This implies that winning and losing trades come in streaks. However, it is easy to show mathematically that successive trades are independent. Hence, on average, it is difficult to justify the premise behind changing bet size. Despite this mathematical fact, most traders will tell you there are psychological benefits to reducing trade size during a drawdown. You can be conservative and assume losing trades will come in bunches, though winning trades may not. Under this assumption, you could generate a smoother equity curve by changing bet size.

A simulation will help us to examine the effect of different betting strategies on the smoothness of the equity curve. We will use the standard error calculations to have a uniform basis for the comparison. We chose ten trades at random, half of them winners, and sampled these trades at random to construct 14 sequences of ten trades each. On each sequence, we then tested the following four strategies:

1. Constant contracts: always trading two per signal.

2. Double-or-half: if the previous trade was a winner, trade four contracts. If the last trade was a loser, trade one contract.

3. Half-on-loss: if the previous trade is a loser, trade one contract. If the last trade was a winner, then trade two contracts again.

4. Double-on-loss: if the previous trade is a loser, trade four contracts. If the last trade is a winner, then trade two contracts again.

We started with $100,000 in each portfolio. Every strategy was tested on precisely the same trades. We ran 14 simulations, for a total of 140 trades, and then averaged the equity curves for each trading strategy. We compared the averaged curves for each strategy to the average curve for trading two contracts per trade. Finally, we used linear regression analysis to calculate the standard error.

You should conduct a larger simulation with your data to find the strategy you like. In particular, be aware that the double-on-loss is the riskiest strategy. If you are hit with an unusually long string of losses, this strategy will produce the largest drawdowns.

Table 7.13 shows the effect of changing the bet size after each trade. The strategy of halving trade size to one contract after each losing trade produced a 21.6-percent reduction in the standard error of the equity curve for only a 2.4-percent profit penalty. Thus, we got a substantially smoother curve for a relatively small reduction in profits.

The double-or-half strategy increased ending equity on average by only 2.1 percent, but the standard error increased by nearly 41 percent. You would expect this strategy to show sharp gains if winning trades come in bunches. Hence, the equity curve will be rougher and the increase in standard error is no surprise.

The double-on-loss strategy was the riskiest, as you can see by a more than 53-percent increase in standard error. The equity curve (see Figure 7.3) shows that this strategy can produce steep drawdowns. Although this strategy had the highest ending average equity, this was only 5 percent greater than the

Table 7.13   Effect of betting strategies on standard error of average equity curve.

Strategy	Number of Contracts after Wins	Number of Contracts after Loss	Average Ending Equity ($)	Percentage Change in Equity	Standard Error ($)	Percentage Change in Standard Error
Constant	2	2	110,377	—	970	—
Half on loss	2	1	107,692	–2.4	760	–21.6
Double or half	4	1	112,699	2.1	1,366	40.8
Double on loss	2	4	115,746	4.9	1,488	53.4

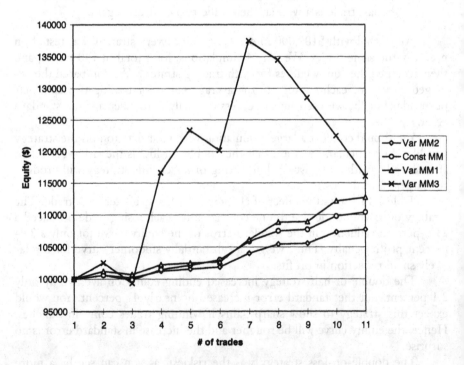

Figure 7.3   Average equity curves for four betting strategies. The "Const MM" curve is for a constant two contracts per trade. The "Var MM1" curve is for the double-or-half strategy. The "Var MM2" is for the half-on-loss strategy. The "Var MM3" curve is for the double-on-loss strategy.

constant contract strategy. Hence, the relative risk reward does not seem worth the aggravation.

This limited simulation supports the opinion expressed by many accomplished traders that they like to reduce trade size during drawdowns. Table 7.13 clearly shows that the half-on-loss strategy had the best reward-to-risk performance. Some traders suggest that they defer accepting new signals during drawdowns, but ignoring new signals may cause you to miss just the signal you need to boost equity.

Table 7.13 shows that the fixed contracts strategy is also a reasonable choice. Certainly, when you are starting off, you may wish to consider this strategy to keep life simple. Eventually, as you feel more confident and have more equity, you can move on to other more elaborate strategies.

Note that when you use a fixed 2-percent stop to calculate a variable number of contracts, you are automatically adjusting position size to equity and volatility. If you have losing trades, equity will drop and bet size will decrease. Similarly, after profits, your bet size will increase. Hence, this strategy will produce a different equity curve. The calculations here should provide a starting point for you to explore other complex strategies, such as continuously varying exposure during a trade. Ultimately, you are the best judge of the betting strategy that suits your style of trading.

Depth of Drawdowns for Actual Performance Records

We saw previously how we could project the expected future drawdown using the standard deviation of monthly returns. We tested those ideas using the hypothetical results of three different trading systems. In this section, we test those ideas using the actual track records of professional money managers, namely commodity trading advisors and hedge fund managers.

If we can show that the ideas of the previous section provide good working estimates for drawdowns using actual performance histories, we would have accomplished a good deal, because objective estimates of future drawdowns would allow comparisons between managers, and assist in formulating and vetting multimanager programs. The estimates can also be used to adjust funding levels to control the depth of expected drawdowns. Note that, because one is making probabilistic statements, there is always the chance, however small, that the estimates will be exceeded in the future. Hence, estimates of future depth and duration of drawdowns must be used with caution.

First, let us look at how we calculate month-end drawdowns and identify drawdown strings. Consider the track record shown in Table 7.14. The table shows monthly returns and the month-end value of an account that started with $1,000. The last column shows a drawdown flag: if the month-end equity is lower than the highest month-end equity since the start of trading, then the flag

Table 7.14   Introduction to calculation of drawdowns.

Month	Return (%)	Reference Equity ($)	Drawdown Flag
	0.00%	$1,000.00	
1	-2.63%	$973.70	-1
2	-6.89%	$906.61	-1
3	-10.71%	$809.51	-1
4	6.93%	$865.61	-1
5	32.42%	$1,146.25	
6	-9.41%	$1,038.38	-1
7	6.85%	$1,109.51	-1
8	2.03%	$1,132.04	-1
9	10.65%	$1,252.60	
10	11.06%	$1,391.13	
11	7.04%	$1,489.07	
12	4.93%	$1,562.48	

= –1 because the account is in a drawdown. If the month-end equity is at the highest level since the start of trading, then the flag is blank.

At the end of month 1, the return is –2.63 percent, and the closing equity is therefore $973.7. Because this is less than the highest equity since starting, the drawdown flag is –1. The program experiences losses for the next two months and then has a positive month. Even though month 4 has a positive return, the month-end closing equity of $865.61 is still less than $1,000, and hence the drawdown flag is –1. In month 5, there is a strong return of 32.42 percent, and the monthly closing equity is $1,146, the highest level since the start of trading. Hence, the drawdown flag is blank. At the end of month 5, we can look back and say that there was a drawdown string of 4 months, and the worst month-end drawdown during that string was –19.05 percent, when the account value dipped down to $809.51 at the end of the third month. Now see if you can explain the subsequent drawdown string of three months with a worst drawdown of –9.41 percent.

Let us now take a step forward and summarize the duration and depth of every losing period or string in a track record. Table 7.15 shows these summary data for an actual track record; it shows the length of drawdown strings and the depth of drawdown (in percent) that occurred in each period. We can now analyze such a summary table in two different ways. First, we find the average and standard deviation of both columns. For example, the standard deviation of the lengths of drawdown strings, (σ_{dd}), was 2 months for this manager, and the standard deviation of the depth of the drawdown (σ_Δ) was 4.94 percent. The longest drawdown was 8 months and the worst drawdown was –20.59 percent. We see that the longest drawdown was about $4*\sigma_{dd}$ and the absolute value of the deepest drawdown was 4.17 percent σ_Δ. Second, we express the absolute value

Table 7.15   Summary of drawdown periods from an actual track record.

		Length of Drawdown (months)	Depth of Drawdown (%)
		4.0	-19.05
		3.0	-9.41
		1.0	-5.42
		1.0	-8.82
		1.0	-8.28
		4.0	-20.59
		2.0	-4.61
		3.0	-1.43
		8.0	-8.58
		6.0	-16.61
		2.0	-6.78
		2.0	-1.93
		3.0	-3.21
		5.0	-8.52
		3.0	-4.63
		2.0	-7.48
		5.0	-6.53
		2.0	-4.25
		1.0	-3.04
		3.0	-7.64
		2.0	-4.30
		4.0	-5.82
		4.0	-7.88
		1.0	-1.29
		1.0	-2.16
		1.0	-0.67
		7.0	-5.40
		7.0	-10.17
		1.0	-0.89
		3.0	-4.15
Average	μ_{dd}	3.07	μ_Δ	-6.65
Standard Deviation (σ)	σ_{dd}	2.00	σ_Δ	4.94
Worst Case (Ω)	Ω_{dd}	8.00	Ω_Δ	-20.59
Ω/σ	Ω_{dd}/σ_{dd}	4.00	$\Omega_\Delta/\sigma_\Delta$	-4.17
Standard Deviation of Monthly Returns (σ_M) %				6.50
Ω/σ_M		Ω_Δ/σ_M		-3.17

of worst drawdown as a multiple of the standard deviation of monthly returns, σ_M. Table 7.15 shows that the absolute deepest drawdown was 3.17 percent σ_M. The calculation using drawdown strings takes a bit longer than the short-cut method of expressing the worst drawdown as a multiple of σ_M. Thus, Table 7.15 gives us two simple rules for estimating the depth and duration of drawdown using monthly performance data. How does this analysis look when applied to a large number of managers?

**Worst Month-End Draw-down Increases as Volatility of
Trading Program Increases**

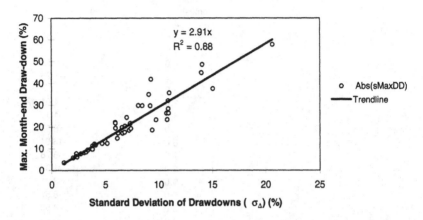

Figure 7.4   The worst drawdown on a month-end basis reported by a manager compared to the standard deviation of the depths of previous drawdowns in the manager's record (σ_Δ) (%).

Let us look at an extension of the above analysis to the performance record of approximately 50 randomly chosen commodity trading advisors, covering a wide variety of trading styles, portfolios, leverages, and lengths of trading records. We analyzed their monthly performance numbers and equity curves to calculate the depth and duration of the absolute value drawdowns. For example, a typical CTA record was 3 to 5 years long and had five or more drawdown periods lasting a month or more during that period. We calculated the standard deviation of the worst month-end drawdown during each losing period. Note that because we used monthly data, the drawdown was measured on a month-end basis, and not on a peak-to-valley basis.

Figure 7.4 shows how the depth of the absolute worst drawdown (on a month-end basis) related to the standard deviation of the losses in drawdown streaks (σ_Δ) in percent. A trend line drawn through the origin had a slope of 2.91 with an R^2 value of 0.88. Figure 7.4 suggests that, to a good approximation, the depth of the worst drawdown was three times the standard deviation of drawdowns. For example, if the standard deviation of the depth of the drawdowns was 5 percent, then the worst drawdown in equity on a month-end basis was typically −15 percent. These data also confirm that volatile managers tend to produce deeper drawdowns.

An application of the short-cut approach is to relate the peak-to-valley drawdown to the standard deviation of monthly returns (σ_M) in percent. For example, Figure 7.5 shows the absolute value of maximum peak-to-valley drawdown (PVDD) figures reported by over 100 CTAs, plotted against the standard deviation of their monthly returns (σ_M). A trend line through the origin had a

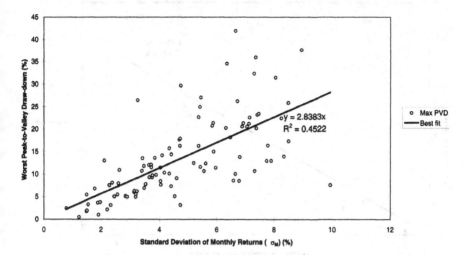

Figure 7.5   An analysis of the actual track record of over 100 commodity trading advisors shows that the worst peak-to-valley drawdown is typically three times the standard deviation of monthly returns (σ_M), as shown by the slope of the line through the origin.

slope of 2.84 and an R^2 value of 0.45. Approximately 90 percent of the data had a ratio of worst drawdown to standard deviation of less than 4. Thus, to a good approximation, PVDD is likely to be less than four times the standard deviation of monthly returns. For example, if the standard deviation of monthly returns is 7 percent, then the worst PVDD is expected to be in the range of 21 to 28 percent.

If the distributions of drawdown depth and duration were truly normal, it would be rare to see values greater than three times the standard deviation, or 3σ. However, the scatter in the data suggests that actual performance data are not truly normal, and an estimate of 3σ to 5σ would be a more conservative multiplier for estimating the depth and duration of drawdowns.

Next, we analyzed the monthly performance of 30 randomly chosen hedge funds from June 1995 through June 1998 for additional confirmation. The results are similar. Figure 7.6 shows the absolute value of the worst peak-to-valley drawdown (Δ) reported by each fund over that 3-year period plotted against the standard deviation of monthly returns for that fund. The Δ generally increases as the standard deviation of monthly returns increases. A best-fit linear regression line through the origin has a slope of 3.0 and an R^2 value of 0.69. For 83 percent of the sample, the Δ was less than four times the standard deviation. Thus, to a good approximation, Δ is less than four times the monthly standard deviation (σ_M). We generalize this relationship as:

$$\Delta = 4\sigma_M \tag{7.1}$$

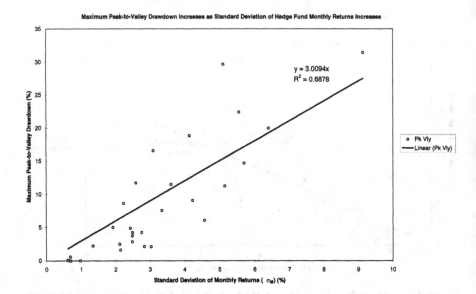

Figure 7.6 The worst peak-to-valley drawdown reported by 30 hedge funds was typcially three times the standard deviation of monthly returns (σ_M) in percent, similar to the result in Figure 7.5 for CTAs.

Thus, we started with a hypothesis using simulated results, and checked it for different trading approaches. We then checked the idea using actual performance data of different money managers using different approaches to trading. We then double-checked this approach using hedge fund data. In every instance, the results confirm that the worst PVDD can be expressed as four times the standard deviation of monthly returns. If you wish to be aggressive, you would use a multiple of $3\sigma_M$ instead of $4\sigma_M$.

Allocators and investors could use the ratio of the worst PVDD to the standard deviation of monthly returns as a figure of merit that measures the quality of risk control techniques used by a manager (see Figures 7.5 and 7.6). For example, the smaller this ratio, the better the design and implementation of risk control methodology followed by an advisor. If, for example, this ratio was greater than 5, then it might suggest the need for a more detailed due-diligence check to understand why a particular drawdown occurred.

The due-diligence process can be simplified if the performance record of CTAs could be "normalized" to allow comparisons on an apples-to-apples basis. The interesting feature of this analysis is that we could combine the performance records of CTAs with many different lengths, styles, portfolios, and leverages on the same curve. Hence, such an approach may provide a uniform framework for normalizing advisor performance records for comparison purposes.

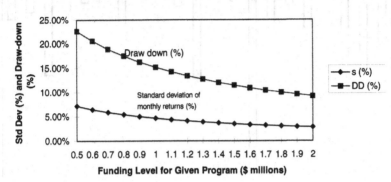

Figure 7.7   The effect of changing the leverage (the funding level) for accounts trading a diversified portfolio of the futures markets. Leverage increases as funding levels are reduced from $2 million to $0.5 million and the standard deviation of monthly returns and the worst peak-to-valley increase nonlinearly. Thus, leverage can be adjusted to obtain the desired level of volatility and drawdown risk.

Figures 7.4 through 7.6 suggest that advisors that are more volatile tend to produce deeper and longer drawdowns. Note that "volatile" is defined rather narrowly here, with particular reference to the standard deviation of the depth and duration of losing periods. Hence, investor or allocator preferences can be used to adjust the capital allocation to an advisor in order to modulate the desired level of volatility derived from the performance record. This idea is illustrated in Figure 7.7 using hypothetical returns.

We now show the effect of "leveraging-up" a trading program. Figure 7.7 shows the changes in the standard deviation of hypothetical monthly returns and the worst month-end drawdown, as the funding of a $2 million trading program is decreased to $0.5 million from $2 million. Observe that the drawdowns and monthly standard deviation increase nonlinearly during the funding decrease, even though their ratio remains approximately constant. Figure 7.7 suggests that funding can be changed to raise or lower the expected volatility of a trading program, simultaneously changing the expected worst drawdown.

The discussion so far has focused on diversified portfolios of futures or futures plus equities. The same logic can be applied to a portfolio of stocks. However, the stocks in a "basket" tend to be more highly correlated to one another than a basket of commodities or futures because stocks as a whole respond to the same macroeconomic data. Thus, we would expect the drawdowns to be more severe. We analyzed the performance of the S&P-500 and the NASDAQ

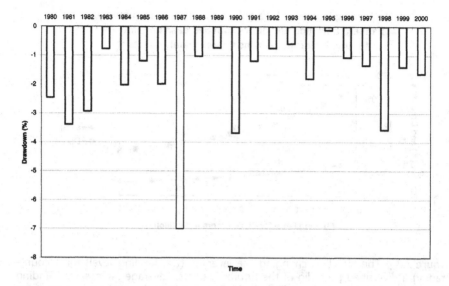

Figure 7.8   Drawdown in the S&P-500 stock index normalized by its monthly standard deviation of 4.31 percent. The worst drawdown since 1980 was approximately $7\sigma_M$ in 1987.

index as a proxy for diversified stock portfolios. The analysis shows that the downside risk for stocks is closer to $8\sigma_M$ than $4\sigma_M$ for diversified futures portfolios. Figure 7.8 shows the worst month-end-basis drawdowns in the S&P-500 cash index for every year since 1980. We normalized the actual drawdown by the 4.13 percent, the standard deviation of monthly returns, σ_M, over the same period. The worst absolute drawdown was in 1987, at approximately $7\sigma_M$.

A similar result is obtained for the NASDAQ composite index. Figure 7.9 shows the worst drawdown on a month-end basis for the index for every year since 1971, normalized by the standard deviation of monthly returns of 5.87 percent. Notice that the figure does not show the intramonth peak-to-valley drawdown data. You may want to use a higher multiple of the monthly standard deviation to account for intramonth data. The average absolute drawdown was $2.4\sigma_M$ on a month-end basis, and the worst was $7\sigma_M$ in 1975.

We then analyzed a convenience sample of 50 mutual funds from four large and popular fund families: Fidelity, Janus, PBHG, and Vanguard Group. This mixture of funds represents equities and bonds, as well as a mixture of styles and market capitalization. The overall results are similar to those obtained for futures, hedge funds, and stock indexes. The worst PVDD in a mutual fund's record from 1994 to 2000 increased as the standard deviation of monthly returns increased. A linear regression through the origin had a slope of 3.85 and $R^2 = 0.75$ (see Figure 7.10). Most funds were typically in the range of $3\sigma_M$ to $5\sigma_M$, as we would expect from our other studies.

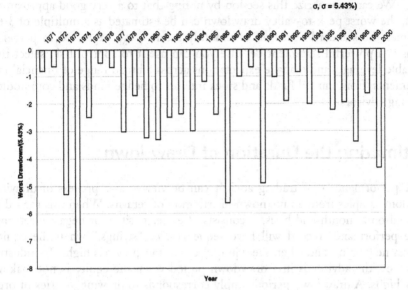

Figure 7.9   The annual losses in the NASDAQ index normalized by the standard deviation of monthly returns of 5.87 percent.

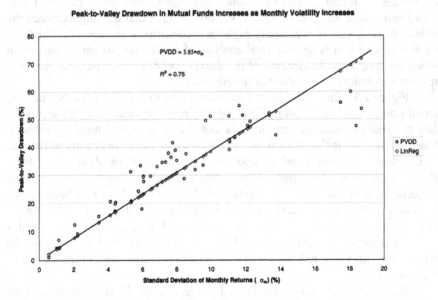

Figure 7.10   A convenience sample of 50 mutual funds from Fidelity, Janus, PBHG, and Vanguard also shows increasing peak-to-valley drawdowns with increasing standard deviation of monthly returns (σ_M). The typical mutal fund reported a worst peak-to-valley drawdown of $3\sigma_M$ to $5\sigma_M$.

We can summarize this section by noting that to a very good approximation, the worst peak-to-valley drawdown can be estimated as a multiple of 3 to 5 times the standard deviation of monthly returns, σ_M, expressed in percent. This is a powerful statement because you can use it to control risk, select the suitable leverage, and manage expectations across a broad range of financial instruments, from mutual funds and stock indexes to hedge funds and commodity trading advisors.

Estimating the Duration of Drawdowns

The performance of a trading advisor can be viewed as a process of drawing random samples from an unknown distribution of returns. When this record is viewed on a month-end basis, it consists of either positive or negative returns. The performance record will have sequences, or "strings," when the equity makes new highs, and when the equity drops below previous highs. In industry parlance, the advisor is in a drawdown period when the equity is not making new highs. A drawdown period simply corresponds to drawing a series of predominantly negative returns from the distribution of the manager's returns.

For every equity curve, we can measure the time to new highs in months, which is the same as measuring the duration of each drawdown period. If an advisor takes 7 months to record a new equity high, then the duration of that drawdown period was also 7 months. We now assume that the time between the arrivals of consecutive new equity highs is exponentially distributed. The basis for this assumption is an empirical analysis of more than 50 equity curves, in which the frequency distribution of the duration of drawdown periods generally appeared to follow an exponential distribution.

Figure 7.11 shows the typical distribution of drawdown periods from the actual track record of a leading CTA. We can now use month-end performance data to make probabilistic statements about the duration of future drawdowns. A key assumption is that the advisor will not change the style of trading that led to the past performance relied upon to make projections about the future. Should there be a substantial change in the advisor's trading process, then the projections from past data will become even less reliable. Note that because one is making probabilistic statements, there is always the chance, however small, that the estimates will be exceeded in the future. Hence, estimates of future duration of drawdowns must be used with caution. Because we are relying on the exponential distribution, here is a brief review of the properties of the exponential distribution.

An exponential distribution is used to describe the distribution of the time between two occurrences of many natural phenomena, such as the time for radioactive decay, or the time between arrivals of a bus at a bus stop, cars at tollbooth, or customers at a teller window. Because we are fitting the duration of drawdowns to an exponential distribution, we are tracking the time between

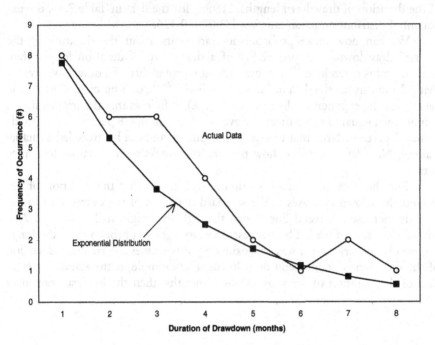

Figure 7.11   The duration of drawdowns for trading managers can be assumed to follow an exponential distribution.

successive arrivals of new equity highs. The distribution assumes that the phenomena being described are uniformly distributed in time, that is, they occur at a constant rate.

A brief mathematical description of the exponential distribution is given here. The probability density function of the exponential distribution is:

$$f(x) = e^{(-\lambda x)}, x \geq 0, \lambda > 0 ,$$

where x is the time interval (in months, say) and λ is the rate at which the event occurs (in occurrences per month, say). The mean value μ of an exponential distribution is $\mu = 1/\lambda$, and the standard deviation of the distribution σ is $1/\lambda$. Note that the range of values that can occur is infinite, that is, the drawdown can last "forever." However, the probability of getting very long gaps between successive occurrences of new equity highs diminishes rapidly.

Consider the summary shown in Table 7.15, in which column one shows the lengths of the different drawdown periods in that track record. The average length of the drawdown period was 3.07 months, or approximately 3 months. In order to fit an exponential distribution to these data, the best estimate of λ, the parameter of the exponential distribution, is given by the inverse of the average of the duration of drawdown lengths. Hence, for the data in Table 7.15, the exponential distribution parameter $\lambda = 1/3.07 = 0.326$.

We can now make probabilistic statements about the duration of the "worst" drawdown. The probability of a drawdown of duration longer than some time t is given by $e^{(-\lambda t)}$. For example, the probability of a drawdown longer than 12 months for the data in Figure 7.11 is $e^{(-0.326 \cdot 12)}$, or 2 percent. Because the average of the exponential distribution is $(1/\lambda)$, it follows that the probability of a drawdown equal to three times the average is e^{-3}, or 4.978 percent, or approximately 5 percent. Note that this only an estimate, and can be exceeded in actual trading. Now let us examine how this analysis works with actual performance data.

For the data of Figure 7.4, Figure 7.12 shows that the duration of the longest drawdown increases as the standard deviation of the duration of losing periods increases. A trend line drawn through the origin had a slope of 2.98 with an R^2 value of 0.85. This suggests that, to a good approximation, the longest month-end drawdown was approximately three times the standard deviation of the duration of month-end drawdowns. For example, if the standard deviation of the duration of drawdowns was 5 months, then the longest drawdown

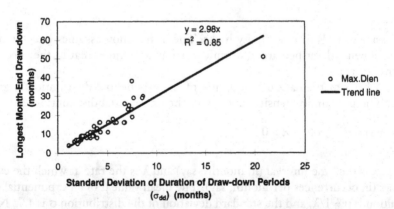

Figure 7.12   Duration of drawdown increases as the standard deviation of the duration of historical drawdown increases, implying that programs that are more volatile tend to have longer-lasting drawdowns. The duration of drawdown depends on the trading system, money management, and portfolio being traded, and the longest drawdown typically lasted three times the standard deviation of the duration of previous drawdowns (σ_{dd}) in the manager's track record.

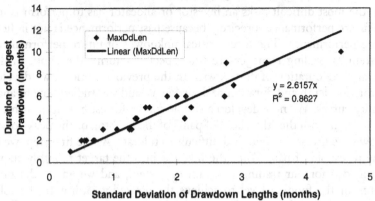

Figure 7.13   The drawdown of hedge funds also increases as the standard deviation of the duration of drawdowns in the track record of a manager increases.

was about 15 months. Thus, the actual performance data seem to fit an assumption that the duration of drawdowns is distributed exponentially. We know from the exponential distribution that there is only a 5 percent probability of getting a drawdown longer than three times the standard deviation of drawdown periods. The data also suggest that due to the variability inherent in trading, an estimate of 4.5σ may be a more conservative estimate of expected "worst case" drawdown.

We also checked the performance of the 30 randomly selected hedge funds in Figure 7.6 for good measure. Figure 7.13 shows the duration of longest drawdown (τ) plotted against the standard deviation of the lengths of losing streaks in a track record (σ_{dd}). Figure 7.13 shows that the duration of longest drawdown generally increases as the standard deviation of the length of losing streaks increases. A best-fit linear regression line through the origin has a slope of 2.62 and an R^2 value of 0.86. Thus, we have additional confirmation about the duration of drawdowns from hedge fund data.

In summary, the duration of drawdowns can be modeled as an exponential distribution, and that allows us to make probabilistic statements about the length of future drawdowns. We can measure the lengths of drawdowns in the track record of a manager and find the standard deviation of drawdown durations (σ_{dd}). The length of future drawdowns (in months) can then be estimated as $3\sigma_{dd}$, knowing that there is only a 5 percent probability that this length will be exceeded. Thus, we have two valuable tools to estimate the length of drawdowns, and these should help resolve another dimension of uncertainty about the future performance of a manager or trading system.

Estimating Future Returns

One of the most difficult tasks an investor or allocator has to perform is to estimate future performance, precisely because past performance is not indicative of future performance. The three critical unknowns of future performance for any system or trading manager are the expected returns, the depth of drawdowns, and the duration of drawdowns. In the previous sections, we developed estimators for depth and duration of drawdowns, and we studied how to analyze the equity curves. We now develop a simple model for estimating returns.

We begin with the "threshold of pain" of the investor, or the peak-to-valley drawdown the investor would find difficult to tolerate. As the first step, we convert the threshold of pain (Δ) of the investor into the target monthly standard deviation (σ_M) for our trading program or system, and we adjust the pricing algorithm or the funding level to achieve the desired volatility. In the following discussion, we will not use the subscript M to denote monthly data, for clarity and simplicity. We now use our results on estimating drawdowns, that the "worst-case" drawdown is four times the monthly standard deviation. Thus,

$$\Delta = 4\sigma, \text{ which implies that } \sigma = \Delta/4. \tag{7.2}$$

Note that the multiplier 4 is a relatively conservative choice; however, you can choose to be more or less conservative than this model. If you wish to be conservative, you could use $\Delta = 5\sigma$, or, if you wish to be aggressive, you may choose to use $\Delta = 3\sigma$. As shown below, your choice will affect your returns as well as drawdown potential.

We can now use some simple equations to show a connection between the thresholds of pain Δ an investor can tolerate and the expected reward for that risk. We begin by defining return efficiency (ρ), which is similar to a Sharpe ratio calculated on a monthly basis with a risk-free rate set to zero.

$$\rho = \mu / \sigma, \tag{7.3}$$

where, ρ = return efficiency, μ is the average monthly return (%), and σ is the standard deviation of monthly returns (%). For example, μ could be 1.5 percent and σ could be 5 percent. In practice, ρ is a measure of the overall quality of the investment strategy and the risk control methodology of the manager, and the larger the value the better. We can use ρ as an internal benchmark for different types of return processes. A good benchmark for return efficiency is $\rho = 0.25$, and this value seems to work well for futures, hedge funds, and equities.

We use equation (7.3) to solve for μ, the average monthly return, and then we substitute for the monthly standard deviation σ from equation (7.2) to express μ in terms of the investor's risk tolerances. Specifically, equation (7.3) can be rewritten as:

$$\mu = \rho\sigma = \rho(\Delta/4). \tag{7.4}$$

The importance of equation (7.4) is that it shows that average returns are determined by investor risk tolerance and the return efficiency of the return generation process (RGP). Thus, higher average returns require the investor to assume more risk (higher Δ) or find a more efficient RGP (higher ρ). All that remains is to convert the expected average return into annual returns by compounding 12 times, once for each month. Thus, we calculate annual returns (R) by compounding the average monthly return μ as:

$$R = 100((1+ 0.01\mu)^{12} - 1) \tag{7.5}$$

Upon substituting from equation (7.4), we can rewrite equation (7.5) as:

$$R = 100((1+ 0.01\rho\sigma)^{12} - 1) = 100((1+ 0.01\rho\Delta/4)^{12} - 1). \tag{7.6}$$

Equation (7.6) shows the direct connection between returns, monthly volatility and the design of the investment process. It shows the annual returns expected for different levels of return efficiency and monthly standard deviation (see Figures 7.14 and 7.15). Clearly, higher returns require greater risk (higher

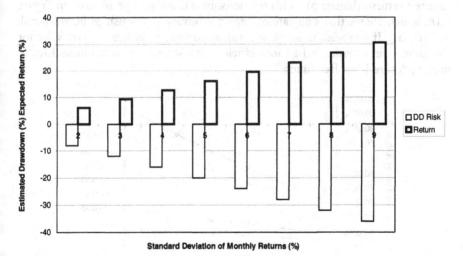

Figure 7.14 Risk and reward implied by equation (7.6) for a return efficiency of 0.25 and standard deviation of monthly returns ranging from 2 to 9 percent. Greater returns require the investor to assume greater risk.

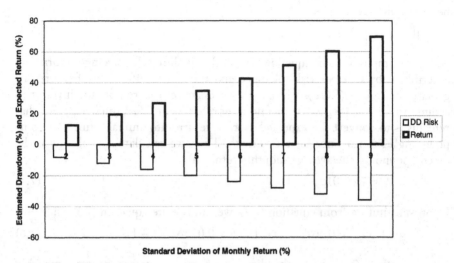

Figure 7.15 Risk and reward implied by equation (7.6) for a return efficiency of 0.5 and standard deviation of monthly returns ranging from 2 to 9 percent. Observe the improvement in the relative magnitudes of reward versus risk because of the higher return efficiency.

σ and Δ), or, for a given level of risk, higher returns require superior risk-adjusted returns (higher ρ). This relationship is illustrated graphically in Figure 7.16, which shows that one cannot expect arbitrary relationships between risk and reward. If you wish to increase returns, you must assume more risk, or for the same level of risk, find a more efficient investment. As economists love to preach, "there is no free lunch."

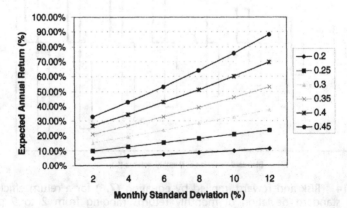

Figure 7.16 Expected annual returns as a function of the return efficiency and the standard deviation of monthly returns. This figure is a graphical representation of equation (7.6). To seek higher returns, one must tolerate higher risk or find a superior return-generation process.

Table 7.16   Calculation of expected return, starting with the threshold of pain of the client.

Item	Symbol	Source	Basis/Formula	Typical Value	Units
Threshold of pain	Δ	Client	Input	20	(%)
Monthly standard deviation	σ	RGP	$\sigma = \Delta/4$	5	(%)
Return efficiency	ρ	RGP	History data/benchmark	0.25	
Average monthly return	μ	RGP	$\mu = \rho * \sigma$	1.25	(%)
Expected annual return	R	Model	$R = 100*((1+\mu)^{12}-1)$	16.08	(%)

Suppose that you can specify a target for the worst peak-to-valley drawdown Δ. For example, if we set our worst PVDD or Δ threshold at 20 percent, then ρ = 0.25 would produce an expected R = 16.08 percent (see Table 7.16). Clearly, a higher ρ or a smaller Δ divisor would improve investment returns. Equation (7.6) is a powerful reason to favor investments with higher return efficiency. Using the results of an earlier section, we can now quantify and relate the downside risk and duration of drawdown to the upside reward.

Chande Comfort Zone

We now have the tools to estimate the three key unknowns about future system performance: the expected returns, the depth of drawdowns, and the duration of drawdowns. Our estimates are of the "upper-bound" of values we can reasonably expect; they do not predict the actual values that will be realized in the future. We can plot these three quantities using a three-dimensional grid to define a "box" or comfort zone (Chande Comfort Zone, or CCZ) within which we can reasonably expect our performance. Remember, it is possible to realize results outside this box under particularly favorable or unfavorable conditions.

Figure 7.17 shows the general shape of the CCZ; its value lies in allowing you to decide if you are comfortable with the proposed dimensions of the box. If you are comfortable, you should be able to stick with your investment strategy for a long time without actively seeking modifications. If you are not happy with the box, you can reshape it to meet your needs.

For example, let us assume that the projected drawdown for a particular strategy is 30 percent, but you want to limit the high probability zone to 20 percent. You can do so by reducing the leverage used in the strategy or increasing the capital allocated to the strategy. Consider now another scenario in which the duration of the drawdown is forecast to be 12 months, but you want it to be 7 months. In this case, you have a portfolio problem: perhaps you can combine

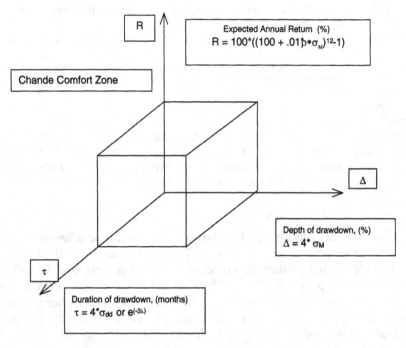

R

Expected Annual Return (%)
$R = 100*((100 + .01 \text{þ}*\sigma_M)^{12}-1)$

Chande Comfort Zone

Δ

Depth of drawdown, (%)
$\Delta = 4* \sigma_M$

τ

Duration of drawdown, (months)
$\tau = 4*\sigma_{dd}$ or $e^{(-3\lambda)}$

Figure 7.17 The Chande Comfort Zone shows estimates for the three key unknowns of future performance for any manager or trading system: expected annual return (%), expected depth of drawdown (%), and expected duration of drawdown (months). Future performance is expected to lie in the "box."

the investment process under review with other return generation processes to reduce the duration drawdowns.

You can also use the CCZ to answer other important questions, such as, has the system stopped working? This is a particularly difficult question because drawdowns are to be expected. However, the shape of the CCZ provides an answer. If the depth and duration of a drawdown both lie outside the projected CCZ, then a detailed review of the RGP is called for, because the system may indeed have "stopped working." Thus, the depth and duration of drawdown provide valuable benchmarks for assessing performance. Let us assume that the CCZ projects a 22 percent drawdown lasting less than 12 months. If you experience a drawdown of 25 percent lasting 13 months, then this is cause for concern and a review is probably necessary; it does not automatically mean that the system has stopping working. You would like to assess if other traders with a similar strategy are also experiencing drawdowns. You should also check for execution errors that may have led to losses. For example, a manager may increase the leverage used in trading in a bid to recover from a drawdown. Any significant deviation from the planned leverage level is certainly a sufficient reason for review and reassessment.

The CCZ also provides valuable clues when the performance has been significantly better than expected. For example, the CCZ projects a 25 percent return, but you are actually up 40 percent. Should you liquidate a portion of this investment? There is no automatic answer, but it is worth a second thought because you have experienced highly favorable market conditions. Once again, it is worth checking if there have been any unusual deviations in execution, such as increasing leverage or changing the portfolio, that may explain the performance.

The CCZ also provides a clue about when to add money to a trading manager, portfolio, or return generation process. Let us further say that the expected duration of drawdown is 8 months, and the manager is 5 months into the drawdown. Let us further assume that the expected severity of the drawdown is 20 percent, and the manager is down 10 percent. This may be a good opportunity to add some assets to this manager because your entry point is significantly below recent equity highs, and the drawdown may be close to ending, assuming the exponential distribution parameters are stable. Additional due-diligence checks would also be necessary, to check if the manager has altered the strategy or reduced leverage.

The CCZ thus performs a useful function by defining the "expected" performance envelope, thus allowing the investor or allocator to take calculated risks while managing their investments.

Dealing with Drawdowns

Dealing with drawdowns is an inevitable part of any investment process. It is easy to understand why it is psychologically difficult to cope with drawdowns because the exact depth and duration of any drawdown period is unknown. It is not difficult to magnify the potential severity of a drawdown when one is faced with this uncertainty. Hence, it would be nice to develop a strategy to deal with drawdowns before initiating the investment program.

The analysis presented in earlier sections provides tools to estimate the depth and duration of the potential drawdowns and allows us to define the scope of the problem. The key money management issues are these: should you cut down or eliminate a strategy or trading manager in a drawdown, or, instead, should you add funds to the strategy or manager? The second part of the problem is the timing of addition or withdrawal of funds. This analysis assumes that the manager does not change trading strategy during the drawdown, because that would further reduce the relevance of historical data used to predict the scope of the drawdown period.

One way to approach the problem is to measure the effect of additions or withdrawals of capital after absolute drawdowns, such as 10 percent, or 15 percent. A better solution might be to measure what the historical performance would have been when capital was added after drawdowns measured in multiples of the monthly standard deviation, such as 2σ or 3σ. We thus ask the question: What would be the return in the 12-month period following the month-end in which the drawdown was 2σ below the previous peak? Because markets often move in cycles of favorable and unfavorable periods, we can expect a period of strong recovery after a sustained drawdown. Note that adding capital during a drawdown would be an "antitrend" strategy or "trend anticipation" strategy, because success is predicated on a strong recovery in performance in the months ahead. The primary risk to such an "add capital when in drawdown" strategy is that markets may change in ways that lead to failure of the underlying trading strategy.

A second approach is to add or withdraw capital after a fixed amount of time in the drawdown, such as after three successive losing months, or 5 months in a drawdown. Here we can use the exponential distribution to estimate the length of the expected worst drawdown, and measure the impact of adding or withdrawing capital when one is, say, half-way through the expected drawdown duration.

We have defined the conditions under which we can determine when a strategy may have failed. If the absolute loss exceeds 4σ and the duration of drawdown exceeds $3\sigma_{dd}$, then an outlier event has occurred, and we may be justified in reducing or withdrawing capital from the trading strategy. By combining both of these approaches, we can add capital with a relatively tight dollar stop and time stop.

A third approach would be to reduce leverage after a specific time in drawdown. Let us say that the expected worst drawdown length is 7 months, and the parameter of the exponential distribution of drawdown strings is 0.6. In this case, the average length of the drawdown period is about 2 months. You could reduce leverage after 2 months in drawdown. This would produce a "soft landing" should the drawdown continue, because the depth of the drawdown will be shallower. Note, however, that the recovery from the drawdown will be slower with reduced leverage and may take longer.

Let us illustrate these ideas with a simple example. Consider the track record shown in Table 7.17, selected because it shows extended drawdowns and uses high leverage. An analysis of the results of the first 36 months of the track record showed that the standard deviation of monthly returns was 11.72 percent, projecting to drawdown potential (4σ) of 46.9 percent of equity. An exponential distribution fitted to the drawdowns in this 36-month period had an exponential parameter of 0.26, projecting to a drawdown period of 11 months with a 5 percent probability. We use the lower probability projection because we are using the drawdown strings only. The trading rule suggested by these data would be as follows: buy on the first occurrence when the drawdown is at least 6 months long, and the depth of the drawdown is at least 1σ, or 12 per-

Table 7.17 Analysis of drawdown performance of an actual track record.

Month	Return(%)	Index Value ($)	Highest Equity ($)	Loss ($)	Drawdown Strings
	0.00%	1000			
Jan-88	26.20%	1262.00	1283.16	-21.16	
Feb-88	-15.90%	1061.34	1283.16	-221.82	1
Mar-88	20.90%	1283.16	1283.16		8
Apr-88	-7.20%	1190.77	1190.77		1
May-88	2.10%	1215.78	1215.78		5
Jun-88	1.00%	1227.94	1227.94		3
Jul-88	-5.40%	1161.63	1227.94	-66.31	8
Aug-88	1.10%	1174.41	1227.94	-53.53	
Sep-88	1.40%	1190.85	1227.94	-37.09	
Oct-88	0.50%	1196.80	1227.94	-31.13	
Nov-88	-1.80%	1175.26	1227.94	-52.68	
Dec-88	18.70%	1395.04	1395.04		
Jan-89	-14.50%	1192.76	1395.04	-202.28	
Feb-89	17.40%	1400.29	1400.29		
Mar-89	-12.60%	1223.86	1400.29	-176.44	
Apr-89	-7.80%	1128.40	1400.29	-271.90	
May-89	-15.70%	951.24	1400.29	-449.06	
Jun-89	21.70%	1157.66	1400.29	-242.64	
Jul-89	5.00%	1215.54	1400.29	-184.75	
Aug-89	16.90%	1420.97	1420.97		
Sep-89	27.90%	1817.42	1817.42		
Oct-89	10.70%	2011.88	2011.88		
Nov-89	5.90%	2130.58	2130.58		
Dec-89	-15.10%	1808.86	2130.58	-321.72	
Jan-90	3.10%	1864.94	2130.58	-265.64	
Feb-90	5.30%	1963.78	2130.58	-166.80	
Mar-90	12.00%	2199.43	2199.43		
Apr-90	8.20%	2379.79	2379.79		
May-90	-6.90%	2215.58	2379.79	-164.21	
Jun-90	-0.30%	2208.93	2379.79	-170.85	
Jul-90	-2.30%	2158.13	2379.79	-221.66	
Aug-90	-1.30%	2130.07	2379.79	-249.71	
Sep-90	7.10%	2281.31	2379.79	-98.48	
Oct-90	-4.90%	2169.52	2379.79	-210.26	
Nov-90	3.80%	2251.97	2379.79	-127.82	
Dec-90	2.50%	2308.27	2379.79	-71.52	

Frequency Distribution

Bin	Frequency	Fitted Frequency
1	2	1.22
2	0	0.93
3	1	0.72
4	0	0.55
5	1	0.42
6	0	0.33
7	0	0.25
8	2	0.19
More	0	

Exponential distribution parameter	0.26
Worst DD Length (months)	11.37

cent. Table 7.18 shows the application of this rule in February 1991 and January 1992. This rule actually provided entries in February 1991, January 1992, August 1994, June 1995, and August 1999. The gains, 12 months later for the first four occurrences, were as follows: 37.6 percent, 22.25 percent, 26.80 percent, and 47.40 percent. At time of writing, the 12-month period for the August 1999 entry was not complete. This example, admittedly an anecdotal one, does illustrate the idea that one can find low-risk entry points by calculating the expected length of drawdown and depth of drawdown.

Table 7.18   Application of trading rule for dealing with drawdowns derived from Table 7.17.

	Monthly Return	VAMI	Equity Peak	Drawdown	% Drawdown	Entry Rule Satisfied	Exit Rule Satisfied
Apr-90	8.20%	2379.79	2379.79				
May-90	-6.90%	2215.58	2379.79	-164.21	-6.90		
Jun-90	-0.30%	2208.93	2379.79	-170.85	-7.18		
Jul-90	-2.30%	2158.13	2379.79	-221.66	-9.31		
Aug-90	-1.30%	2130.07	2379.79	-249.71	-10.49		
Sep-90	7.10%	2281.31	2379.79	-98.48	-4.14		
Oct-90	-4.90%	2169.52	2379.79	-210.26	-8.84		
Nov-90	3.80%	2251.97	2379.79	-127.82	-5.37		
Dec-90	2.50%	2308.27	2379.79	-71.52	-3.01		
Jan-91	1.60%	2345.20	2379.79	-34.59	-1.45		
Feb-91	▮	1951.20	2379.79	-428.58	-18.01	Yes	
Mar-91	0.40%	1959.01	2379.79	-420.78	-17.68		
Apr-91	18.20%	2315.55	2379.79	-64.24	-2.70		
May-91	0.20%	2320.18	2379.79	-59.61	-2.50		
Jun-91	1.90%	2364.26	2379.79	-15.52	-0.65		
Jul-91	28.20%	3030.99	3030.99				
Aug-91	-12.30%	2658.17	3030.99	-372.81	-12.30		
Sep-91	-15.20%	2254.13	3030.99	-776.85	-25.63		
Oct-91	1.10%	2278.93	3030.99	-752.06	-24.81		
Nov-91	-3.90%	2190.05	3030.99	-840.94	-27.74		
Dec-91	-1.90%	2148.44	3030.99	-882.55	-29.12		
Jan-92	▮	2288.09	3030.99	-742.90	-24.51	Yes	
Feb-92	17.40%	2686.21	3030.99	-344.77	-11.38		Yes
Mar-92	6.10%	2850.07	3030.99	-180.91	-5.97		
Apr-92	-5.30%	2699.02	3030.99	-331.97	-10.95		
May-92	-1.60%	2655.83	3030.99	-375.15	-12.38		
Jun-92	-0.20%	2650.52	3030.99	-380.46	-12.55		
Jul-92	-0.10%	2647.87	3030.99	-383.11	-12.64		
Aug-92	1.70%	2692.89	3030.99	-338.10	-11.15		
Sep-92	16.60%	3139.91	3139.91				
Oct-92	2.90%	3230.96	3230.96				
Nov-92	6.60%	3444.21	3344.21				
Dec-92	1.50%	3495.87	3495.87				
Jan-93	1.00%	3530.83	3530.83				Yes

"Rescaling" Volatility

One of the most frequently asked questions about any trading program is its daily volatility. Many risk-control programs closely monitor daily volatility of all managers or systems in a portfolio for risk-control purposes. Fortunately, the daily, monthly, and annualized volatility are related, and one can be scaled from the other. It is important to note the calendar period over which the volatility has been calculated, because the volatility is a summary statistic and does vary over time.

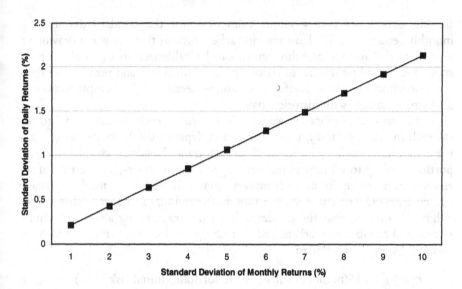

Figure 7.18   Volatility measured by the standard deviation of returns can be easily scaled from a larger time frame to a shorter time frame, or vice versa, providing useful guidance for traders and managers.

We use stochastic calculus or the theory or Brownian motion to scale from a shorter time to a longer time. If we assume 22 trading days to a month, the conversion from daily to monthly (Figure 7.18) works as:

$$\sigma_{monthly} = \sigma_{daily}\sqrt{22} \qquad (7.7)$$

Similarly, we can scale up monthly volatility into annualized volatility by multiplying by the square root of 12. For example, a monthly volatility of 5 percent implies a daily volatility of 1.07 percent and an annual volatility of 17.32 percent. These conversions are useful in monitoring the daily operation of a return generation process.

The conversion of monthly into daily volatility can be used to extend the ideas of peak-to-valley drawdown. Because there is less smoothing in the daily data (versus monthly data, for example), one has to use a larger multiple. For example, a good scaling for the worst daily drawdown is $5\sigma_{daily}$, or approximately equal to the monthly standard deviation. Similarly, the worst monthly drawdown is approximately equal to the annualized standard deviation.

A Calibration for Leverage

In this section, we review simple rules to adjust the standard deviation of monthly returns, σ_M. We have seen in earlier sections that the worst drawdown as well as the average monthly return can be calibrated to σ_M, and we need some understanding of how to change σ_M to control risk and reward. We limit the discussion here to a portfolio of futures because it is a simple matter to simulate portfolios with historical data.

The simplest calibration we want is how much each market "adds" to the σ_M each month. Naturally, this contribution depends on the trade sizing algorithm and how much equity is risked on each trade. Historical calculations with portfolios of up to 80 futures markets suggest the following simple rule: if we risk 1 percent of equity on each market, then a single futures market typically contributes 0.15 percent to σ_M per month, depending on the trade sizing algorithm. This means that the σ_M depends on the trade sizing algorithm, equity risked, and number of markets traded in the portfolio. Thus, the rule for estimated σ_M may be written as:

$$\sigma_M(\%) = 0.15(\text{number of markets in portfolio})(\text{initial risk in \%}) \qquad (7.8)$$

For example, if you risked 1 percent of $1 million per trade, then with a 60-market portfolio, you would expect to see a standard deviation of monthly returns of 9 percent, given by equation (7.8). This simple equation suggests that we can reduce the volatility by reducing the percentage of initial equity risk, or cutting back on the dollar risk (see Figure 7.19). We can also reduce volatility by reducing the size of the portfolio. If you change the money management algorithm or the fee structure, then the constant of 0.15 may increase to, say, 0.3 or decrease to 0.08. Overall, the changes are nearly linear, although some non-linearity exists as the size of the account increases. The relationship can be more complex for multisystem portfolios, but can be restated in the above form.

Return-Efficiency Benchmarks

We defined return efficiency (ρ) as the ratio of the average monthly return (μ) to the standard deviation (σ) of monthly returns ($\rho = \mu/\sigma$). Return efficiency is a useful measure of risk-adjusted performance because it can be used to make apples-to-apples comparisons without being overly sensitive to the leverage used in different return generation processes. It would be immensely useful to develop a benchmark for return efficiency because it can be used to compare and contrast different RGPs.

We begin by examining equity performance for the period 1979–1999, which includes one of the greatest bull markets in history. The following data (see Table 7.19) appeared in the *Chicago Tribune* on May 30, 2000, courtesy of

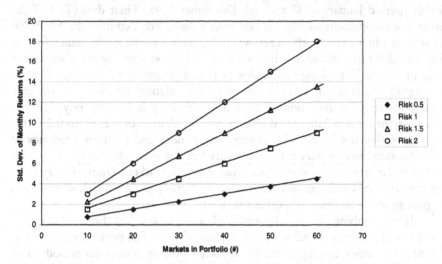

Figure 7.19 The relationship between the standard deviation of monthly returns, initial risk, and number of markets in the portfolio is practically linear for a given trade sizing algorithm for a portfolio of futures markets—a useful feature for adjusting risk and reward.

T. Rowe Price and Company. The table shows the performance of various stock "cash" indexes that do not have management fees or expenses. The Diversified Equity performance consisted of 37.5 percent Russell 1000 Growth index, 37.5 percent Russell 1000 Value index, 10 percent Russell 2000 Small Cap index, and 15 percent MSCI EAFE index. The data are useful for two reasons. First, they show that the typical monthly standard deviation for a stock index is around 5 percent. Second, they show that the return efficiency was between 0.2 and 0.32 percent, and about 0.26 percent on average, during a period with a roaring bull market.

Table 7.19 Summary of risk-adjusted performance of U.S. stock indexes.

1979–1999	Annual Stdev	Avg Annual Return	Avg Monthly Return	Monthly Stdev	Return Efficiency
MSCI EAFE Index	17.41%	14.79%	1.16%	5.03	0.23
Russell 1000 Growth index	17.02	17.82	1.38	4.91	0.28
Russell 1000 Value index	14.12	16.78	1.30	4.08	0.32
Russell 2000 Small Cap index	18.90	13.96	1.09	5.46	0.20
Diversified Equity	14.46	16.90	1.31	4.17	0.31

Schneeweis and Spurgin reported data for many equity and CTA indices for the period January 1987 through December 1995. Their data (Table 7.20) provide a comparison among various asset classes. For example, the S&P-500 total return index return efficiency was 0.29, similar to the performance for the Russell 2000 Growth index. The data from Schneeweis and Spurgin show that only the T-bill had a long-term value of return efficiency greater than 1, a direct result of the steady returns with very low volatility provided by Treasury bills. Note that the definition of the return efficiency favors precisely this type of consistent return. The return efficiency of CTA indexes is close to 0.25. It is significant that the MAR CTA Discretionary index had a return efficiency of 0.49, because discretionary traders can vary bet size more efficiently, putting on relatively large positions when they expect smooth markets. Discretionary traders are often strikingly correct at pinpointing turning points, which allows them to post superior risk/reward performance.

If we combine Tables 7.19 and 7.20, a reasonable benchmark for return efficiency is 0.25, which reflects performance of diversified portfolios across different asset classes, trading strategies, leverage levels, and calendar periods. The return efficiency is clearly not constant; it varies between asset classes and with time for the same return generation process. Setting up a benchmark has profound implications for evaluating trading manager performance and managing investor expectations. We have seen from the previous sections that, risk tolerance being equal, you should favor an RGP with a "better" return efficiency.

The value of return efficiency used will vary with the calendar period for a given RGP. For example, if you used rolling 24-month periods or rolling 36-month periods, then the return efficiency calculated over these rolling intervals

Table 7.20   Return efficiency data for variety of indexes and instruments from Schneeweis and Spurgin (1997).

	January 1987–December 1995		
	Monthly Arithmetic Average Return (%)	Monthly Standard Deviation (%)	Return Efficiency
T-bill	0.44	0.14	3.14
Salomon U.S. Bond index	0.71	1.36	0.52
S&P-500 total return	1.22	4.27	0.29
GS Commodity index	1.14	4.42	0.26
CRB index	0.17	2.37	0.07
TASS CTA index	1.10	4.23	0.26
Barclay index	1.11	4.77	0.23
MAR CTA dollar weighted	1.45	4.21	0.34
MAR CTA discretionary	1.98	4.08	0.49

Source: Schneeweis and Spurgin, *J. Derivatives,* Summer 1997.

would change. Hence, as suggested earlier, the R3RE, or rolling 3-month return efficiency, may be a good way to smooth the data. Yet another approach to data smoothing is to calculate the return efficiency of the return efficiency. A manager with a smoother equity curve will have a high value for the second-order return efficiency.

Empty Diversification

Diversification is a commonly proposed antidote to the variability of returns experienced in trading. Diversification can increase returns and reduce variability, but is there some point of diminishing returns? We examine this question by recognizing that there are many kinds of diversification. One can diversify across markets (or sectors), trading philosophies (or systems), and various money management and risk control algorithms. The goal is to improve the risk-adjusted performance of the portfolio of system-market combinations.

Figure 7.20 shows the effect of adding futures markets in random order to a portfolio traded using a simple channel breakout-style system. The figure shows that as expected, when markets are added to this portfolio, the standard deviation of monthly returns increases steadily. However, the risk-adjusted performance, as measured by the return efficiency, first increases and then levels out, increasing at a slower rate as markets are added (Figure 7.21). Thus, the incremental benefits of adding markets to this portfolio are decreasing. What would happen if we add even more markets to this portfolio?

When we add another 26 or so markets to this portfolio, the standard deviation of returns keeps increasing steadily without any noticeable saturation in the rate of increase (Figure 7.22). However, the return efficiency reaches a peak and declines, suggesting that there may be a point of diminishing returns in futures portfolios (Figure 7.23). There are two possible reasons for this decline:

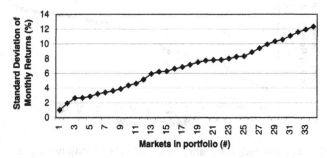

Markets vs. Portfolio Volatility

Figure 7.20 Adding markets in random order to a portfolio of futures markets monotonically increases the standard deviation of monthly returns.

Return Efficiency vs. Portfolio Size

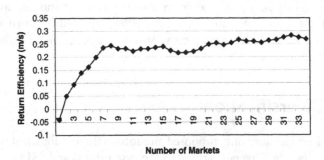

Figure 7.21 Adding markets in random order to a portfolio of futures markets increases return efficiency, but the gains get progressively smaller as number of markets in this data set increases.

(1) adding markets that are unprofitable over the test interval, and (2) adding markets that are structurally correlated to those already in the portfolio.

A number of factors can influence the shape of the return efficiency curve shown in Figure 7.23. For example, if all market sectors perform strongly during the test period, then the return efficiency curve may flatten out, or even increase slowly instead of declining. As global economies become ever more closely connected, the effects of structural correlation are more difficult to overcome.

Some factors that can potentially limit the benefits of diversification are that new markets added are correlated to markets in the portfolio, correlation shifts from historical correlations among markets in the portfolio, markets stay in a nontrending mode longer than historical norms, or drawdowns from usually noncorrelated systems occur coincidentally in a narrow time window. In

Portfolio Volatlity with Size

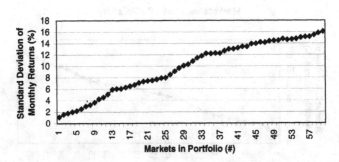

Figure 7.22 As expected, the standard deviation of monthly returns continues to increase monotonically as we add even more markets to the portfolio shown in Figure 7.20.

Return Efficiency vs. Portfolio Size

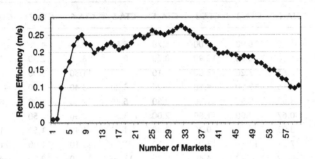

Figure 7.23   As we add even more markets to the portfolio in Figure 7.20, the return efficiency actually decreases significantly because the new markets were, on the whole, unprofitable over this data set.

essence, the diversification logic assumes that history will repeat itself, which it might, but in ways that negate some of the benefits of diversification.

Comparing Money Managers

Comparing the performance of money managers is more art than science because you have to evaluate historical data to fearlessly forecast future performance. You have to factor in your risk tolerance and expectations of profitability, and temper them with the uncertainties associated with selecting managers based on historical data. In this section, we focus on the performance records of a convenience sample of nine commodity trading advisors and apply the tools developed in previous sections to differentiate among them.

Table 7.21 shows the monthly performance data for nine CTAs from January 1998 through December 1999. The length of the track records is arbitrary, and you could choose to analyze 36 months of data instead if you so desire. We compute the average monthly return (μ), the standard deviation of monthly returns (σ), and the return efficiency ($\rho = \mu/\sigma$). You can use the built-in spreadsheet functions for the average and the standard deviation for this calculation. Return efficiency measures risk-adjusted performance and is insensitive to the order in which the returns were realized. It is a good measure of the overall structure of the trading program (systems and markets), with a higher ratio indicating a better system. However, your returns as an investor are affected by the order in which returns are realized.

We quantify the actually realized returns by calculating the net profits and net losses after fees and interest for an account starting at $1,000 at the beginning of the test period, and then calculate the ratio of the two quantities to get the net profit factor (NPF). The NPF is sensitive to the order in which returns

Table 7.21 Comparing managers based on multiple criteria.

	CTA-1	CTA-2	CTA-3	CTA-4	CTA-5	CTA-6	CTA-7	CTA-8	CTA-9
Jan-98	−1.29	16.90	2.00	5.70	5.80	−0.70	−4.20	1.50	4.71
Feb-98	6.06	3.00	12.90	0.20	−0.40	−3.70	2.80	3.27	1.74
Mar-98	3.65	7.20	13.60	5.10	−0.40	11.30	3.00	8.02	−0.39
Apr-98	−2.16	−9.00	4.10	−0.20	−3.20	−3.40	−5.20	−1.48	−2.61
May-98	3.62	9.50	1.30	0.50	6.40	2.40	1.90	8.53	0.07
Jun-98	−0.67	9.00	−1.80	2.00	−3.20	0.50	−0.50	3.23	−3.62
Jul-98	3.03	−6.60	10.70	−2.30	−1.00	−1.40	1.50	1.35	2.23
Aug-98	7.27	14.30	3.00	11.50	21.90	15.10	11.00	11.06	12.39
Sep-98	−0.59	6.90	4.40	9.00	11.90	12.30	2.20	4.52	3.98
Oct-98	−3.21	−7.20	3.40	−4.10	−6.20	−1.60	−7.10	−5.65	−3.96
Nov-98	−1.68	−2.40	8.30	−0.10	1.20	−0.90	2.10	1.18	0.40
Dec-98	1.80	0.90	−4.90	4.70	−0.80	0.70	3.50	9.19	0.97
Jan-99	−1.65	2.60	−2.20	−0.90	0.50	0.40	−4.20	−1.51	−2.46
Feb-99	2.64	1.90	10.80	0.70	5.90	−6.10	5.20	3.55	3.62
Mar-99	−2.20	−2.50	−2.80	−0.70	0.50	3.80	−5.70	−4.24	1.59
Apr-99	7.70	6.10	16.30	−5.10	−1.50	8.70	11.40	10.09	6.48
May-99	−6.60	7.40	−10.30	−4.20	−5.20	−1.30	−4.20	−8.58	−5.02
Jun-99	2.90	4.40	−9.00	−2.20	4.20	2.62	−3.40	5.31	−0.95
Jul-99	−4.61	−5.00	−13.40	6.47	4.03	−9.67	−5.56	−1.93	−0.74
Aug-99	3.86	−2.90	−7.60	2.50	1.15	−6.87	−4.22	−3.64	−1.00
Sep-99	1.78	−8.20	−10.90	−0.35	0.07	−1.67	4.76	−0.16	−1.33
Oct-99	−7.31	−6.20	−14.20	−2.67	−3.46	−1.56	−5.47	−6.13	−5.91
Nov-99	3.66	6.50	14.60	5.06	5.04	−2.76	5.93	13.00	−0.50
Dec-99	8.45	−13.30	−4.60	2.35	1.50	2.28	2.92	9.13	5.00
Average μ (%)	1.02	1.39	0.99	1.37	1.86	0.77	0.35	2.48	0.61
Std. dev. (σ) (%)	4.31	7.78	9.27	4.23	5.95	5.99	5.27	5.97	4.07
Return efficiency (ρ)	0.24	0.18	0.11	0.32	0.31	0.13	0.07	0.42	0.15
Net profits (NP) ($)	626.79	1262.39	1460.27	655.27	831.05	680.08	589.54	1244.61	466.65
Net losses (NL) ($)	377.94	961.95	1311.84	295.10	330.13	524.67	535.01	512.02	330.05
NPF = NP/NL	1.66	1.31	1.11	2.22	2.52	1.30	1.10	2.43	1.41
Expected worst drawdown duration (months)	7	12	7	12	10	9	7	8	10
Expected worst drawdown depth (%)	17.24	31.13	37.07	16.93	23.80	23.96	21.08	23.89	16.27
Expected annual return (%)	12.93	17.98	12.52	17.78	24.81	9.64	4.31	34.23	7.60
Gain/pain	0.75	0.58	0.34	1.05	1.04	0.40	0.20	1.43	0.47

are realized, and measures the money management process. The NPF measures how much money the managers make when they are right, versus how much they lose when they are wrong. It may be interpreted as a composite measure of the money management process, including risk control, trade sizing, and speed of exits. NPF is not sensitive to the absolute value of leverage because increasing leverage will generally increase both the net profits and the net losses. The NPF thus recognizes those managers who use leverage more effectively to the upside, that is, managers who are not penalized for a greater volatility in winning months. At a minimum, NPF should be greater than 1, and the higher the value the better. In theory, if there were no losing months during a test period, then the NPF would be infinite because there would be no net losses. Similarly, if there were no winning months, the NPF would be zero because the net profits would be zero. We illustrate the calculation of the net profit factor for CTA-3 in Table 7.22.

We started with an account of value $1,000. In January 1998, there was a net gain of 2.0 percent, or $20, so the ending account value was $1,020. In February 1998, there was a gain of 12.90 percent, which was applied to the previous month's ending index value of $1,020, giving a new ending index value of $1,151.58. Thus, the net gain for the month was $131.58. The 1.8 percent loss in June 1998 came on an index value of $1,379.53 at the end of May, and the net loss for the month was $24.83. After all the monthly calculations are done, we add up the total dollars gained and lost. For example, for the 2-year period ending December 1999, a $1,000 account would have gained $1,460.27 and lost $1,311.84, for a net return of $148.43 or 14.84 percent. The net profit factor is thus (1,460.27/1,311.84), or 1.11.

We next calculate the expected duration of the worst drawdown. We use the same methodology discussed earlier, but we use all the strings in the data, both runups and drawdowns, because the overall length of the data being evaluated is relatively short. In general, the shorter the length of the expected drawdown, the more attractive a manager's record. Table 7.23 shows a sample calculation for CTA-3. Table 7.21, which shows the net profit factor calculations, is used to find the duration of all strings in the equity curve. For example, the track record for CTA-3 starts with a string of 5 winning months, then 1 losing month, followed by 5 winning months, and so on. This raw data on strings is tabulated in the first column of Table 7.23. These are then converted into a histogram, using the built-in data analysis tools in Microsoft Excel 2000®. For example, there are six strings of one-month duration and one string of six-month duration. We next use an iterative procedure to fit an exponential distribution to the frequency distribution of strings. We guess the parameter value to be 0.5, and fit an exponential distribution to the data. Then we calculate the squared deviations of the fitted frequency from the actual frequency. The solver tool in Excel 2000 is then used to minimize the sum of squared deviations while adjusting the parameter of the exponential distribution. The solver solution is assumed to provide the best-fit exponential distribution parameter. The last step

Table 7.22   Calculation of the net profit factor for CTA-3 from Table 7.21.

	Monthly Return (%)	Index Value ($)	Net Gain ($)	Net Loss ($)
		1000		
Jan-98	2.00	1020.00	20.00	
Feb-98	12.90	1151.58	131.58	
Mar-98	13.60	1308.19	156.61	
Apr-98	4.10	1361.83	53.64	
May-98	1.30	1379.53	17.70	
Jun-98	−1.80	1354.70		24.83
Jul-98	10.70	1499.66	144.95	
Aug-98	3.00	1544.65	44.99	
Sep-98	4.40	1612.61	67.96	
Oct-98	3.40	1667.44	54.83	
Nov-98	8.30	1805.84	138.40	
Dec-98	−4.90	1717.35		88.49
Jan-99	−2.20	1679.57		37.78
Feb-99	10.80	1860.96	181.39	
Mar-99	−2.80	1808.86		52.11
Apr-99	16.30	2103.70	294.84	
May-99	−10.30	1887.02		216.68
Jun-99	−9.00	1717.19		169.83
Jul-99	−13.40	1487.08		230.10
Aug-99	−7.60	1374.06		113.02
Sep-99	−10.90	1224.29		149.77
Oct-99	−14.20	1050.44		173.85
Nov-99	14.60	1203.81	153.36	
Dec-99	−4.60	1148.43		55.38
	Sum		1460.27	1311.84
	NPF		1.11	

is to find the drawdown length with 0.1 percent probability of occurring, which is obtained by dividing 6.9 by the parameter of the exponential distribution. In the case of CTA-3, the estimated exponential parameter value is 1.04. Hence, the expected worst drawdown duration is 6.9/1.04, or 6.63 months, which rounds up to 7 months. The worst expected drawdown is estimated at four times the standard deviation of monthly returns in Table 7.2. Therefore, CTA-3, with a monthly standard deviation of 9.27 percent (see Table 7.21) has a worst expected drawdown of 37.08 percent. The expected annual returns are obtained by compounding the average monthly returns 12 times.

Table 7.23 Calculation of duration of worst drawdown.

Duration of
Strings   Frequency Histogram

5.00 Duration (months)	Frequency	Fitted Frequency	Squared Deviation
1.00	1.00	6.00	3.68	5.40
5.00	2.00	1.00	1.29	0.09
2.00	3.00	0.00	0.46	0.21
1.00	4.00	0.00	0.16	0.03
1.00	5.00	2.00	0.06	3.78
1.00	6.00	1.00	0.02	0.96
6.00	7.00	0.00	0.01	0.00
1.00 More		0.00		
1.00			Sum Squared	10.46

Exponential Distribution Parameter (λ)   1.04

"Worst" Duration: 0.1% probability (months)   7

The gain/pain ratio is simply the ratio of expected annual returns divided by the worst expected drawdown. A higher ratio is obviously preferred to a lower ratio. It is similar to an annualized Sharpe ratio with the risk free rate of zero. A manager that produces consistent returns with short and shallow drawdowns will have a larger gain/pain ratio.

As an investor or allocator, you can focus on the particular measurement that meets your objectives. For example, you can rank managers on the basis of return efficiency or NPF or any of the other measures. It is also possible to derive a composite measure by scoring managers relative to one another. For example, we can average the expected duration of drawdowns, the worst depth of drawdown, and expected annual returns across all managers. Table 7.24 shows that for the group of CTAs under review, the average length of worst expected drawdown is 9.11 months, the average depth of drawdown is 23.48 percent, and the expected annual return is 15.76 percent. We can calculate relative scores as follows. Because a shorter drawdown duration is more attractive than a longer one, we divide the expected average drawdown duration (9.11 months) by the expected duration of the individual CTAs. Hence, for CTA-1, the duration score is 9.11/7, or 1.30. Because a smaller drawdown is preferred to a larger drawdown, we divide the average worst drawdown by the expected drawdown for each manager. For CTA-1, the drawdown score is 23.48/17.24, or 1.36. By design, the drawdown score favors managers with a lower volatility. However, they will be penalized in the return score because their return will generally be lower, accounting for differences in return efficiency. Because a higher return is preferred to a lower return, we divide the expected return for every manager by

Table 7.24   Ranking on the basis of total performance score of expected future performance.

	Draw-down Duration (Months)	Worst Draw-down (%)	Expected Annual Return (%)	Duration Score	Draw-down Score	Return Score	Total Perform-ance Score (TPS)	Rank
CTA-1	7.00	17.24	12.93	1.30	1.36	0.82	3.48	2
CTA-2	12.00	31.13	17.98	0.76	0.75	1.14	2.66	8
CTA-3	7.00	37.07	12.52	1.30	0.63	0.79	2.73	6
CTA-4	12.00	16.93	17.78	0.76	1.39	1.13	3.28	4
CTA-5	10.00	23.80	24.81	0.91	0.99	1.57	3.47	3
CTA-6	9.00	23.96	9.64	1.01	0.98	0.61	2.60	9
CTA-7	7.00	21.08	4.31	1.30	1.11	0.27	2.69	7
CTA-8	8.00	23.89	34.23	1.14	0.98	2.17	4.29	1
CTA-9	10.00	16.27	7.60	0.91	1.44	0.48	2.84	5
Average values	9.11	23.48	15.76					

the average expected return for the group. Thus, for CTA-1 the return score is given by 12.93/15.76, or 0.82. Note that because CTA-1 had a lower monthly volatility than some of the other CTAs, CTA-1 had a higher drawdown score but a lower return score, than, say, CTA-2 or CTA-5. We can now build the total performance score (TPS) by summing the duration score, drawdown score, and return score. Note that this is a performance score of expected *future* performance, and such rankings can be quite useful.

Table 7.24 shows that CTA-8 was the highest-rated CTA based on the total performance score of expected future performance. CTA-8 had the highest return efficiency and the second highest NPF (see Table 7.21). The importance of a low duration of expected drawdowns is reflected in the number 2 ranking for CTA-1 on the TPS because CTA-1 had the fourth best return efficiency and NPF (see Table 7.21). Thus, the TPS adds value by factoring duration of drawdowns in addition to the quality of returns. The importance of the duration score also explains why CTA-2 narrowly beat out CTA-7 to avoid the lowest ranking.

The calculation of the length of the expected drawdown can be time consuming. A quicker approach would be to rank the managers based on the depth of drawdown score and the expected return score. To explore this idea, we selected another convenience sample of 10 CTAs with a technical trend-following trading strategy on diversified futures portfolios. Only two managers from the sample of nine CTAs used earlier were included in the sample of ten we discuss now. The primary reason to change the sample is to find CTAs whose track record extends to January 1993. We would also like to check if there is any

Table 7.25   Ranks based on composite drawdown depth and expected return score.

	1993-94	1994-95	1995-96	1996-97	1997-98	1998-99
CTA-1	1.00	3.00	5.00	6.00	4.00	2.00
CTA-10	5.00	8.00	8.00	7.00	5.00	9.00
CTA-2	9.00	6.00	4.00	1.00	3.00	3.00
CTA-3	7.00	10.00	10.00	10.00	10.00	10.00
CTA-4	3.00	5.00	7.00	8.00	8.00	6.00
CTA-5	6.00	1.00	3.00	4.00	7.00	7.00
CTA-6	2.00	4.00	9.00	9.00	6.00	5.00
CTA-7	10.00	7.00	2.00	3.00	2.00	1.00
CTA-8	8.00	9.00	1.00	2.00	1.00	4.00
CTA-9	4.00	2.00	6.00	5.00	9.00	8.00
Spearman's Rho		0.53	0.12	0.90	0.71	0.78
Significant		Yes	No	Yes	Yes	Yes

predictive value to this ranking strategy. We use rolling 2-year calendar intervals starting with January 1993 and ending with December 1999. Thus, we use overlapped samples 1993–1994, 1994–1995, and so on. The calculations in Table 7.25 are the same as Table 7.24, except that we do not calculate the length of the expected drawdown, and we rank the managers using relative performance on the sum of expected return score and expected worst-case drawdown score. We then use the nonparametric rank correlation test, Spearman's rho, to check for statistical significance.

The relative ranking of the 10 CTAs is summarized in Table 7.25 for the overlapped two-year intervals starting in 1993 and ending in 1999. The correlation between successive periods was statistically significant in four of the five intervals. For example, if you examine the last two columns, a CTA with a high ranking (low number) is associated with a high ranking (low number) in the subsequent period, and a CTA with a low ranking (high number) is associated with a low rank in the subsequent period. For example, CTA-3 was the lowest ranked CTA in both the 1997–1998 and 1998–1999 periods, and CTA-7 was ranked number 2 and number 1 in the two periods, respectively. The relationship in the rankings between the two periods was not random. Statistically, the ranking was significant at better than the 5 percent level.

In the 1994–1995 period compared to the 1995–1996 period, however, the numbers do not follow a pattern: CTA-8 was ranked number 9 in the first period and number 1 in the subsequent period. This period was marked by "rotation" in the rankings, and hence the rankings in the two periods are not significant statistically. The rotation is easier to see in Table 7.26, which shows the same results as the previous table by substituting the name of the CTA for its rank. The rotation may be because of a change in trading strategy and portfolio

Table 7.26   Ranks based on composite drawdown depth and expected return score.

	1993-94	1994-95	1995-96	1996-97	1997-98	1998-99
	CTA-1	CTA-5	CTA-8	CTA-2	CTA-8	CTA-7
	CTA-6	CTA-9	CTA-7	CTA-8	CTA-7	CTA-1
	CTA-4	CTA-1	CTA-5	CTA-7	CTA-2	CTA-2
	CTA-9	CTA-6	CTA-2	CTA-5	CTA-1	CTA-8
	CTA-10	CTA-4	CTA-1	CTA-9	CTA-10	CTA-6
	CTA-5	CTA-2	CTA-9	CTA-1	CTA-6	CTA-4
	CTA-3	CTA-7	CTA-4	CTA-10	CTA-5	CTA-5
	CTA-8	CTA-10	CTA-10	CTA-4	CTA-4	CTA-9
	CTA-2	CTA-8	CTA-6	CTA-6	CTA-9	CTA-10
	CTA-7	CTA-3	CTA-3	CTA-3	CTA-3	CTA-3
Significant		Yes	No	Yes	Yes	Yes

tactics. Notice how CTA-8 rose from the lower rankings in 1995–1996 and stayed as one of the top performers through 1997–1998. Notice also how CTA-3 remained the lowest-ranked CTA from 1994–1995 through 1998–1999. Even if you picked the best-performing CTA in one interval, your downside risk was three rankings; in this sample, the slippage was usually only two slots. Thus, the rankings based on expected future performance may be a useful way to find CTAs likely to perform well in the future. For example, you could build a portfolio of the top four CTAs at the end of each year and hold it for the next year. Table 7.27 shows how the portfolio would rotate; managers in highlighted boxes are held over from the prior year.

These calculations can be repeated using the Hotelling-Pabst test with identical results of statistical significance. The fact that this method can provide statistically significant rankings has great practical significance. As always, we must use caution must because the rankings are not guaranteed to persist, and are not an assurance of improved performance. There is also the issue of sample size: we have examined a relatively small sample over a moderately long period.

Table 7.27   Portfolio of top four CTAs at the end of the previous year. Managers in highlighted cells are held over from the previous year.

1995	CTA-1	CTA-6	CTA-4	CTA-9
1996	CTA-5	CTA-9	CTA-1	CTA-6
1997	CTA-8	CTA-7	CTA-5	CTA-2
1998	CTA-2	CTA-8	CTA-7	CTA-5
1999	CTA-8	CTA-7	CTA-2	CTA-1

You should crosscheck these ideas on a larger sample if possible. Our discussion in this section shows that we can integrate the ideas underlying the Chande comfort zone that estimate the expected return and the depth and duration of future drawdowns into a composite score for ranking money managers. Remember that the process of evaluating a manager is complex, and a quantitative analysis of performance can be only one small part of the total picture.

Risk and Reward in Stocks and Mutual Funds

Just how much risk is there in a stock or mutual fund? There is the relative risk that you may underperform other stocks or funds in the peer group. However, you are also bearing an absolute risk—the risk that you will lose 25 percent or more of your value in a week or less. In the end, the absolute risk is more important to your investment success—in fact, your survival—than relative risk. The spread of online trading and real-time data feeds has led to a culture that punishes bad news with a summary execution. These "trigger-happy vigilantes" proudly espouse the philosophy of "shoot first, ask questions later." A review of the sharp declines in market leaders such as Intel and Apple in September 2000 suggests that market capitalization and liquidity are no protection against an avalanche of sell-orders. The price moves that previously occurred in months can now be completed in a matter of hours. In this section, we extend the ideas of estimating the depth of drawdowns to daily events. You will remember that the peak-to-valley drawdown can be estimated to a good approximation as four times the standard deviation of monthly returns (σ_M). On daily data, we will use the standard deviation of daily closes over 22 days (σ_{22}) as our estimate of the standard deviation of monthly returns. Implicitly, we are assuming that there are 22 trading days in a month.

We begin by examining the decline in Intel Corp. (INTC) stock in September 2000 following an earnings warning. The company issued a warning after the close on a Thursday, and the stock declined in after-hours trading, opening down about $15 the next day. Figure 7.24 shows that the 22-day standard deviation of the daily close was $6.15 as of Thursday close. The closing price of Thursday does not show after-hours trading. Hence, the decline amounted to approximately $2.2\sigma_{22}$ on a closing basis. This suggests that the price decline, although instantaneous, was relatively well contained.

Apple (APPL) followed a few days later with its own announcement of declining revenues and falling sales of its flagship products. The market took a large bite out of AAPL, sending the stock down 7.44 σ_{22}, considerably worse than Intel's woes (see Figure 7.25). AAPL's drop was in line with the worst stock market declines, as shown in Figures 7.8 and 7.9 for the S&P-500 and NASDAQ. Thus, 8 σ_{22} is probably a better estimate of the daily risk in a stock today, given the speed of movement and liquidity constraints.

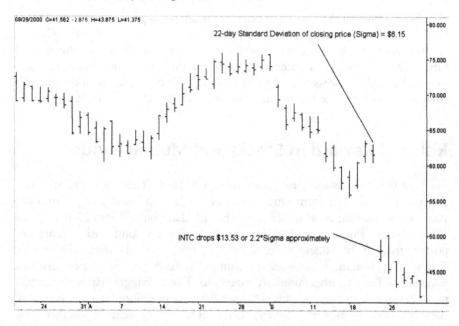

Figure 7.24   Intel gapped lower after the company surprised analysts by lowering earnings forecasts. The decline amounted to approximately 22 times the standard deviation of returns over the previous 22 days.

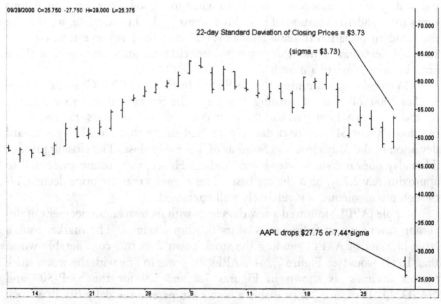

Figure 7.25   Apple Computer stock declined a stunning seven times the standard deviation of daily returns over the previous month after announcing weak sales.

Are mutual funds subject to similar risks? As shown previously in Figure 7.10, the peak-to-valley drawdown increases with increasing monthly standard deviations (σ_M). The average drawdown was $4.3\sigma_M$, suggesting that the diversification afforded by owning 50 or more stocks tends to smooth out the equity curve. An analysis of the daily data of more than 50 funds suggests that the severest daily declines are typically less than $2.5\sigma_{22}$ and closer to $1.5\sigma_{22}$, primarily due to smoothing effects of a diversified portfolio.

An analysis of the return efficiency of a convenience sample of 50 mutual funds used to create Figure 7.10 suggests that return efficiency is insensitive to monthly volatility (see Table 7.28). Return efficiency is the ratio of average monthly return to the standard deviation of monthly returns and can be used to estimate expected returns using equation (7.6). The average return efficiency of this sample was 0.37. You can use this figure to weed out funds with lower return efficiency for a given range of monthly volatility. Because increasing volatility leads to larger drawdowns, you can start by estimating a target standard deviation of monthly returns as your threshold of pain divided by 4. If your threshold of pain is 32 percent, then the target standard deviation is 8 percent. You should avoid funds with much higher standard deviations or much lower standard deviations because you have identified a risk level you can tolerate. The next step is to select those funds that exceed the average return efficiency at the same or similar level of risk in order to maximize your returns for the level of risk you are willing to bear.

You should remember that the return efficiency is not cast in stone, but will vary from year to year. However, this approach will help you find funds that meet your risk exposure limits and yet provide superior absolute returns versus funds of similar absolute risk. This approach of using absolute risk to select mutual funds is probably more meaningful than other commercial approaches based on performance relative to an entire category of funds or relative to riskless investments such as U.S. Treasury bills.

Summary

In this chapter we discussed key money-management ideas. We began by examining the risk of ruin. Those calculations show that there is little incentive to overleverage a trading account. The risk-of-ruin calculations assume that your bet size, payoff ratio, and fraction winners are fixed. However, you can vary bet size if you could identify an extraordinary opportunity in the markets.

We then looked at the interaction between system design and money management. The design philosophy is for you to protect the downside and let the market take care of the upside. We then used the standard deviation of monthly equity to project future drawdowns at four to five times the standard deviation.

Table 7.28

Fund	Return Efficiency
FBALX	0.34
FBIOX	0.27
FCNTX	0.35
FCVSX	0.46
FDCAX	0.28
FDCPX	0.31
FDEGX	0.43
FDEQX	0.34
FDGFX	0.35
FEQIX	0.34
FEQTX	0.35
FEXPX	0.32
FFIDX	0.4
FFTYX	0.18
FMAGX	0.36
FPURX	0.23
FSINX	0.16
FSPCX	0.21
FSPTX	0.47
FSTCX	0.36
FSTGX	0.55
FSUTX	0.47
JABAX	0.41
JAEIX	0.41
JAENX	0.43
JAFIX	0.32
JAGIX	0.44
JAHYX	0.18
JAMPX	0.49
JANSX	0.44
JAOLX	0.48
JAOSX	0.34
JASSX	0.41
JATEX	0.21
JAVLX	0.46
JAWWX	0.46
JAXBS	0.76
PBCRX	0.31
PBEGX	0.21
PBHEX	0.38
PBHGX	0.29
PBHLX	0.44
PBLDX	0.31
PBMCX	0.39
PBTCX	0.41
PLCPX	0.52
PSSCX	0.28
TWCGX	0.42
VFINX	0.43
VGXTX	0.43

We examined how betting strategies affect the smoothness of the equity curve. The fixed-contracts per signal is a reasonable choice for most traders. You can get a smoother curve by reducing position size after a losing trade. Your other strategies, such as double-on-win or double-on-loss, greatly increased equity curve roughness. You should understand this material well, because each of these money-management strategies can significantly affect future portfolio performance.

We then shifted gears and examined in detail factors affecting the depth and duration of drawdowns. The depth of drawdowns is generally less than four times the standard deviation of monthly returns for many asset classes, such as futures, hedge funds, and mutual funds. The duration of drawdowns can be estimated from an exponential distribution or as three times the standard deviation of the duration of drawdown "strings," or periods. These are extremely valuable tools to estimate two critical aspects of future performance. We discussed how return efficiency could be used to create a model for expected returns. Together these models help define the Chande comfort zone, a powerful tool for managing risks and expectations.

We next studied the difficult issues of how to deal with drawdowns, and showed how to identify low-risk entry points when a manager is in a drawdown. Next, we looked at practical issues dealing with rescaling volatility, and a calibration for leverage. These will help you determine how much volatility to expect and how to estimate the volatility from the number of markets traded and leverage used. These ideas form essential building blocks no trader, investor, or allocator can afford to ignore.

We addressed a critical issue by proposing a benchmark for return efficiency that can be used for futures, stocks, mutual funds, and hedge funds. A return efficiency of 0.25 is an excellent benchmark of risk-adjusted performance among these diverse asset classes. Diversification is often touted as the best pathway for superior risk-adjusted performance. However, how many markets are too much? We showed how it is not difficult to obtain empty diversification by trading too many markets.

We then gave a detailed example of the application of these ideas by examining how money managers can be compared. In this discussion, we proposed several new measures of ranking managers to better handicap their future performance. This section should be of much interest to investors and allocators. We ended by showing how individuals could apply the ideas introduced in this chapter to define the risk in individual stocks or to identify superior mutual fund investments.

Chapter

Data Scrambling

There are never enough data of the kind you want.

Introduction

Our focus continues on understanding how our system will do in the future. In this chapter we introduce a new method to generate synthetic data that can produce unlimited amounts of data for system testing. The new method, called data scrambling, will help you overcome the restrictions imposed by the relatively small amount of data on futures markets. Data scrambling can create the new price ranges and new price patterns necessary to test your system under the widest possible range of market activity. This is true out-of-sample testing. We explain this procedure in detail using a spreadsheet and S&P-500 data. We then use a 7-year long Swiss franc continuous contract to generate 56 years of synthetic data. We then test a volatility system on the synthetic data so you can appreciate the advantages of such testing.

What You Really Want To Know about Your System

What you really want to know about your trading system is how it will do in the future. Ideally, you want to know what the profits and the drawdowns may be. Since you cannot foresee the future, a good option is to test your systems on many data sets that "simulate" future market action. You can then simply average the results to get reasonable estimates of future profits and drawdowns. We emphasize, however, that it is difficult to get precise figures for both your profitability and your drawdowns.

You can also use good estimates for the average and standard deviation of the monthly equity changes. We looked at interval equity change and its standard deviation when we studied equity curves. The standard deviation is useful for projecting future drawdowns.

As a trader, you also want to get a feel for how well the design philosophy of a particular system works on a variety of markets. Your comfort level with a system's design approach is even more valuable than performance numbers because you can implement a familiar system without hesitation. One way to gain this confidence is to test the system on many different data sets, of the type you are *likely* to come across in the future.

Remember that all the computer testing occurs in a sterile, unemotional environment, without any great stakes riding on the outcome. You become emotionally involved with the system in real trading because the stakes are higher. However, you never feel this pressure when you test a system. A solution is to test the system on many data sets so you can experience, at least indirectly, many different market environments. You will then have a better understanding of the variability of system performance over those markets.

Note that your system-testing efforts tell you only how your system would have done in the past. Your results are hostage to the particular data set you use. So you would like to test dozens, even hundreds, of data sets that simulate future market action. However, since most of the active futures markets have traded for less than two decades, the amounts of market data are finite. Add the complication that futures contracts expire, and your big challenge is to find sufficient data to thoroughly test your system. The more data sets you can use, the better off you are, both from a quantitative and from a psychological perspective.

This chapter discusses a new method to generate unlimited amounts of data that "simulate" future market action. This new method allows you to generate an unlimited number of data sets from historical market data. These synthetic data encapsulate knowledge about market volatility and trading patterns. You will see that once you can generate such data, you are free to thoroughly test your system in a way better than ever possible before. What is more important, you can "live through" many types of markets, and build confidence in the system that could be vital to your success.

Past Is Prolog: Sampling with Replacement

The idea of sampling with replacement is basically as follows. Imagine a situation in which you take 100 disks, number them from 1 to 100, and then mix them up in a bag. You then shake the bag, and pull out a disk with, say, #21 on

Table 8.1 Illustrating sampling with replacement; note how the average and standard deviation of the 11 samples move toward the values for the original sample.

Original	#1	#2	#3	#4	#5	#6	#7	#8	#9	#10	#11
1	7	2	8	3	9	6	2	8	6	1	7
2	6	6	9	6	10	7	8	10	3	4	3
3	2	3	6	4	1	8	4	1	4	1	0
4	3	7	7	10	5	9	1	8	6	6	5
5	10	3	7	10	7	9	10	7	8	5	4
6	9	6	3	8	7	10	4	10	10	8	3
7	5	4	5	1	3	3	10	6	5	6	3
8	5	7	3	10	9	2	6	9	7	8	5
9	4	1	8	2	3	10	9	4	2	4	8
10	5	7	8	4	7	5	1	1	1	9	2
Average	5.50	5.60	4.60	6.40	5.80	6.10	6.90	5.50	6.40	5.20	6.10
Std dev	3.03	2.50	2.27	2.12	3.49	3.00	2.85	3.60	3.37	2.78	2.73

| Average (all) | 5.72 |
| Std dev (all) | 2.81 |

it. Now, before pulling out a second disk, you have two options. You can put #21 back into the bag so that all 100 disks are in the bag, or you can select another number out of the remaining 99 disks, without replacing #21 in the bag.

If you put #21 back, there is a 1 chance in 100 you will pull it out the second time. This is the process of sampling with replacement. The probability that you will get #21 the first time is 1 percent. The probability that you will get #21 twice is 0.01 percent. Thus, the probability of getting #21 three times in a row is 0.0001 percent, or once in 1,000,000 tries. Remember, just because the probability of getting #21 three times in a row is small does not mean it cannot happen.

An example will illustrate the idea behind sampling with replacement (see Table 8.1). Using the numbers from 1 to 10 as our "original" sample, we calculate its average (5.5) and standard deviation (3.03). We then use the sampling-with-replacement algorithm in Microsoft Excel® 5.0 to generate 11 additional samples. If you study the samples for a minute, you will see that the same value often occurs more than once. The values are being drawn at random from the original sample, so that each of the 11 samples is different. At the same time, we retain the "signature" of the original data set, as measured by the difference between the highest and lowest value.

We have also computed the average and standard deviation for each sample. These values range from 4.30 to 6.90 for the average and 1.95 to 3.60 for the standard deviation. Thus, each sample is only a rough estimate of the average and standard deviation of the original sample. However, when we calculate the average (5.72) and standard deviation (2.81) for all 11 samples, those values are closer to the statistics of the original sample. The more samples we generate, the better our estimates for the statistics of the original sample.

Applying the same principle to system testing, we could use sampling with replacement to generate synthetic data. The extra data will improve our estimates of the average and standard deviation of, say, the monthly equity changes. The new data will allow true out-of-sample testing and extend the variety of market conditions exposed to the system.

The idea of sampling with replacement leads to another statistical idea, called bootstrapping, in which you use sampling with replacement from the results of some experiment to develop the statistical distribution for the quantity of interest. For example, say you had the results of 200 trades from a trading system. You can use sampling with replacement to generate different possible outcomes, and then average those data to develop a distribution for future trading results. In the example above, the different values of average and standard deviation from each sample give us a distribution for the average and standard deviation of the original sample.

You can revisit our discussion of the results for the 65sma-3cc system to look at the distribution of all trades. Those 2,400 tests led to a particular histogram or distribution of trades. We could use sampling with replacement from the 2,400 trades to develop other potential distributions or histograms, and try to estimate future performance.

One difficulty in using sampling with replacement is that we can select data only from within the original sample. Hence, you can "see" only those events that have occurred in the original sample. The procedure developed here tries to overcome this problem so you can create new price ranges and price patterns.

Let us see how we can use sampling with replacement on a continuous contract to generate other continuous contracts that encapsulate market information. Once we can replicate market data, we are on the way to freedom from data set limitations.

Data Scrambling: All the Synthetic Data You'll Ever Need

Data from scrambled continuous contracts are termed synthetic data because these data are not from actual trading in the open market. The phrase data scrambling is used because this method randomly rearranges the data to create new sequences.

Let us first see how to encapsulate market information. We place two daily bars next to each other. Then, we observe the relationship between the open (O), high (H), low (L), and close (C) of the second bar by using the close of the first bar as the reference. We can write the relationship as follows:

deltaO = O – C[1],

deltaH = H – C[1],

deltaL = L – C[1],

deltaC = C – C[1].

Here [1] denotes the close of the previous day. These equations encapsulate market trading behavior since they capture price patterns versus the previous close. Over a period of years, each market will have some characteristic values for these equations, based on its volatility, liquidity, and other trading patterns. When we sample with replacement using these formulas, we create patterns that bear the market's signature as defined by relative price relationships.

The next step is to use a random number generator to scramble the bars. Once you have a new sequence, you need a starting point, usually the prior close. You can use any number for the first bar. The new bar is derived from the prior close as follows (new synthetic values are indicated by the Syn prefix):

Syn-Close = Close[1] + delta C,

Syn-High = Close[1] + delta H,

Syn-Low = Close[1] + delta L,

Syn-Open = Close[1] + delta O.

So the calculations are easy to put into a program or a spreadsheet. We will first calculate the interbar relationships in Table 8.2, which is based on the actual bar sequence of the December 1995 S&P-500 (Figure 8.1). The interbar relationships appear in the last four columns. The difference between the daily close of 11/30 and 11/29 was –0.80 points. The differences between yesterday's close and today's open, high, low, and close are shown for each day. These calculations encapsulate price relationships. Now we can scramble these bars using a random number generator.

To scramble these data, number them from 1 to n, where n is the last bar. Then, use the random number generator to pick a number between 1 and n. That number is the next bar in the sequence. Suppose on the tenth pick, you pick bar 5. Then the original bar 5 becomes bar 10 of the new sequence. The bars may repeat more than once. For example, on the twenty-seventh pick, you may draw bar 5 once again. You can generate as long a sequence as you desire.

Here we used the 11/29/95 close of 608.05 as reference, and generated a new sequence of bars using the sampling function in Microsoft Excel®. The new

348   Data Scrambling

Table 8.2   Spreadsheet based on December 1995 S&P-500 data.

Bar #	Date	Open	High	Low	Close	O– C[1]	H– C[1]	L– C[1]	C–C[1]
	11/29/95	608.6	608.85	606.3	608.05				
1	11/30/95	608.07	610	606.1	607.25	0.02	1.95	–1.95	–0.8
2	12/01/95	608	609.4	605.9	608.3	0.75	2.15	–1.35	1.05
3	12/04/95	608.87	615.5	608.05	614.8	0.57	7.2	–0.25	6.5
4	12/05/95	614.02	619.5	613.85	618.75	–0.78	4.7	–0.95	3.95
5	12/06/95	619.85	622.65	617.35	619.8	1.1	3.9	–1.4	1.05
6	12/07/95	618.95	619.8	615.7	616.65	–0.85	0	–4.1	–3.15
7	12/08/95	618.5	619.5	614.3	618.3	1.85	2.85	–2.35	1.65
8	12/11/95	618.9	621.7	617.75	619.8	0.6	3.4	–0.55	1.5
9	12/12/95	618.9	620	618.2	618.8	–0.9	0.2	–1.6	–1
10	12/13/95	619.4	622.6	618.65	621.35	0.6	3.8	–0.15	2.55

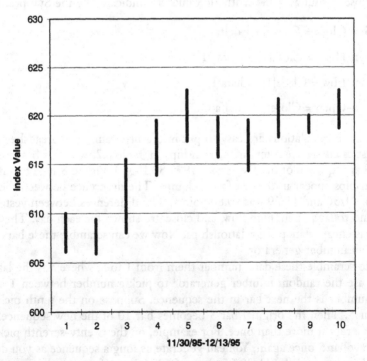

Figure 8.1   Actual price bars from the December 1995 S&P-500 contract.

Table 8.3   Scrambled data for S&P-500 using relationships calculated in Table 8.2. I assumed that the close before the first bar (bar 4 below) was 608.05.

Bar #	O– C[1]	H– C[1]	L– C[1]	C– C[1]	Syn–O	Syn–H	Syn–L	Syn–C
4	–0.78	4.7	–0.95	3.95	607.27	612.75	607.1	612
5	1.1	3.9	–1.4	1.05	613.1	615.9	610.06	613.05
8	0.6	3.4	–0.55	1.5	613.65	616.45	612.5	614.55
1	0.02	1.95	–1.95	–0.8	614.57	616.5	612.6	613.75
3	0.57	7.2	–0.25	6.5	614.32	620.95	613.5	620.25
10	0.6	3.8	–0.15	2.55	620.85	624.05	620.1	622.8
10	0.6	3.8	–0.15	2.55	623.4	626.6	622.65	625.35
8	0.6	3.4	–0.55	1.5	625.95	628.75	624.8	626.85
9	–0.9	0.2	–1.6	–1	625.95	627.05	625.25	625.85
1	0.02	1.95	–1.95	–0.8	625.87	627.8	623.9	625.05

sequence was: 4, 5, 8, 1, 3, 10, 10, 8, 9, 1. Therefore, starting with the previous close of 608.05, we put in the fourth bar of the original data, then the fifth bar, and the eighth bar, and so on.

Table 8.3 presents the spreadsheet used to calculate the new synthetic data. The first column is the bar number drawn by sampling with replacement. The next four columns are the inter-bar relations previous calculated for each bar in Table 8.2. The last four columns are the synthetic data derived from the previous close by adding the interbar relations.

In Table 8.2, the data for 12/05 converts to bar 4, and the market gained 3.95 points on the close. In Table 8.3, bar 4 is the first bar of the new sequence. The previous close was assumed to be 608.05. So the new close is 3.95 + 608.05, or 612.00. The new low is 608.05 – 0.95, or 607.10. The new high is 4.7 + 608.05, or 612.75. These are the numbers for the synthetic contract in the first row. The close for the second bar is 612.00 + 1.05 or 613.05. You can now complete the rest of the calculations. The new scrambled data created a synthetic bar pattern plotted in Figure 8.2.

The new bar sequence (Figure 8.2) shows an upward bias, getting up toward the 630 area. Note how it does not show the consolidation in the last six bars of the original data. The last bar from the original data (bar 10 on Figure 8.1) occurs in Figure 8.2 as bars 6 and 7, and you can see that the relative appearance of the high and low versus the previous bar in the sequence is similar in both cases. Thus, we have encapsulated the market behavior in the original bar 10 and reproduced it in another sequence to create new synthetic data.

Of course, the more samples you generate, the greater the variety of patterns you will see. Another synthetic pattern derived from original December 1995 S&P-500 futures data is shown in Figure 8.3 to illustrate the variety of

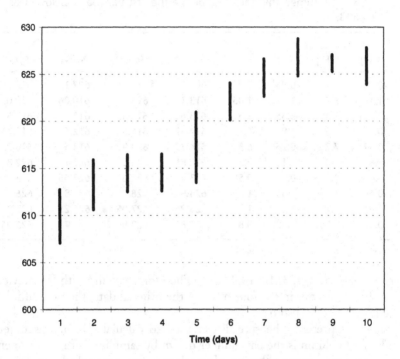

Figure 8.2 Synthetic data from Table 8.3 for the S&P-500 contract.

possible patterns. The new patterns cover a narrower price range than the original data, and appear like a breakout at the end.

Thus, you can generate a variety of chart patterns using data scrambling. Continuous contracts work well to create synthetic data because they represent a long history of market action. If you prefer, you can use this method on individual contracts, and then string them together for testing using rollovers at the appropriate dates.

The power of data scrambling increases as the number of bars of data increases because you can create a greater variety of patterns. Thus, if you had, say, a 5-year or 7-year long continuous contract, you could generate 100 years of data and test your system against a variety of market conditions. Since these are the type of patterns you are *likely* to see in the future, this is the most rigorous out-of-sample testing you can achieve.

Figure 8.4 shows how data scrambling can overcome the limitation of insufficient data. First, the original data had several trading ranges, whereas the synthetic data has several trends, indicating you can generate new price patterns. Second, the synthetic data exceeded the price range of the original. Thus

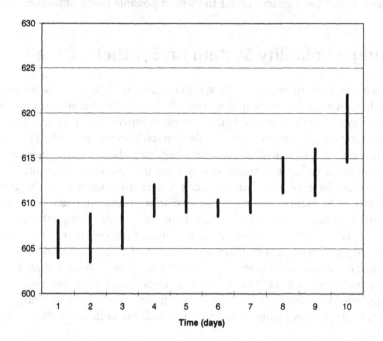

Figure 8.3   Synthetic data for S&P-500 contract using the bar sequence 6, 5, 4, 2, 1, 9, 10, 8, 7, 3.

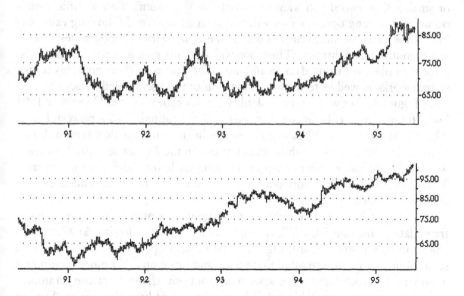

Figure 8.4   Swiss franc synthetic contract (lower curve) generated from daily data using continuous contract (upper curve).

data scrambling can create new price ranges and new price patterns, which are necessary to test your system under the widest possible range of market activity.

Testing a Volatility System on Synthetic Data

Here we test a volatility system on synthetic data to illustrate how to use data scrambling. A volatility system is a good choice for this because the currency markets have recently seen sudden, compressed moves. You may feel that sudden, compressed price moves are a staple in today's futures markets. However, a historical review will convince you that they have also occurred before. Such moves are often difficult to trade with systems that use heavily smoothed data. Many traders have observed that sudden moves also occur near the turning points of trends. Hence, you may find a volatility-based approach also suitable for identifying tops or bottoms. You can define volatility in many different ways.

The usual practice is to use some multiple of the recent true range to define the edges of price moves. Here we take a simpler approach and use just the difference between today's high and low as the measure of price range. The buy stop for tomorrow is today's high plus two times today's high-low range. Similarly, the sell stop is today's low minus two times today's high-low range. It is quite unlikely (but not impossible) that you will hit both entry orders on the same day.

The above definition of entry points is quite generic and not optimized to any specific market. You can use a multiple larger than two to get fewer entries, or smaller than two if you want more entries. We assume these volatile swings occur near turning points, so we will test an arbitrary trend following exit: exiting on the close of the twentieth day in the trade. First we look at test results using continuous contracts. Then, we will test this system on synthetic Swiss franc data obtained using data scrambling. The goal is to show how this simple system works as well as to illustrate how you can use scrambled data.

Figure 8.5 shows how the volatility entries appear on the December 1995 Swiss franc contract. In September, this system profited from a powerful rally. The exit at the end of 20 days got you out in the consolidation region. However, the system did not go short soon enough in the August sell-off. That trade was barely profitable. Note the previous long trade hit the $3,000 initial stop. Therefore, by design, a short burst out of one consolidation into another consolidation or trend works best with this system.

We tested the system first on a continuous contract using actual Swiss franc data from June 30, 1989, through June 30, 1995, allowing $100 for slippage and commissions and using a $3,000 initial stop. We then used the data scrambling routine to scramble these data, and made up eight more continuous contracts. We tested the same system without any changes on the scrambled data, as summarized in Table 8.4. The synthetic data have the letters "Syn" in their name for clear identification.

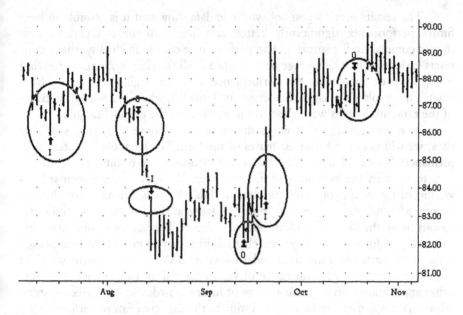

Figure 8.5   Stops at two times the high-low range above and below today's high and low provide good entries into compressed moves. However, the market can often make big moves without volatility.

Table 8.4   Comparison of volatility system on actual and scrambled data.

Market	Profit ($)	Maximum Intraday Draw-down ($)	Profit Factor	Number of Trades	Number of Winners	Average Win/ Loss	Average Trade ($)
SF Contract	5,800	−17,600	1.06	121	43	1.92	48
SF Syn #1	33,624	−12,732	1.42	81	39	1.60	415
SF Syn #2	35,563	−19,550	1.38	97	45	1.59	367
SF Syn #3	−713	−21,388	0.99	99	37	1.53	−8
SF Syn #4	14,350	−14,938	1.16	86	39	1.92	167
SF Syn #5	8,937	−20,425	1.11	98	44	1.36	91
SF Syn #6	−22,625	−27,050	0.79	101	40	1.21	−224
SF Syn #7	13,550	−22,463	1.14	97	42	1.49	139
SF Syn #8	−13,212	−30,750	0.9	97	42	1.19	−136
Average SF Syn data	8,684	−21,162	1.11	95	41	1.49	101

The results over 56 years of synthetic data show that it is possible to have future performance significantly better or worse than the test period. This should come as no big surprise. The performance over individual synthetic contracts varies widely. The average performance of all the eight synthetic series (last row), however, approaches the performance over the original test period (first row). This result is similar to that shown in Table 8.1, where the average statistics of the random samples were close to the statistics of the original sample.

In essence, when we average the results over more and more synthetic data, we will get ever better estimates of the "true" or most likely system performance. We can also find the standard deviation of the results over synthetic data to quantify the variability of future results. For example, the standard deviation of the profits on synthetic data in Table 8.4 was $20,523 (not shown). Armed with this data, we can use mean-variance analysis to make portfolio decisions using the ideas of modern portfolio theory. We can try to find the portfolio weights for a group of systems that might achieve a given level of expected return for a particular expected standard deviation. We can also use the standard deviation to input a relevant range of values for risk of ruin calculations. Another application is to estimate a range of future drawdowns for a given system. Thus, synthetic data can be used to estimate the expected future performance.

There is one important limitation of scrambled data. Since we are using a random sampling with replacement approach, our new patterns do not represent actual market behavior. For example, synthetic data can create patterns that do not represent market psychology or any real supply-demand forces. Hence, you should create many data sets and average your system performance across those sets. The averaged performance will probably be more representative of potential system performance in the future.

Summary

In summary, scrambled data provide a new method to test a system over many different market conditions. You can observe the model's performance under such simulations, and gain much needed confidence on how it works and learn to recognize when it does not. You can then use your insight to create filters that may improve system performance, reduce the number of trades, and create a neutral zone for system trading. You can also develop equity curves to check your interval estimates of standard deviation and therefore improve your projections of future drawdowns. You can also perform a subjective evaluation of market conditions under which the system does particularly well or poorly.

Chapter

A System for Trading

A speculator's trade plan is often little more than greedy entries, hopeful risk control and fearful exits.

Introduction

Trading is analysis in action. If you thought building a trading system was easy, here comes the difficult part: implementing it. In this chapter we examine the factors you should consider when you implement your trading system. If you have followed all the principles outlined earlier, you have created a trading system that is just right for you. Now, all you have to do is to execute it. We will attempt to close the gap between system design and implementation. Hence, in this chapter we focus on a system for trading.

Surprisingly, there are only two steps necessary to implement a trading system: (1) you need to have a specific trading plan, and (2) you need to execute the plan. You will be surprised how easy it is to trade without a plan and without a system to monitor implementation.

The first hurdle you must overcome is that system testing does not solve all your problems. Second, you must understand something about your interaction with the markets when you start trading. Third, there are other key issues such as risk control and money management that need attention. Last, you need a tool to organize your trading.

The Problem with Testing

Even though trading occurs in a pressure cooker of emotion, testing is performed in an emotional vacuum. Imagine an aerodynamically slick race car designed in a wind tunnel that handles poorly in the turbulent wake of other cars on race day. Similarly, a high-performance system based on historical data can provide a bumpy ride in actual trading.

Your computerized system testing occurs unemotionally, without any fear of losing money. All you see are a summary of the results and colorful up or down arrows pointing out entries and exits. You do not have to suffer through losing streaks during testing. Nor do you have to agonize as the system is late to enter or slow to exit. You do not have to create orders, enter orders, track fills, remember rollovers, monitor margin, or read the daily equity run. What is more important, you do not have to actively monitor position risk or make any money management decisions.

During computer testing, you do not have any fear of losing money or missing opportunities. Thus, system testing using software is a sterile environment that fails to capture the emotional components of system implementation. Hence, if you use all your creativity to develop a trading system that considers all the factors we have discussed, then all you have to do is to focus on system implementation.

Trading is an acquired skill. Perhaps the only way to acquire and maintain a new skill is to endure endless repetitions. Computerized testing does not allow you to build any skills in implementing the system. Thus, no amount of testing can give the repetitions needed to develop the many skills necessary to physically implement a system. Clearly, you need some more tools to address these key limitations of system design and testing.

Paper Trading: Pros and Cons

A traditional answer to the limitations of system design is to use a trial period during which you trade the system "on paper." Paper trading will certainly help you address and understand the mechanics of actual trading. You can practice all the steps of implementing the system, such as creating portfolios, generating orders, tracking fills, monitoring risk, and scoring profits and losses. In addition, you can keep a diary of your emotions, which is very useful to track your trading beliefs and patterns.

Another valuable way to use paper trading is to analyze your system results trade by trade. You should try to relive the trades, scanning through the chart one day at a time, writing your reactions to chart patterns, equity levels, volatility, and so forth. Even though this is not a perfect solution, reviewing historical trades in detail will give you valuable insight into system performance.

The extra insight will enable you to deal with the ups and downs of the system in actual trading.

However, paper trading does not tell you much about actual system performance. Thus, you will gain little additional insight into system performance that you have not already gleaned from system testing. Let us assume that during testing your system produced eight successive losing trades. If the system produces three successive winning trades during paper trading, this does not mean it is a great system. Similarly, if it generates ten successive losing trades, it does not mean it is a useless system. Precisely because successive trades are unrelated, you cannot use the results observed in paper trading to make sweeping generalizations about overall system performance.

Another disadvantage of paper trading is that it still lacks the fear of losing that afflicts trading with real dollars. Thus, paper trading can still insulate you from the emotional demands of real trading. In spite of these limitations, paper trading offers a reasonable means to close the gap between system design and implementation.

Do You Believe in Your System?

The market will challenge your faith in your system in every way possible. The market uses the well-known maxim of war: "Lure them with greed, conquer them with confusion." The markets will constantly create new chart patterns that can confuse your analysis. Unless you have absolute faith in your system, the markets will push you to meddle with your system. They will push you to override your signals, alter your plans, bend your system rules, invent new exceptions—all in the name of "improving performance." The only place to improve system design is with rigorous back testing and prospective paper trading. Any untested deviation provides short-lived gratification, which can seriously erode long-term performance.

You should pour all your creativity and emotional needs into creating a system that works for you. Your system should have the time horizon, trading frequency, market sensitivity, and profitability that you consider essential. Once you have rigorously tested the system on historical data, you should test it on scrambled data. You will quickly discover the type of markets the system likes and dislikes when you test it on scrambled data. You will also have greater confidence in the system's future performance by testing it over many sets of scrambled data. You can follow up system testing with paper trading to clarify the mechanics of the process. Once you are satisfied that this is the system you want, you should resist all unchecked attempts to modify it.

The markets push you to reexamine your faith in your system. You should not use a system unless you can reaffirm your full faith and confidence in that system every day. If you do not believe in your system, the market will quickly push you into deviating from it. Once you deviate from a system, you are trading an untested system, and all bets are off. Of course, you can ask why you should stick to a tested and true system. The answer is found in the next section.

Time Is Your Ally

The market giveth, and the market taketh away. You should recognize that in all markets, there will be time periods when money is easily made and other periods when most models will show losses. Your goal, as a system trader, is to survive the unprofitable periods so you can enjoy the good times when they roll around. In essence, your risk-control strategy, money-management practices, and overall system design will all play major roles in determining your ability to survive difficult market conditions. Hence, it is advantageous to take the long view and remember that the current trade is just one of many to come. Therefore, you need not get emotionally involved in the outcome of each trade.

Suppose you are trading many markets and more than one system in a diversified trading account. Let us assume that your average probability of winning is 35 percent. Since we can show that successive trades are independent, the probability of having ten successive losing trades is $(0.65)^{10}$, or 0.0135, or 13 in 1,000. Thus, if you opened 1,000 new accounts, only 13 of them would show ten successive losing trades. Now, suppose you put on the trades all at the same time. If you risked 2 percent per trade, you will experience a 20-percent drawdown at the very beginning about 13 times in 1,000 attempts. If you risked 1 percent per trade, your chance of reaching a 20-percent drawdown is approximately 18 in 10,000.

A 20-percent loss of capital, although not pleasant, is not irreversible. You should also recognize that unlikely events can and do occur. Thus, do not get emotionally involved in each gyration of every trade. You should take the long view: enforce rigid risk control, follow money-management guidelines, and focus on implementing your system.

No Exceptions

A good way to assure long-term success is to follow your system without exceptions. If you want exceptions, write them down and test them thoroughly instead of relying on your intuition alone. If you want to override your model, it probably means you are not comfortable with it and should do more testing and refining.

Many traders will use rising volatility as a measure of impending market change. They will reduce their positions when volatility is "high." You should define this scenario precisely. For example, you could say that volatility is "high" if the 50-day standard deviation of closing prices is more than $1,500. Then, you could test historical price data to check what the markets have done when volatility has risen to this level.

You could choose to increase market exposure to 4 percent of account equity if conditions are "right." Instead of relying on intuition, you could define a specific condition as "right," such as a 25-bar breakout accompanied by a 5-day RSI value greater than 70 or less than 30. You can then check historical data and develop some statistics on what to expect.

We saw in the tests with the 65sma-3cc model in Chapter 4 that only 4 percent of the trade were the home runs that made all the difference in portfolio performance. If you routinely deviate from your system, there is no assurance that you will not manage to miss all the important trades in a given period.

The no-exceptions policy is necessary for another reason: traceability, which is discussed in the next section.

Full Traceability

You should be able to trace back in time the precise reasons for a particular trade or trading action. For example, you should be able to recall why you made a particular trade or move. If you have a well-defined mechanical system, and you follow a strict policy of no exceptions, then you have assured traceability.

If you use subjective chart analysis, then the best way to understand your trading patterns is to keep a diary and a copy of your charts. You should record all the emotions and analyses you used to make a certain decision.

If you have no traceability, you will have little information to monitor your implementation, and you will lose valuable information that could improve your trading. Let's assume you have a tendency to get in late and get out too soon. If you do not keep detailed records, it is difficult to correct such tendencies. If you have good records, you can calculate the impact of your late entries and early exits. Specifically, you can determine the type of market conditions that push you into exiting early. Say you find that a sharp 3-day sell-off often pushes you to exit your trades. Then, after a brief consolidation, the markets have resumed their previous trend. You now have reliable information you can use to overcome your fear that every 3-day countermove is going to escalate into a major correction.

Traceability is also important if you notice errors in your account statements and want to get them corrected. For example, your broker may fail to report a fill, or give you a fill far away from your desired prices. If you have good records, it is relatively easier to make the changes you desire. If you called in to check a fill and were given a certain fill price, but your equity run shows a different fill price, or worse, does not show a fill at all, you can correct such mechanical errors if you keep good records.

"Guaranteed" Entry into Major Trends

Over the long run, your overall performance will be greatly influenced by less than 5 percent of your trades. You only have to miss a few big trades to seriously degrade overall performance. Your entry method and trade implementation should be focused on ensuring entries into the major trend. If one does not have a position in a particular market, that seems to increase the odds for the onset of a major trend.

When you design your system, try to use orders that will ensure you an entry into the desired trade. For example, an order to trade at the market, trade on the open, trade on the close, or trade on a stop will usually get you into a trade. Of course, the amount of slippage will vary, but if you are not doing great size, you will consistently enter the trade. If you rely on limit orders, you could easily miss a major trading opportunity by a few ticks. The cost of a lost opportunity is often greater than the few ticks you save using a limit order. However, if you are trading liquid markets and have a real-time data feed, you could try to fine-tune your entries. But for most traders, an order entered with a broker seems to work best.

The greatest slippage occurs not in the markets, but at the source: with the trader. If you fail to place an order, or place a wrong order, or place the order incorrectly, then these errors will often cost you more than any slippage in the markets. Hence, you should strive to control slippage at the source. The no-exceptions policy will help to reduce slippage at the source.

It is a good idea to prepare an order entry sheet the previous day, and transmit it to your broker before the markets open. There are many advantages to preparing your orders when the markets are closed. (1) You can create your order entry sheets calmly and unemotionally. (2) You can stick to your trade plans and avoid deviations. (3) You can double-check your orders for mechanical errors. (4) You can avoid trades made at the spur of the moment, without detailed analysis. (5) If you do plan subjective trades, you can write down detailed entry points or exit points, or other cues for trading. You can ensure entries into major trends by preparing your orders in advance and entering them before trading begins for the day.

Starting Up

When you begin trading your account for the first time, you must resolve some "start-up" issues. Let us assume you are using a mechanical system, and trading 20 markets. The first question is how to put on trades to match existing positions of your trading system. For example, the last signal in deutsche mark may be a buy signal that occurred 15 days ago. Now, should you put on the long position, or wait for a new signal? The preferred approach is to put on all positions as soon as possible, scaling them by the current volatility. You may not want to wait for the next signal if your system trades infrequently. Another reason to put on the trade immediately is to capture the remainder of the current move. There are several other ways to resolve this issue. (1) You can trade just one contract instead of multiple contracts. If you usually trade ten contracts, you can initiate your position with just one or two contracts to enter the position cautiously. (2) You can scale into the position. For example, you would buy ten contracts gradually over the next 5 days. (3) You can wait for the last day of the month and put on the entire position on the close. The benefit of putting on the position on the last trading day of the month is that then the month-to-month equity changes will accurately reflect the actual system results.

You must also decide where to place your initial stop on a start-up trade. You can go with the usual initial stop at 1 or 2 percent of account equity. Your other option is to set it slightly wider than usual, but trade a proportionately smaller number of shares.

Risk Control

It is essential that you always maintain rigid risk control. Your risk control strategy may be entering a stop-loss order every day, and with each new position. You can also use more elaborate strategies around market correlation and volatility. The key is to always control your risk. Risk control and money management go together. Using good money management guidelines will place reasonable limits on position size and promote diversification. These will prevent one bad trade from wiping out your account.

Do You Have a Plan?

You should avoid trading without a plan. A common cause for trading problems and failures is the lack of a trading plan. Your trading plan should explain clearly how you will trade. You must specify the markets, number of contracts, type of orders, entry rules, exit rules, and risk-control rules. The more specific you can be, the easier it is to implement the plan. If you have specified and designed your system properly, defining and implementing a plan should be relatively easy.

Every football team makes elaborate plans for their games. For example, one championship football team would "script" the first 15 plays for every game. After careful research, the coaches would pick the first 15 plays ahead of time. Then, the players would practice these plays many times so that they all knew them well. On game day, every one could concentrate on executing those plays, with excellent results. This example points out the benefits of preparation. You can plan your trades, visualize how you will execute those trades, and then monitor how you executed the trades. This process of auto-feedback can help you improve as a trader.

You should plan for adversity. For example, are you ready to absorb a 20-percent drawdown in equity? Do you have a plan to cope with this sort of drawdown? For example, you may not be prepared to experience a 20-percent drawdown in the first 3 months of your trading. If such losses occur, would you modify your trading system, change your money-management and bet-size algorithms, or change the portfolio mix? Similarly, if you are up 20 percent, will you alter any of the same variables?

Scenario planning is common in the military across the world. You, too, should use your imagination to explore good and bad scenarios about your trading. You can then develop detailed plans that will help you cope with the ever-changing markets.

How Will You Monitor Compliance?

It is one thing to have a plan, and another to actually implement it. You cannot properly implement a plan if you do not have a way to monitor and record how well you are implementing your plan. A good way to measure compliance is to keep a daily diary. An electronic diary is a fast and easy way to record your compliance or deviations. Later, you can analyze the diary entries to measure how well you are executing your plans. You can also find out which elements are easy or difficult for you to implement. You can then work to strengthen your weak spots.

If you do wish to deviate from your system, write down your reasons in detail, and then test them rigorously. That is the best approach to ensure consistent, long-term performance. Let us suppose there is a news event or political development that suggests you should exit the position. You should observe a noticeable market reaction to such events, such as a gap, a large range day, an outside day, or a key reversal day. You can then identify such bars on daily data and test them systematically. This will give you a historical database to formulate your strategy.

Get It Off Your Chest!

One big plus of keeping a diary is that you can get your concerns off your chest simply by writing them down. Let us say you wanted to apply the ideas of total quality management or continuous improvement to your trading. You must have detailed records of your trading, including how your orders were generated and what factors affected your implementation. You can keep a diary to get rid of any bottled-up emotions resulting from trading. A diary will add to the full traceability we discussed above by providing data on your emotional state.

Focus on Your Trading

It is difficult to avoid distractions and to focus sharply on your trading. Focus means you can execute your system without deviations. Focus means you can enter your orders, follow your risk-control guidelines, and reduce variations from your system. If you have a plan and a system you believe in, it is easier to focus on your trading. You should try to automate your analysis and order generation as much as possible. This will minimize variations from your system. Try to develop a routine that includes checking account equity, fills, new orders, rollovers, trailing stops, market volatility, and so forth.

The best way to focus on your trading is to separate analysis from trading. You should set aside a fixed time each day when you generate your trading sheets. You should try to be relaxed when you are generating your sheets. You should avoid circumstances that affect your concentration, since it is easy to make a mistake in your order entry process.

Applications of Sports Psychology in Trading

Sports are often used as a metaphor for trading. After a winning trade, traders are quoted as saying that they "vanquished" the market. Conversely, a losing period brings out comments to the effect that the market "beat me." Many similarities exist between trading and participating in sports, with the exception that trading is rarely a team sport. For example, the mental focus needed to succeed at all levels of sports is also necessary for trading success. Sports psychologists have developed several approaches to deal with the psychological dimensions of winning and losing games. In this section, we examine how some those ideas can be applied by traders to gain the "winning edge."

The first key idea is that athlete/trader must accept responsibility for his or her performance. Traders have it in their power to make the changes necessary to improve their trading performance. Psychologists have developed an attribution theory that describes the broad factors to which success or failure can be attributed by players, based on research into what is called locus of control.

Players or traders can attribute the reasons for their success or failure to any of four boxes, shown in Table 9.1. Athletes might say that they lost because of luck (bad call by a referee) or the difficulty of the task ("We never play well in that arena"). Alternately, they may ascribe credit to internal factors such as effort ("The only way to get me off that court was to drag me off ") or superior ability ("I was in the zone tonight"). A study of successful athletes suggests that

Table 9.1   Psychologists use attribution theory in sports to analyze the attitudes of consistent "winners." The most successful players are internal attributors, who take personal responsibility for their success.

	Attribution Theory for Athletes	
	Internal Factors	**External Factors**
Stable Factors	Ability	Task
Variable Factors	Effort	Luck

more often than not, losers tended to blame external factors, and winners, as a group, tended to focus on internal factors. For example, winners ascribed success to ability and effort, but pointed to a lack of total effort in losses. A study of sports legends indicates that they all were "internal attributors": they assumed responsibility for their performance and looked to improve their ability and increase their effort in order to be successful. Professional teams, playing in championships, focus on the task (their opponents and the perceived strengths and weaknesses) to develop a game plan, practice those abilities that will help implement the game plan, hope to take care of luck with careful pregame rituals, and then mentally "psych-up" at game time to maximize their effort. Even a casual perusal of the sports pages will show that the mental aspect of the game is probably more important than the physical requirements at the highest level of every sport, and the attribution theory seems to be a good approach to classify the responses of athletes to the mental demands of their sports.

We can generalize and extend the attribution theory for athletes to traders by separating events into those the trader influences and those influenced by the market or other external factors (see Table 9.2). Traders control their ability, or more broadly, the technology used to trade, which includes the tools (data feeds, computers, software) as well as the trading systems, risk control principles, and money-management algorithms. When traders speak of self-improvement, they are implying an improvement in the technology they use in their trading. The category of effort is converted to A2D (attention to detail) in the trading context. Trading can be a messy affair with many loose ends, and the trader must pay passionate attention to detail to be successful. Various factors can affect the level of concentration each trader brings to the table every day, but traders must remember that it is very easy to make costly mistakes. As in tennis, the difference between winning and losing is often this category of "unforced errors."

The primary role of the markets is price discovery, and elaborate infrastructures have been built to discover and disseminate trading information, such as prices, volume, and open interest. These processes are relatively stable, and can be used to broadly refer to the "technology" used by each market. Each

Table 9.2 The attribution theory model adapted for traders. Winning traders should focus on their trading technology and pay attention to the details of executing their trading plan. Most traders can do little about external events controlled by the markets, such as settlement prices and random noise.

	Attribution Theory for Traders	
	Trader Factors	**Market Factors**
Stable Factors	Technology	Price discovery
Variable Factors	Attention to Detail	Noise

trader can approach a market in his or her own way, and ascribe profitable months to "easy" markets and unprofitable months to "tough" or "difficult" markets. The one unstable part of trading is market noise, generated by the markets themselves as they try to digest data, information and news that bombards them everyday. Traders can easily ascribe losses to intraday volatility or noise. For example, the bond markets often wait anxiously for reports on economic activity; immediately after release, the snap judgment of the market may cause a big move one way, which can be quickly reversed as cooler heads prevail or the analysts get more time to sort through the data.

If we extend the attribution theory to traders, then successful traders should take personal responsibility for their gains and losses, and should focus on understanding the task (trends in price discovery), improving the technology of market analysis (ability), and paying full attention to the details of trading (effort). Market noise (luck) should be a factor in their overall results only occasionally, if at all, because even the best prepared trader can be surprised by the market. For example, many traders cut down the size of their position before the release of reports and may even be completely out of the market. Then they will have separate specific plans for each situation, whether the reported numbers are well below expectations, at or near expectations, or well above expectations. They will map the size of their positions in each instance, their entry points and exit points, as well as what they will do in the case of sharp reversals from the initial reaction. This kind of preparation clearly shows that traders are internal attributors, and have accepted the responsibility for their own performance.

The next important idea in sports psychology is goal-setting. Goal-setting is considered a highly effective motivational technique: hence, goal-setting really requires a player (read trader) to set up many layers of goals, leading from the long term (the "dream") to the short term (for the next trading day). The goals must be specific, achievable, and tied to a definite timetable. The objective is to develop a hierarchy of tasks that are tied together in a purposeful sequence in order to attain specific goals. The tasks can be evaluated regularly and can be

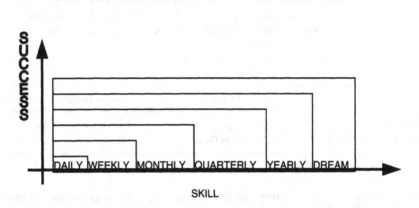

Figure 9.1 Goal-setting is a powerful motivational tool in sports psychology. Here it is adapted for traders, who should set specific daily, weekly, monthly, quarterly, and yearly goals as they progress toward their dreams.

altered as necessary. As shown in Figure 9.1 for traders, tasks will lead to greater skill levels over time, which should result in greater trading success as well.

The very process of developing a list of tasks and actually writing them down has been found to be an effective motivational tool. Teams will often write these goals on their caps, where they can be read easily and often. To traders who accept personal responsibility for their trading results, goal-setting offers a tool to identify those tasks that can lead to ever-greater improvements in their arsenal of trading technology, or their ability to improve A2D by process automation, or their ability to understand market trends. In the short run, goal-setting can lead to specific trading plans, a critical element in trading success. One psychologist who has studied traders reports that losing traders, without exception, were operating without a trading plan. Another part of goal setting is an analysis of strengths, weaknesses, opportunities, and threats (SWOT), applicable to both sports and business. The hierarchy of goals is developed to improve weaknesses, mitigate threats, and build on strengths to take advantage of opportunities.

Psychologists studying athletes, scientists, and other high achievers have developed a concept called "flow," which describes a period of effortless action that tends to occur when a person faces a clear set of goals that require action (see Csikszentmihalyi, 1997) . Most people experience a variety of mental states in response to the activity they are doing, based on their skill level and the difficulty of the task, as shown below in Figure 9.2. People experience flow when they are highly skilled at a task and are in a situation that challenges those skills. A basketball player asked to take a last-second shot may experience flow, as may a surgeon faced with a complication during a well-known procedure, although a surgical resident may experience anxiety at the same procedure. For many

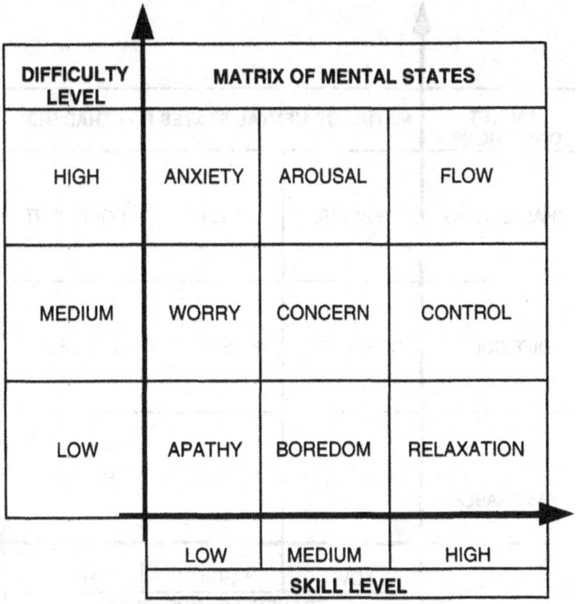

DIFFICULTY LEVEL	MATRIX OF MENTAL STATES		
HIGH	ANXIETY	AROUSAL	FLOW
MEDIUM	WORRY	CONCERN	CONTROL
LOW	APATHY	BOREDOM	RELAXATION
	LOW	MEDIUM	HIGH
	SKILL LEVEL		

Figure 9.2   A matrix of mental states observed by psychologists studying the phenomena of "flow," in which a period of effortless action is experienced by highly skilled people challenged by a difficult task requiring their skills. The chart shows the type of emotion experienced by subjects when they faced familiar and unfamiliar tasks and challenges. Adapted from *Finding Flow* by Mihaly Csikszentmihalyi, 1997.

traders, especially market makers, online or on the floor, trading the market just before and after the release of an important report or an unexpected news story may create the opportunity to experience flow.

Trading is an emotional business, and Csikszentmihalyi's concepts of mental states can be adapted to describe the experiences of trading. There seems to be a consensus in the literature that highly skilled traders have strong belief systems, are resilient and confident, and exhibit a high degree of "mental toughness." They remain confident in the face of market adversity and do not deviate easily from their trading process. They are focused through difficult trading conditions and are relaxed when trades are going their way. New traders tend to be the most emotional as a group, being overoptimistic when market conditions are favorable and downright fearful when losses begin to accumulate. Traders with intermediate skills, as a group, show greater variation in their emotional states. They seem happiest and engaged with trading when market conditions are favorable. Intermediate traders often know what they need to do under difficult market conditions, but are unable to "pull the trigger." They tend to turn defensive or angry under challenging market conditions and are quick to change methodologies. These traits are summarized in the Figure 9.3. Note that this is

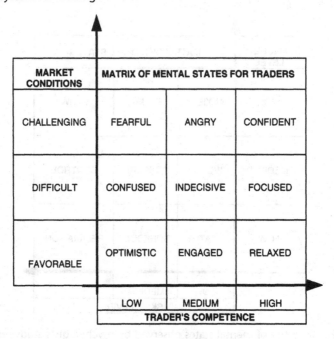

MARKET CONDITIONS	MATRIX OF MENTAL STATES FOR TRADERS		
CHALLENGING	FEARFUL	ANGRY	CONFIDENT
DIFFICULT	CONFUSED	INDECISIVE	FOCUSED
FAVORABLE	OPTIMISTIC	ENGAGED	RELAXED
	LOW	MEDIUM	HIGH
	TRADER'S COMPETENCE		

Figure 9.3   A matrix of mental states adapted for trading, which tries to depict various emotional states that could occur in traders. Note the gradation in emotions horizontally, vertically, and along the diagonals.

but a simplified depiction and is not meant to be an exhaustive description of all possibilities. Figure 9.3 allows traders to measure their reactions and understand where they may be in their evolution as a trader.

Traders can become stressed when they perceive a mismatch between their competence level and the degree of difficulty of the markets. Stress can be manifested in many forms—mental, physiological, and behavioral. Relaxation techniques and mental imagery can be used to match our competence level as traders to the difficulty posed by the markets. Relaxation techniques can be learned easily from a variety of sources. The simplest approach is to sequentially clench or tense the large muscle groups of the body for 10 seconds followed by 20 seconds of relaxation. After each muscle group is relaxed, you should feel the sense of relief flooding through your body. A few deep breaths after the relaxation exercises should set you up for practicing mental imagery. Mental imagery in sports involves recreating images of the optimal moves necessary to win. The imagery can be extensive, vivid, and detailed, covering every phase of the game, pregame, and postgame activities. There is anecdotal as well as scientific evidence that mental imagery can enhance performance in athletes. It can also improve concentration, the connection between the mind and the body. Mental imagery can also be connected to ancient disciplines of meditation.

As traders, mental imagery can be used to reinforce or modify belief systems, rehearse the mechanics of trading, or even prepare for the release of market moving data. Mental imagery can be used to finesse fear, diffuse anger, clarify confusion, and transform indecisiveness. The goal of relaxation and mental imagery is to become more relaxed when approaching the trading day, regardless of what the markets have to offer.

Unlike players, who need to concentrate on peak performance for short periods from a few minutes to a few hours, traders are like marathoners, who must keep their focus day after day for hours on end. A study of marathoners found that they are internally focused during the run, focusing on their own internal environment, their aches and pains, and how their body is doing. This is opposed to focusing on the course, other runners, or distractions from the fans. Positive self-talk is another sports psychology technique that may help the trader maintain focus and morale during challenging markets.

In summary, the attribution theory for traders, goal setting, mental imagery, and the matrix of mental states provide a framework for traders to apply the principles of sports psychology to trading. This research suggests that traders need to become internal attributors, concentrating on those factors within their control, such as trading technology and A2D, or attention to detail. They should trade what they test and test what they trade in order to increase their skill level and increase their confidence in their trading systems and methods. They should apply the risk control methods discussed in Chapter 7, especially the Chande comfort zone, to prepare for drawdowns and to manage their expectations. Markets will come and go, but traders must go on forever.

Trading with Your Head and Heart

Every trader has an analytical part (head) and an emotional component (heart). A system that suits you will engage both aspects of your personality. When you start trading a system, you face two expectations. One is the statistical expectation, which we have discussed in detail. The other is your emotional expectation from the system. If the two expectations are not coherent, then you will not be happy trading the offending system.

This raises questions about why you trade. For many people, the only reason to trade is to make a profit. However, you could have many other reasons, such as the excitement of trading or the intellectual challenge of competing with other traders. You should check to see if the following are consistent: your profit objective, trading horizon, mathematical expectations, and emotional expectations.

If these are not consistent, then you may not have the mental edge. Probably fewer than 25 percent of traders have the mental edge, and perhaps only 2 percent can maintain the edge year after year.

There are many contradictions between mathematical and emotional expectations. The mathematical expectation covers 2 to 3 years of data, but the emotional expectation covers only 2 to 3 months. Emotional expectations can be complex, and they cannot be represented by a single number. In the worst case, a system could have a positive mathematical expectation but a negative emotional expectation. In this case your head and heart disagree, and the inevitable tension will make it impossible for you trade this system.

Your emotional expectations may be based on an inaccurate or incomplete understanding of system test results. You should make it a point to study the evolution of each trade day by day. You should be comfortable with the dollar amount of the average trade, the winning percentage, and the length of the average trade. You should also be comfortable with the dollar amount of the initial risk-control stop. If you understand the "signature" of the system, then each trade will reinforce your belief in the system. If you have unreasonable emotional expectations, then each trade will diminish your faith in the system.

You may expect big successes, with few losing streaks and many exciting trades. The reality is that only 5 percent of the trades are big successes, you can have many losing streaks, and most of the trades are dull. You can use the "rule of two," as follows, to modulate your emotional expectations:

1. Expect half as many winning trades in a row as you project from your testing.

2. Expect twice as many losing trades in a row as your testing may show.

3. Prepare for half the expected profits.

Let us continue with the "head and heart" analogy. What you "think" you believe is in your head. What you "truly" believe is in your heart. Your head may be clear or confused. Your heart may be confident or fearful. If your head and heart disagree, and the stakes are low, then the head wins any conflicts. However, if the stakes are high, then the heart wins any conflicts. Thus, you can trade comfortably only if your head and heart agree. So spend the time and effort to understand system performance so that your mathematical and emotional expectations will agree. This is the key to long-term success.

Summary

You should integrate all the ideas of this chapter to create a system for trading. A trade plan is at the heart of a system for trading. You should monitor compliance with your plan and try to provide full traceability. You should also follow the principle of no exceptions to your trading rules. To win, trade with your head and heart.

Appendix to Chapter 9: Creating an Automated Diary of Trading Emotions

A diary of your emotional states as you trade will help you improve as a trader over a period of many months. One difficulty with jotting down your thoughts is that it may be difficult to graph or analyze trends in your emotions. Many diarists sometimes find it difficult to read their own handwriting months later because stress has way of distorting how you write. A solution to this problem is to use a database or spreadsheet and keep a numerical score of your emotions. All spreadsheets are equipped with graphing capabilities and statistical functions, so you can easily chart your emotional states. You may even be able to use the principles of technical analysis to spot breakouts, consolidations, and trends in your feelings about a particular trading strategy.

In this section, we show how to use a Microsoft Excel 2000® spreadsheet to build a simple application that will allow you to record a numerical score of your feelings about your current trading strategy. To do this, we use Figure 9.4, which shows a matrix of trader reactions as market conditions change, and the trader's belief in the trading system fluctuates. Figure 9.4 identifies nine emotional states, ranging from relaxed, confident, and patient, to eventually ignoring signals and finally stopping trading altogether. The two variables being used

MARKET CONDITIONS	MATRIX OF TRADER REACTIONS WITH SCALES		
CHALLENGING [10]	STOP TRADING [10, 1]	ABANDON SYSTEM [10,5]	PATIENT [10,10]
DIFFICULT [5]	IGNORE SIGNALS [5, 1]	MODIFY SYSTEM [5, 5]	CONFIDENT [5, 10]
FAVORABLE [1]	OVER CONFIDENCE [1, 1]	RELIEF [1, 5]	RELAXED [1, 10]
	LOW [1]	MEDIUM [5]	HIGH [10]
	BELIEF IN TRADING SYSTEM		

Figure 9.4   The matrix of trader reactions is converted into pairs of numbers by assigning numerical values to the levels of market conditions and trading system belief. The numerical assignments are low = 1, medium = 5, and high = 10 for each axis.

to map mental states are belief in the trading system and trading conditions in the market. Each variable is divided into three levels, low, medium and high. These levels can be converted to numerical values as follows: the low level converts to a number less than or equal to 3, the medium level ranges from 4 to 7, and the high level varies from 8 to 10. A simpler alternative is to equate the low level to 1, the medium level to 5, and the high level to 10.

Once you have a numeric scale for your belief in the trading system and market conditions, you can easily convert the nine cells in Figure 9.4 into corresponding paired numerical values. If you perceived that the market conditions were challenging and wanted to stop trading, then the paired values quantifying this mental state are [10, 1], where the value 10 implies challenging market conditions (high = 10) and the value 1 derives from your low belief in the trading system (low = 1). You can record quantitative values of your mental state in a spreadsheet after each trade is closed out or at frequent time intervals, such as daily or weekly. If you wish, you can use a more refined numerical scale from 1 to 10, as indicated in the previous paragraph. After a few months, you will have detailed information that can be graphed and analyzed.

A convenient way to enter this information in a spreadsheet is to create buttons on the sheet and attach macros to those buttons. You can then just press the appropriate button to record your mental state. In Microsoft Excel®, you can add buttons to a spreadsheet by clicking on the Controls toolbar, which can be accessed from the View→Toolbars menu selections. You can then click on the Command button icon and draw a button at a convenient spot. After drawing the button, place the mouse pointer on the button and click the right mouse button. On the pop-up menu, select Properties to see a window with the properties assigned to the button. The property values can be edited directly in the pop-up window. You can edit the name, change the caption, and set the Placement property to 3. The advantage of setting the Placement property to 3 is that the button will stay "fixed" to the location you used even if you add rows to your spreadsheet. If you wanted to program the "RELIEF" reaction button, you would edit the Caption property to read "RELIEF" and name the button cmdRelief, using a popular naming convention. You can draw nine buttons for each of the reactions, as shown in Figure 9.5. You can then add some code to make the button add values to the spreadsheet as discussed in the following paragraphs.

Let us now assume that you want to store the data on your mental states. You want to record the date, the market condition, and the strength of your belief in the trading system. You would also like to store the data in reverse chronological order, so that the most recent data are near the top of the spreadsheet. You would thus add a new row at the top of the spreadsheet and enter the date, market condition, and belief strength in adjacent columns. It is easy to automate this procedure by writing a simple macro and attaching it to each of the buttons in Figure 9.5 so that the correct values are entered in your spreadsheet.

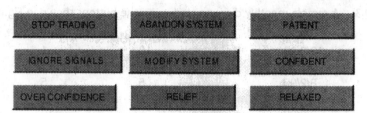

Figure 9.5   A group of command buttons in a Microsoft Excel 2000® spreadsheet that can be programmed to enter values of market condition and belief in the trading system into designated cells. These entries can be tracked and analyzed to understand your trading patterns.

You can program the buttons to add values to the spreadsheet with the following procedure. After you have drawn the button on the spreadsheet and edited its properties, double click on the button. This opens the Visual Basic editor. If you were programming a button called cmdRelief, then you will see a blank page with blue words "Private Sub cmdRelief_click()" followed by a blank line and then another line with the words "End Sub." You can now type in the following lines just above the line with the words "End Sub," just as you would in any text editor. Here is how the Visual Basic editor should look to you:

```
Private Sub cmdRelief_Click()
        Application.Goto Reference:="R2C2"
        Selection.EntireRow.Insert
        Range("B2").Select
        ActiveCell.FormulaR1C1 = "=TODAY()"
        Range("C2").Select
        ActiveCell.FormulaR1C1 = "1"
        Range("D2").Select
        ActiveCell.FormulaR1C1 = "5"
    End Sub
```

The program lines shown above are the instructions for the RELIEF button. Remember that the three columns we want to enter are the date, the market condition, and the strength in trading beliefs. The first line of code moves to the cell in row 2, column 2 (cell B2) and then inserts an entire row. The cursor then enters today's date in cell B2. The cursor moves to cell C2 and enters the value 1 for favorable market conditions (see Figure 9.4) followed by an entry of the value 5 in the column for strength of belief in the trading system (cell D2). Once you have finished entering the code, simultaneously press the Alt-Q keys to return to the spreadsheet. You can access the Visual Basic editor again by pressing the Alt-F11 key sequence or from the menu by choosing

Table 9.3   A sample monthly diary created using the buttons shown in Figure 9.5.

Date	Market Condition	Bellief in System
10/3/00	10	1
9/2/00	10	1
8/2/00	5	5
7/2/00	1	1
6/2/00	5	10
5/2/00	10	10

Tools→Macros→Visual Basic editor. You can copy this code into each of the other buttons, and change values for cells C2 and D2 as needed. You will then be able to enter values for each mental state simply by clicking the appropriate button (see Figure 9.5). For completeness, the program lines for the STOP TRADING button are shown so you can observe how the values for market condition (10) and trading beliefs (1) are edited in after copying the code for the button RELIEF:

```
Private Sub cmdStopTrading_Click()
     Application.Goto Reference:="R2C2"
     Selection.EntireRow.Insert
     Range("B2").Select
     ActiveCell.FormulaR1C1 = "=TODAY()"
     Range("C2").Select
     ActiveCell.FormulaR1C1 = "10"
     Range("D2").Select
     ActiveCell.FormulaR1C1 = "1"
End Sub
```

A sample set of monthly diary entries is shown in Table 9.3. You could keep a more detailed diary if you wish, or use a more refined scale for the variables being tracked. You can also enter the data directly into the spreadsheet without using buttons. You can even program the buttons to store any other data you wish to track. These data can then be tracked and analyzed via graphs or statistical functions built into spreadsheets to spot trends.

Selected Bibliography

Babcock, Bruce: *Business One Irwin Guide to Trading Systems*, Business One Irwin, Homewood, Illinois, 1989.

Balsara, Nauzer J.: *Money Management Strategies for Futures Traders*, John Wiley & Sons, New York, 1992.

Chande, Tushar S.: "Estimating depth and duration of drawdowns from past performance data," *The MFA Reporter*, September, 1998, Managed Funds Association, Washington, DC.

Chande, Tushar S.: "Controlling risk and managing investor expectation by modeling the dynamics of losses in hedge funds and alternate investment strategies," *Derivatives Quarterly*, 5(3): 52–58, Spring 1999.

Chande, Tushar S., and Stanley Kroll: *The New Technical Trader*, John Wiley & Sons, New York, 1994.

Chande, Tushar, and Stanley Kroll: "Stochastic RSI and dynamic momentum index," *Technical Analysis of Stocks and Commodities*, 11(5), Technical Analysis, Inc., Seattle, 1993.

Connors, Larry, and Linda Bradford Raschke: *Street Smarts: High Probability Trading Strategies for the Futures and Equities Markets*, Oceanview Financial Research, Malibu, California, 1996.

Csikszentmihalyi, Mihaly: *Finding Flow*, Basic Books, New York, 1997.

De Mark, Thomas R.: *The New Science of Technical Analysis*, John Wiley & Sons, New York, 1994.

Edwards, Franklin R., and Jimmy Liew: "Hedge funds versus managed futures as asset classes," *Journal of Derivatives*, 45–67, Summer 1999.

Hayden, John H.: *The 21 Irrefutable Truths of Trading*, McGraw-Hill, New York, 2000.

Henry, J. W.: Commodity trading advisor has good information packages, at www.jwh.com

Hull, John C.: *Options, Futures and Other Derivative Securities*, 5th ed., Prentice Hall, Saddle Brook, New Jersey, 2000.

Irwin, Scott H., Carl R. Zulauf, and Barry W. Ward: "The predictability of managed futures returns," *Journal of Derivatives*, 20–27, Winter 1994.

Jessen, Raymond J.: *Statistical Survey Techniques*, John Wiley & Sons, New York, 1978.

Kaufman, Perry J.: *Smarter Trading*, McGraw-Hill, New York, 1995.

Kaufman, Perry J.: *Trading Systems and Methods*, John Wiley & Sons, New York, 1998.

Kroll, Stanley, and M. J. Paulenoff: *The Business One Irwin Guide to the Futures Markets*, Business One Irwin, Homewood, Illinois, 1993.

Krutsinger, Joe: *The Trading Systems Toolkit*, Probus Publishing, Chicago, 1993.

Lane, George C.: "Lane's stochastics," *Technical Analysis of Stocks and Commodities*, 2(3): 87–90, Technical Analysis, Inc., Seattle, June 1984.

Le Beau, Charles, and David W. Lucas: *Technical Traders Guide to Computer Analysis of the Futures Markets*, Business One Irwin, Homewood, Illinois, 1992.

McCarthy, David, Thomas Schneeweis, and Richard Spurgin: "Investment through CTAs: An alternative managed futures investment," *Journal of Derivatives*, 36–47, Summer 1996.

Murphy, John J.: *Intermarket Technical Analysis*, John Wiley & Sons, New York, 1986.

Pardo, Robert: *Design, Testing and Optimization of Trading Systems*, John Wiley & Sons, New York, 1992.

Rotella, Robert P.: *Elements of Successful Trading*, N.Y. Institute of Finance, New York, 1992.

Schneeweis, Thomas, and Richard Spurgin: "Comparisons of commodity and managed futures benchmark indexes," *Journal of Derivatives*, 33–50, Summer 1997.

Schwager, Jack D., *Managed Trading: The Myths and Truths*, John Wiley & Sons, New York, 1996.

Schwager, Jack D.: *Market Wizards*, Harper & Row, New York, 1990.

Schwager, Jack D.: *The New Market Wizards*, Harper Business, New York, 1992.

Schwager, Jack D.: *Schwager on Futures: Technical Analysis*, John Wiley & Sons, New York, 1995.

Smith, Aynsley M.: *Power Play*, 3rd ed., Power Play Inc., Rochester, Minnesota, 1999.

Sweeney, John: "Where to put your stops," *Technical Analysis of Stocks and Commodities*, 10(13): 30–32, Technical Analysis, Inc., Seattle, December 1992.

Tewles, Richard J., C. V. Harlow, and H. L. Stone: *The Commodity Futures Game*, McGraw-Hill, New York, 1974.

Tharp, Van K.: *Trade Your Way to Financial Freedom*, McGraw-Hill, New York, 1998.

Vince, Ralph: *Portfolio Management Formulas*, John Wiley & Sons, New York, 1990.

Vince, Ralph: *The Mathematics of Money Management*, John Wiley & Sons, New York, 1992.

Wilder Jr., J. Welles: *New Concepts in Technical Trading Systems*, Trend Research, Greensboro, North Carolina, 1978.

Index

variable-contract strategy, 55–58, 224–
226, 292–294
Veritas Software Corp., (VRTS), 192, 193
VIDYA (Variable Index Dynamic Average), 33–35
volatility, 55–58, 137, 277, 292
volatility-based barrier, 212
volatility-based stops, 81, 83, 136, 137,
144, 204–208
volatility-based system (VOL), 295–297
volatility breakout system, 97
volatility-exit, 204, 206, 210, 218, 240

weighted moving average, 26
whipsaw losses, 78–79
whipsaw signal, 141
whipsaw trades, 213
Wilder Jr., J. Welles, 66, 139, 253
win-loss ratio, 223, 228
winning edge, 363
winning intervals, 250
winning percentage, 287, 288
winning trades, 91–93, 126, 154

yardstick, 238, 265